THE Church MAY ICE IN THE Summer

Dr. Selvon Seebran

The Church May Ice in the Summer

Trilogy Christian Publishers
A Wholly Owned Subsidiary of Trinity Broadcasting Network
2442 Michelle Drive, Tustin, CA 92780

Copyright © 2022 by Dr. Selvon Seebran

Scripture quotations marked NIV are taken from the Holy Bible, New International Version®, NIV®. Copyright © 1973, 1978, 1984, 2011 by Biblica, Inc.TM Used by permission of Zondervan. All rights reserved worldwide. www.zondervan.com. The "NIV" and "New International Version" are trademarks registered in the United States Patent and Trademark Office by Biblica, Inc.TM

Scripture quotations marked NKJV are taken from the New King James Version®. Copyright © 1982 by Thomas Nelson. Used by permission. All rights reserved.

Unless otherwise noted, all Scripture quotations are taken from the King James Version of the Bible. Public domain.

No part of this book may be reproduced, stored in a retrieval system, or transmitted by any means without written permission from the author. All rights reserved. Printed in the USA.

Rights Department, 2442 Michelle Drive, Tustin, CA 92780.

Trilogy Christian Publishing/TBN and colophon are trademarks of Trinity Broadcasting Network.

For information about special discounts for bulk purchases, please contact Trilogy Christian Publishing.

Cover Artwork Element Credit: Realistic transparent blue ice cubes with berries inside Free Vector. Designed by macrovector / Freepik. https://www.freepik.com/free-vector/realistic-transparent-blue-ice-cubes-with-berries-inside_2870215.htm

Trilogy Disclaimer: The views and content expressed in this book are those of the author and may not necessarily reflect the views and doctrine of Trilogy Christian Publishing or the Trinity Broadcasting Network.

Manufactured in the United States of America
10 9 8 7 6 5 4 3 2 1
Library of Congress Cataloging-in-Publication Data is available.

ISBN: 978-1-63769-752-8
E-ISBN: 978-1-63769-753-5

TABLE OF CONTENTS

Chapter 1, Part 1: *God* 5
Chapter 1, Part 2: *Jesus* 15
Chapter 1, Part 3: *The Holy Spirit* 29
Chapter 2: *Peter or Jesus?* 37
Chapter 3: *The Church* 49
Chapter 4: *The Ministry Gifts in the Church*. 63
Chapter 5: *The Gifts of the Holy Spirit* 83
Chapter 6: *The Fruit of the Holy Spirit* 93
Chapter 7: *In the Image of God* 99
Chapter 8: *What Jesus and the Apostles Taught* 111
Chapter 9: *The Church May Ice in the Summer* 161
Chapter 10: *Prophecy: Where We At!* 177
Chapter 11: *Revival Is Not!* 189
Chapter 12: *Revival: What Is It?* 195
Chapter 13: *Revival! Returning to Your First Love* 211
Chapter 14: *How to Keep Your First Love* 217
Chapter 15: *Staying Revived* 223
Chapter 16: *When the Price Is Right* 229
Chapter 17: *Strong or Agonizing Praying* 245
Chapter 18: *Purity Is the Key to Revival* 263
Chapter 19: *Manifestation of God's Power* 273
Chapter 20: *You're Assurance for Heaven* 289
Chapter 21, Part 1: *Stranger in His Own House* 297
Chapter 21, Part 2: *Stranger in His Own House* 313
Chapter 22: *Peter's Shadow: An Embarrassment or a Challenge* 329

CHAPTER 1, PART 1
God

The universe contains objects of incredible size and mass at distances that the human mind cannot fully comprehend. The moon is the nearest (natural) celestial body. It is approximately 238,855 (1,737.5 kilometers) in diameter—roughly the size of the continental United States. The Moon orbits at an average distance of 240,000 miles (380,000 km) from the earth. On the one hand, this is a tremendous distance. The moon orbits the earth in a roughly circular path, taking about one month from start to finish. In fact, that is where we get the idea for a "month." According to Scripture, one of the reasons God created the celestial bodies was to be for signs, seasons, days, and years, in other words, to mark the passage of time. The moon does just that. It continually orbits the earth every month with clockwork precision.

> *And God said, "Let there be lights in the firmament of the heaven to divide the day from the night; and let them be for signs, and for seasons, and for days, and years."*
>
> — Genesis 1:14

Additionally, the moon, the "lesser light" created on day four, was designed to "rule the night," Indeed, the moon does rule the night; it outshines every other nighttime celestial object. In fact, when the moon is out, it tends to "wash out" most other astronomical objects, making them more difficult to see. This effect is particularly evident when the moon is near its full phase. At that time, the moon is over 2,500 times brighter than the next brightest nighttime object—Venus. Let us move farther out into space and consider the "greater light" that God created on day four—the Sun. The Sun, like other stars, is a glowing hot ball of hydrogen gas. It derives energy from the fusion of hydrogen to helium in the core. The sun is effectively a stable hydrogen bomb. It is an extremely efficient source of energy, placed at just the right distance to provide the right amount of light and heat for the earth. The distance from the Earth to the Sun is approximately 92 935,700 miles.

The Sun is about 400 times more distant than the moon. Remarkably, it is also 400 times larger. So it has the same angular size as the moon—meaning it appears the same size and covers the same portion of the sky. It is interesting that God made both "great lights" the same angular size and far larger (in angle) than any of the other celestial objects. There is no naturalistic reason why the sun and moon would be at just the right distances to have the same apparent size as seen from earth. As far as we know, the earth is the only planet for which this is the case. The Sun is over 100 times the diameter of the earth. If it were hollow, it could hold over 1 million earths. At first, it seems almost "wasteful" to create such a massive globe merely to provide light for earth: until we consider that God created the Sun just as easily as the rest of the universe. It was not all difficult for Him, and it demonstrates His great power.

> *Ah Lord God! behold, thou hast made the heaven and the earth by thy great power and stretched out arm, and there is nothing too hard for thee.*
>
> — Jeremiah 32:17

At the incredible distance of 93 million miles (150 million km), we cannot fully appreciate just how far away the sun is. An analogy may be helpful. How long would it take to drive 93 million miles? If we were to drive 65 miles per hour (105 km/hr), it would take 163 years to drive this distance. We couldn't drive this far in our lifetime. The sun is far from the earth, and yet the earth is much closer to the sun than many of the other planets. Consider Pluto, a tiny frozen world at the outer edge of the planets of the solar system. Pluto (on average) is about forty times farther away from the sun than the earth is. Earth is much closer to the sun than many of the other planets. Pluto (on average) is about forty times farther away from the sun than the earth is.

Traveling at 65 miles per hour, it would take about 6,500 years to reach Pluto. This is comparable to the age of the universe. The solar system is truly vast; if it had been the only thing God had made, Yet, God has created on even larger scales. Consider the distances between the stars. Let's start with the nearest star system to the earth (besides the sun), the Alpha Centauri system. Unlike the solar system, Alpha Centauri contains more than one star. Two bright stars (comparable to the sun in size and color) revolve around each other every eighty years. A third faint red dwarf star called "Proxima" lies farther away. The distance to this system is about 25 trillion miles. Such a number has little meaning to most of us; who can comprehend 25 trillion miles? This is about 6,800 times farther away from the earth than Pluto is. To help grasp this to some extent, let's imagine that we had a miniature scale model of the solar system with Pluto's orbit being only one foot (about 30 cm) in diameter. The sun would be approximately in the center, and the earth would be just over an eighth of an inch (3.8 mm) away from the sun. The sun itself would be smaller than the period at the end of this sentence. Where would we place the next nearest star in our one-foot scale model solar system? At this scale, Alpha Centauri would be over half a mile (about one km) away, and that's just the nearest star system. Our galaxy is comprised of countless numbers of stars at much greater distances. With our one-foot-scale model solar system, the galaxy would be larger than the Pacific Ocean!

Our galaxy is shaped like a disk with a bulge in the center. Earth is shaped like a disk, closer to the edge than the center. The disk has spiral arms; we cannot directly see this spiral structure because we are within it. To us, the galaxy looks like a faint cloud band stretching across the sky on (northern hemisphere) summer nights (or winter nights for the southern hemisphere). This is how our galaxy gets its name—the "Milky Way." Our galaxy contains over 100 billion stars; the Bible says that God calls them all by their names. How amazing that God has a name for each and every one of those stars! Some of these stars are far separated from their nearest neighbor, much like the sun. Some stars come in binary or multiple star systems, such as Alpha Centauri. Some stars come in large clusters. Consider the M80 star cluster. This cluster within our galaxy is estimated to contain over 100,000 stars.

> *He telleth all the stars He calleth them all by names.*
>
> — Psalm 147:4

> *Lift up your eyes on high and behold who hath created these things, that bringeth out their host by number, He calleth them all by names, by the greatness of His might, for that He is strong in power, not one falleth.*
>
> — Isaiah 40:26

That means that the Milky Way has roughly a million times as many; imagine one million stars for every single star in this cluster! The galaxy contains more than stars. It also contains nebulae—the same stuff as stars, but whereas stars are compact spheres, a nebula is spread out over a much larger region of space. When a nebula is heated by nearby stars, it glows, often with vivid and beautiful colors. Consider the beauty of the nebulae shown, but keep in mind how enormous these objects are. The Rosette Nebula is not only beautiful; it is estimated to be more massive than 10,000 suns. The section of the Eagle Nebula shown below is several thousand times larger than our solar system. It is incredible to realize that our solar system would not even be visible in this image. God paints beautiful artwork, and He does it on a canvas of unimaginable size.

When we consider the immensity of the Milky Way, with its 100 billion stars, countless nebulae, and star clusters, the overwhelming power of the Creator becomes clear. Yet, our galaxy is not the only one. God has created innumerable galaxies with a wide range of shapes and sizes. Some galaxies are spiral, like the Milky Way and M31. Others are elliptical in shape, and some galaxies have shapes that can only be described as "irregular." Many galaxies come in clusters. The Milky Way belongs to a cluster of a few dozen galaxies called the "Local Group." Some clusters are much larger than this. The Virgo cluster has about 2,000 galaxies. Clusters of galaxies are organized into even larger superclusters, clusters of clusters. Superclusters show organization on the largest scales we can currently observe; they form an intricate web of strings and voids throughout the visible universe.

Just think about the quantity of energy involved when God created all this. The sun alone gives off more energy every second than one billion major cities would produce in one year. Yet, our entire galaxy is 20 billion times more luminous than the sun; it is estimated that there are at least as many galaxies as there are stars in the Milky Way 100 billion. Just consider such energy and mass filling a volume of space that is immense beyond our ability to fathom. How does the Bible describe the creation of all this? States simply that God also made the stars (Genesis 1:16).

It is astonishing that the creation of the entire universe beyond earth is described so casually by such a simple statement. The biblical description makes it sound like the creation of all the hundreds of billions of galaxies was so trivially easy for God that it barely deserves to be mentioned. How awesome is the Lord when we contemplate all this which God created; it brings to mind how great our God is.

> *When I consider your heavens, the work of your fingers, the moon and the stars, which you have set in place, what is man that you are mindful of him, the son of man that you care for him?*
> — Psalm 8:3–4

It is amazing that the God who created such a universe would be concerned with something as small as human beings. Yet, Scripture makes it clear that humans are more important to God than anything; the reason is humans are created in His image and have an everlasting soul. Who would have thought from a casual glance at the night sky that the universe would be so majestic and so enormous? Certainly, the night sky is stunningly beautiful, even to the unaided eye. Who could have known that it would contain hundreds of billions of galaxies, each with millions to trillions of stars, along with countless clusters and nebulae of immense size and breathtaking beauty? It seems that the more we zoom in on the universe, the more beautiful it becomes, and the more we realize how truly vast and amazing it is. The more we "magnify" the universe, the more amazed we are by its beauty and complexity. The same is true of the Creator of the universe.

The more we magnify God, the more we realize just how amazing He is. It seems that God has constructed the universe to reflect this aspect of His character. Romans one twenty indicates that many of the invisible attributes of God can only be understood from the things which He made:

> *For the invisible things of Him from the creation of the world are clearly seen, being understood by the things that are made, even His eternal power and Godhead so that they are [mankind] without excuse.*
>
> — Romans 1:20

Who else could have put together the vast universe, its magnitude, which comprises of the earth with all its riches, the oceans with all of the sea creatures and its wonders? The firmament, which consists of a conflagration of billions of stars, galaxies, planets, the Milky Way, including the sun and moon, all canopied inside this universe.

The ground you are standing on, which is being taken for granted by billions; have you considered the earth, its picturesque grandeur beauty, and scenery throughout this entire earth's globe, the rainbow's multicolor rays of light piercing through deep down in the valleys, revealing the awesome beauty of the mountains with its array of different trees shrubs and plants, the rivers?

Silhouettes the mountains ranges, valleys, and plains. Have you ever considered the vast riches on the Earth? Who else could have done all of this? No one but *Jehovah, the True and Living God*.

God, Theo, the sole Supreme Being, eternal, spiritual, and transcendent, who is the Creator and Ruler of all. God was, is, and forever. He is the future and always will be God. He exists as *El Olam*, which means the Everlasting God. The Hebrew name, *El Olam*, also means *forever*, *perpetual*, *old*, and *ancient*; God is infinite past, present, and future.

> *Before the mountains were brought forth the earth and the world, from everlasting to everlasting you are God.*
>
> — Psalm 90:2

He was before time and everything that was made. The apostle Paul so eloquently stated as he was inspired by the Holy Spirit to write these words,

> *For the invisible things of him from the creation of the world are clearly seen, being understood by the things that are made, even his eternal power and Godhead; so that they are without excuse.*
>
> — Romans 1:20

This actually means from the creation of the world, His invisible attributes, that is, His eternal power and divine nature, are clearly seen by the things that He created from the beginning. Anyone in their right mind would obviously attribute everything that we see was created by a Supreme Being, and He is God.

Here are some of the names applied to God: *Yahweh, Elohim*.

> *In the beginning God created the heavens and the earth.*
>
> — Genesis 1:1

The heavens declare the glory of God and the firmament sheweth his handiwork.

— Psalm 19:1

El-Olam—meaning "God," a reference to God's power and might. "Hast thou not known? Hast thou not heard, that the everlasting God, the Lord, the Creator of the ends of the earth, fainteth not, neither is weary? There is no searching of his understanding" Isaiah 40:28.

- *Jehovah-Rapha*, Exodus 15:26, meaning "The Lord our healer."
- *Jehovah-Tsidkenu*, Jeremiah 23:6, "The Lord our righteousness."
- *Jehovah-Jireh*, Genesis 22:13–14, meaning, "The Lord will provide."
- *Jehovah Nissi*, Exodus 17:15, meaning "The Lord our banner."
- *Jehovah-Shalom*, Judges 6:24, meaning "The Lord is peace."
- *El-Elyon*, Genesis 14:17–20, Isaiah 14:13–14, meaning "The Most High God."
- *El-Roi*, Genesis 16:13, meaning "The all-seeing God."
- *El-Shaddai*, Genesis 17:1, Psalm 91:1, meaning "The God of the mountains or God Almighty."

God is a spirit, and His power is limitless. His power fills the universe. The being or essence of God is intrinsically sublime and resplendent. This inherent brilliance is often referred to in scripture as light and glory. Light emphasizes the splendor of who He is comprehended by some as unapproachable and immaculate, "Every good gift and every perfect gift is from above, and cometh down from the Father of lights, with whom is no variableness, neither shadow of turning" James 1:17.

He revealeth the deep and secret things: he knoweth what is in the darkness, and the light dwelleth with him.

— Daniel 2:22

God who alone possesses immortality and dwells in unapproachable light, which no man has ever seen. God's being transcends the physical universe. He is not limited or bounded by material issues or concerns. God is not subject to matter in any way. God is not made of matter; God created matter and employs it however He desires.

The study of physics tells us that matter, time, and space must all occur together. Without matter, there can be neither space nor time. Therefore, "time," the succession of moments one after another, did not exist before God created the universe, but before there was a universe or time, God always was there and existed. As described in His Word, "Who only hath immortality, dwelling in the light which no man can approach unto; whom no man hath seen, nor can see: to whom be honour and power everlasting. Amen" 1 Timothy 6:16.

From the record of the Bible, His being is best considered in terms of who He is, even His nature character; God is spirit, infinite, perfect in character; people talk about truth. God is truth. His being transcends the physical universe; however, He desires, God is Eternal. He is a supernatural being and transcends God's own way, "To whom will ye liken me and make me equal, and compare me, that we may be like" Isaiah 46:5.

Uniqueness comes from God's infinite nature. No one else in the universe can reasonably be compared to Him. He is absolutely unique within His own creation and, therefore, the one Person to whom all honor is due. Uniqueness thus speaks to God's natural authority and ability to order the universe however He chooses. From the standpoint of His transcendence of the physical universe, He is unique by virtue of His spirituality, eternity, and immeasurability. From the standpoint of His supremacy within the physical universe, God is Omnipotent, which means He is all-powerful God, is Omniscient; He knows all things, and God is Omnipresence, He is everywhere, this means He is all-powerful God is good, and the word "good" came from the word "God." God is good to all. His love, mercy, kindness, and compassion reach out to all of humanity.

God is Sovereign; He has no authority over Him. He is the authority over all. God is omniscient; He knows the past, present, and future; minutes, hours, months, years, decades, and millenniums are like nothing to Him. He, Himself, is greater than time. He made time.

He does not wait on time (even though He has a set time for the human race on this earth); time surrounds and waits on Him. God has time in His hands, and He is able to see the whole span of history as if it were a brief moment. Nothing that occurs in our lives He does not know; as a matter of fact, God is Omnipotent, Omniscient, and Omnipresent. God is a supernatural being who has existed from the beginning of time, based on the fact of a revelation we have of Him and His existence. As humans who were created by God, we can only comprehend certain things from beginning to end, but when it comes to God, we are limited as humans. Scientists and scientific researchers can believe the universe and planets exist with the explanation of the origin, but some of them cannot accept the fact and concept of God, who is a supernatural being that exists within the past, present, and future. It is easier for some of mankind to believe in an alien from another planet or galaxy than to believe in the True and Living God.

This book is not about Christian apologetics (even though the author understands what Christian apologetics is all about), but the Christian world does not have to apologize to anyone about God because God knows how to take care of Himself, the universe, and everything He created within the universe. God has set patterns and laws that govern this universe and everything He placed within this universe. The question about God is not God's problem; it is a human dilemma combined with the devil's influence for human beings to disbelief there is a God, God already exists, but whether some people believe there is a God or not (there is a God) rests upon the human race whom He allowed to be alive until this present time. The big question is whether you believe in God or not; this would determine your destiny in eternity. There are three kinds of people in this world, (1) unbelievers, (2) make-believers, and (3) believers. Believers have nothing to lose believing in God, His righteousness, His plan, purpose program, and timeline for humankind; yes, God even created time because His Word says,

> *In the beginning God created the heaven and the earth. And the earth was without form, and void; and darkness was upon the face of the deep. […] And God said, Let there be light: and there was light. [Everything that is on this earth, under the earth, and in the heavens were created.]*
>
> — Genesis 1:1–3

Billions of people know Him as the Creator of everything and endeavor to worship Him in some way. God imbedded within the spirit of mankind a desire for God, even though some of them are searching and implementing their own ways to come to God. Believe it or not, God has already provided a way. God used the Jewish people to reveal and teach the world about God. God revealed Himself to Old Testament individuals in different names and ways from the beginning of time; some of these names of God indicated His love for fallen mankind. If we, humans, will choose to respond to God's love and live for Him, most of all accept God's provided way to come to Him, worship Him, love Him, obey Him, and fit into His plan and program, we would be blessed in every way and at times be despised or hated.

Two thousand years after the fall of mankind, the human race became so polluted, perverse, and perverted; certain of the human race had become so unrecognizable as humans because the devil and his angels had intermingled with humans that produced a type giant size monster called Nephilim, a type of people who had no desire for the true and living God. During this time, the people became a generation of idol worshipers, murderers, a generation who had no fear of God; they were loose and licentious in their living as they practiced human sacrifice. At this point, the Bible says that it grieved the heart of God that He had made mankind.

> *And it came to pass, when men began to multiply on the face of the earth, and daughters were born unto them,*
>
> *That the sons of God saw the daughters of men that they were fair; and they took them wives of all which they chose.*
>
> *And the LORD said, My spirit shall not always strive with man, for that he also is flesh: yet his days shall be an hundred and twenty years.*
>
> *There were giants in the earth in those days; and also after that, when the sons of God came in unto the daughters of men, and they bare children to them, the same became mighty men which were of old, men of renown.*
>
> *And God saw that the wickedness of man was great in the earth, and that every imagination of the thoughts of his heart was only evil continually.*
>
> — Genesis 6:1–5

God, who is a God of righteousness, could not allow the human race to continue in their perverse and perverted ways and condition. God destroyed this generation of people besides Noah, his wife, three sons, and their wives.

After the flood, God spared Noah, his wife, and out of Noah, three sons, Shem, Ham, and Japheth, out of whom were born the nations of the world.

> *And the sons of Noah went forth from the Ark, were Shem, and Ham, and Japheth: and Ham is the father of Canaan. These are the three sons of Noah: and of them was the whole earth overspread.*
>
> — Genesis 9:18–19

At the present time, the world population is approximately seven billion people of different nations of races and color. From the descendants of Shem, one man found favor with God. God called and told him to take his wife and family separate from his father's home, family, and idolatry. Abraham obeyed God's voice and moved out of his father's household. After Abraham obeyed, God revealed Himself to Abraham, and Abraham taught Isaac about the true and living God, then Isaac taught Jacob about God. Jacob, in turn, taught his twelve sons, the patriarchs, about God; then, from Jacob's twelve sons came the Hebrew nation, who ended up in bondage for four hundred years in Egypt. Recorded in the Pentateuch, or the first five books of the Bible—*Genesis*, *Exodus*, *Leviticus*, *Numbers*, and *Deuteronomy*, which is also called the five books of Moses—these books give us a revelation of the beginning of the Jewish people who, in turn, introduced the True and Living God to the people of our world, especially those who desire and want to know Him.

Moses had a supernatural experience with God on Mount Horeb, and then God gave him the message, the ministry, and the miracles to go to Egypt and deliver the children of Israel who were in bondage for four hundred years. Moses was inspired as he asked God whom he should tell the Hebrew people (under Egypt's bondage) sent him. God, in His all-knowing wisdom, told Moses to tell his people, "'I Am that I Am' sent you." It was quite some years since these words were translated from the Hebrew language, "*ehyeh asher ehyeh*," which means "I Am that I Am." During the time that God spoke these words to Moses, certain of the Hebrew people understood the meaning of these words, "*ehyeh asher ehyeh*." Moses, the messenger and deliverer of the children of Israel, went to Egypt and told the people that he was sent by God to deliver them, then some of them would ask who sent him, and he spoke these words—"*ehyeh ahser ehyeh*." "*The I Am that I Am* that sent me," then Moses got their attention, and they opened their hearts to Moses and God, His Messenger, the message as they saw the supernatural power of God as God brought their deliverance. This supernatural act of God gave birth to the Hebrew people, out of whom the Messiah would be born.

God created everything in beauty, grandeur, and splendor, and when Lucifer (the fallen morning star angel) tried to destroy creation and our first parents, Adam and Eve, this is where the plan of God to redeem mankind was implemented. God is not a tyrant like certain predominant religion thinks that God wants them in the name of their religion to hate, kill, and destroy. But God is a God of love, and the purpose of this book, from the inspiration of the Scriptures, is to reveal God to you and that God wanted to show who He is—"*the Great I Am*" (Exodus, chapter 3). The "*Great I Am*" who came down to deliver the children of Israel through Moses' leadership from spiritual, physical, social, and financial bondage also came to deliver the human race through His Son, Jesus Christ.

> *For God so loved the world [the people He allowed to be born through Adam and Eve], that he gave his only begotten Son, that whosoever believeth in Him should not perish, but have everlasting life.*
>
> —John 3:16

God has shown He is a God of judgment (corrective measures), but generally, God is a God of love, and Jesus is where God's love is expressed for us human beings. God exists and is timeless; all the prophets beginning, such as Moses and other prophets, instructed the Israelites to honor and seek after God first. Contrasts God's beginning throughout eternity with man's frail and brief life. Man must come to terms with the small number of his days in comparison to a holy, everlasting God.

[Elihu says of God] "How great is God—beyond our understanding! The number of his years is past finding out."

— Job 36:26, NIV

God's years are innumerable and unending in contrast to men's few years. God is love, and His love knows no limits. His love reaches out to all people of every race, color, and creed. Love is not love until it reaches out to someone, even though they might not realize that someone loves them. There are two kinds of love. The first is Greek, "*phileo love.*" Phileo love is a love of our affections, a warm feeling that comes when touching someone he or she has affections for.

Then the second one is what you call "*agape love.*" Agape love is God's kind of love. It is seeking the welfare and betterment of another regardless of how they feel. Except for a few men and women in the Old and New Testament, Jesus was the first person that expressed "*agape love.*" When it seemed like the ceremonial, civil, and religious laws had reached their pinnacle and could do nothing for mankind, plus the rule of the stone-hearted Roman government who controlled the Jews, and everyone else with an iron fist, here came Jesus and preached "*agape love*" to one of the most religious men of that day named Nicodemus and, obviously, to the people of the world: to the Jews first, then the Gentiles.

These words of Jesus burst through like gleaming sun rays through centuries of dark clouds of ceremonial, civil, religious, and political darkness as He announced in the Gospel of Jesus Christ,

For God so love the world, that he gave his only begotten Son, that whosoever believeth in Him, should not perish, but have everlasting life.

— John 3:16

CHAPTER 1, PART 2

Jesus

Seven hundred years before Jesus was born, the prophet Isaiah prophesied the birth of Jesus Christ.

"Therefore the Lord Himself will give you a sign: […] a virgin shall conceive and bear a Son and shall call His name Immanuel [translated 'God with us']."

— Isaiah 7:14, NKJV

Fulfillment:

Now the birth of Jesus was as follows, after His mother Mary betrothed to Joseph before they came together she was found with child of the Holy Spirit.

— Matthew 1:18, NKJV

Mary's pregnancy was a supernatural act of God; being pregnant in those days without being married had very serious repercussions.

[…] the angel of the LORD appeared unto him [Joseph] in a dream, saying, Joseph, thou son of David, fear not to take unto thee Mary thy wife: for that which is conceived in her is of the Holy Ghost.

And she shall bring forth a son, and thou shalt call his name JESUS: for he shall save his people from their sins.

— Matthew 1:20–21

If Jesus was not God or the Son of God, then He deserves a diamond-studded Oscar trimmed with billions of dollars worth of diamonds and gemstones. With all the conflicting ideas that are being written and circulated about Jesus, without a shadow of a doubt, Jesus is God, but He also became a man. He was with God the Father from the beginning; He was born in the similitude of a human being because this was the only way God could have redeemed humankind from sin. Jesus had to become the God-man, the Son of God, and He was called the Son of Man in the Bible because He was the first God-man that was born of a woman.

In the beginning God created the heaven and the earth. And the earth was without form, and void; and darkness was upon the face of the deep. And the spirit of God moved upon the face of the waters. And God said, Let there be light: and there was light.

— Genesis 1:1–3

The earth was already here, but without form and void (nothing); the Spirit of God was brooding over the earth, and God said, "Let there be light, and there was light"; after God spoke, the Holy Spirit moved on the earth, and creation occurred; well, He is the same Holy Spirit that moved upon Mary and created a body that grew in Mary's womb after which she gave birth to Jesus; only the godly mind could comprehend the virgin birth of Jesus Christ. There was no human contact here; the virgin birth of Jesus Christ was an act of the creative power of God through the moving of the Holy Spirit.

Then said Mary unto the angel, "How shall this be, seeing I know not a man?"

— Luke 1:34

Human beings were sick and in need of a doctor, spiritually speaking, a spiritual doctor to perform spiritual surgery on the human race to get rid of the imbedded sinful nature that we inherited from Adam and Eve. Jesus had to become a man to redeem mankind. If you are in need of a doctor, you do not need the doctor's mother, but you need the doctor himself. In addition to this statement, Jesus will be the central focus of this book to help the modern-day church to get back to the place it ought to be. The Doctor is Jesus, and He is the only One who has the answer for this modern-day church. Mary was not the doctor, but she was chosen by God as a vessel to bring forth Jesus. Jesus is the doctor; spiritually speaking, for God to save mankind, His Son, Jesus Christ, had to be born of a woman, and here lies the key to this entire book: the birth of Jesus Christ was supernatural, His ministry was supernatural, His death and resurrection were supernatural, the outpouring of the Holy Ghost who Jesus promise to send back to earth was supernatural.

The word "supernatural" would be used as often and needed in this book, and when speaking of the supernatural, the author is referring to the supernatural power and acts of God from a godly and biblical point of view. Not a hocus-pocus state of mind or walking around like zombies and insinuating being involved in witchcraft, voodoo, magic, Satan worship, etc. The word "supernatural" originated and was first used in medieval times, of which some ungodly English people referred to the acts of the devil, but this word was predominantly used by the church in England when they were experiencing a revival and the power of God was being manifested in supernatural signs and wonders.

By the way, the word "supernatural" was never mentioned in the Bible because the miraculous was expected; the word "supernatural" being mentioned in this book is obviously necessary and is mentioned from a godly and biblical point of view; the reason is, generally speaking, 90 percent of the church world today goes to church for Sunday ritual, tradition, and formality. Thank God you are going to church, but prayerfully, it would dawn on you that you need more than ritual, formality, and tradition but the power of God like the apostles, which is in the book of Acts.

> *And when the day of Pentecost was fully come, they were all with one accord in one place.*
> *And suddenly there came a sound from heaven as of a rushing mighty wind, and it filled all the house where they were sitting.*
> *And there appeared unto them cloven tongues like as of fire, and it sat upon each of them.*
> *And they were all filled with the Holy Ghost, and began to speak with other tongues, as the Spirit gave them utterance.*
> — Acts 2:1–4

What this is referring to is if the church, in general, would impact the people of our world in its present condition and rise beyond the norm like the book of Acts church with a few men, we must go beyond the norm. There is a great need within the Body of Christ to get back to the basics of Christianity, but there is a greater need within the church to contend for the faith that was once delivered to the saints. God's divine intervention to redeem the human race from sin and to provide salvation (means to be free from sin) to have peace of mind, real joy, and happiness, to be set from the bondage of the sicknesses, diseases, devil, demons, evil spirits, and to give *eternal life or everlasting life* to all that believe. The redemption of the human race was solely dependent upon God; He had a perfect plan from the beginning of time after the devil caused Adam and Eve to plunge the entire human race into sin. This plan began with Abraham, Isaac,

Jacob, and then the Hebrew people, which produced the Judges, Prophets, Kings, King David, and then a Virgin by the name of Mary, who came from the lineage of David.

Every leader of all religions came to live; Jesus was the only God-man or leader who came to die. He came to die to bring us life, everlasting life, yes, the life of God, which is the only thing that would be able to sustain and keep us in these last and closing days as we are noticing every word or prophecy that the prophets, Jesus, and the apostles spoke, is being fulfilled in our day. The beginning of Jesus' ministry was an indication to bring changes in the religious order of that day to the present time, especially spiritual change, and change is what every leader of every religion, denomination, and organization is afraid of. Why? Because change for the betterment in every area of life, especially spiritually speaking, would mean self-denial, sacrifices, pain, and this would interfere with the traditional ritualistic formalistic ideologies of serving and leading men and women to God.

This is what Jesus did; He caused change in the church world of His day. Let it be said the change He brought about in the church world of His day. Religious leaders are the ones that tried to hinder Him, but eventually, His life, words, and teachings ministry changed the lives of a few men who shook then the known world. It was the religious leaders of that day, who engineered His death, but even in death, Jesus was triumphant. God vindicated His death by raising Him from the dead and now sitting at the right hand (authority) of the Father God to make intercession for us; in other words, Jesus is representing us to or before the Father God.

The *death and resurrection of Jesus is the foundation of the Christian faith*, and this is why almost every religious leader, people of every religion, some denominations, organizations, cults, far independent out-groups, some news media, atheists, agonistics, and the new age movement and modernism of this day and age are endeavoring to disprove that Jesus did not die on the cross and did not rise from the grave. Because the death of Jesus on the cross and the resurrection of Jesus Christ is a slap in the devil's face, that God is alive and well, and so are His true followers. Jesus is my example, my hero, and my God. His way was God's way for us. Jesus came to fulfill all that the law and the prophets spoke and wrote about, but in doing what He came to do, this was to give mankind a choice to a better way of life, also life eternal.

Believing and choosing His way of life, His teachings, and accepting Him will bring us inner peace, real joy, happiness, contentment, and, most of all, eternal or everlasting life. Jesus came to die so that we might live. He came to bring us life, everlasting life. Yes, Jesus came to show us the way to God, which was different than what we are accustomed to; why so many prominent people and thousands of people are turning to the mystical religions of the east? It's because Jesus' way in a way that is straightforward and contradicts the lifestyle so many want to live; if they adhered to the lifestyle of Jesus and His teachings, millions would experience salvation and inner peace and assurance of eternity, and the church would experience one of the greatest moves of God and a revival like we have never seen, which, in turn, would result in unprecedented evangelism of souls being reached with the Gospel of Jesus Christ around the world, which would usher in the second return of Jesus.

One of our finest pastors in America asked, "Yours truly, what is your vision, mission, goal, and purpose in the ministry?" He thought I was going to tell him that I would like to build a magnificent church building seating ten thousand or more people, comprising of every type of facility with my name and the name of my ministry in a digital flashing neon sign above this complex. Also, a type of building to facilitate every age group to reach all people with different needs and teach the things pertaining to the kingdom of God. Nothing wrong with this idea; God blesses the ministers and ministries who are fortunate to have this opportunity. But what surprised him was my answer, "My only desire, vision, mission, purpose, and goal is to try to be like Jesus in every way and to have the prayer life, power, the word, the boldness, the faith, miracles, signs, and wonders that Jesus had following the Word that He preached. To unconditionally love my brothers and sisters in the Lord, to have the compassion for lost souls that Jesus had (which I do), and to reach this generation for Jesus Christ before Jesus Christ returns to earth the second time."

There are over one hundred names that relate to Jesus; here are some of them. He is called:

- Alpha and Omega
- the Beginning and the Ending
- Bread of Life
- Bright and Morning Star
- Christ of God
- Counselor
- Creator
- Deliverer
- He is the Door
- Great High Priest
- Heir of all things
- Holy One of God
- Horn of Salvation
- I Am
- Image of God
- Immanuel
- King of the Jews
- King of Kings
- Lamb
- Lamb of God
- He is Life
- Light of the World
- Lion of the Tribe of Judah
- Lord of Host
- Man of Suffering
- Mediator
- Messenger of the Covenant
- Messiah
- The Anointed One
- Mighty God
- Nazarene
- Prince of Peace
- Prophet
- Redeemer
- Resurrection of Life
- Rock
- Savior
- Wonderful
- the Way

Jesus is God because He was with God from the beginning.

"In the beginning was the Word, and the Word was with God, and the Word [living Word, not written word] was God.

—John 1:1

"[…] Most assuredly, I say to you, before Abraham was, I Am."

—John 8:58, NKJV

Here are two of the most convincing scriptures concerning Jesus as God:

He is the image of the invisible God, the firstborn over all creation. For by Him were all things created that are in heaven and that are on earth, visible and invisible, whether thrones or dominions or principalities or powers. All things were created through Him and for Him. And He is before all things.

— Colossians 1:15–17a, NKJV

"In Him dwells the fullness of the Godhead bodily."

— Colossians 2:9, NKJV

Jesus was God in the flesh. Amazingly so, the baby that was born in a manger, who grew up in Nazareth and worked in the sawdust and shavings of Joseph the carpenter shop, was convincingly the Son of God or God in the flesh.

The Gospel of *Matthew*, *Mark*, *Luke*, and *John* takes us to the beginning of the ministry of Jesus, especially the Gospel of Luke, "And Jesus being full of the Holy Ghost returned from Jordan, and was led by the Spirit into the wilderness" Luke 4:1. "The next day John saw Jesus coming unto him, and saith, Behold the Lamb of God, which taketh away the sin of the world" John 1:29.

It is recorded where Jesus went into the wilderness to fast and also pray to be alone with God, this is where the devil attacked Jesus with three temptations, and He overcame every single one of them and the devil. These temptations were pertaining to the world, flesh, and the devil and his evil deeds. Jesus' fasting in the wilderness was an example to us that we should fast and pray and be alone with God; the author is not insinuating that anyone should go in some wilderness somewhere and fast and pray for forty days but to emphasize fasting once in a while, which crucifies the flesh, purifies the mind, and increases the power of God in an individuals life. More will be dealt with in another chapter pertaining to fasting. But here is the record from the Bible.

> *And Jesus being full of the Holy Ghost returned from Jordan, and was led by the Spirit into the wilderness,*
>
> *Being forty days tempted of the devil. And in those days he did eat nothing: and when they were ended, he afterward hungered.*
>
> *And the devil said unto him, If thou be the Son of God, command this stone that it be made bread.*
>
> *And Jesus answered him, saying, It is written, That man shall not live by bread alone, but by every word of God.*
>
> *And the devil, taking him ups into an high mountain, shewed unto him all the kingdoms of the world in a moment of time.*
>
> *And the devil said unto him, All this power will I give thee, and the glory of them: for that is delivered unto me; and to whomsoever I will I give it.*
>
> *If thou therefore wilt worship me, all shall be thine.*
>
> *And Jesus answered and said unto him, Get thee behind me, Satan: for it is written, Thou shalt worship the Lord thy God, and him only shalt thou serve.*
>
> *And he brought him to Jerusalem, and set him on a pinnacle of the temple, and said unto him, If thou be the Son of God, cast thyself down from hence:*
>
> *For it is written, He shall give his angels charge over thee, to keep thee:*
>
> *And in their hands they shall bear thee up, lest at any time thou dash thy foot against a stone.*

And Jesus answering said unto him, It is said, Thou shalt not tempt the Lord thy God.
— Luke 4:1–12

And Jesus returned in the power of the Spirit into Galilee: and there went out a fame of him through all the region round about.
— Luke 4:14

Jesus' way to fame was not to be popular but to meet the people's needs, glorify, and do God's will. Today's way to fame is the person with a magnificent name, with degrees behind his or her name, and being popular with the crowd.

And he taught in their synagogues, being glorified of all.
— Luke 4:15

Jesus was already preaching the good news of the kingdom of God, which is peace and salvation through Him, healing the sick, casting out devils with miracles, signs, and wonders, following the word He preached. But up until this present time, hardly anyone really understood who He really was, and they began following Him by the thousands; why? Because of the word, the truth, and the power of miracles, there was something different about Jesus, supernaturally different, plus their souls were being nourished by the word He preached, their spirits were being lifted, their faith began to increase to believe God for greater things.

The dawn of a new Sabbath day had broken. The sun was with rays of sunlight protruding through the clouds, shining majestically with multicolored rays of sunshine upon the hills and valleys and upon the little town of Nazareth as everyone else was walking to the synagogue, including Jesus. This is the first time Jesus had returned to Nazareth, where He was born. Jesus walked majestically into the synagogue, and the presiding priest had respect and honor for Jesus. As Jesus entered the synagogue and sat down, the priest gave Him the book of the prophet Isaiah to read, and here is the written account from Luke, chapter 4,

And he came to Nazareth, where he had been brought up: and, as his custom was, he went into the synagogue on the sabbath day, and stood up for to read.

And there was delivered unto him the book of the prophet Esaias. And when he had opened the book, he found the place where it was written,

The Spirit of the Lord is upon me, because he hath anointed me to preach the gospel to the poor; he hath sent me to heal the brokenhearted, to preach deliverance to the captives, and recovering of sight to the blind, to set at liberty them that are bruised,

To preach the acceptable year of the Lord.
— Luke 4:16–19

Everyone in the synagogue suddenly felt a ray of hope and praised God as they said these words, "Alas! Deliverance has come. This homegrown boy, now one of their own ministers, was going to deliver us from our sins, sicknesses, diseases, problems, poverty, and depression and give us peace of mind. Also, He will definitely deliver us from the oppression of the Roman government and be at peace with our neighboring cities."

Jesus continued reading:

And he closed the book, and he gave it again to the minister, and sat down. And the eyes of all them that were in the synagogue were fastened on him.
And he began to say unto them, This day is this scripture fulfilled in your ears.
And all bare him witness, and wondered at the gracious words which proceeded out of his mouth. And they said, Is not this Joseph's son?

— Luke 4:20–22

The local congregation was so proud that this home-raised young man, now in the prime of His life, was going to be their Elite Rabbi, but they did not as of yet see Him as God and Savior. They were looking at Him as Joseph and Mary's son, but not as the God who came to redeem them and mankind from their sins, and this is where they began to miss out on whom Jesus really was. Some of them missed their visitation from God. Losing sight of who Jesus really is can cause the church world of today to reduce Him to a little baby born in a manger (nothing wrong with celebrating His birth). Generally speaking, the church world is birthing, crucifying, and resurrecting Jesus every year, but something is radically wrong when the church cannot move beyond this and recognize Jesus as God, praise and worship Him as the same who is the center of our lives.

"For in him we live, and move, and have our being."

— Acts 17:28a

Understanding who Jesus is will cause you and millions of people to experience the revelation that Jesus is God and not just as a baby born in a manger (anything wrong with celebrating His birth, no), but the conclusion is up to you, with the billions of dollars being spent for the wrong reason in the wrong place instead of centering our minds on Jesus Christ.

There was no room for Him in the Inn.

— Luke 2:7

The drop of a pin could have been heard throughout the entire synagogue; silence was golden and everywhere as every eye was fastened on Jesus after Jesus read these words:

And he closed the book, and he gave it to the minister, and sat down. And the eyes of all them that were in the synagogue were fastened on him,
And he began to say unto them, This day is the Scripture fulfilled in your ears.
And all bare him witness and wondered at the gracious [encouraging] words which proceeded out of his mouth. And they said, Is not this Joseph's son?

— Luke 4:20–22

This is what they wanted to hear: the man Jesus, who was born and then grew up among them, is now their earthly deliverer; Jesus took the opportunity to woo and win the gathering in the synagogue. I can hear some of the sisters in the synagogue saying, "Finally, we have someone who can show us the way of

God." Listen to how He is speaking; as the brothers responded, I have never heard anyone who can preach like Him, but there is a problem here, as they commented and said, "Is this not Joseph's son!"

They were surprised by the words that were coming from the mouth of the carpenter's son, and another part of the congregation looked speechless because these words did not sound like a prepared, polished, homiletically preached sermon. Mumbled words from the mouth of the hearers within the synagogue rippled throughout the temple. The words of Jesus were a direct fulfillment of prophecy from the Holy Scriptures. The announcement He made in the temple in Nazareth that was spoken by the prophet Isaiah seven hundred years ago caused every the high priest, priests, scribes, lawyers, doctors, Pharisees, Sadducees, and other religious leaders and all the people within the temple on that day to look upon Him, as some were in shock, as God's eternal plan for the redemptive work of mankind was about to be unfolded and implemented. Jesus came for a purpose, a mission of love, grace, and deliverance, but to them, it was coming from the carpenter's son. With the announcement that Jesus made in the temple of Nazareth.

The Spirit of the Lord is upon me because He (God) hath anointed me to preach the Gospel to the poor, deliverance to the captives, recovering to sight to the blind, heal the brokenhearted, set at liberty to them that are bruised. All eyes were fastened on Jesus, and He concluded His reading Scripture with these words, "This day is the scripture fulfilled in your ears" Luke 4:21. Everything else that Jesus read and said was music to the ears of His hearers.

Shockwaves went through the synagogue as some of them murmured as their forefathers did, who does He think He is. Since Jesus was baptized in the River Jordan, really, there was no other person to recognize and introduce Jesus; there are times that a minister has to talk about himself, and this was one of those occasions that the Son of God had to introduce Himself. The onus rested on Him; He wanted them to understand that the Son of God was standing among them. "Hey, guys, certainly I grew up among you, but please do not look at me as a little baby born in a manger and grew up among you as a carpenter son and your carpenter, open your eyes and look beyond my birth and growth. God in the flesh is standing right before your very eyes, and I am come to bring you something beyond the tradition of the Scribes and Pharisees and religions of your day. I am come to manifest God's life and power among you; most of all, do not look at me from a fleshy point of view, I am God in the flesh, and I am here to bring life, not death."

From the very beginning or proclamation of Jesus' ministry recorded in the Bible, Jesus wanted the people to understand that He is the one who came to fulfill all the laws and prophets. He was the one to look to. Now, here it comes, He was before any religion, denomination, organization, pope, priest, king, or kingdom; a kingdom without Jesus is not a kingdom; Jesus was before a kingdom. Thank God for dedicated leaders, but we are living in a day and time when certain men, even women, claim that they are the head of their particular religion, ministry, denomination, or organizations with man-made rules without direction from God, God's Word, and leading of the Holy Spirit.

At this point, Jesus could have seen and sensed an antagonistic spirit emitting from most attendees in the synagogue towards Him. But He zeroed in anyhow as He continued speaking in the synagogue.

> *And he said unto them, Ye will surely say unto me this proverb, Physician, heal thyself:*
> *whatsoever we have heard done in Capernaum, do also here in thy country [hometown]. […] I*
> *say unto you, No prophet is accepted in his own country.*
>
> — Luke 4:23–24

In this particular crowd, some of them had witnessed His birth, probably helped Mary, washed His diapers, gave Him a bath, changed His clothes, and fed Him. Some of them had gone with Him to the well to draw water, ran around the neighborhood with other kids, went to the market, some went to school with Him, and some had taught Him in the temple, even though they were astounded at the way He answered their questions and how He knew of the law and the prophets. Now, He is standing among them, and He is telling them He came to deliver them. This is all right, yes, we need help; we have heard how the blind saw, the deaf heard, the lame walk in Capernaum and other surrounding villages and cities, but You are one of us, and we know You as the carpenter son, You read well, You spoke well, but claiming that You are the one that the law and the prophets spoke about, claiming that You are the one the Scriptures spoke about, this is susceptible and difficult to digest. We know of Your life: You were born in a manger, You grew up among us. We know what You are thinking and saying.

PHYSICIAN, HEAL YOURSELF

Jesus discerned they were looking at His human side, but He broke the icy spirit and said these words, which surfaced what was within the hearts of this congregation, as He continued speaking,

> *But I tell you of a truth, many widows were in Israel in the days of Elias, when the heaven was shut up three years and six months, when great famine was throughout all the land;*
>
> *But unto none of them was Elias sent, save unto Sarepta, a city of Sidon, unto a woman that was a widow.*
>
> *And many lepers were in Israel in the time of Eliseus the prophet; and none of them was cleansed, saving Naaman the Syrian.*
>
> — Luke 4:25–27

All Jesus was trying to tell the people who were in the synagogue at the time of His inauguration, the woman of Zarepath received a supernatural miracle of survival in spite of the famine because she received and believed the prophet Elijah; Naaman, the Syrian King, received and believed the prophet Elisha, obeyed and went to the River Jordan and dipped seven times, and he received a supernatural miracle of healing after he dipped in River Jordan seven times. Both of them were strangers to the Jewish people; they were not schooled or taught in the feast days, Sabbaths civil, and ceremonial laws. But they believed and received the prophet of God and were delivered, healed, and blessed.

When I announced:

> *The Spirit of the Lord is upon me, because he [God] hath anointed me to preach the Gospel to the poor, [...] deliverance to the captives, recovering of the sight to the blind, [heal the broken hearted], to set at liberty them that are bruised.*
>
> — Luke 4:18

The congregation in the synagogue was elated and very happy, but when Jesus said:

> *And he began to say unto them, This day is this scripture fulfilled in your ears.*
> *[What Jesus was telling them: I am the one, the Messiah, that Isaiah prophesied about; I am standing here now; Isaiah chapter 61 is fulfilled by God sending Me.]*
>
> — Luke 4:21

Few of them believed; some of them were puzzled, but most of them were adamant and apoplectic. Jesus also felt an atomistic spirit coming from the religious leaders and most of the people; the people were looking at how He was born among them, His growing up, and how He was raised, He was Mary and Joseph's Son, but they did not realize that He was God in the flesh.

> *"Physician, heal thyself."*
>
> — Luke 4:23

Jesus discerned their thoughts and now their attitude towards Him. All Jesus was trying to get them—to see that He was God, He came down in the flesh to deliver them. "If you receive me like the widow of Zarephath received Elijah and survived the famine, as Naaman received Elisha and was healed of his leprosy; if you receive me, you will be saved, healed, and delivered." All Jesus was telling them was—"Your time of visitation had come."

As God, Jesus was knowing what was in the heart of mankind, but from a human point of view (just speculating), maybe He did not anticipate this kind of attitude from this crowd this early. He did not get a handshake from the mayor of the city; the ecclesiastical governing board of the religious organization of that day did not ordain and present Him with an ordination certificate. The welcoming committee was not too welcoming after all towards Jesus; He did not get the recognition or the covering from the presidents of the denominations, organizations, or the ministerial association of that time (this did not mean anything to Jesus, but inevitably so, He was also human and might have appreciated all of the above), but Jesus did not compromise and did not pull any punches He was bold about whom He was. They did not like Jesus proclaiming Himself as the Son of God in this His inaugural service.

This is the welcome Jesus received:

> *And all they in the synagogue, when they heard these things, were filled with wrath, And rose up, and thrust him out of the city, and led him unto the brow of the hill whereon their city was built, that they might cast him down headlong.*
> *But he passing through the midst of them went his way [disappeared].*
>
> — Luke 4:28–30

This antagonistic spirit did not deter Jesus from what He came to do.

One of the greatest revelations I heard about Jesus was when yours truly attended one of Billy Graham's meetings when I was fifteen years old. I stood right in front of him and heard him tell that he and his son were walking through the woods on a certain day. He said he stepped on an ant bed, and his son noticed that his daddy hurt and killed some of the ants; his son, being a little kid, said to him, "Daddy, can you help these ants that are hurting, even though some of them are dead?" Billy Graham spoke back and said, "For me to help those ants, I will have to become an ant myself."

This is exactly what God did for us. So many people would like to see God but miss the simplicity of the Gospel of Jesus Christ, and Jesus Christ became one of us in order to deliver us.

People spend millions of dollars traveling to different places and visiting religious shrines, rivers statutes, and magnificent buildings with idols to which they bow down. Some of them hold on to trinkets, count beads, chains, and crosses, so many people are being deceived into the religions of some Asian countries. People are delving more into the new age movement and mysticism; why? It's all because they are searching for God; they want to know God. But God made it so simple; all we have to do is look to Jesus, study the Gospels, read the writings of the prophets, the apostles, and get a picture of Jesus in your spirit; seeing Jesus, you will see and understand who God is.

Ever since God created the universe, He has billions of insignias or proofs within the universe that He created that can be seen night and day and, of course, anywhere you go. All of this signifies He made them and that He exists. And since the glory of His power and wisdom shine more brightly above, the heavens and heaven is His palace. There is no place in the universe where you cannot see His glory. Here are some Scriptures from the Word of God that give a vivid, magnificent, and majestic description of our Lord and Savior who reveals God.

> *And in the four and twentieth day of the first month, as I was by the side of the great river, which is Hiddekel;*
>
> *Then I lifted up mine eyes, and looked, and behold a certain man clothed in linen, whose loins were girded with fine gold of Uphaz:*
>
> *His body also was like the beryl, and his face as the appearance of lightning, and his eyes as lamps of fire, and his arms and his feet like in color to polished brass, and the voice of his words like the voice of a multitude.*
>
> *And I Daniel alone saw the vision: for the men that were with me saw not the vision; but a great quaking fell upon them, so that they fled to hide themselves.*
>
> *Therefore I was left alone, and saw this great vision, and there remained no strength in me: for my comeliness was turned in me into corruption, and I retained no strength.*
>
> *Yet heard I the voice of his words: and when I heard the voice of his words, then was I in a deep sleep on my face, and my face toward the ground.*
>
> — Daniel 10:4–9

> *I was in the Spirit on the Lord's day, and heard behind me a great voice, as of a trumpet.*
>
> — Revelation 1:10

> *Saying, I am Alpha and Omega, the first and the last: and, What thou seest, write in a book, and send it unto the seven churches which are in Asia; unto Ephesus, and unto Smyrna, and unto Pergamos, and unto Thyatira, and unto Sardis, and unto Philadelphia, and unto Laodicea.*
>
> *And I turned to see the voice that spake with me. And being turned, I saw seven golden candlesticks;*

And in the midst of the seven candlesticks one like unto the Son of man, clothed with a garment down to the foot, and girt about the paps with a golden girdle.

His head and his hairs were white like wool, as white as snow; and his eyes were as a flame of fire;

And his feet like unto fine brass, as if they burned in a furnace; and his voice as the sound of many waters.

— Revelation 1:11–15

Let not your heart be troubled: ye believe in God, believe also in me.

In my Father's house are many mansions: if it were not so, I would have told you. I go to prepare a place for you.

And if I go and prepare a place for you, I will come again, and receive you unto myself; that where I am, there ye may be also.

And whither I go ye know, and the way ye know.

— John 14:1–4

And after six days Jesus taketh Peter, James, and John his brother, and bringeth them up into an high mountain apart,

And was transfigured before them: and his face did shine as the sun, and his raiment was white as the light.

And, behold, there appeared unto them Moses and Elias talking with him.

— Matthew 17:1–3

Philip saith unto him, Lord, show us the Father, and it sufficeth us.

Jesus saith unto him, Have I been so long time with you, and yet hast thou not known me, Philip? he that hath seen me hath seen the Father; and how sayest thou then, Show us the Father?

— John 14:8–9

Seeing Jesus is the most awesome experience that any human being can encounter it would reshape anyone's life. This does not mean, especially if you are a Christian, that you would go around entertaining the idea that you want Jesus to appear to you, just live your daily Christian life; I heard a certain TV preacher say that Jesus does not appear to anyone unless He returns again in the Rapture then all eyes shall see Him; this is true, but this does not limit an individual from having an experience with Jesus or even seeing Him. Jesus appeared to certain people in the Old Testament of the Bible. After the resurrection, Jesus appeared to them; Paul, the apostle, saw Him and had a supernatural experience with Him on the road to Damascus. I have personally heard realizable pastors, missionaries, evangelists, and other ministers; even certain people shared awesome experiences of seeing Jesus. At the present time, it is reported that within the Moslem population, angels, Jesus, and other supernatural occurrences are happening, and they are being saved by the thousands upon thousands.

The prophet Daniel and the apostle John describe their experiences of seeing Jesus. This was hundreds of years before He was born in Bethlehem and about thirty years when John saw Jesus; both of them wrote of their supernatural encounter with Jesus Christ and saw Him as who He really is.

DANIEL 10:4-9, COMMENTARY

- 534 BC, while in captivity, the prophet Daniel was standing by the river Hiddekel in meditation and prayer, and he lifted up his eyes and looked and saw a man standing who obviously was Jesus Christ. His clothes were of fine linen, and from His stomach or His loins down, He was girded with the fine gold of Uphaz. Uphaz is the Ophir of other passages; in the times of the prophets, it was the gold region of the earth, whence the most abundant supplies of the finest gold were obtained in certain regions of India. Even though the gold on Jesus that Daniel saw was superb, the gold of Uphaz was the only words that Daniel could have thought of to describe what Jesus was wearing. His body also was like the beryl (the color of beryl ranges from a transparent blue, sometimes a mixture of green, yellow, red, and white), His face as the appearance of lightning, and His eyes as lamps of fire, and His arms and His feet like the color to polished brass, and the voice of His words like the voice of a multitude. When Jesus speaks, His voice could be heard over a multitude talking.

- AD 33—John, the last of the apostles who was banished on the Isle of Patmos, the only apostle to die a natural death, before dying, saw a vision of Jesus in His glory, which was similar to that of Daniel five hundred and thirty-four years earlier. John said he looked in the midst of the seven golden candlesticks and saw Jesus clothe with a garment down to the foot and dressed from His chest down with gold clothing (note the similarity of Daniel's vision). His hair was white like wool and snow, His eyes were as a flame of fire, and His feet unto fine brass and if they were heated up in a furnace to shine more and His voice of many waters. What is the author's intent? Is it to allow you to see really who Jesus Christ is?

CHAPTER 1, PART 3

The Holy Spirit

Before writing on the Holy Spirit, the author would like the reader to consider these Scriptures taken from the Old Testament, one of the most intriguing books of the Bible.

And it came to pass on the third day in the morning, that there were thunders and lightning's, and a thick cloud upon the mount, and the voice of the trumpet exceeding loud; so that all the people that was in the camp trembled.

And Moses brought forth the people out of the camp to meet with God; and they stood at the nether part of the mount.

And mount Sinai was altogether on a smoke, because the LORD *descended upon it in fire: and the smoke thereof ascended as the smoke of a furnace, and the whole mount quaked greatly.*

— Exodus 19:16–18

And when the voice of the trumpet sounded long and waxed louder and louder, Moses spake, and God answered him by a voice.

And all the people saw the thunderings, and the lightnings, and the noise of the trumpet, and the mountain smoking: and when the people saw it, they removed, and stood afar off.

And they said unto Moses, Speak thou with us, and we will hear: but let not God speak with us, lest we die.

And Moses said unto the people, Fear not: for God is come to prove you, and that his fear may be before your faces that ye sin not.

And the people stood afar off, and Moses drew near unto the thick darkness where God was.

And the LORD *said unto Moses, Thus thou shalt say unto the children of Israel, Ye have seen that I have talked with you from heaven.*

— Exodus 19:19, 20:18–22

Reading the book of Exodus has always had a profound impact on me; the awesomeness of God expressed in these pages of the Bible is like no other book except for the miracles that Jesus was recorded in the Gospels and the works of the Holy Spirit recorded in the book of Acts.

Reading the above Scriptures always leaves an indelible impression on my mind about the reality of God and who He *is*. God is Awesome. But here comes a question of questions, how would you like to experience this event of God appearing on Mount Horeb for one week, a day, or night?

The children of Israel could not look at this awesome visitation of God for a few moments; they told Moses, "Please you speak to us, but do not let God speak to us," what was their dread! "Lest we die!" God, in His divine wisdom, knew that His people could not sustain or survive this manifestation of Himself, so in due time He sent Jesus Christ, who, in turn, sent the Holy Spirit. We, human beings (even though some think they are gods), could not accommodate God as He did on Mount Horeb for one week, more or less; God realized this, which is why He sent the Holy Spirit.

Notice the similarity in the book of Acts, chapter 2, wind and fire.

The Holy Spirit and exclusively so is an inexhaustible subject; thousands of books have been written about the Holy Spirit; it is true that we respect the ideas, views, and writings written about the Holy Spirit, but please remember whatever is written must correspond with the Bible, the Word of God. Within the past years, there have been hundreds of different translations of the Bible, but if there is going to be any validity of doctrinal teachings, especially pertaining to God, Jesus, and the Holy Spirit, we must adhere to the original KJV version, which was translated from the original Aramaic (Hebrew) and Greek languages. Thank God for men and women of high scholastic standards pertaining to the Scriptures, but please remember it takes the Holy Spirit to reveal books, chapters, and verses within the Bible.

The contents within the next pages contain a brief study of "who the Holy Spirit *is*" in another chapter that contains what the Holy Spirit does, including the gifts and fruits of the Holy Spirit.

In the Old Testament, God manifested Himself as the Father; in the New Testament, God manifested Himself through Jesus Christ, His Son. In our day and time, God is manifesting Himself through the Holy Spirit. One God manifesting Himself as God the Father, God the Son, and God the Holy Spirit; please note God the Holy Spirit. On many occasions, yours truly had the opportunity to meet certain rabbis, some by appointment, others in meetings, and some by coincidence. In conversation with these rabbis, the subject of God would automatically and obviously come up. With no intention of theological discussions on my behalf, these rabbis, of course with love, would inject these words into our discussion and conversation, "You, Gentiles, Christians, believe in three Gods," with no intention to continue the conversation, these rabbis would affirm their conviction as they quoted Scripture from Deuteronomy 6:4.

"Hear, O Israel: the Lord thy God is one God."

— Deuteronomy 6:4

Thank God for the Jews or the Hebrew people. They are the first people that God revealed Himself to, the first people that accepted Jehovah as one God while other nations around them worshiped idols and man gods of gold, silver, brass, stones, and wood. But most Jews, even to this present time, refuse to accept Jesus Christ as their Messiah (but in due time, they will); most of them do not accept the Gospels, which contain the records of the birth, life, and ministry of Jesus on earth two thousand years ago, in particular, most of them refuse to accept the death of Jesus Christ on the cross and His resurrection and the Holy Spirit with us and in us today, when we believe. To some of them, God is always the God of the Old Testament, but they forget that God sent His Son, Jesus Christ, and Jesus or God sent the Holy Spirit.

The Holy Spirit is not a force, energy, or power. The Holy Spirit must *not* be referred to as "*it*" because He is a Person, and He is *God* at work, moving, creating, convicting, comforting, speaking, leading, guiding, empowering, anointing, and drawing men and women to God if they will open their hearts and listen to Him. The Holy Spirit is God; His power and presence extended actively working in the universe to bring about God's plan and purpose through His servants within the Church of Jesus Christ. The Holy Spirit was also sent to hinder Satan's plan from hindering God's work. The Holy Spirit contributes and has the attributes of God and does the work of God. The Holy Spirit is omnipresent, omnipotent, and omniscient. He anoints God's servants in ministry and empowers miracles; when the Holy Spirit moves and does something, this means God has done and doing it.

When the Holy Spirit speaks, this means God is speaking because He, the Holy Spirit, is God; God's Spirit is moving on the earth today, moving, working in Spirit form, striving and moving to bring men and women back to God and to bring about God's plan and purpose. Most of all, the Holy Spirit wants to dwell in all those who will believe in God through Jesus Christ. The Church, or the Body of Christ, desperately needs to understand who the Holy Spirit is. He is God, the same Jehovah God of the Old

Testament and the same Jesus Christ of the New Testament, and now He is the same God in the Holy Spirit. As has been taught by some, especially a particular organization that carries the name Christians and the church who labeled the Holy Spirit as the third person, but nowhere in the Bible does it mention the Holy Spirit as the third person, this trend of thinking limits the Holy Spirit and takes away from a biblical fact that He is God.

The Holy Spirit is God with us and in us. God with us and in us, the carnal mind would not be able to comprehend this statement. How could a Holy God dwell in a sinful man? It is an age-old question! Such thinking and thinkers, little do they realize (unless we teach or preach to them the Gospel of Jesus) that God was manifested in Jesus Christ, who died on the cross and opened the way for all mankind to come to God. While Jesus was alive, He promised to send the Holy Spirit, and when He arose from the grave, He did send the Holy Spirit on the Day of Pentecost.

From that time to the present, the Holy Spirit was outpoured and is with us and in us who believe not carnal-minded and unbelieving people. The only time they will understand (unbelievers, that is) is when they repent of their sins and accept Jesus Christ as Lord and Savior.

> *The next day John seeth Jesus coming unto him, and saith, Behold the Lamb of God, which taketh away the sin of the world.*
>
> *This is he of whom I said, after me cometh a man which is preferred before me: for he was before me.*
>
> *And I knew him not: but that he should be made manifest to Israel, therefore am I come baptizing with water.*
>
> *And John bare record, saying, I saw the Spirit descending from heaven like a dove, and it abode upon him.*
>
> — Gospel of John 1:29–32

While John was baptizing Jesus, he saw or witnessed the Holy Spirit descending on Jesus like a dove. The Holy Spirit descending on Jesus like a *dove* was a sign that Jesus was the Son of God and to further authenticate and confirm that Jesus was the Son of God and God sent Him, this sign of the dove on Jesus' baptism to reconfirm that this was so. Jesus was baptized in water and with the Holy Spirit also attested to the fact He was anointed with the Holy Spirit to do the works of God. The crowd that was standing by the River Jordan witnessed Jesus being baptized in the River Jordan. There were people from every walk of life, including Scribes, Pharisees, and Sadducees, leaders and other religious sects, and obviously, people from every facet of society.

There are no records of the number of the people standing on the banks of the River Jordan, but they did not see the Holy Spirit descending on Jesus; John saw the Holy Spirit like a "*dove.*" This was a supernatural and sacred event, but with reverence and the fear of God, this statement would be made. Could you imagine if the crowd had seen this supernatural event, they might have gone into some type of hysteria, frenzy, or hallucination, some might even have passed out, and some religious leader or leaders from that crowd might have started what might have been called the dove movement.

What happened at the River Jordan—"*the dove descending of Jesus*"—was of God and a supernatural act of God to verify who Jesus was and His baptism with the Holy Spirit; the author does not mean to take away from the seriousness, sacredness, and godliness of that moment, but people are so quick and gullible about accepting symbols, relics, signs, chains, beads, wafers, etc., instead of the real.

There are occasions when the Holy Spirit manifests Himself, and He comes like *a dove, wind*, or *fire*, but the Holy Spirit is not a dove, wind, or fire, even though He comes as these, but the Holy Spirit is God and God among us when we are baptized like the apostles on the day of Pentecost with the evidence of speaking in other tongues.

> *For with stammering lips and another tongue will he speak to this people.*
>
> — Isaiah 28:11

> *And they were all filled with the Holy Ghost and began to speak with other tongues, as the Spirit gave them utterance.*
>
> — Acts 2:4

After Jesus was baptized, He immediately went into the wilderness to fast and pray; during fasting and praying, He was tempted by the devil and overcame all of the temptations the devil threw at Him. Jesus came down from the mountain and started His ministry; the Holy Spirit was evident in the life and ministry of Jesus.

> *He went to Nazareth, where he had been brought up, and on the Sabbath day he went into the synagogue, as was his custom. He stood up to read, the scroll of the prophet Isaiah was handed to him. Unrolling it, he found the place where it is written:*
>
> *The Spirit of the Lord is on me, because he has anointed me to proclaim good news to the poor. He has sent me to proclaim freedom for the prisoners and recovery of sight for the blind, to set the oppressed free.*
>
> — Luke 4:16–18, NIV

The Holy Spirit is not *peculiar* and wired sounds, sensations, and emotions, but there are some people in receiving the Holy Spirit who might react differently emotionally, but this is not the Holy Spirit but only people reacting to the baptism of the Holy Spirit or signs that are baptize with the Holy Spirit. There are some who proclaim that the Holy Spirit is a wafer. This is not so; how could the Holy Spirit be a dry piece of cracker or wafer? Foremost, the Holy Spirit is God with and in you; this thought should make us walk holy, reverently (not pious), and humbly in our Christian life and before God. Here is a word of warning for those who think there should be no type of emotion when an individual receives or is baptized with the Holy Spirit. There would be some type of emotion. When the hundred and twenty disciples were baptized with the Holy Spirit in the Upper Room, first of all, there was a rushing wind, then cloven tongues of fire sat or lighted on each one of their heads, and they began to speak in other tongues as the Spirit of God gave them utterance or as they were inspired to speak. After this, some of them behaved like drunken men; these were signs that they had received the Holy Spirit; and the rushing mighty wind, cloven tongues like a fire, behaving like drunken men were outer evidence they were baptized with the Holy Spirit.

After the crucifixion and resurrection of Jesus Christ, Jesus gave the apostles specific instruction before ascending to heaven that they should go to Jerusalem and wait for the promise of the Father, which is the Holy Ghost or Holy Spirit; here is the Bible record:

And, behold, I send the promise of my Father upon you: but tarry ye in the city of Jerusalem, until ye be endued with power from on high. [This they did, and while fasting, praying and waiting in the Upper Room.]

— Luke 24:49

There came a sound of a rushing mighty wind, and there appeared cloven tongues as of fire, and it sat each upon their heads, and they began to speak in other tongues.

— Acts 2:2

Sound of a rushing mighty wind, cloven tongues as of fire that appeared on each of the apostles' and other disciples' heads were signs that the Holy Spirit was outpoured for the first time; their speaking in tongues was a sign that they were baptized with the Holy Spirit. The Holy Spirit is God because He is God. He can move as He will; He can move and bring about changes in the atmosphere and hinder the power of Satan; He can move within the Church or the Body of Christ in signs, miracles, healing, and the gifts of the Spirit and many other manifestations, most of all He was sent to help believers in Christ live a successful Christian life. He can move for us in the atmosphere, nature, our circumstances, situation, healing, and problems. The Holy Spirit is a Person, and He is at work in the world we live in, as He lives in the Church and in us. The Holy Spirit was sent to bring about God's plan and purpose through the Church.

There is divineness when someone is baptized with the Holy Spirit combined with salvation. This can be sometimes unexplainable but can only be experienced. The Holy Spirit is God's way of working in and through us; the Holy Spirit does not bear witness of Himself but of Jesus Christ; the "face" of the Father is revealed by the Son; the "face" of the Son is revealed by the Holy Spirit. Theology is vague in explaining God through the Father, Son, and the Holy Spirit, but God in His divine wisdom has limits for us here on earth; all He asks us to do is to believe, and we would see and experience God working through the Son and the Holy Spirit.

Two thousand years have gone by since the outpouring of the Holy Spirit on the day of Pentecost, but it seems like most of the modern-day Church lacks the understanding of who the Holy Spirit really is! It's all because some of them labeled the Holy Spirit as the third person. There is no intent by the author of this book to create any controversy, but nowhere in the Bible does it state that the Holy Spirit is the third person, and I would rest my thoughts right here, but the Holy Spirit is God. Going back to the beginning of the study on the Holy Spirit, we read in Exodus 19 and 20, where God manifested His glory in fire, thunders, lightnings, fiery clouds, and smoke to the Hebrew people. So great and marvelous was this sight that Moses and the people were in immense fear that they trembled. This was God in His glory visiting the Hebrew people and preparing them as a nation to bring forth the coming Messiah, Jesus Christ.

The outpouring of the Holy Spirit on the Day of Pentecost was God manifesting Himself in the Holy Spirit (Acts chapter 2), this time when God manifested Himself in the Upper Room, instead of one an open appearance where He manifested Himself on the mountain (Exodus 19 and 20), on the day of Pentecost He manifested Himself through the Holy Spirit. Again it must be reiterated in the Old Testament times; God manifested Himself as the Father; in New Testament time, He manifested Himself through His Son, Jesus Christ, and from Pentecost (Acts 2) to the present time, He manifested Himself through the Holy Spirit.

He came to be *with us, in us, where our flesh and spirit could contain Him and manifest Himself through us.* The responsibility of the Church is to be baptized with the Holy Spirit and seek the fullness of the Holy Spirit, which has been outpoured since the day of Pentecost so that we would be effective witnesses in bringing mankind to God. Obviously, by doing this, we would be fulfilling the plan of God. Even though the author at this juncture wrote on "who is the Holy Spirit," in another chapter, the author would continue to teach on "what the Holy Spirit does."

Now that you understand that the Holy Spirit is God (and not just a third person), thinking the Holy Spirit is the third person leaves a physiological afterthought in people's minds that He is limited because He is not first and cannot be like God. This kind of thinking, therefore, limits the believer, the minister, and of course, the Church. The author certainly realizes that there are revival fires in certain areas in the Body of Christ, but most of all, in some areas, and some congregation is as cold as ice; even in other countries, they are dead and lifeless.

It is a fact this is due to the absence of the Holy Spirit, even certain ministries who claim the Holy Spirit is working in their midst, but everything they do seems dry, lifeless, fleshy, worldly, and has no power, no presence of God, no anointing, no miracles, no gifts of the Spirit in operation, no altar calls, no laying hands on the sick, no supernatural occurrences (not that you go around with a spooky attitude); it's all due to the fact some of them profess they are baptized with the Holy Spirit but does not allow the Holy Spirit to work and manifest Himself in their lives and ministry.

The Holy Spirit is life because God is life, which means something can be created from nothing; there is no greater example than in creation recorded in the book of Genesis.

> *In the beginning God created the heaven and the earth.*
> *And the earth was without form, and void; and darkness was upon the face of the deep. And the Spirit of God moved upon the face of the waters.*
> *And God said, Let there be light: and there was light.*
>
> — Genesis 1:1–3

Throughout the Old Testament and the New Testament, especially what's recorded in the book of Exodus, the ministry of Jesus in Matthew, Mark, Luke, and John, and in the book of Acts, the Holy Spirit was the agent in all of the miracles that Moses, Jesus, and the apostles did. Certainly, this would include all of the miracles that happened in the Bible. Since we now comprehend that the Holy Spirit is God, the conception and birth of Jesus Christ is nothing but an act of God through the working of the Holy Spirit to bring about the Messiah, Jesus Christ.

Here are some Scriptures concerning the Holy Spirit and who He is. It would be beneficial to the believer in Christ or anyone, as a matter of fact, to search out these Scriptures.

- The Spirit of God (Genesis 1:2),
- Spirit of glory (1 Peter 4:14),
- Spirit of the Lord (1 Thessalonians 3:5),
- God (Acts 5:3–4),
- Spirit of revelation (Ephesians 1:17),
- Spirit of the Son (Galatians 4:6),

- Spirit of God (1 Corinthians 2:11),
- The Spirit of God, the breath of the Almighty (Job 33:4),
- Eternal Spirit (Hebrews 9:14),
- Spirit of the Lord (Isaiah 11:2; Acts 5:9),
- Spirit of wisdom (Isaiah 11:2, Ephesians 1:17),
- Spirit of counsel (Isaiah 11:2),
- Spirit of might (Isaiah 11:2),
- Spirit of understanding (Isaiah 11:2),
- Spirit of knowledge (Isaiah 11:2),
- Spirit of the fear of the Lord (Isaiah 11:2),
- Spirit of judgment (Isaiah 4:4; 28:6),
- Spirit of burning (Isaiah 4:4),
- Spirit of the Lord God (Isaiah 61:1),
- Comforter (John 14:16, 26; 15:26),
- Spirit of truth (John 14:17; 15:26),
- Power of the Highest (Luke 1:35),
- Spirit of the Father (Matthew 10:20),
- The Spirit (Matthew 4:1; John 3:6; 1 Timothy 4:1),
- Good Spirit (Nehemiah 9:20; Psalm 143:10),
- Holy Spirit (Psalm 51:11; Luke 11:13; Ephesians 1:13; 4:30),
- Free Spirit (Psalm 51:12),
- Spirit of prophecy (Revelation 19:10),
- Seven Spirits of God (Revelation 1:4),
- Spirit of holiness (Romans 1:4),
- Spirit of adoption (Romans 8:15),
- Spirit of life (Romans 8:2; Revelation 11:11),
- Spirit of Christ (Romans 8:9; 1 Peter 1:11),
- Spirit of grace (Zechariah 12:10; Hebrews 10:29)

CHAPTER 2

Peter or Jesus?

After several months of ministry, Jesus, being human, was concerned about the fact of how the populace of Jerusalem and surrounding areas were thinking and saying about Him. Recorded in the Gospel of Matthew is one of the most important Scriptures concerning the church and its foundation?

> *When Jesus came into the coasts of Caesarea Philippi, he asked his disciples, saying, Whom do men say that I the Son of man am?*
>
> *And they said, Some say that thou art John the Baptist: some, Elias; and others, Jeremias, or one of the prophets.*
>
> *He saith unto them, But whom say ye that I am?*
>
> *And Simon Peter answered and said, Thou art the Christ, the Son of the living God.*
>
> *And Jesus answered and said unto him, Blessed art thou, Simon Barjona: for flesh and blood hath not revealed it unto thee, but my Father which is in heaven.*
>
> *And I say also unto thee, That thou art Peter, and upon this rock I will build my church; and the gates of hell shall not prevail against it.*
>
> *And I will give unto thee the keys of the kingdom of heaven: and whatsoever thou shalt bind on earth shall be bound in heaven: and whatsoever thou shalt loose on earth shall be loosed in heaven.*
>
> — Matthew 16:13–19

There are multitudes of professing Christians, not the words professing Christians who do not have a clue or even a vague idea as to whom is the head of the Church. Ask some of them, and in a heartbeat, they would say the bishop, superintendent, cardinal, pope, etc. Before going any further, there should be some clarity concerning this particular subject, and please, reader, pay particular attention as you read these particular verses of Scripture. As you continue reading, I ask you earnestly to consider the word "revelation." The word "revelation" here means the Holy Spirit, revealing the Word of God like it should be interpreted. There is another type of revelation that will be dealt with later on.

As you might have noticed in reading the Gospels, after Jesus started His ministry most of the time in different towns, cities, and villages, He came to Caesarea Philippi.

Now please pay particular attention to what Jesus is saying; these are His words concerning Peter's confession (not a confession to a man but the word or answer that Peter gave to Jesus). Peter answered and said unto Him, "Thou art the Christ the Son of the living God, The Messiah, the hope of Israel, the anointed one."

> *Then Jesus, in turn, responded to the revelation that God gave to Peter. Because of the word or confession that Peter spoke: "Thou are the Christ the Son of the living God."*
>
> — Matthew 16:16

> *"And Jesus answered and said unto him upon this rock."*
>
> — Matthew 16:17

The confession Peter made or what he said in response to Jesus' question is *that Jesus Christ is the Son of the living God.*

Then in response to Peter's answer, Jesus replied, "I will build my church and the gates of hell shall not prevail against it" Matthew 16:18.

God could not build the church on a man; He had to build the church on Jesus; Jesus is the head of the Church.

Here lies the truth about who is the head of the Church, instead of some misguided leadership and unscriptural headship for the Church. There are too many heads in the Body of Christ, even though the true Church of Jesus Christ here, in America, and in other countries of the world has increased in numbers and grown spiritually and otherwise, but to some extent, millions of people in this world even to this present time do not recognize Jesus as the Head of the Church. To make matters worse, millions of people, especially of the Middle East and some other countries, cannot differentiate or even do not understand who really the head of the Church is and who are real Christians. Some of them are thinking the pope (he is a wonderful human being, but he is not the head of the church), the Crusaders, who marched against other religious people in the year of AD 1096, were just as religious as the other people they marched against and destroyed them, and now these other religions are trying to return the favor; both religious factions are wrong.

On the day of Pentecost, the apostle Peter experienced a miraculous transformation in his life; God used him in a miraculous way to minister to thousands of people, as recorded in the book of Acts. Reading the book of Acts, you must have discovered that Peter, in the earlier phase of his ministry, had a problem with the Gentiles, this means the Samaritans and other people; to put it plainly, he had a prejudiced spirit against the Gentiles and other people because this spirit was imbedded in him from youth. Could you imagine that even though he was baptized with the Holy Spirit, this spirit continued to bother him until he had an experience with God that changed his life?

Here is the biblical record from the book of Acts.

> *There was a certain man in Caesarea called Cornelius, a centurion of the band called the Italian band,*
>
> *A devout man, and one that feared God with all his house, which gave much alms to the people, and prayed to God alway.*
>
> *He saw in a vision evidently about the ninth hour of the day an angel of God coming in to him, and saying unto him, Cornelius.*
>
> *And when he looked on him, he was afraid, and said, What is it, Lord? And he said unto him, Thy prayers and thine alms are come up for a memorial before God.*
>
> *And now send men to Joppa, and call for one Simon, whose surname is Peter:*
>
> *He lodgeth with one Simon a tanner, whose house is by the sea side: he shall tell thee what thou oughtest to do.*
>
> *And when the angel which spake unto Cornelius was departed, he called two of his household servants, and a devout soldier of them that waited on him continually;*
>
> *And when he had declared all these things unto them, he sent them to Joppa.*
>
> *On the morrow, as they went on their journey, and drew nigh unto the city, Peter went up upon the housetop to pray about the sixth hour:*

And he became very hungry, and would have eaten: but while they made ready, he fell into a trance,

And saw heaven opened, and a certain vessel descending unto him, as it had been a great sheet knit at the four corners, and let down to the earth:

Wherein were all manner of fourfooted beasts of the earth, and wild beasts, and creeping things, and fowls of the air.

And there came a voice to him, Rise, Peter; kill, and eat.

But Peter said, Not so, Lord; for I have never eaten any thing that is common or unclean.

And the voice spake unto him again the second time, what God hath cleansed, that call not thou common.

This was done thrice: and the vessel was received up again into heaven.

Now while Peter doubted in himself what this vision which he had seen should mean, behold, the men which were sent from Cornelius had made enquiry for Simon's house, and stood before the gate,

And called, and asked whether Simon, which was surnamed Peter, were lodged there.

While Peter thought on the vision, the Spirit said unto him, Behold, three men seek thee.

Arise therefore, and get thee down, and go with them, doubting nothing: for I have sent them.

Then Peter went down to the men which were sent unto him from Cornelius; and said, Behold, I am he whom ye seek: what is the cause wherefore ye are come?

And they said, Cornelius the centurion, a just man, and one that feareth God, and of good report among all the nation of the Jews, was warned from God by an holy angel to send for thee into his house, and to hear words of thee.

Then called he them in, and lodged them. And on the morrow Peter went away with them, and certain brethren from Joppa accompanied him.

And the morrow after they entered into Caesarea. And Cornelius waited for them, and had called together his kinsmen and near friends.

And as Peter was coming in, Cornelius met him, and fell down at his feet, and worshipped him.

But Peter took him up, saying, Stand up; I myself also am a man.

And as he talked with him, he went in, and found many that were come together.

And he said unto them, Ye know how that it is an unlawful thing for a man that is a Jew to keep company, or come unto one of another nation; but God hath shewed me that I should not call any man common or unclean.

Therefore came I unto you without gainsaying, as soon as I was sent for: I ask therefore for what intent ye have sent for me?

And Cornelius said, Four days ago I was fasting until this hour; and at the ninth hour I prayed in my house, and, behold, a man stood before me in bright clothing,

And said, Cornelius, thy prayer is heard, and thine alms are had in remembrance in the sight of God.

Send therefore to Joppa, and call hither Simon, whose surname is Peter; he is lodged in the house of one Simon a tanner by the sea side: who, when he cometh, shall speak unto thee.

Immediately therefore I sent to thee; and thou hast well done that thou art come. Now therefore are we all here present before God, to hear all things that are commanded thee of God.

Then Peter opened his mouth, and said, Of a truth I perceive that God is no respecter of persons:

But in every nation he that feareth him, and worketh righteousness, is accepted with him.

The word which God sent unto the children of Israel, preaching peace by Jesus Christ: (he is Lord of all:)

That word, I say, ye know, which was published throughout all Judaea, and began from Galilee, after the baptism which John preached;

How God anointed Jesus of Nazareth with the Holy Ghost and with power: who went about doing good, and healing all that were oppressed of the devil; for God was with him.

And we are witnesses of all things which he did both in the land of the Jews, and in Jerusalem; whom they slew and hanged on a tree:

Him God raised up the third day, and shewed him openly;

Not to all the people, but unto witnesses chosen before of God, even to us, who did eat and drink with him after he rose from the dead.

And he commanded us to preach unto the people, and to testify that it is he which was ordained of God to be the Judge of quick and dead.

To him give all the prophets witness, that through his name whosoever believeth in him shall receive remission of sins.

While Peter yet spake these words, the Holy Ghost fell on all them which heard the word.

And they of the circumcision which believed were astonished, as many as came with Peter, because that on the Gentiles also was poured out the gift of the Holy Ghost.

For they heard them speak with tongues, and magnify God. Then answered Peter.

Can any man forbid water, that these should not be baptized, which have received the Holy Ghost as well as we?

And he commanded them to be baptized in the name of the Lord. Then prayed they him to tarry certain days.

— Acts 10:16–48

It was imperative that the entire chapter, ten of the book of Acts, had to be printed so that the reader could comprehend the topic of the second chapter of this book after Cornelius had a visitation from God. God instructed him to send for Peter to emphasize and zero into a very important point that must be brought to the readers' attention; when Peter arrived with some followers of Christ to Cornelius' house, he met Peter at the door; again here is Peter's reaction to Cornelius:

And the morrow after they entered into Caesarea. And Cornelius waited for them, and had called together his kinsmen and near friends.

And as Peter was coming in, Cornelius met him, and fell down at his feet, and worshipped him.

But Peter took him up, saying, Stand up; I myself also am a man.

— Acts 10:24–26

Why should Jesus make a *man* the head of the church? But this was not the born-again blood, washed, filled with the Holy Ghost church. This was a man-made, man-ordained church. The Roman Catholic Church, which is one of the largest church organizations, was established in AD 33, then they recognized and elected Linus as the successor to Peter, whom they affirmed was the first pope, and this trend continued to the present time.

The most important part of the body is the head. Within the head, there is the brain; the anatomy of the brain is intrinsically complex due to its intricate structure and functions; this amazing organ acts as a control center by receiving, interpreting, and directing sensory information throughout the body. There are three major divisions of the brain; they are the forebrain, the midbrain, and the hindbrain. The forebrain is responsible for a variety of functions, including receiving and processing sensory information, thinking, perceiving, producing and understanding language, and controlling motor function.

There are two major divisions of the forebrain, but before going any further, it has been proven by scientists and scientific research that the forebrain that lies in front of the brain triggers a desire for God, worship, prayer, and the word of God. Then you have within the brain the diencephalons and the telencephalon; the diencephalon contains structures such as the thalamus and hypothalamus, which are responsible for such functions as motor control relaying sensory controlling automatic functions. The telencephalon contains the largest part of the brain. The cerebrum, most of the actual information processing in the brain, takes place in the cerebral cortex. The hindbrain extends from the spinal cord and is composed of the metencephalon and myelencephalon. The metencephalon contains structures such as the pons and cerebellum. These regions assist in maintaining balance and equilibrium, movement coordination, and the conduction of sensory information. The myelencephalon is composed of the medulla oblongata, which is responsible for controlling such autonomic functions as breathing, heart rate, and digestion. The cerebrum, most of the actual information processing in the brain, takes place in the cerebral cortex. The hindbrain extends from the spinal cord and is composed of the metencephalon and myelencephalon. The metencephalon contains structures such as the pons and cerebellum. These regions assist in maintaining balance and equilibrium, movement coordination, and the conduction of sensory information.

The above paragraph shows the importance of the head in the human body. Could you imagine a body without a head? The answer is obvious, death. Where there is no head, and when there is no head, there is no life. Life can only be in the body when the head is on the body. Jesus is the head of the church, and if He is the head of the church, He is leader, controller, ruler, director, executer, and planner of the church. Every word or the words of Jesus mean the written word, the Bible, and the Rhema word, and actions must come from the head. Jesus is the head of the church. He is the authority and at the head of the church. The church has only one head, and He is Jesus. We must recognize Jesus is the head in the order of all things;

He is the head of the church and the Bishop of our souls, "For ye were as sheep going astray, but are now returned to the Sheppard and Bishop of your souls" 1 Peter 2:25.

There are 330,000 denominations and organizations; it is a fact that each of these has a representative, leader, or head; the pope is the head of the Roman Catholic Church, then there are religions and religious sects and cults that have a man like all other who has one man or woman, whom they have named as their head, all of them have chosen a leader to represent them in some religious or political form. The biggest problem is Jesus is not a head but a man, and their ministers, officers, leaders, and parishioners have to listen to the dictates of head office, superintendents, bishops, archbishop, and obviously, Rome; the reason? Jesus is not the head. Some of these leaders are so dictatorial that it resembles or it's like a country or nation with a communistic government.

The head is essential and the most important and vital in the human body—so is Jesus Christ in the Church. It is the crowning and ruling organ in the human body, the source of actions, expressions, emotions, and the seat of intellect. It is at once the palace and the throne of the soul whence that invisible occupant issues his mandates to the body, impels its motions, and regulates and controls all its members. Of Christ, it is said that His headship originated before time; Jesus was there before and during the creation of the world.

> *Who is the image of the invisible God, the firstborn of every creature:*
>
> *For by him were all things created, that are in heaven, and that are in earth, visible and invisible, whether they be thrones, or dominions, or principalities, or powers: all things were created by him, and for him:*
>
> *And he is before all things, and by him all things consist.*
>
> *And he is the head of the body, the church: who is the beginning, the firstborn from the dead; that in all things he might have the preeminence.*
>
> — Colossians 1:15–18

> *In the beginning was the Word [Jesus], and the Word was with God, [...] and without Him was not anything made that was made.*
>
> — John 1:1–3

Jesus Christ is not only the legislator; He is the supreme executive head of the church. The head and the body should be one and function as one; this means He should be the *one and only head for the Body of Christ universal.*

Lucifer, the devil, the usurper (note the word "usurper"), was already here on earth. But Lucifer, Satan, manipulated and used the serpent; this creature was unlike all other animals that God created because the serpent walked upright like a human being. This is how everything transpired in the Garden of Eden.

> *Now the serpent was more subtil [crafty, witty, or tricky] than any beast of the field which the* LORD *had made. And he said unto the woman, Yea, hath God said, Ye shall not eat of every tree of the garden*
>
> *And the woman said unto the serpent [she knew what God hath spoken], We may eat of the fruit of the trees of the garden:*

But of the fruit of the tree which is in the midst of the garden, God hath said [she knew what God hath said], Ye shall not eat of it, neither shall ye touch it, lest ye die

[now notice how slick the devil is and what he is doing, usurping authority from the Head who is God].

And the serpent said unto the woman, Ye shall not surely die [here it comes]:

For God doth know that in the day ye eat thereof, then your eyes shall be opened, and ye shall be as gods, knowing good and evil.

— Genesis 3:1–5

From the verses above, we now can understand the diabolical, satanic, demonic spirit of trying to usurp authority from the Head, who is Jesus Christ. The devil craftily engineered and devised a plan to manifest himself throughout the ages that will constantly be endeavoring to usurp authority from the True and Living God. The devil's perceptional keyword to Adam and Eve was, "Both you would become like God," which means knowing all things or being knowledgeable like God in everything. Eve took the bait and then passed it on to Adam, and this same spirit continues today along with the blame game.

Who are the worst enemies of God in this day and age? Almost all educated people? In most of America's educational system, God is not God anymore; why? Because all of these educational systems think that they are too educated to acclaim or recognize God as God. Because they think they are smarter than God. Most of the Church world and religions with so many heads within their organization and now more educated, to them the leading of the Holy Spirit remained with the apostles and our early church fathers who believed in the Holy Spirit and His leading, but the excuse is for some of them the Holy Spirit is not for today, which is to modernize to let Jesus be the head and to be led by the Holy Spirit.

From the beginning to the present time, there are some people with the devil's inspired aspirations of wanting to be gods, or like God, especially in this day and time, refusing God and God's law or the word of God.

This spirit was very prevalent in Nimrod's case, which is recorded in the Bible, Genesis, chapter 11.

Nimrod decided to build a tower as high as the heavens, which was his motive to be like a god among his people. Over the past centuries to the present time, this same spirit that the devil used to usurp authority away from God by telling Adam and Eve they would be like God, "For God doth know that in the day ye eat thereof, then your eyes shall be opened, and ye shall be as gods, knowing good and evil" Genesis 3:5.

Reading the above is very vital in understanding who the head of the Church is. The forebrain is responsible for a variety of functions, including receiving and processing sensory information, thinking, formation, perceiving, producing, and understanding language. Even though this subject is being dealt with of who is the head of the Church, here are some facts and functions of the head of a human body. The functions of the brain in the human body and what it does are vague in comparison to Jesus Christ, who is the Head of the Church. He is responsible for a variety of functions, spiritually speaking, such as sensory information (inspiration or revelation) from Jesus or the leading Jesus, the Head, or the Holy Spirit, thinking formation, perceiving, producing, and understanding all people. He, who is the perceiving, producing, and understanding all people, all language, and all nations, He, who is the head, wants to communicate to the Church, which is His Body, whom He left here, on earth, as His representative to communicate to ungodly people who God is and teach them His ways and purpose and His plan for the human race. Most of all, to bring mankind back to God through the preaching of the cross, on which Jesus died for the sins of the world.

Besides true Christians worldwide, most of the people of the world do not recognize God as God, and inevitably so, but want to be like a god, so educated and high-minded, egotistical alienated from God, and instead of pointing mankind to God, certain of mankind is wanting the human race to look to them as God, this is the spirit of the Antichrist.

Therefore, the head of the Church is not the head of a denomination, organization, religion, or independent groups; the head of the church is not a man who sits in his office and dictates who should go, where and when to go, and what to do. The head of the Church is not someone sitting on a throne so that men and women should bow down to a man, and it is not someone who desires or forces to be worshiped as God; Jesus is the Head of the Church, and He, alone, is worth that all mankind should bow down to Him. Something is radically wrong with a denomination, organization, religions, and some independent and so-called Christian organizations that bow down and worship a man and treat him, and now her, like God. This was the devil's tool from the beginning to usurp authority from the Head Jesus Christ, even God.

Suppose every representative of every organization, denomination, and religion would recognize Jesus as the Head of the Church and follow His life, His word, His teachings, His prayer life, His power, His ministry, His love, His compassion, His soul-winning, His miracles, His care for human beings, His outreach, His purpose, His sacrifice on the cross, His resurrection, His intercessory ministry before the throne of God for us, and most of all lead people to Jesus this world would have already been evangelized. In that case, this is worth being reiterated right here "when an individual is sick, they are not in need of the doctor's mother; they need the doctor," who is He, doctor, Jesus. In most cases, so goes the world, and so goes the church. Almost every leader today is consumed by building his or her utopia or kingdom; it's all because they want to be the head. Look what I have done to build a tower to the sky. This is the reason there is so much confusion in the Church today. It seems like the majority of Christendom does not know where they at; it's all because the Head, who is Jesus Christ, is not being recognized as the Head of the Church, and it is from Him we receive leadership and direction through and by the power of the Holy Spirit.

Respect to who respect is due, honor to who honor is due, there are men and women within the church of Jesus Christ whom God has blessed with God-given talents and gifts to edify and be leaders in the church. But in this day and age, we must be aware of the spirit that has overtaken some key people whom I consider to have a tremendous ministry in the world, and they are blessed to have a worldwide ministry; in other words, the modern-day term for these ministries is that they are popular. I witnessed or looked at an ordination service or meeting some years ago of one of the most prominent speakers in America, whom I respect because of the word that this individual preaches weekly. I did not mind the confirmation, ordination, and exultation into a new position; even though the coordinator of this entire ceremony meant well, but the robes, gowns, and biretta they wore and the words and phrases that were mentioned, all of this resembled and carried the spirit of the Apostate Church. There are times some leaders will go to the extreme innocently or deliberately to attract attention to themselves instead of Jesus Christ or God. By the way, the individual on whom the honor was conferred seemed a bit disillusioned about the entire ceremony because Jesus Christ was not exalted in this ceremony.

These are the words of the apostle Paul, indicating Jesus is the Head of the Church. "And hath put all things under his feet, and gave him to be the head over all things to the church" Ephesians 1:22. "And he is the head of the body, the church: who is the beginning, the firstborn from the dead; that in all things he might have the preeminence" Colossians 1:18.

There is no mention in scripture that Peter was the rock. Jesus said to Peter because of the confession that Peter made, "*Jesus was the Christ,*" that Jesus was the head of the Church,

> *He [Jesus] saith unto them [his disciples], But whom say ye that I am?*
> *And Simon Peter answered and said, Thou art the Christ [the Messiah, the hope of Israel, the anointed one], the Son of the living God.*
>
> — Matthew 16:15–16

Upon this word or confession that Peter spoke, Jesus said that He would build His Church. This means the born again Church (John, chapter 3), The Holy Spirit Church (*John 4*; *Acts 2*), the church that is like Jesus' life, words, and miracles, as recorded in the Gospels, like the apostles recorded in the book of *Acts*.

Jesus is the firm foundation of all truths; this is the rock on which Peter knew that Jesus was the Christ. Yes! Peter was one of the leading apostles in the book of Acts, but he was not the head of the Church. Bible study indicates that when Paul wrote to the Romans towards the end of his third missionary journey, about AD 58, no mention was made of Peter. He had not known that he would become a prisoner at Jerusalem but planned to stop in Rome on his way from Jerusalem to Spain.

> *This is the reason why I have so often been hindered from coming to you. But now, since I no longer have any room for work in these regions, and since I have longed for many years to come to you.*
>
> — Romans 15:22–23

When Paul finally arrives at Rome AD 63, no mention is made of Peter among the brethren that came to meet him.

No further mention is made during the two years Paul was in in-house arrest and received guests,

> *Where we found brethren, and were desired to tarry with them seven days: and so we went toward Rome.*
> *And from thence, when the brethren heard of us, they came to meet us as far as Appii forum, and The three taverns: whom when Paul saw, he thanked God, and took courage.*
>
> — Acts 28:14–15

The book of Acts has Peter ministering in Jerusalem, Judea, and Samaria. Peter wrote to churches throughout Asia Minor, and he indicates that he was in Babylon at the time; he never wrote to Rome, nor does the Scripture indicate anywhere that he ever even visited there. James, the half-brother of Christ, took charge at Jerusalem in the council convened to discuss a legalistic problem. Peter was there but simply reported how God opened the door to preaching to the Gentiles with Cornelius. Then Paul and Barnabas reported on their ministry. James then led the meeting to a conclusion, Peter was not in charge, whereas Peter indicates that he is an elder of the church, he puts himself on a level with other church elders. Much has been made of Peter feeding the flock of God, but Peter tells the elders of the Asia Minor churches to feed their flocks. No mention in Scripture is not made of Peter having charge over the entire church at large, nor indicates that supposed position, nor is he ever called Papa (Pope). The Greek word "*papa*" is not in the Bible.

The infallible, inspired word of God is the final authority that, without question, vindicates who is the Head of the Church; everyone reading these scriptures should have no doubt about who is the Head of the Church, and He is Jesus Christ.

It is true that some within the church convincingly recognize and believe that Jesus Christ is the Head of the Church, but there are people who gather together within the confinements of magnificent structures, edifices worth millions of dollars, who innocently think that the building is the most important thing and does not even recognize Jesus is the Head of the Church. They have been taught He is a man. Embarrassingly so, this situation exists even after two thousand years after Jesus died on the cross, was resurrected from the tomb, went back to heaven, and is now sitting at the right hand of God to make intercession for us, and now Jesus is about to return the second time. Some think the head of the Church is in Cleveland, Springfield, Utah, or Rome, but the Head of the Church is Jesus Christ and now manifesting Himself through the power of the Holy Spirit everywhere or all over the world through those believers that are born again and baptized with the Holy Spirit (John, chapters 3 and 4, and Acts, chapter 2).

Another convincing Scripture that should make some so-called leaders of some denomination, organization, and religions recognize Jesus is the head of the church, exalt and lift Jesus up is, "And as Moses lifted up the serpent in the wilderness, even so must the Son of man be lifted up" John 3:14.

The apostle Paul, who was the last of the apostles that God called and raised up, had a revelation of Jesus Christ, who convincingly, through his writings of the Epistles, revealed Jesus is the head of the Church; here are some Scriptures to remind the Body of Christ that Jesus is the only head of the Church.

> *In whom we have redemption through his blood, even the forgiveness of sins,*
>
> *Who is the image of the invisible God, the firstborn of every creature:*
>
> *For by him were all things created, that are in heaven and that are in earth, visible and invisible, whether they be thrones or dominions or principalities or powers, all things were created by him and for him:*
>
> *And he is before all things, and by him all things consist.*
>
> *And he is the head of the body, the church: who is the beginning, the firstborn from the dead [Jesus was the first and only one that rose from the dead]; that in all things he might have the preeminence [always should be exalted in the body the church].*
>
> — Colossians 1:14–18

> *[...] who is the blessed and only Potentate, [no man] the King of kings and Lord of lords;*
> — 1 Timothy 6:15b

CHAPTER 3

The Church

Within the past years, biblical knowledge has increased and is increasing more and more daily; ministers and members of the Body of Christ have more understanding of the Scriptures today than at any other time in history. But mention the word church, and there are some people who think that the church is a huge multimillion complex with carpeted floors, padded pews, stained glass windows, chandeliers' high steeples (sometimes these sharp-pointed steeples remind me of the spear that pierced the side of Jesus' chest, which caused blood and water to flow out of His body), and now computers with projectors flashing with countless illustrations on fancied painting walls and just to see one preacher.

Please understand there are privileged and honored ministers because their ministry warranties the convenience of a huge building and all of the trimmings that go with the building and ministry. Because of the growth of their particular congregation, of which they are pasturing, they need the space to accommodate thousands of people. But it must be realized that all of this is not the church; people that are born again, saved, baptized with the Holy Spirit, ready for the second return of Jesus Christ, comprise the Church.

While this book is being edited, we're in the midst of a worldwide pandemic pandemonium called COVID-19; notice what it's called—COVID-19. This was already planned in 2019; this coronavirus is killing thousands, but what has caught the author's attention is the fact that the Church of Jesus Christ is targeted. My heart and prayer are for these pastors. Still, in church buildings seating twenty thousand people more or less, the congregants or members cannot gather together for regular meetings, whoever, whenever. Whatever this COVID-19 was targeted to and for, with the devil's craftiness and certain of men's ingenuity, with a platform being laid for the Antichrist and money in mind, all of this was aimed at the Church. But little do the devil and his company realize that the building is not the Church. The Church is you and me, and that God we can pray to, at home or anywhere, people who do not know God, are in a crisis, fearful mood, or spirit.

With the topic of this paragraph, this statement should remain and leave an indelible, lasting, burning impression on your mind when Jesus returns. He is not coming back for the building but for people that are ready to go to be with Him. Let it be understood that the author of this book does not entertain the idea that people ought to worship in an outdated, dilapidated building! Yes, it costs to build church building, necessary conveniences for people to gather and worship God, to teach children and young people, to accommodate God's people, and operate a ministry. But in this day and time, build a building that costs less, which can seat the congregation that exists with the intention of expanding to anticipate some growth. Thank God for what is being done to reach lost souls, but with the world's ongoing population growth, 49 percent of the world's population has not heard of the Gospel of Jesus Christ; instead of concentrating on huge edifices, for namesake, if not necessarily more time and money should be spent on missions, evangelism, and winning lost souls.

There are times that God speaks directly to people, He reveals Himself and speaks by dreams, visions, and revelations, which is a direct Word or message from God, but revelation is also the revealed Word of God, the Bible. Here is a revelation from the Word of God, the Bible. When John the Baptist started his ministry, he preached a message that was different than the Scribes, Pharisees, and all other religious sects of that day.

John the Baptist was the forerunner of Jesus' ministry; John the Baptist's message was: "Repent: the Kingdom of God is at hand" John 3:2. And then Jesus came preaching: "The Kingdom of God shall be in you" Luke 8:12. "Seek ye first the kingdom of God, […] and all these things shall be added unto to you" Matthew 6:33.

These words came directly from the mouth of Jesus as a solemn warning that we should avoid being caught in the trap of going after material things and building unnecessary buildings. This does not mean that people should not work and make a living to care for their families, to buy food, clothing, pay their bills, etc. What did Jesus mean when He spoke the above words? Here is your answer and a God-inspired revelation in relation to just material things and buildings.

There are two twelve-year-old children in your church; we are going to call them James, who is a boy and twelve years old, and Cindy, who is a girl and she is eleven. Every week you see them in Church and in Sunday school, time and money are spent to get them to the church building; let's use the terminology they are growing up in church, the goal is to reach these children for Jesus. You teach them and pray with them, then finally, you lead them to Jesus Christ. They get saved and receive the baptism of the Holy Spirit. But let's suppose the church spends approximately one million dollars, more or less, taking these children back and forth from home to church, then teaching, preaching, giving them refreshments, raising them in the ways of God, and then finally, you lead them to Jesus Christ. They get saved, you baptize them in water, and they receive the Holy Spirit (before or after they are baptized in water). This is what Jesus meant by—"The Kingdom of God shall be in you" Luke 8:12.

Here is the point of this revelation that is most important: these two children have something worth more than all the money and material things in this world. Time and money were not wasted getting these children to church and then preaching, teaching, caring for them, and leading them to Jesus. So what is worth more—"the building or these two children's souls"? Don't think the author is crazy or losing it, but put this on Jesus because this is what He said, "For what is a man profited, if he shall gain the whole world, and lose his own soul? or what shall a man give in exchange for his soul?" Matthew 16:26.

One soul being saved and baptized with the Holy Spirit is worth more than all the monies of this world, material things, or a five-million-dollar church building. Yes, souls can be saved in a building, but more time and money should be spent reaching people with the Gospel of Jesus Christ than material things or buildings. A building is not made in the image of God and does not have a soul, but all human beings are made in the image of God and possess a never-dying soul. Every Church member should read the words of Jesus over and over.

> *"For what is a man profited, if he shall gain the whole world, and lose his own soul? or what shall a man give in exchange for his soul?"*
>
> — Matthew 16:26

The above thoughts and words correlate with the words of Jesus, and it seems that the modern-day church or people need to take a closer look at the words of Jesus and let the Holy Spirit burn brand and sink it within your spirit so we can get the message. Personally speaking, I know of some multimillion buildings that the people who spent millions on building, some of them rarely enter these buildings but once on a Sunday morning, while the mid-week prayer and Sunday night soul-winning meeting has died or is dying.

The church is not the building; the church is you, whether there be few or thousands; the church is comprised of people of all nations and every race and color of people, who are born again, according to the Gospel of John, chapters 3 and 4, baptized with the Holy Spirit (Acts, chapter 2), and living a sanctified life, according to the book of Romans, chapter 7. Sad to say, here, in America, when referring to a gathering or congregation, words like these are mentioned: it's a black church, white church, Spanish church, Indian, Korean church, etc.; yes, culture and language are understood as people of the same country and language normally would want to congregate together. Bur every effort should be made to accommodate one another without prejudice. There are people of all races and cultures with the same blood running through their veins who desire to gather together along with other people to worship and praise the *One* and true living *God*.

Even though Jesus attracted large crowds at the beginning of His ministry, His method of building the church from the beginning of His ministry was Spirit-led and methodical by this; it means He chose them one or two at a time. His purpose was to get a few men that were humble enough to follow Him, learn from Jesus about God, His plan, and the purpose of salvation for mankind, pray like Him, and have the power to reach their generation with the Gospel of Jesus Christ. This also means men and women who have the call of God upon their lives in every ongoing generation to reach their generation.

And I saw, and bare record that this is the Son of God.

Again the next day after John stood, and two of his disciples;

And looking upon Jesus as he walked, he saith, Behold the Lamb of God!

And the two disciples heard him speak, and they followed Jesus.

Then Jesus turned, and saw them following, and saith unto them, What seek ye? They said unto him, Rabbi, (which is to say, being interpreted, Master,) where dwellest thou?

He saith unto them, Come and see. They came and saw where he dwelt, and abode with him that day: for it was about the tenth hour.

One of the two which heard John speak, and followed him, was Andrew, Simon Peter's brother.

He first findeth his own brother Simon, and saith unto him, We have found the Messias, which is, being interpreted, the Christ.

And he brought him to Jesus. And when Jesus beheld him, he said, Thou art Simon the son of Jona: thou shalt be called Cephas, which is by interpretation, A stone.

The day following Jesus would go forth into Galilee, and findeth Philip, and saith unto him, Follow me.

Now Philip was of Bethsaida, the city of Andrew and Peter.

Philip findeth Nathanael, and saith unto him, We have found him, of whom Moses in the law, and the prophets, did write, Jesus of Nazareth, the son of Joseph.

And Nathanael said unto him, Can there any good thing come out of Nazareth? Philip saith unto him, Come and see.

Jesus saw Nathanael coming to him, and saith of him, Behold an Israelite indeed, in whom is no guile!

Nathanael saith unto him, Whence knowest thou me? Jesus answered and said unto him, Before that Philip called thee, when thou wast under the fig tree, I saw thee.

Nathanael answered and saith unto him, Rabbi, thou art the Son of God; thou art the King of Israel.

Jesus answered and said unto him, Because I said unto thee, I saw thee under the fig tree, believest thou? thou shalt see greater things than these.

And he saith unto him, Verily, verily, I say unto you, here after ye shall see heaven open, and the angels of God ascending and descending upon the Son of man.

—John 1:34–51

What is it that attracted Nathaniel to Jesus? He noticed there was something different most of all, discerned that Jesus was the Son of God; what is it that attracted Jesus to Nathaniel? It was the gift of God, the supernatural power of God manifesting through Jesus Christ, that caught his attention. This is so important in understanding where this book is taking you (the reason Jesus said the son of man, He was the first and only God-man to be born of a woman); from this point on, all of the other disciples came to Jesus because they discerned He was the Son of God and witnessed the supernatural gift of God in Him. They witnessed the supernatural miracle healing power of God manifesting through Jesus. The blind saw the dumb spake, lepers were cleansed or healed, storms stopped, trees dried, the dead raised, and now He is telling them that they would see the angels of God ascending and descending on Him. These supernatural events strengthened their faith in Him.

The church of Jesus Christ is comprised of people of all nations, countries, and, of course, people of all races and colors. The Bible never speaks of a particular people that comprise the Church; the apostle Paul had enough boldness to correct the supposedly head of the church, Peter. Peter was used of God as miracles and signs followed his ministry, and honor is due to the apostle Peter, but the apostle Paul corrected him because Peter, being a Jew, developed a prejudice spirit that was imbedded in him from youth. When he grew up, got saved, and received the Holy Spirit, it was difficult for him to comprehend how the Gentiles could be saved and receive the Holy Spirit just like he did. This spirit is one of the greatest hindrances to revival and a move of God here and in other countries of the world. And this spirit can be vise versa and can be witnessed at times from all races; there are times this spirit can be seen within a country of its own people, such as class and the caste system in India and the tribal divisions in some other countries.

The Word of God supports the above statements. When the early Church, which is the book of Acts, experienced the outpouring of the Holy Spirit in the Upper Room, of course, it was an act of God to birth the church in power to live for Christ. The Holy Spirit was given to empower them to be anointed to preach the Gospel of Jesus Christ to the Jews and Gentiles.

They were given power to perform the works of Christ with miracles and healing on those that were sick, most of all to confirm that Jesus was alive. This power was almost short-circuited by a prejudiced spirit against people of a different race. God, Himself, had to intervene from the very beginning of the Church to correct this spirit, or else the early book of Acts church would have missed why Jesus came and died on the cross. This was to forgive the sins of all people and for them to experience salvation through the redemptive work of Jesus on the cross. God made every human being with the same red blood running through their veins, even though with different blood types, the culture of different races and people of every nation world must and should be taken into consideration. If a nation or people's customs and culture are not the same as yours, this should not interfere with your faith and belief in God through Jesus Christ, do not turn your nose up against them. But you should endeavor to understand them so that you can influence and win them to Jesus Christ.

The apostle Paul said these words,

> *For though I am free from all men, I have made myself a servant to all, that I might win the more,*
>
> *and to the Jews I became as a Jew, that I might win Jews; to those who are under the law, as under the law, that I might win those who are under the law,*
>
> *to those who are without law, as without law (not being without law toward God, but under law toward Christ), that I might win those who are without law,*
>
> *to the weak I became as weak, that I might win the weak. I have become all things to all men that I might by all means save some.*
>
> *Now this I do for the gospel's sake, that I may be partaker of it with you.*
>
> — 1 Corinthians 9:19–23, NKJV

I have often seen certain people run from other people than themselves because of people of different color and culture. God placed you here to solve problems, not to create problems or riots and wars. Godly wisdom is to avoid creating problems, riots, or wars, God blessed Solomon with the greatest gift, which is wisdom, and these are his words, "Our responsibility as Christians is to win souls, not to despise, run, or cause them to go hell."

> "[…] he that winneth souls is wise."
>
> — Proverbs 11:30b

In many countries of the world, even among Christian denominations and organizations, God has held back His blessing because of this spirit. Certain countries of this world and its people at this moment are missing the blessing of God and revival because they are not willing to bend for the good of another people who are made in the image of God and possess a never-dying soul.

There are people here in the United States who know of our work and ministry in over fifty-five countries of the world. I have ministered in almost every State of this Union. Individuals would approach me during my revival meetings in different churches, seminars, and conferences and request that they want to travel with my wife and me to the mission field. In one of our scheduled meetings overseas, I consented to certain people that they could travel with us. The moment they landed in the country where our meetings were being held, we gathered our luggage and started driving to the hotel. Instead of looking for the best in the country they were traveling through, my wife and I would hear comments like this, "How hot it is." "What is that smell? "This place is so filthy." After we checked in the hotel, they would talk about how bad the room was; the bed was uncomfortable, the food was no good and the kind of car they had to ride to the meeting. Most of all, some of them that went with us had a controlling or a takeover or bossy attitude; there are times we regretted taking anyone with us overseas unless we really knew them. When going overseas, I want to be at peace to preach the Gospel of Jesus Christ. Overall it is understood that we have to be careful in every way but not to the extent of scorn and contempt for other people's customs, culture, and ways.

Christians, in general, must never lose sight of the fact that people of different nations, cultures, customs, and languages have a body, spirit, and soul just like you and I. This is the main reason Jesus died on the cross and shed His precious blood for all people of the world. Most of all, when He rose from the dead and proved He was alive in many different ways, His final words were to, "Go into the entire world and preach the Gospel to every creature" Mark 16:15, NKJV.

This means every human being is created in God's image and should have the opportunity to hear the Gospel of Jesus Christ, regardless of their race, color, and condition.

Jesus started the Church with twelve men; one of them betrayed Him. This is the reason God raised up the apostle Paul. Jesus taught these twelve men for three years, and then the Church of Jesus grew to seventy men; then, according to the Gospels of Matthew, Mark, Luke, and John, the Church of Jesus grew to one hundred and twenty and more.

The apostles and the other disciples that walked, talked, and learned from Jesus knew what He intended to do: raise up a Church that should have an experience with God. He wanted them to realize that He did not come to start another religion, organization, or denomination; there was a lot of that in His day. He came to start the Church of which He would be the head. Within the head of a human being, the forebrain is responsible for a variety of functions, including receiving and processing sensory information, thinking, forming, perceiving, producing, and understanding language.

The functions of the brain in the human body and what it does are vague compared to what Jesus Christ, the head of the Church, does. He is responsible for a variety of functions, spiritually speaking, such as sensory information, thinking formation, perceiving, producing, and understanding all people, all languages, and all nations.

He, who is the head, wants to communicate to the Church, who is His Body, whom He left here on earth as His representative to communicate to people who do not know God, as we teach them His ways, plan, and purpose. Jesus dying on the cross is the only message that would keep the Church focused. It is God's mandate for reconciling and bringing mankind back to God. Within the human body, there are five senses; four of them originate from the head; these are sight, hearing, smell, and taste. Our hands symmetrically reach out to feel or to touch; amazing is the word for this revelation. He is the head. We are His body, our hands are attached to our bodies, so this brings us to the point that feelings and touch can only be transmitted by the hands. Within the human neck is one of the most intricate fabrications of the veins that connect to the human body, and only our Omniscient God has the creative ability to create such a network of veins that connects from the head of a human to the neck and then to the heart and other parts of the body. Study with me in the next few paragraphs as we study the connection from the head and neck to the body.

The neck of a human being is attached to the head, and so is Christ to the Church. Studies about the head, neck, and body are relevant to the Church. Within the neck are all of the intricate parts such as the external jugular, anterior jugular, post external, internal jugular, and vertebral obviously connect to the heart, which pumps the blood to every other organ within the body through a network of other veins, plus the vertebral system which goes from the back of the head and neck right on down to your tail bone. This, of course, entwines a network of a threadlike network system that controls the sensory nervous system from the brain back and forth throughout the body of a human being.

The apostle Paul used his God-given knowledge as he was inspired to write these words two thousand years ago.

> *From whom the whole body fitly joined together and compacted by that which every joint [part] supplieth according to the effectual working in the measure of every part, maketh increase of the body unto the edifying of itself in love.*
>
> — Ephesians 4:16

The idea seems to be that the group of Christians in the world constitutes the physical representation of Christ on earth. If a person is not in the church, he is not among those whom Jesus has saved from sin. So the people who have been saved and purchased by that blood of Christ are the people who comprise the church!

> *And he is the head of the body, the church: who is the beginning, the firstborn from the dead; that in all things he might have the preeminence.*
>
> — Colossians 1:18.

So the people who have been saved and purchased by that blood of Christ are the people who are in the church!

"Jesus is head of the church and He is savior of his body. [...] He gave himself up for the church" Ephesians 5:23, 25. So the church is the body of all people who have been saved by Christ.

> *The Lord added to the church daily those who were saved.*
>
> — Acts 2:47b

The "universal" church consists of all saved people everywhere because when God saves people, He puts them in the church. In this sense, the church is always singular. This also shows us why it is important to be in the church. It is true that Jesus is the Savior, so the church does not save us. Nevertheless, all those whom Jesus has forgiven are in the church. If a person is not in the church, he is not among those whom Jesus has saved from sin.

> *For by him were all things created, that are in heaven, and that are in earth, visible and invisible, whether they be thrones, or dominions, or principalities, or powers: all things were created by him, and for him:*
> *And he is before all things, and by him all things consist.*
> *And he is the head of the body, the church: who is the beginning, the firstborn from the dead; that in all things he might have the preeminence.*
> *For it pleased the Father that in him should all fulness dwell; and, having made peace through the blood of his cross, by him to reconcile all things unto himself*

And you, that were sometime alienated and enemies in your mind by wicked works, yet now hath he reconciled

In the body of his flesh through death, to present you holy and unblameable and unreproveable in his sight:

If ye continue in the faith grounded and settled, and be not moved away from the hope of the gospel, which ye have heard, and which was preached to every creature which is under heaven; whereof I Paul am made a minister;

Who now rejoice in my sufferings for you, and fill up that which is behind of the afflictions of Christ in my flesh for his body's sake, which is the church:

— Colossians 1:16–24

In whom we have redemption through his blood, the forgiveness of sins, according to the riches of his grace.

— Ephesians 1:7

And from Jesus Christ, who is the faithful witness, and the first begotten of the dead, and the prince of the kings of the earth.

Unto him that loved us, and washed us from our sins in his own blood, [So the people who have been saved and purchased by that blood are the people who are in the church!]

— Revelation 1:5

For the husband is the head of the wife, even as Christ is the head of the church: and he is the saviour of the body..

Therefore as the church is subject unto Christ, so let the wives be to their own husbands in every thing.

Husbands, love your wives, even as Christ also loved the church, and gave himself for it.

— Ephesians 5:23–25

[…] And the Lord added to the church daily such as should be saved.

[The people who have been saved and purchased by that blood are the people who are in the church! We must be reminded the Church of Jesus Christ comprises of people who are truly born again.]

— Acts 2:47b

Jesus answered and said unto him, "Verily, verily, I say unto thee, Except a man be born again, he cannot see the kingdom of God."

Nicodemus saith unto him, "How can a man be born when he is old? can he enter the second time into his mother's womb, and be born?"

Jesus answered, "Verily, verily, I say unto thee, Except a man be born of water and of the Spirit, he cannot enter into the kingdom of God. That which is born of the flesh is flesh; and that which is born of the Spirit is spirit. Marvel not that I said unto thee, Ye must be born again. The wind bloweth where it listeth, and thou hearest the sound thereof, but canst not tell whence it cometh, and whither it goeth: so is every one that is born of the Spirit [people that are saved and baptized with the Holy Spirit].

— John 3:5–8

But you will receive power when the Holy Spirit comes on you; and you will be my witnesses in Jerusalem, and in all Judea and Samaria, and to the ends of the earth.

— Acts 1:8, NIV

And when the day of Pentecost was fully come, they were all with one accord in one place.
And suddenly there came a sound from heaven as of a rushing mighty wind, and it filled all the house where they were sitting.
And there appeared unto them cloven tongues like as of fire, and it sat upon each of them.
And they were all filled with the Holy Ghost, and began to speak with other tongues, as the Spirit gave them utterance.

— Acts 2:1–4

People who recognize Jesus and accept Him as their Lord and Savior according to the Bible are cleansed from all their sins.

But if we walk in the light, as he is in the light, we have fellowship one with another, and the blood of Jesus Christ his Son cleanseth us from all sin.

— 1 John 1:7

People who are washed in the blood of Jesus Christ, who recognize Jesus as their Lord and Savior, and are transformed by the power of God and now living a life (even though they live in this world) sanctified and separated from sin and have a daily walk and relationship with God. These are people who comprise the Church, people who read their Bibles, go to the house of God, these people work with their pastor, pray, attend church, study the Word, support the work of God for the expenses of the church, for the ministry, outreaches, missionary programs, and other outreaches, world evangelization. People who are preparing themselves by living clean and holy lives are ready for the second return of Jesus Christ when He returns the second time. These people are called the Church; the church can be a few, hundreds, thousands, and millions. The church is in every continent, nation, country, city, and town in every country of the world. They constitute people of every race, every color, and this is all because of God's love towards the human race, "For God so loved the world [people] that he gave his only begotten Son, that whosoever believeth in Him should not perish, but have everlasting life" John 3:16.

The church of Jesus Christ is God's representative on earth. This means in every way that Jesus Christ was and *is*. His life, words, power, anointing, works, ministry, compassion, love, and winning souls should be carried out through the Church. The church of Jesus can and should be the greatest power on earth, power from God to stop, not just talk, preach, or write about the evil that's occurring around us and in the world, but power to stop the devil and the works of the devil—sin, which is correctly termed the attributes of sin murder, adultery, lust, fornication, witchcraft, Satan worship and much more.

The country of Haiti is one of the neediest countries in the world. We do have pastors, churches, and ministries in Haiti, and here is a true modern-day story that does not come from the history of revivals from the seventeenth and eighteenth centuries, but the author wanted to write about something that would be relevant to the paragraph above to emphasize the power that Jesus gave to the church and the power that is allotted to us.

From Port-au-Prince, Haiti, driving north, which my wife and I have done time and time again, driving throughout some interesting cities and towns like Duvalierville, Gonaives, Saint Mark, then some beautiful cascading mountains ascending and descending onto the city of Cap Haitian, where one out of several of our churches or congregation exists. Pastor Charles Genard, who is one of our pastors, I received a telephone call from him one morning. He sounded very troubled on the phone; as I asked him what was going on, here is what he shared with me, "Pastor Seebran," he said to me as he was choked up, "the church building, school, and distributing center that you are helping us to build…every morning we go back to continue working on the building, we would discover part of the building is broken down. Worst of all, we would find at the front door and inside the building—chicken feathers and blood and a dead chicken, incenses, ashes, and every type of fetishes; the voodoo priest, who lives right next door to the church, is the one who is doing all of the damages; and worst of all, he is doing witchcraft and voodoo against us. He is trying to stop us, pastor." He continued, "We have done everything possible to talk and witness to this voodoo priest trying to get him saved, but he is getting worse. He said, "Pastor, you have taught us how to fast and pray; we are going on seven-day fasting and praying for God to stop this voodoo priest because he does not want to change." I told him we were going to fast and pray with him.

He called during the week and said the situation with the voodoo priest had gotten worse; I told him, "You and the church keep fasting and praying; God knows how to deal with this situation." He called back at the end of the seven-day fasting and praying, and he said the voodoo priest was dead.

The church of Jesus Christ has power, either way, to change the situation so that souls can be saved, the community can be changed for the better, the clubs of ill repute centers can be shut down, the perverted spirit can be stopped, the ungodly spirit in our country can be hindered, the atheistic millionaires who are using their monies and demoniac influences to organize ungodly adults and young people who are being told and has the attitude if it feels good to do it, and some who are now succumbing to the devilish demonic agenda of not knowing what gender they are, and a man can enter a woman's public bathroom as long as he feels he is a woman, or the woman can do the same. While same-sex marriage is lauded by some leaders of governments, cities, and towns, some of them have rejected God and His righteousness. Then if the church leaders and leaders of governments believe in God and do not condone it, He is lambasted by the left and fake news media.

This same demonic spirit that caused the Bible, prayer, and all godly plaques and the Ten Commandments to be removed from our schools and public places is the same spirit that is manifesting itself in all of these loose rallies and marches, while some entertainers, movie stars, and news media late-night show hosts, who have no respect for the office of the president, who openly shout out of blowing up the White House how nasty they are, use profanity with no fear of God.

Yes, the Church of Jesus Christ has the power to stop all of this. But like the preacher in Haiti who stopped the voodoo priest from destroying his church and building, we can stop what is going on in our day and have one of the greatest revivals with signs, wonders, and miracles following. There can be no excuse for the Church in the light of what Jesus has done for us on the cross, His resurrection, and the power He gave to the Church. But the church, in general, has to come out from its modern-day mentality that is being preached from pulpits today, that is, Jesus has done it all; we have to do nothing. Most of the church has become too lazy and lackadaisical. Remember what happened to the five foolish virgins that Jesus spoke about in Matthew, chapter 26. The statement that Jesus made after Peter made the confession that Jesus was Christ, the Son of the living God, Jesus continued as He spoke these words: *"And Simon Peter answered and said, Thou art the Christ, the Son of the living God"* Matthew 16:16.

> *And I will give unto thee the keys of the kingdom of heaven: and whatsoever thou shalt bind on earth shall be bound in heaven: and whatsoever thou shalt loose on earth shall be loosed in heaven.*
>
> — Matthew 16:19

On the day of Pentecost (Acts, chapter 2), after Peter received the baptism of the Holy Spirit, Peter and the other apostles received the keys to the kingdom of heaven, which means power from God to stop the works of the devil here on earth. This power was passed down from Jesus to Peter and to all the other apostles, the book of Acts Church, and to all believers within the past centuries to the present time. God used Peter to be the spokesman on the day of Pentecost, but this does not mean that the power of God was limited to Peter alone but to all the other apostles and all believers from that time to the present. By the way, have you ever thought about what the keys to the kingdom of heaven or power from God were? The keys that God gave to Peter, all of the other apostles, and the church from that time to the present time are the (1) power of the Holy Spirit, (2) the name of Jesus, and (3) the Word of God, the Bible. With all of these biblical keys, most of all, we have the power of the blood of Jesus.

Here are the keys to stopping the flood tides of evil for a sweeping revival in our day; this is the power that the Church has.

> *"Whatsoever ye shall bind on earth shall be bound in heaven: whatsoever ye shall loose on earth shall be loosed in heaven."*
>
> — Matthew 16:18

Combine these words with the great commission to the Church.

> *And he said unto them, Go ye into all the world, and preach the gospel to every creature.*
>
> *He that believeth and is baptized shall be saved; but he that believeth not shall be damned.*
>
> *And these signs shall follow them that believe; In my name shall they cast out devils; they shall speak with new tongues;*
>
> *They shall take up serpents; and if they drink any deadly thing, it shall not hurt them; they shall lay hands on the sick, and they shall recover.*
>
> *So then after the Lord had spoken unto them, he was received up into heaven, and sat on the right hand of God.*
>
> *And they went forth, and preached every where, the Lord working with them, and confirming the word with signs following. Amen.*
>
> — Mark 16:15–20

Again, the question is, who are the ones supposed to do the binding and losing? It is the members of the Body of Christ. The lame excuse is that so many ministers and churches (congregation) are going around saying we have to do nothing. "Jesus did it all" sometimes can be an excuse not to pray or bind and lose. How do we bind and lose? This is done while in prayer. Besides meditating and waiting on God, it is opening our mouths and talking to God, and this is where binding and losing come in.

Jesus already gave the Church the power on earth to bind and loose; this means all believers in Jesus Christ. Residue power and power unleashed can only be activated by prayer and the spoken word. This brings us to the point where members of the Church of Jesus Christ must realize that the ungodly politicians, news media, hollywoodites, entertainers, late-night show hosts, social media, and atheist billionaires financing ungodly agendas do not have the key; the church has the key to change things for the better and to bring about a revival of righteousness and evangelization of the world, which would usher in the second return of Jesus.

Instead of members of the Body of Christ and ministers spending time and money just to talk: seminars, conferences, prophecy conferences, just to talk about the intricacies of prophecy and the fulfillment of prophecy, nothing wrong with this, but thank God for the pastors, ministers, churches, and TV ministries that are winning souls. And I mean getting down to the nitty-gritty of soul-winning; it seems like many or 89 percent of the church world, in particular, prophecy teachers, have forgotten these words of Jesus,

> *But he that shall endure unto the end, the same shall be saved.*
> *And this gospel of the kingdom shall be preached in all the world for a witness unto all nations; and then shall the end come.*
>
> — Matthew 24:13–14

CHAPTER 4

The Ministry Gifts in the Church

Jesus chose twelve men while He was here on earth. For three and a half years, He taught them, He taught and prayed with them, they learned as He ministered to the people, and the apostles witnessed the supernatural as signs and wonders testified of His divinity. Three of them witnessed Him in His real glory as He outshined the sun on the Mount of Transfiguration. There was no doubt in their minds that He was the Son of God. After His crucifixion, His resurrection, ascension, and sitting at the right hand of God to make intercession for us, the apostles' time came to represent Jesus on Earth.

The word Jesus taught them impregnated their spirit, soul, mind, and bodies; now it was their God-given responsibility to pick up where He left off; they solemnly recollect the words of Jesus as we term it today "The Great Commission," as recorded.

> *And he said unto them, Go ye into all the world, and preach the gospel to every creature.*
>
> *He that believeth and is baptized shall be saved; but he that believeth not shall be damned.*
>
> *And these signs shall follow them that believe; In my name shall they cast out devils; they shall speak with new tongues;*
>
> *They shall take up serpents; and if they drink any deadly thing, it shall not hurt them; they shall lay hands on the sick, and they shall recover.*
>
> *So then after the Lord had spoken unto them, he was received up into heaven, and sat on the right hand of God.*
>
> *And they went forth, and preached every where, the Lord working with them, and confirming the word with signs following. Amen.*
>
> — Mark 16:15–20

We were given the instruction to carry out "The Great Commission" and preach the word in such a manner as we manifest a Christ-like life with healings, miracles, signs, and wonders that will cause people to believe the Gospel of Jesus Christ.

While on earth, Jesus chose twelve apostles who are foundational leaders of the New Testament Church; before and after Jesus ascended to heaven, they carried on their ministry exalted where Jesus left off, as they exalted Jesus with the power of God as miracles, healings, signs, wonders, divine supernatural interventions as they carried the great commission (Mark, chapter 16).

There must be an understanding of the ministry gifts within the Church of today, their qualifications, attitude, message, vision, lifestyle, prayer life, their handling of the Word of God, and their motive and purpose in the ministry. It's so simple, all God intended for the church of today is to carry out and escalate where Jesus and the twelve foundational apostles left off. Most of all, to preach and teach the Gospel of Jesus Christ, with signs, healings, and miracles, following so that men and women would accept Jesus and be saved. The twelve apostles that followed Jesus who were used of God in such an unusual and mighty way are recorded in Acts. Their apostolic gifts should not be limited and minimized for their day. The Church of Jesus Christ was established on the day of Pentecost (Acts, chapter 2), beginning with the ministry of Jesus recorded in Matthew, Mark, Luke, and John, and then the twelve apostles continued and did exactly what Jesus did through the power of the Holy Spirit. Other believers were added down throughout the ages to the present time, so "The Church Continues Today," not the building but "Born Again" washed in the blood of Jesus believers, baptized in Christ, and the power of the Holy Spirit.

Here are the words revealed to the apostle Paul, and he was inspired to write: "And he gave some, apostles; and some, prophets; and some, evangelists; and some, pastors and teachers" Ephesians 4:11. "And God hath set some in the church, first apostles, secondarily prophets, thirdly teachers, after those miracles, then gifts of healings, helps, governments, diversities of tongues" 1 Corinthians 12:28.

The gift of *help* is one of the most overlooked ministries in the Body of Christ. All we see and hear is the first fivefold ministry gift in the Church; the apostle Paul was inspired by the Holy Spirit to be certain that the gift of *help* was included because the fivefold ministry gifts could not really function without the ministry gift of *help*.

Before going any further comparison of the same mentioned ministries recorded in the book of *Acts* and the apostle Paul's writings are so foreign to the men and women who claim the same ministries today. All of these ministry gift titles should be backed up by the high standard of biblical living, such as purity, holiness, and cleanliness with the power of the Almighty God manifesting and working through their lives. Names and titles and degrees do not deliver anyone, so what's the point of people who claim these titles must be real and have the power of the Holy Spirit working through their lives before claiming to be an apostle, prophet, evangelist, pastor, teacher, or *help*.

A title with degrees on a piece of paper wherever it can be bought from over the counter, the internet, or any form of media that offers them. Competition rages on in an open market for all types of religious paraphernalia, that is, if the price is right. Just go online and punch in a credit card, and your credentials card, diploma, doctorate, master's, bachelor's, ordination, and certificates will be on their way.

Those who profess to have a ministry, even so with degrees, some of these individuals snub and shun lost souls (with no compassion and disrespect of the one who died on the cross), men and women who do not know what a prayer closet looks like and the prayer that is being referred to is not a few seconds of prayer! Praying and giving thanks for a meal or at the ball games is commendable; education is important but must be preceded with a born again experience, baptism with the Holy Spirit, a dedicated Christ-like life with a desire to see Matthew, Mark, Luke, John, and the book of Acts fulfilled in our day.

The twelve apostles did not care for the title apostles; they did not carry a chain with a cross or a card or a badge and did not have people register at the front door and charge them enormous or exorbitant fees to get in at the front door so people can attend their conference, seminar, or meeting, neither did they charge an advance fee for their services. Ignorant, someone might say no, but these words are without the understanding that there are expenses involved in different types of meetings, but titles and money (even though money is needed for the evangelization of the world) should not be a priority. Jesus wept because of the unbelief at Lazarus' grave; if he were in the flesh today, he would be flat on face, weeping for the thousands upon thousands of gimmicks and schemes that are going on in the name of Jesus Christ.

This paragraph might be termed nit-picking, but it's not directed toward the real people of God who desire and mean well in advancing the kingdom of God. There are people within some denominations, organizations, and independents who blatantly deny and plainly preach and teach that there is no need for apostles and prophets today. Some even deny miracles, healings, speaking in unknown tongues, and the gifts of the spirit. Some of them spend more time fighting and adamantly denying as they constantly affirm that there is no need for apostles, prophets, and the gifts of the spirit in the church today. I presume that they are not reading the same Bible that I am reading, this would not surprise yours truly, and it's all because of some of these modern-day translations they are reading.

And he gave some, apostles; and some, prophets; and some, evangelists; and some, pastors and teachers.

— Ephesians 4:11.

APOSTLES

Who are they? The Greek word for apostle or apostles means "*Apóstolo.*" An apostle is a messenger of Jesus Christ who has seen Jesus and has all of the gifts of the Spirit operating through their ministry (1 Corinthians, chapter 12); this will be dealt with later on working and manifesting through His life and ministry as they minister with the purpose strengthening the Body of Christ. The word "*apostle*" also means "a sent out one," sent out on a mission; what mission? The mission of leading men and women to Jesus Christ. The first prominent Christian missionary to a region or group is a person who initiates a great moral reform or who first advocates an important belief or system apostle and apostol, both from Late Latin "apostolus," from Greek "apostolos," from "apostellein," to send away, from "apo—stellein" to send. An apostle does not necessarily build upon another man's foundation.

"Yea, so have I strived to preach the gospel, not where Christ was named, lest I should build upon another man's foundation.

— Romans 15:20

Like Paul, they prefer to build by laying a solid foundation or preferably what you would call the original or the basics of Christianity, or exactly what Jesus Christ taught apostleship is a basic and foundational ministry, "And are built upon the foundation of the apostles and prophets, Jesus Christ himself being the chief corner stone" Ephesians 2:20.

The true apostles of Christ are not interested in titles, hierarchy, or positional authority. It is not a glamorous ministry, nor is it a walk of glory or honor. On the contrary, the apostle must be willing to endure great personal sacrifice and hardship, walking at the end of the procession. In many cases, the apostle has taken a personal walk through the wilderness in preparation for his ministry. Apostles must set aside self-ambition in order to commit to the service and promotion of others' thoughts. Here are the qualifications of an apostle. Apostles are trailblazers, spiritual pioneers who must be able to think this way in order to plant and establish new churches. They are often the first to go into new territories, cutting a path for others to follow. These new territories can be geographical or areas of new knowledge and understanding. An apostle is a chosen vessel of God to penetrate deep into different countries, cities, villages, and towns, and with that apostle's anointing from God through Jesus Christ and the power of the Holy Spirit upon their lives. With God's help, they break the spirit of darkness and bring the light of Jesus Christ into an area of darkness where people who have never heard of Jesus.

Most self-claim apostles of today, all they do is preaching to a few people or more every Sunday morning who have heard the same thing preached over and over (sometimes their gospel) but not the Gospel of Jesus Christ. An apostle is Christ conscious, Christ sent, Christ powered, Christ-exalting, and Christ purposed; real apostles are men of prayer and are dedicated to God's plan and program. Most of all, real apostle carries a deep yearning for God and the things of God and has a driving passion within their spirit to win lost souls in every area they are and take the Gospel of Jesus Christ to places where people have never heard of Jesus. The life of an apostle is a totally sold-out to Jesus Christ, a sacrificial life, and a life given over to God's plan and purpose.

PROPHETS

The Hebrew word for prophet is "*Nabi,*" from the root meaning to bubble forth like a fountain. *Nabi*, in general, is used when speaking of a prophet. Also another Hebrew word that is used in naming a prophet is "*Ro'eh,*" the root meaning a "*seer.*" The scriptural reference for this is about Samuel the prophet (1 Chronicles 29:29); *Samuel the "seer," Nathan the prophet "Nabi,"* the word "*nabi*" is centered up the fact like Nathan, the spokesperson for God. A prophet is a direct spokesman for God, who receives a direct revelation message from God and communicates that message to an individual, certain people, or nation. The apostle and the prophet possibly can have all of the nine gifts operating and manifesting through their lives to confirm that what they are speaking is directly from God.

A true prophet does not assume, guess, sense, or feel suspect. Set people up within their ministry to snoop and find out from different ones what's going on in their lives, where they live, their house numbers, etc., then they bring back information to the so-called prophet, then he can call out people with the information that was given to him or her or mention the same information on the radio, TV, or meetings. True prophets do not sit down on a TV set speaking or telling a TV audience there is a person out there who is suffering from a migraine headache being healed. Believe me, this might work because a person has faith to be healed, etc. Prophets do not have someone in the audience transmitting people's names and addresses to the so-called prophet as they call it out while names and addresses are being transmitted to them. A prophet does not take news from informants and then gets up in front of a crowd and speaks what they heard from the informant. In fifty years of ministry, you truly have witnessed every type of gimmick, scheme, and trick from so-called prophets who want the name of a prophet to gain the favor of people and make a profit financially.

But a prophet is direct and has a direct word from God that will produce results, and his word from God will be confirmed by the gift of God manifesting through him, which will bring everlasting results, miracles, healings, deliverance, and healing in the Body of Christ. Yes, sometimes a prophet's word from God will shake, rattle, and disrupt some agendas, plans, and programs, but his or her prophetic message will not produce hate, division, and strife but will bring healing to an individual and the Body of Jesus Christ, yes! Sometimes a prophet's word will be a warning to a nation, people, or church to repent and turn to God, which will bring about a change for the better if they turn to God; God will spare in individual, people, community, city or nation. There are times that a word from God is delivered by a prophet, which will contradict everyone else.

Too many times, it's been seen that so-called prophets cause division in the Body of Christ. Yes, Jesus took a whip and drove out the tax collectors, money changers, traders and sellers from making the house of God a marketplace, but his final message after cleaning the house of God was, "[…] My house shall be called a house of prayer" Matthew 21:13a.

What was Jesus' message to them about God's house? It is a place where we should get together and pray; a prophet's message always ends up with the word "together," "pray," "answers," "results"; a prophet's message should not leave people hanging in doubt and confusion. A word of caution here, God can give a pastor, teacher, or evangelist a dream, vision, revelation, or they can speak a word, and if it comes to pass, this does not make them prophets, and they should not go around claiming that they are prophets. It is true that, as recorded in the Bible, certain prophets in the Bible, their word or message seemed divisive, but it was when a nation, people, kings, priests, and leaders strayed away from God, and the message got back to God or judgment.

Concerning the office of an apostle or prophet, it must be understood that most of our generation of ministers and Christians are so prone to thinking that anyone who claims to be an apostle or prophet is false. But there are men who have this qualification in the Body of Christ, the church, today. The church continues from the day of Pentecost till now, the church did not cease to exist, but the church of Jesus is existing today; the ministry gifts, the gifts of the Spirit, are for us today.

The apostle and prophet are the most watched, ostracized, and fought against ministry gift in the church today; why? Satan fights these ministries more than all ministries because they are what you might call the bulldozer, icebreaker, and pioneer ministries for the church. God ordained the apostle and the prophet as the forefront ministries to pioneer, establish and be the seer in the church. Why accept pastors, teachers, and evangelists and reject apostles and prophets.

The author is cautious from calling the names of certain men whom he knows personally who fit and qualify as apostles or prophets because we have a generation of ministers and people who will deliberately do everything possible to separate you from their company because they are afraid to be identified with these great men of God. If Jeremiah, the prophet, and Paul, the apostle, were alive today, they would have a rough time getting into some of these churches to minister because both of them would not qualify as to the expectations of some denominational, organizational, and religious standards. Both of them would have been branded jailbirds, prisoners, and not fit to minister to their congregation. The minds of so many are intuitionally tuned to the false that they do not recognize when God sends the real combined with the truth. A bank teller is trained in getting the feel of real money or currency bills that when a counterfeit bill touches his or her hands, they know it's false or counterfeit.

Spiritually speaking, it's time to get our minds conditioned to the truth, so when the ministries that are not real come by, we will know them. Jesus had more problems with the Scribes, Pharisees, and other religious sects of that day than He did with some religious leaders. But real apostles and prophets do not really care for these titles.

All they want to do is deliver men and women from darkness, bring them into the light of God's salvation, and speak a word that will bring deliverance to an individual, city, or nation. When this is done, they certainly give God the glory and praise and do not go around looking for men's praise for what was done.

How do you recognize a true prophet? How do you confirm a true prophet? What are the qualifications of a true prophet? First of all, a prophet lives a godly and Christ-like life. A prophet does not have to be a graduate from a university with degrees following his name (this does not mean that God cannot use an educated person); most of all, God would raise up nothing and use them for His purpose. A prophet's message or word from God would be direct, uncompromising, with the intention of bringing an individual, people, church, or nation back to God. Most of the time, when God sends a prophet to a people with a word from God, that prophet's word would be backed up with a sign or signs back up the word of that particular prophet. If people listen to that God sent a prophet and pray and turn to God, this will result in a supernatural visitation, miracles, and blessings, or if they refuse, judgment will be an inevitable result.

Most of all, when a prophet speaks a word, predicts, or prophesies an event, and it comes to pass, they are true prophets, and if what they speak, predict, or prophesy does not come to pass, then they are false prophets.

> *And if thou say in thine heart, How shall we know the word which the LORD hath not spoken?*
> *When a prophet speaketh in the name of the LORD, if the thing follows not, nor come to pass, that is the thing which the LORD hath not spoken, but the prophet hath spoken it presumptuously: thou shalt not be afraid of him.*
>
> — Deuteronomy 18:21–22

A true prophet stands in the gap (intercessory pray) for a person, people, or nation and prays for them until they come to know God.

"Moreover as for me, forbid that I should sin against the Lord in ceasing to pray for you: but I will teach you the good and the right way" 1 Samuel 12:23.

A true prophet always has a direct word from God; God also visits him or her through dreams, visions, and when a prophet speaks a word, prophesies, or predicts that an event would happen, he always backs it up with, "*Thus said the Lord*," and it comes to pass.

EVANGELIST

Even though the scriptures placed the evangelist before the pastor, there is a reason why the ministry of the evangelist is mentioned at this point. The ministry of the evangelist is one of the most important ministries in the Church, but the ministry of the evangelist is the most despised ministry in the church today, even though the ministry of the evangelist is least respected by some pastors' ministries and people today. If the evangelist does not have a church, this means he is not important, especially in the eyes of other ministries, most of all by some pastors. These words were mentioned to get the attention of the Body of Christ, or the Church, to appreciate once more the gift of the evangelist that God has set in the Body of Christ, the Church.

The evangelist and the ministry of the evangelist have taken a beating but thank God they keep ticking. Disrespected and despised by some other ministries, the ministry of the evangelist needs to gain back the godly respect they deserve because God lists them as one of the fivefold ministries in the Church. No name will be mentioned here, but there is a popular TV minister whom I respect and still do look and listen to him. This particular evangelist and TV minister spoke some words about the evangelist, and God knows if he realized what he said had such a negative impact on you truly. Of course, this happened many years ago, God knows that his attitude must have changed by now, but these words should have never been mentioned; here are the words of this TV minister, "I am not some evangelist traveling with my family looking for someone to buy me some new tires," not because he is on TV and people see and support him but still have a heart for the ministry of the evangelist because he is God-ordained.

Yours truly has pastored many congregations or churches (churches for modern-day terms) and have had so many evangelists and missionaries conduct revivals in the churches I have pastored. It is true that as far as I can remember, one or two of them did not do like I expected them to do, but with a Christ-like spirit, I prayed and spoke to them and also supported their ministry; some of them were a blessing to me, lifted the spirit of the church as people were saved, healed, and delivered, also left the church in a great state of revival.

Here is a simple illustration of the heart yours truly has; while pastoring, one of the churches that I founded also had assistant pastors while I was on the mission fields; this church, in particular, was not a large congregation (name of church and city withheld for personal reasons), the congregation comprised predominantly simple people of the Caucasian race. I invited a black preacher (again, name withheld for personal reasons); he was supposed to speak for one night, the congregation received him, and the meeting was great, and everyone was blessed. He was supposed to minister on a Wednesday night, but the meeting was so good that I asked him to continue until Sunday night.

The people were so blessed as I asked them to bring a love offering on Sunday night for the preacher; as the meeting continued, souls were saved, people were healed, backsliders came back to God, the congregation was revived, and the man of God did a great job as an evangelist, God anointed and used him. Sunday night came by as I remember this meeting closed out with a spiritual revival and God's blessings.

With no reservation, I picked up the offering for the evangelist, with a congregation of less than a hundred people; when the deacons and secretary counted the offering, they gave it to me to present it to the evangelist, the amount of offering that the people gave this evangelist was six thousand five hundred dollars. This was many years ago when money was scarce and when most churches and pastors hardly had money. The evangelist was quite surprised and a bit shocked; the evangelist, in turn, asked me as he said, "Dr. Seebran, how do you want to split this offering?" I smiled, looked at him, and said, "This offering is yours; the people gave it to you; please accept this love offering from us as an expression of our love." Tears filled his eyes as he said, "No pastor ever did this for me." I told him, "I am an evangelist; even though I have had the opposite done to me by certain pastors, the church or congregation wants to be a blessing to you." And he said, "You are one of the most big-hearted pastors I have ever had met."

Yours truly feels for the ministry of the evangelist because I am one of them, as a missionary—evangelist in fifty-five years of ministry, ministered in over fifty-five countries of the world, ministered to over six to seven hundred thousand people or more in a single meeting each night. When I give an altar call, especially overseas, hundreds of thousands of souls respond; I have been the pastor to about ten different congregations. My wife and I, as missionary-evangelist, have the responsibility of supporting schools, orphans, planted hundreds of churches; at the present time, my wife, Sherry, and I are conducting large crusades in stadiums, parks, large and small churches in South America, particularly Brazil.

We are ministering to the people who live on the banks of the Amazon River, where we are building a church, school, and medical center. I shy away from the television ministry, not that yours truly does not want to be on TV, but it costs to be on TV, but I would rather take the money God blesses me with and go to the people that have never heard of Jesus, God opens the way a TV ministry; thank God I would be happy to oblige.

One of the greatest preachers of our time has his own church and TV ministry and claims he is an evangelist, and God has blessed him immensely. He is reaching multitudes daily with the Gospel of Jesus Christ. Because of the ministry of an evangelist, multitudes of thousands have been saved, healed, and delivered. Governments and nations have been shaken and changed, some of the most Jesus-like miracles have occurred, the devil's territory shaken, and poverty-stricken people, countries, and areas started prospering because of the ministry of this evangelist. I have witnessed congregations that were down spiritually and never seen the light of day in steep traditions, rituals, and man-made dogmas. One of their pastors invited this evangelist to minister for a few nights, which extended into a move of God or revival that lasted for several weeks or months.

Yours truly will never forget in the earlier days of my ministry; I planned a few nights of meeting in a certain church; the pastor and I spoke, and arrangements were made; date and time were scheduled for three nights of meetings. The day came for these meetings; I spent my own money and drove about two hundred miles to get to the city where this meeting was supposed to be held, checked into a hotel, then called the pastor, informing him that I was at this particular hotel; told him the room I was in; he said fine. After informing the pastor, I was there, ready to start the revival that night; one hour later, I heard a knock on my hotel door, one of the deacons was standing in front of the door, and these were his words to me, "Our pastor said he could not have you to minister tonight and the other two nights," then the deacon left. Well! I was disappointed but thanked God yours truly never depended on pastors and did not have a beggar mentality, just in case. We drove to another meeting, but anyone reading this book might wonder what the reason for mentioning this is; here is your answer—this is an example of what the evangelist has to go through. Now in this day and time, it seems that the ministry of the evangelist is totally vanished and vanquished.

Another experience yours truly would like to share with the readers with the intention of making a very important point. Many years ago, my wife, Sherry, and my daughter Lisa were invited to conduct a week's revival meeting at one of Detroit's largest Churches or congregations of seven thousand or more people; our host pastor was one of Detroit's most admired and prominent pastors.

Upon our arrival in Detroit, I will never forget we were met by this host pastor who gave us one of the warmest welcomes we had ever received from a pastor who took us to one of the best seven-star hotels in Detroit. Our room was already paid for, plus arrangements were made for all our meals, etc. After a day and night's rest in one of the most comfortable rooms, the next day, we got dressed and went down to the lobby, waiting for someone to give us a ride to the church where I was the guest speaker. While waiting in the lobby, I thought some brother from the church with an ordinary car would come and pick us and take us to the Church; as we looked outside the lobby, one of the finest huge limousines pulled up in front of the hotel. Surely I thought there was a really important guest or VIP staying at the same hotel. Immediately after the limo pulled up, the door opened from the driver's side, and a well-dressed stately looking gentleman came towards the lobby and entered the door with a huge umbrella in his hand (as it was raining). I thought he was going to someone else but us. Being well dressed, he walked up to us and asked, "Are you Dr. Seebran and family?"

Yes, was the reply: he said to follow him; as we walked towards the limo, he graciously opened the door as we got inside the limousine and drove to the church. When we arrived, there were two ministers standing at the door to welcome us; they took our briefcase, shoes that I wear to preach and minister, our Bibles, etc.; with respect, honor, and love, they spoke these words, "It's an honor to have you here at our church. Is there anything we can do for you? Or if there is anything you need, please inform us." They ushered us to the platform as thousands of people were in attendance. Right after this, two of the finest women who were also nurses and ministers were introduced to us as someone told us, "These are your nurses; they are here to help and take care of you." The pastor, of course, seated us close to his chair on the platform (he did not seat us with everyone else but treated us like we ought to be treated like ministers); in this day and time, it's like pastors treat other ministries like nothing, and by the way, if they do have visiting ministers, some of them do not care to mention a word about them and lose them in the crowd. It is true that some pastors are taping for television, etc., but what about the majority of other times. This illustrious man of God gave a synopsis of our ministry, highly recommended us to the congregation, and graciously beaconed me behind his pulpit to minister the word of God; of course, we had one of the greatest revivals.

During this revival, I did not have to push, beg, or promise the congregation the blessings of God. If they give, believe me, there are some meetings where I had to do this because there was no guarantee that I would leave some churches getting gas money, so much for expenses and ministry. Anyhow after the meetings in Detroit, the pastor called me into his office and handed me a large check, of which I thanked him as I expressed my love and gratitude for his kindheartedness.

Some evangelist has indeed disrespected the office of some pastors. There are times certain evangelists have been dishonest; some of them caused division in different congregations, but this does not mean that the evangelist's ministry should be shut out from the church. Most of them are honest, and their ministry is desperately needed in the church. These two unforgettable experiences, the first experience exposes the inexperience and immaturity of an untrained pastor, and the second experience attests to the fact of a pastor with the love of God, trained and mature, who understands the need of the ministry of an evangelist in his church, the ministry of the evangelist is desperately needed in the church, and by the way, a pastor cannot be both at the same time.

What makes some pastors think that the congregation they are pasturing does not need a change of voice, or is it that some pastors do not want the ministry of the evangelist who might outdo his? Or hers. Again, which is a sign of immaturity or jealousy? All of the ministry gifts were placed by God in the Church, and each ministry should make every effort to work together with one another, which would be beneficial to God's people and in every way do everything possible that one soul or souls would be saved and come into the kingdom of God. The second experience is a perfect example of how an evangelist should be treated; of course, it might not be to the level of this minister from Detroit, but what's the point? He had godly respect for one of the ministry gifts within the Body of Christ; the first pastor had truth on ice, and the second one had truth on fire.

The New Testament word for "evangelist" comes from the Hebrew word "*basar*." Before we consider the Hebrew word, we recall that the word "evangelist" is an English form of the Greek word "*euangelistes*," which is derived from the Greek. The Greek word is a translation of the Hebrew noun "*mevasser*," which is an action-packed word Hebrew "*basar*," meaning "to announce cheerful news." When the verb "*basar*" is used in the noun, it means "*gospel*," "*good news*," and "*joyful news.*" The word "*basar*" also means "*the beginning point to stir to bring about a change in what's existing to greater heights and completion.*" The word "*basar*" gives meaning to the ministry of the evangelist as one who "*stirs*" up stagnant water and causes it to run again.

Matthew, Mark, Luke, and John were the first evangelists in Jesus' Church after He died and rose again and ascended into heaven. What would have happened if there were no evangelists like them? Paul, the apostle, was not only an apostle but an evangelist who did not stay in Jerusalem and rambled over doctrinal differences, fighting over who was right or wrong and trying to keep the other apostle straight with a bunch of rules and regulations. Of course, he had the ministry of a missionary-evangelist; there was a burning desire in his soul to win the world to Jesus; read the record in the book of Acts, chapter 9, about Phillip the evangelist, who stirred cities, towns, and villages.

Thomas the apostle, who asked Jesus to let him place his fingers in the scars of His hands, traveled to South India. (My wife and I were there.) As an evangelist, he won thousands of souls to Jesus. It cost him his life, but up to this present day and time, millions of Indians remember and gather by his grave to celebrate Thomas going to India two thousand years ago to bring the Gospel of Jesus Christ to India. This certainly was the ministry of an apostle but also a missionary-evangelist whom God ordained like some evangelists of today, not because the evangelist does not have a megachurch; this should not indicate that he or she is not a God-ordained ministry.

PASTORS

Of all the ministry gifts in the Church, the ministry of the pastor or pastors is a ministry that interacts with all the other ministries within the church; in simple language, the pastors can be the other entire ministry gift in the church, that is, if he wants to be. He is also constantly in contact with more people more frequently than the other ministries. A pastor's responsibility does not end after he preaches a sermon, but it is a twenty-four-hour job. A pastor's work never stops; "profession" is not the word to describe the work of a pastor, but this is a calling to lead, help, and minister to people night and day.

The original word for a "pastor" from Middle English is "*pastour,*" from Anglo-French, from Latin—"*pastor,*" which means herdsman, from "*pascere,*" to feed. The Greek word for "pastor" is "*poi men,*" herdsmen and shepherd. Also, some added meaning to the word "pastor" is one who cares for, feeds, guides, and protects. The word for a pastor in Greek is "*poimhn,*" also "*poimen,*" and means shepherd. It is used sixteen times in the New Testament and translated as shepherd. Only is it translated pastor. The word is as a shepherd, one who tends the herds or flocks, not merely one who feeds them. It is used metaphorically by the Christian pastors. Christ said to be the Great Shepherd and the Good Shepherd.

> *And he gave some, apostles; and some, prophets; and some, evangelists; and some, pastors and teachers.*
>
> — Ephesians 4:11

Now the God of peace, that brought again from the dead our Lord Jesus, that great shepherd of the sheep, through the blood of the everlasting covenant.

— Hebrews 13:20

"I am the good shepherd: the good shepherd giveth his life for the sheep."

— John 10:11

Speaking to the Jews uses this word—"poimen"—in reference to Christ, stating, "For ye were as sheep going astray; but are now returned unto the Shepherd and Bishop of your souls" 1 Peter 2:25.

The word "bishop" means "overseer." Therefore, the word "*poimen*" refers to the man God calls to oversee the local congregation. A pastor then is the Lord's "under-shepherd," the overseer of the Lord's congregation. He is called a "pastor-teacher," which denotes his twofold ministry. He is to shepherd the Lord's flock and to be a teacher of God's Word.

Here Jesus is referred to as the Shepherd and Bishop of our souls. The terms "bishop" and "elder" denote the position or duties of the pastor. It would be correct to use the title bishop or elder for the pastor. But it is not biblical for a minister to use the title "reverend." The word is found only once in the Bible and is not a reference to a man but to Almighty God.

He sent redemption unto his people: he hath commanded his covenant for ever: holy and reverend is his name.

— Psalm 111:9.

The Hebrew word "*yare*" means to fear; morally, to revere, to reverence. Clearly, only God is to be revered, and in holding the reverence of God, we exercise godly fear, knowing that who knows who He is and of His absolute power over all things. That is certainly not an attribute of a minister of the Gospel, an under-shepherd who pastors a local congregation of believers. We are to respect our pastors who minister unto us. The reverence this word speaks of is reserved for God alone, to respect mingled with fear and affection; the word reverent is applied solely to the Supreme Being who is the Almighty God to His laws or institutions. The use of the title "reverend" came from the Roman Catholic Church and its unbiblical church politics. In the Roman Church, it is distinctly used to denote people in religious positions. Note that the title was applied to "reverend fathers; abbesses, prioresses and reverend mothers." All of these titles are unbiblical or are not mentioned in the Bible.

Each of these refers to a position in the Roman Church that has no biblical precedent. No man in the Bible is called by the title "reverend" or even so revered. In the true New Testament assembly, *ekklesia*, or church, there were no reverend fathers; abbesses, prioresses, reverend mothers, archbishops, cardinals, vicars, etc., they were simply called bishop overseers, and it should be the same today, or pastor-teacher, who is the leader of a local congregation. He is to be respected and honored.

Remember them that have the rule over you, who have spoken to you the word of God, whose faith follow, considering the end of their conversation.

Obey them that have the rule over you and submit yourself, for they watch for your souls, as they might give account, that they may do it with joy and not with grief: for that is unprofitable for you.

— Hebrews 13:7, 17

This does not mean a pastor has to get into all of his members' business and rule with an iron rod; then, some church and board members seem like they are ordained and cut out to cause the pastor problems and trouble. Honor the pastor or pastors who teach and preach the Word of God. If God truly calls the pastor, he then is God's man and messenger to the local congregation.

"Reverend" is a title that the religious world has conjured up, but it is not a biblical term used to describe a minister of the Gospel of Jesus Christ or a shepherd of a local congregation. The biblical term is pastor, and I think it honors the Lord and is an act of obedience to use the term He used. The use of the word reverend has its roots in the unbiblical practices of the Roman Catholic Church, which is the apostate church. It is not used in the Bible to refer to God's ministers and is not a proper description of the position. The title "reverend" to men seems to denote a touch of pride in one's position and elevates the man.

The term "pastor" correctly denotes one who humbly serves and cares for the people of his congregation. I think it is clear that using the term "reverend" sends the wrong message as to what God's leader in the local church is to be. So, I do not use the term "reverend," nor do I use it in addressing ministers. Only God is to be revered.

There are times when the pastor is a carpenter, yard keeper, electrician, plumber, secretary, janitor, yard keeper, cook, bus driver, planner and organizer, councilor, chairman of the board, sound man, musician, worship leader, and more. This is one of the ministries in the Body of Christ that can be more demanding and stressful than all of the other ministries; this is the reason why a pastor, as well as all other ministries, should be a man and woman of prayer. Samuel Chadwick, one of the greatest Bible teachers, taught in many universities, colleges, and Bible schools. When he became older, he uttered these words, "I wish I had spent more time in prayer and fewer hours in study." Surrounded by people most of the time, most of the ministry gifts, especially a pastor, can be the loneliest man in the world. There are times in the life of a pastor when absolutely no one seems to understand what he or she goes through.

Yes! There would be a smile for the TV camera, in front of the congregation, in the office counseling different families and individuals, the pressure of executing his pastoral duties, raising funds to pay the staff, seeing to it that all the bills are paid on time, the church building conducive always for worship, the different ministries outreach in from the church must be carried out with precision, all the departments functioning as one unit with the purpose of reaching the goal of the church and ministry, most of all dealing with countless problems each week, at times having to deal with problematic board members sometimes call *b-o-r-e-d* members. Thank God for prayerful and dedicated board members, committees, leaders, etc., who are dedicated to work of God.

A word of encouragement to pastors, a pastor's job, as well as all other ministries, is one of the most important jobs (if I may call it such) in the world; why such a bold statement, lost souls is what the ministry is all about. Remember Jesus died on the cross for our peace, joy, happiness, satisfaction, a daily walk or relationship with God, but most of all, Jesus died on the cross for *lost souls*. Again, there is no greater job than saving lost souls from going to hell. If every other ministry and the pastors in America and other parts of the world let lost souls be their focus, we would experience one of the greatest soul-winning revivals in America and other countries. I would let the words of the apostle Peter speak to pastors,

> *The elders which are among you I exhort, who am also an elder, and a witness of the sufferings of Christ, and also a partaker of the glory that shall be revealed:*
> *Feed the flock of God which is among you, taking the oversight thereof, not by constraint, but willingly; not for filthy lucre, but of a ready mind;*
> *Neither as being lords over God's heritage, but being ensamples to the flock.*
> *And when the chief Shepherd shall appear, ye shall receive a crown of glory that fadeth not away.*
>
> — 1 Peter 5:1–5

Please note the words "neither being lords over God's heritage"; this is what some pastors have become in this day, lords over God's people; a domineering, controlling spirit has overtaken so many pastors that the members of some churches cannot make a move without permission from the pastor; this is what is called the spirit of witchcraft.

Pastors, the words of the apostle Peter should be imbedded deep down within your being as you carry the responsibility of a pastor; from the godly advice of the apostle, from behind the pulpit, this is not a place to mess up people's minds, separate, divide, breakdown, lead astray, get involved in politics and opinions of individuals and the world. It is not to incite hate or strife, regardless of what happens inside, this is not a place for self-satisfaction and personal vindication but your responsibility to feed the flock, overseer, lead or guide the sheep, not with remorse and a controlling spirit but with love lead God's people.

TEACHERS

The definition of the word "teacher" is someone who causes another to think, learn, pursue, and attain their desired goal in life. Who, in turn, would impart knowledge they attained to someone else. Teaching is to cause to know something, to cause to know how. Teaching means accustoming to some action or attitude and teaching students to think for themselves consequences of some action. To guide, impart knowledge to instruct by precept, example, or experience. To make known instruction regularly in teaching school to provide instruction act as a teacher. To show, instruct, educate, indoctrinate, school, train, tutor, coach, mentor; drill, fit, ground, habilitate, prepare, prime, qualify; direct, guide, lead, rear; catechize, lecture, moralize, preach; implant, inculcate, instill, home school; edify, enlighten; brief, familiarize, inform, verse; initiate, introduce, show; reeducate, preschool, instruct, educate, train, discipline. "School" means to cause to acquire knowledge or skill. "Teach" applies to any manner of imparting information or skill so that others may learn taught us a lot about our planet. "Instruct" suggests methodical or formal teaching by instructing raw recruits in military drill.

"Educate" implies development of the mind more things than formal schooling serves to educate a person, train stresses instruction, and drill with a specific end in view. Biblically speaking, if every ministry gift would seriously consider and study the above-mentioned paragraph, this world would have already been evangelized. Teaching, especially in relation to the Gospel of Jesus Christ, is not limited to the gift of the teacher solely, even though this ministry gift to the church has his or her responsibility to teach the Gospel of Jesus Christ. All of the other ministry gifts to the Church should always inculcate the teaching method to communicate the Gospel of Jesus Christ to their hearers. After Jesus rose from the grave, He requested His followers meet Him in Galilee on the Mount; these are His specific words,

> *And Jesus came and spake unto them, saying, All power is given unto me in heaven and in earth.*
> *Go ye therefore, and teach all nations, baptizing them in the name of the Father, and of the Son, and of the Holy Ghost:*
> *Teaching them to observe all things whatsoever I have commanded you: and, lo, I am with you always even unto the end of the world.*
>
> — Matthew 28:18–20

Jesus commands preaching but also teaching of the Gospel; good preaching is an art by itself and very important. Screaming might be all right (even though we have a generation of people that needs to be screamed at) and might appeal to people's emotions for the present moment, but teaching produces and has lasting results. Jesus said, "Go and make disciples of all nations, teaching them to obey everything that I have commanded you." Teaching is a means of reproductive process, a means of adding to the church daily. This is where most of the Church of Jesus Christ, to an extent, made a mistake. Personally speaking, I have witnessed some organizations, religions, and cults set up a tent for three to six months and teach, or I might add their leaders would indoctrinate the attendees night after with their tracts, magazines, books, videos, and before they leave, a church building is erected with a congregation and an ordained pastor.

While most full gospel preachers and leaders and TV ministries pop in and pop out of town to preach and shout, some pray for the sick with some miracles (thank God), as they think that God would send revival in one or two nights.

> *And the things you have heard me say in the presence of many witnesses entrust to reliable people who will also be qualified to teach others.*
>
> — 2 Timothy 2:2, NIV

Sitting down and learning from a qualified teacher is a sign that you are on the way to maturity; maturity in Christ is a sign that you were and are willing to learn. This is the reason so many mess up in ministry; they heard a bird say tweet, tweet, tweet and thought the bird said to preach, preach, preach, a little oil on their head. Grandmother or mother's (why not father) prayers are a great incentive to deliver sons, daughters, grandsons, and granddaughters, but be certain God is the one who called you and is willing to learn through teaching.

> *Let the word of Christ dwell in you richly.*
>
> — Colossians 3:16a

The Hebrew word for teacher is rabbi, meaning teacher, developed in the Pharisaic and Talmudic eras when learned teachers assembled to codify Judaism's written and oral laws. In more recent centuries, the duties of the rabbi became increasingly influenced by the duties of the protestant Christian minister; hence the title pulpit rabbis, and in nineteenth-century Germany and the United States, rabbinic activities, including sermons, pastoral counseling, and representing the community to the outside, all increased in importance. God bless the pastors and other ministries who will encourage and teach others within their ministries.

A Church might be doomed when pastors and other ministries fail to teach the people what God Almighty has entrusted to them. I know of some ministries whose leaders passed away or went on to be with Lord, and their entire ministry folded up, including their followers who were dispersed each and everywhere because they failed to teach their people what they knew, and at the present time, they are nowhere to be found.

Besides "*rabbi*," who refers to a Hebrew teacher, there is another word for teacher in the Hebrew language, which is "*lamad*," which means a teacher who teaches with the intent to learn. This common Semitic term is found throughout the history of the Hebrew language and in ancient *Akkadian* and Urgartic. *Lamad* is found eighty-five times in the text of the Hebrew Old Testament. In its simple active form, this verb has meaning to learn, but it is also found in a form giving causative sense "*to teach*" by a teacher with the intent to impart knowledge to another, hence the reason in times past that every Hebrew child was knowledgeable of the first five books of Moses.

The Greek word for "teacher" or "teachers" is *didaskalos*, meaning an individual or teacher who teaches to impart knowledge for a cause or purpose. This is why Nicodemus, when he came to Jesus, called Him a Teacher or Master because Nicodemus saw how He took time with His disciples and taught and trained them with the intention of the disciples preaching and teaching what He taught them.

Every ministry in the Body of Christ should have the ability to teach with the intention of imparting Christ-life knowledge, power, and ministry with the intention of teaching and training others to reach the world with the Gospel of Jesus Christ. How could anyone ignore the fact, especially looking and listening to the news to see children and young people? This means boys and girls carry weapons, even arming themselves with bombs on their bodies with the push of a button, which can explode and kill scores of people and themselves; why? Because from a child to young men and women, they have been taught the Moslem cause is right, and they would have to kill to get the doctrine of the Moslem religion across to the people of the world. It's called teaching.

Here we are in America; in some areas of Christianity, we think that a little bit of hollering, screaming, and shouting and just a healing meeting would cause a move of God. What is needed in the church today is some dedicated teachers who will pray combined with some fasting to teach and preach what Jesus taught in Matthew, Mark, Luke, and John, and teach what the apostles taught in the book of Acts, including the ministry of the apostle Paul, this surely will produce a revival like they had and bring about a move of God's power.

HELPS

Within the church of Jesus Christ, the ministry of *helps*, in particular at times, has been innocently, mistakenly, and deliberately has been overlooked by other ministries and members of the Body of Christ. The apostle Paul mentions all of the fivefold ministries within the church in another Scripture; he added the gift of *helps*.

> *And he gave some, apostles; and some, prophets; and some, evangelists; and some, pastors and teachers.*
>
> — Ephesians 4:11

> *And God hath set some in the church, first apostles, secondarily prophets, thirdly teachers, after that miracles, then gifts of healings, helps, governments, diversities of tongues.*
>
> — 1 Corinthians 12:28

Please note the above scripture, the apostle Paul mentioned the gift of *helps*. While writing, the author considered leaving out some scriptures that particularly referred to the gift of helps but was inspired by the Holy Spirit to mention the ministry of *helps*. Let us consider the writing of the apostle Paul concerning the ministry of helps within the church, which has been overlooked for decades by leaders of the church.

> *I commend unto you Phebe our sister, which is a servant of the church which is at Cenchrea:*
>
> *That ye receive her in the Lord, as becometh saints, and that ye assist her in whatsoever business she hath need of you: for she hath been a succourer of many, and of myself also.*
>
> *Greet Priscilla and Aquila my helpers in Christ Jesus:*
>
> *Who have for my life laid down their own necks: unto whom not only I give thanks, but also all the churches of the Gentiles.*
>
> *Likewise greet the church that is in their house. Salute my well-beloved Epaenetus, who is the firstfruits of Achaia unto Christ.*
>
> *Greet Mary, who bestowed much labour on us.*
>
> *Salute Andronicus and Junia, my kinsmen, and my fellow-prisoners, who are of note among the apostles, who also were in Christ before me.*
>
> *Greet Amplias my beloved in the Lord.*
>
> *Salute Urbane, our helper in Christ, and Stachys my beloved.*
>
> *Salute Apelles approved in Christ. Salute them which are of Aristobulus' household. Salute Herodion my kinsman. Greet them that be of the household of Narcissus, which are in the Lord. Salute Tryphena and Tryphosa, who labour in the Lord.*
>
> *Salute the beloved Persis, which laboured much in the Lord.*
>
> *Salute Rufus chosen in the Lord, and his mother and mine.*
>
> *Salute Asyncritus, Phlegon, Hermas, Patrobas, Hermes, and the brethren which are with them.*
>
> *Salute Philologus, and Julia, Nereus, and his sister, and Olympas, and all the saints which are with them.*
>
> *Salute one another with an holy kiss. The churches of Christ salute you.*
>
> *Now I beseech you, brethren, mark them which cause divisions and offences contrary to the doctrine which ye have learned; and avoid them.*
>
> — Romans 16:1–17

The apostle Paul painstakingly took the time to mention the names of the Christians in Rome and, of course, other cities that helped him in the work of God or ministry. Considering the day and time he was faced with the inconvenience of not having the modern-day method of pen, ink, ballpoints, and computers, it must have taken him months to write these names with a feather tip dye, papyrus, or leather he wrote their names anyhow.

It is true that within a congregation or ministry that some people do not like their names to be mentioned, but how many times I have been to a conference, revival meetings, seminar, etc., and the superintendent, bishop, evangelist, TV minister, special guest speaker, and other ministries who are held in high esteem, be recognized and given a standing ovation. Nothing wrong with this, but what about the people who supported, prayed, and saw to it that their clothes and food were taken care of? What about the sound man, the workers, the organizers, worship leaders, soloists, choir, the janitor, teachers, supporters, the ushers. But not once have I heard leaders in general mention these precious people or their names. Yes! They are doing their work, help, or ministry unto God, who will reward them. Then why did Paul mention their names in all of his writings? It was to encourage them. Obviously, this must not be done in each meeting, but once ever so often, it must be done.

I remember pasturing a church in Orlando, Florida, and a certain associate pastor plus some board members and deacons would always come up to me with an attitude and sometimes vehemently say to me, "I should not mention the names of the people in the service who did something good for the church and ministry." Well! Go back two thousand years ago and tell the apostle Paul that he would have given you one of the sharpest rebukes; not commending and encouraging and being thankful to the people who help your ministry is a sin (the sin of omission).

Helps, this word comes from the Greek word *Sunergeoto*, which means helping a minister or ministry to accomplish a goal in God's work. Your talent, ability, gift, and insight contribute greatly to the work of the ministry. The Hebrew word for help is "*Azar*." The word "*Azar*" can also mean where we can be supportive to one another in giving aid, help, support, give material or nonmaterial encouragement; it often refers to aid in the form of military assistance and, in many instances, refers to help from as illustrated by the uses below. To help means to aid, assist, succor to lend strength or means towards effecting a purpose to change for the better; actually, "helps," at times, could mean problem solvers, not problem creators.

Here is another Hebrew word for "helps"—"*Boetheo*." "*Boethos*" means assisting, helping, and being supportive to all of the fivefold ministries. With the help in their lives, ministry, and projects, this same word can also mean to run to and so to run to support, to go to the aid of, to help or relieve when in difficulty, want, or distress. To assist in suffering, or if some minister is under stress or strain, it means someone would run to help them in whatever they are doing.

No apostle, prophet, pastor, evangelist, or teacher can be successful without the ministry of *helps*; examples of the ministry of *helps* are far too many, but yours truly can mention a few of them that will give some perfect examples of the ministry of *helps*. A pastor or congregation is building a church building, even though they might have a contractor to build, but the members of the body should do everything possible to offer manual labor to help build that building. A country, city, town, or village is in need of salvation, members of the Body of Christ should be invited, even though they might be from another area, or they should volunteer to help reach those lost souls. Remember, all fivefold ministries are human, especially a pastor; they should already have trained people to stand in the gap and assist; should they have to travel, important appointments, they become tired or weary and even become sick.

Helps can also mean being faithful in the church (congregation), where an individual Christian member who is in response in the ministry they are called to serve, such as a Sunday School teacher, bus ministry, worship leader, choir director, choir member, assistant pastor, youth leader, organist, musician, deacon, usher, nurse, pastors aid, treasurer, secretary, janitor, outreach minister or ministries, financial supporter to a church or ministry; believe me, just going to church and being a church member sitting in the pew and worshiping God is a ministry because no ministry gift can function with empty pews.

Four of the most important ministry of *helps* in congregation or church is giving, soul-winning, missions, and intercessory prayer. When you mention the word intercessory prayer, some pastors and people do not understand what you are talking about and are difficult to find in this modern-day Church. Some think the ministry of help is only standing in front of a crowd with one of these intricate, sophisticated microphones hooked up to your belt and mouth, strutting and doing your stuff in front of a crowd. It is *so* difficult to find helps these days in this modern-day church, especially in the area of intercessory prayer; this ministry is seldom seen in the eyes of the public but has its rewards here and in eternity and produces great results.

Please take the time to read prayerfully about the ministry of intercessory prayer, for example, Abraham (Genesis 20:12), Moses (Exodus 12:13), Hannah (1 Samuel), and Elijah (1 Kings, chapter 17). The early church for Peter while he was in prison (Acts, chapter 12) is but a few examples from the Bible, but these saints of God set aside themselves, prayed, and got answers.

As the apostle continues honoring the ministry of *helps*, inspired by the Holy Spirit, he interjects the word *governments* and *diversities of tongues*. In this case, governments come from the Hebrew word "*misrah*," which means *the gift of the ability to rule* or *rule, lead, or govern*. The Greek word for governments is "*kubernesis*," which is the divine calling that empowers someone in particular or a Christian man or woman within the Church that possesses the gift to lead, rule, wisdom, and the ability to govern without complications. There are people within the church who are blessed with this God's gift or ability to guide, lead, and steer so that the church would be of a greater blessing to the community, city, or country. This gift to the church is not limited to just members of the Body of Christ, but it's been witnessed that many pastors and other ministry gifts are blessed with the ability to lead the church so they can be of a greater blessing to the church and in leading many souls to Jesus Christ.

Governments come under the ministry of *help* and obviously are not limited within the church, but God can place this ministry gift in the realms of political environment, take into consideration that the apostle Paul was addressing some of the Christian people who worked for the Roman Government. He commended these saints for their dedication to the Lord Jesus Christ; the apostle Paul recognized their gift and ability to serve or work in compounds as is, known today as offices of the Roman Governments.

Certainly, they had to keep their identity as a Christian from the scrutiny of some of the leaders within the Roman government and, with wisdom, work alongside other Roman citizens, but some of them had the ability to lead, which contributed to helping the Roman leader, they worked odiously and gathered each Lord's day, and most of all studied the word of God, prayed and worshiped God, supported the local church, prayed and financed the ministry of the apostle Paul to help him in his missionary work or to win souls. Studying all of the apostle's writings in the New Testament, we come to a conclusion that the saints took care of the apostle Paul and financed his ministry in reaching lost souls. In other words, their attitude was we must care for the missionary before there can be missions or winning souls. In so many ministry circles, it's been noticed and with an attitude by some leaders; forget the missionaries just concentrate on the missions, but it doesn't work that way; the point is to take care of the missionary, and you will get the missions or soul winning done.

DIVERSITIES OF TONGUES

Differences of opinion thought expressed in speech, preaching, and teaching or in writing is certainly welcome by the author; during much research, diversities of tongues are not referring to when an individual receives the Holy Ghost or the Holy Spirit and speaks in other tongues and has the gift of interpretation. Yours truly had the opportunity to be in the southern part of India. The only language I speak is English; obviously, I needed an interpreter, a man or a woman who spoke English but also speaks the language of the Indian people. In different states of India, I always had to get a new interpreter.

One of my interpreters, who spoke five different languages, interpreted while I was preaching to seven hundred thousand or more people; the beautiful thing about this was that he was able to translate my English into two different languages so that the people could understand what I was preaching about the Gospel of Jesus Christ.

Opposed to diversities of tongues as recorded in 1 Corinthians 12:10, people like this man had the education or ability to speak different languages. What the apostle is referring to from the scripture above is that certain people within the church who have the gift of the Holy Spirit to speak and interpret different languages as the Holy Spirit gives the utterances to do so.

> *Now there are diversities of gifts, but the same Spirit.*
> *And there are differences of administrations, but the same Lord.*
> *And there are diversities of operations, but it is the same God which worketh all in all.*
> — 1 Corinthians 12:4–6

CHAPTER 5

The Gifts of the Holy Spirit

Two thousand years ago, while Jesus was on earth, His ministry, the words He taught and preached were backed up by every type of miracle and supernatural act of God. Most of all, the nine gifts of the Holy Spirit were evident and were manifested through the life of Jesus as people were mystified in amazement and awe as they witnessed the gifts of the spirit operating in and through the life of Jesus. To begin with, at the very beginning of Jesus' ministry, as He began to build the Church, the gifts (notice gifts) of the Holy Spirit were operational and evident in His life. After Jesus was baptized by John, Jesus began the process of recruiting disciples. He recruited twelve men that He, Himself, would train and teach. He taught these men words that no man ever taught their followers. Anyone reading Matthew, chapters 5, 6, and 7, of course, would conclude no man spoke like this man. As a matter of fact, whoever heard about loving your enemies? The words He imparted to them were to become part of Him with the same supernatural miracles and signs and wonders following, who, in turn, would pass it on to their generation, and for those who follow Jesus Christ, the same principle would be carried out to every ongoing generation.

After Jesus' baptism in the River Jordan, He wasted no time; as recorded, the Holy Spirit guided the life of Jesus as He began to recruit men whom He would teach about the kingdom of God, His words, life, and purpose, and do the miracles which He did. From the very beginning of the ministry of Jesus, if you would closely observe, the *Gifts of the Spirit* were in operation, which was followed later by signs, wonders, and miracles, plus the supernatural power of God. Here is the record from the Bible,

> *Again the next day after John stood, and two of his disciples;*
>
> *And looking upon Jesus as he walked, he saith, Behold the Lamb of God!*
>
> *And the two disciples heard him speak, and they followed Jesus.*
>
> *Then Jesus turned, and saw them following, and saith unto them, What seek ye? They said unto him, Rabbi, (which is to say, being interpreted, Master,) where dwellest thou?*
>
> *He saith unto them, Come and see. They came and saw where he dwelt, and abode with him that day: for it was about the tenth hour.*
>
> *One of the two which heard John speak, and followed him, was Andrew, Simon Peter's brother. He first findeth his own brother Simon, and saith unto him, We have found the Messias, which is, being interpreted, the Christ. And he brought him to Jesus. And when Jesus beheld him, he said, Thou art Simon the son of Jona: thou shalt be called Cephas, which is by interpretation, A stone.*
>
> *The day following Jesus would go forth into Galilee, and findeth Philip, and saith unto him, Follow me. Now Philip was of Bethsaida, the city of Andrew and Peter. Philip findeth Nathanael, and saith unto him, We have found him, of whom Moses in the law, and the prophets, did write, Jesus of Nazareth, the son of Joseph.*
>
> *And Nathanael said unto him, Can there any good thing come out of Nazareth? Philip saith unto him, Come and see. Jesus saw Nathanael coming to him, and saith of Behold an Israelite indeed, in whom is no guile!*

Nathanael saith unto him, Whence knowest thou me? Jesus answered and said unto him, Before that Philip called thee, when thou wast under the fig tree, I saw thee. Nathanael answered and saith unto him, Rabbi, thou art the Son of God; thou art the King of Israel.

Jesus answered and said unto him, Because I said unto thee, I saw thee under the fig tree, believest thou? thou shalt see greater things than these. And he saith unto him, Verily, verily, I say unto you, Hereafter ye shall see heaven open, and the angels of God ascending and descending upon the Son of man.

— John 1:35–51

Verses 45 to 49, please notice that the gift of the Holy Spirit was in operation through Jesus Christ. What were these gifts of the Holy Spirit operating through the life of Jesus that caught the attention of Nathanial? The word of knowledge and discernment. Generally speaking, Jesus was a prophet or seer; this, in turn, caused Nathaniel to believe even more that Jesus is the Messiah. There was no assuming, guessing, like I feel something or sense something or a bunch of uh-uh-hu-hu, the Gifts of the Spirit operating through the life of Jesus were straight to the point and accomplished their purpose. Look at the results they produced.

The Gifts of the Holy Spirit are not for a show but to manifest God's power, produce results and, most of all, to attract and win people to Jesus Christ. Most of all, the gifts of the Holy Spirit are to attract people to Jesus Christ, build faith in them for healing, miracles to convict of sin and win souls to Jesus. When people see a minister of the Gospel who is real, honest, and the gifts of God are operating in their lives, this builds confidence and confirms that God is real, and they will want to serve, live, and serve God. The gifts of the Holy Spirit operated in Jesus; for example, when the woman of Samaria met Jesus at Jacob's well, here is how this transpired, "There are nine gifts of the Holy Spirit" John, chapter 4.

Now concerning spiritual gifts, brethren, I would not have you ignorant.

Ye know that ye were Gentiles, carried away unto these dumb idols, even as ye were led.

Wherefore I give you to understand, that no man speaking by the Spirit of God calleth Jesus accursed: and that no man can say that Jesus is the Lord, but by the Holy Ghost.

Now there are diversities of gifts, but the same Spirit.

And there are differences of administrations, but the same Lord.

And there are diversities of operations, but it is the same God which worketh all in all.

But the manifestation of the Spirit is given to every man to profit withal.

For to one is given by the Spirit the word of wisdom; to another the word of knowledge by the same Spirit;

To another faith by the same Spirit; to another the gifts of healing by the same Spirit;

To another the working of miracles; to another prophecy; to another discerning of spirits; to another divers kinds of tongues; to another the interpretation of tongues:

But all these worketh that one and the selfsame Spirit, dividing to every man severally as he will.

— 1 Corinthians 12:1–11

God uses dedicated men and women of God and moves through ministers or individuals in this day and time in the Gifts of the Holy Spirit. Rejection of these gifts of the spirit is like rejecting the Holy Spirit. Some denominations, organizations, and independents reject these gifts, which is saying to a certain extent that I am educated enough by this world's education standards that I do not need God nor His Gifts. Even though an individual has the talent or ability by human standards, we do need the Holy Spirit to empower us. These gifts were given by God through the power of the Holy Spirit to empower any minister to bring people closer to God; they or these gifts are not our gifts; these gifts come from God. If some pastors or congregations do not understand these gifts, it is the church's responsibility to study and teach them to the people they are ministering to. This will bring back the life of God in the Church. These gifts of the Holy Spirit begin with the baptism of the Holy Spirit, as recorded in the book of Acts, chapter 2.

Here is a breakdown or synopsis of the gifts of the Holy Spirit.

REVELATION GIFTS

Word of wisdom, Word of knowledge, Faith

First is *wisdom*. The word wisdom which comes from the Hebrew word "*khohkh-mat*," which means of or from God. There are so many who thinks that the gift of wisdom is perfection, ability, skill, a human standpoint, but this is not so. The gift of wisdom is a gift that cannot be gained through man's educational standards (even though important), but God's wisdom is a gift that comes from God. The gift of wisdom is the wisdom of God. It is the supernatural impartation of facts that are not natural but for the natural. You can't earn it; this gift comes from and can be manifested through dedicated vessels. The gift of the word of wisdom is seeing life from God's perspective; it is speaking hidden truths of what is not known. It is a supernatural perspective to ascertain the divine means for accomplishing God's will in a given situation and is a divinely given power to appropriate spiritual intuition in problem-solving.

The gift of wisdom can be explained in this way: I have experienced, in fifty-five years of ministry, congregations that were in total disarray or confusion; here comes a dedicated praying leader who speaks a word of wisdom to the church, and within minutes the problem is solved. There are times I have witnessed people who are hurting financially, and God gave them the gift of wisdom to make something, do something, go somewhere, and they would be blessed financially. There are times when a minister is ministering, someone would need a word of wisdom about their soul, and the word of wisdom spoken to them can save their soul. The gift of the word of wisdom can be imparted to any believer in Christ that can change every difficult situation in their life.

The gift of the *Word of knowledge* is supernatural insight or understanding of circumstances, situations, problems, or a body of facts by revelation; that is, without assistance by any human resource but solely by divine aid. Furthermore, the gift of the word of knowledge is the transcendental revelation of the divine will and plan of God. It involves moral wisdom for right living and relationships, requires objective understanding concerning divine things in human duties and refers to knowledge of God or of the things that belong to God, as related in the Gospel. The Hebrew word for the word of knowledge is "*veda'at*," which means God revealed through the person who is preaching and ministering to the needs of people; God would give them the name of the sickness, problem, situation they are in, the minister in whom the Holy

Spirit is using can say or speak exactly to that individual and by the gift of knowledge tell the problem the individual is going through, even before they say anything; this, of course, builds faith and they can be healed.

It is supernatural insight or understanding of circumstances, situations, problems, or a body of facts by revelation; that is, without assistance by any human resource but solely by divine aid. Furthermore, the gift of the word of knowledge is the transcendental revelation of the divine will and plan of God.

Faith, the gift of faith, is not just the faith that a person exercises when they repent of their sins and confess and accept Jesus Christ as Lord and Savior; it is not the faith they exercise for receiving the baptism of the Holy Spirit; it is not the faith a person needs to live and have a daily relationship with God. But the gift of faith can be imparted to a believer in Christ who is faced with an immediate unusual, difficult situation; they would suddenly be imparted with the gift of faith, they would pray a prayer, speak a word, degree a thing, command the extreme situation to change, and it will come to pass. The gift of faith is the supernatural ability to believe God without doubt, overcome unbelief, and visualize what God wants to accomplish. It is not only an inner conviction impelled by an urgent and higher calling but also a supernatural ability to meet adverse circumstances with trust in God's words and messages.

POWER OR DUNAMIS GIFTS

Gifts of healing, Working of miracles, Discerning of spirits

The gift of healing—the Greek word for healing is "*iaomai,*" which means to attend to someone until they are cured, become better, or to be made whole. The believer in Christ—this means a minister or any Christian can lay hands and pray for anyone who is seriously sick in the name of Jesus (*Mark, chapter 16*), and they can be supernaturally healed. This, of course, is without human aid. The gift of healing is a special gift to pray for specific diseases. Healing can come through the touch of faith, by speaking the word of faith (James 5:14–15), or by the presence of God being manifested (Luke 7:1–10).

> *And whithersoever he entered, into villages, or cities, or country, they laid the sick in the streets, and besought Him that they might touch if it were, but the border of his garment: and as many as touched him were made whole.*
>
> — Mark 6:56

Of course, there are different types of healing that human beings need, emotional, mental, social, and most of all, physical. Still, most of all, the gift of healing generally applies to a member of the Body of Christ. He specifically prays for people when they are sick, even if it's cancer or any other serious sicknesses, and the person that they pray for will be healed. Mentioned must be made that according to the apostle Mark in the Gospel of Mark 16:17–20, the gift of healing really is for all believers in Christ Jesus.

> *And these signs shall follow them that believe; In my name shall they cast out devils; they shall speak with new tongues;*

They shall take up serpents; and if they drink any deadly thing, it shall not hurt them; they shall lay hands on the sick, and they shall recover.

So then after the Lord had spoken unto them, he was received up into heaven, and sat on the right hand of God.

And they went forth, and preached every where, the Lord working with them, and confirming the word with signs following. Amen.

— Mark 16:17–20

The second set of gifts of the Holy Spirit is generally called the *manifested power gifts*. The first, these are the working of miracles; the reason it is called the manifested power gifts is when a minister or any believer in Christ is ministering, and the need arises for God to work miracles of any kind as they pray, command, or speak a miracle is an act of God that happens immediately. The working of miracles is the performance of something which is against the laws of nature; it is a supernatural power to intervene and counteract earthly and evil forces.

The word "miracles" comes from the Greek word *dunamis*, which means "power and might that multiplies itself." The gift of miracles operates closely with the power gifts of faith and healings to bring authority over Satan, sickness, sin, and the binding forces of this age. Miracles can also be defined as supernatural interventions of God. God exhorts us with energy to do something that is not natural or normal to us. Some hold the view that the working of miracles has reference to the ability to impart to others miracle-working ability. The Greek words "*energemata, dunameon*," working of miracles, can be translated as the effective working of God's power through believers to bring about an immediate change in all in ever adverse circumstances and situations.

Discerning of spirits is not suspicion; most of the time, the only gift that seems to operate in the church is suspicion. Discerning of spirits is the supernatural ability given by the Holy Spirit to perceive the source of a spiritual manifestation and determine whether it is of God, or of the devil, or of the Word of God.

And Cornelius said, Four days ago I was fasting until this hour; and at the ninth hour I prayed in my house, and, behold, a man stood before me in bright clothing,

And said, Cornelius, thy prayer is heard, and thine alms are had in remembrance in the sight of God.

Send therefore to Joppa, and call hither Simon, whose surname is Peter; he is lodged in the house of one Simon a tanner by the sea side: who, when he cometh, shall speak unto thee.

Immediately therefore I sent to thee; and thou hast well done that art art come. Now therefore are we all here present before God, to hear all things that are commanded thee of God.

Then Peter opened his mouth, and said, Of a truth I perceive that God is no respecter of persons:

But in every nation he that feareth him, and worketh righteousness, is accepted with him.

— Acts 10:30–35

…or of man of the devil,

And it came to pass, as we went to prayer, a certain damsel possessed with a spirit of divination met us, which brought her masters much gain by soothsaying:

The same followed Paul and us, and cried, saying, These men are the servants of the most high God, which shew unto us the way of salvation.

And this did she many days. But Paul, being grieved, turned and said to the spirit, I command thee in the name of Jesus Christ to come out of her. And he came out the same hour.

— Acts 16:16–18

And when Simon saw that through laying on of the apostles' hands the Holy Ghost was given, he offered them money,

Saying, Give me also this power, that on whomsoever I lay hands, he may receive the Holy Ghost.

But Peter said unto him, Thy money perish with thee, because thou hast thought that the gift of God may be purchased with money.

Thou hast neither part nor lot in this matter: for thy heart is not right in the sight of God.

Repent therefore of this thy wickedness, and pray God, if perhaps the thought of thine heart may be forgiven thee.

For I perceive that thou art in the gall of bitterness, and in the bond of iniquity.

— Acts 8:18–23

Discerning of spirit is not mind reading, psychic phenomena, or the ability to criticize and find fault. The power of the Holy Spirit must do discerning of spirits; He bears witness with our spirit when something is or is not of God. The gift of discerning of spirits is the supernatural power to detect the realm of the spirits and their activities. It implies the power of spiritual insight; it is the supernatural revelation of plans and purposes of the enemy and his forces. It is a gift that protects and guards your spiritual life. The recipient of discerning of spirits could miraculously determine the truth being taught by the teacher. We have the charge of trying the spirits whether they are of God: because many false prophets are gone out into the world, "Beloved, believe not every spirit, but try the spirits whether they are of God: because many false prophets are gone out into the world" 1 John 4:1.

THE PROPHETIC GIFTS

Prophecy, Diverse kinds of tongues, Interpretation of tongues

Prophecy, there are times that the gift of prophecy is addressed to the prophet or seer prophesying. The gift of prophecy is definitely not predicting or foretelling catastrophic events. Prophecy in the New Testament church carried no prediction of future events whatsoever; It is the ministry of the Holy Spirit to convict of sin, of righteousness, and of judgment to come,

And when he is come, he will reprove the world of sin, and of righteousness, and of judgment:

Of sin, because they believe not on me;

Of righteousness, because I go to my Father, and ye see me no more;
Of judgment, because the prince of this world is judged.

— John 16:8–11

Prophecy is divinely inspired and anointed utterance, a supernatural proclamation in a known language. It is the manifestation of the Spirit of God, not of intellect, and it may be possessed and operated by all who have the filling of the Holy Spirit, "For ye may all prophesy one by one, that all may learn, and all may be comforted" 1 Corinthians 14:31.

The gift of prophecy is the power of the Holy Spirit expressing in the gift of prophecy utterances directly from the Holy Spirit, not drawing attention to the individual who is being used in the prophetic, but this individual is being used of God by the Holy Spirit to speak utterances that would encourage, admonish, lift, edify, warn, rebuke, correct the Body of Christ that is present or in the presence of the pastor and congregation. The gift of prophecy is not limited to an established congregation and pastor. Still, this gift can be operational through individuals who are dedicated to God gathered in a prayer meeting or other gatherings with the purpose of worshiping God. Still, it does not have to be a particular individual who always seems to be used in this gift and no one else. God's gifts are for everyone who believes, and if God works through that individual, he or she must give glory to God and exalts Jesus Christ.

At this juncture, it is imperative that the reader read the entire chapter from his or her Bible (1 Corinthians 14).

The Holy Spirit convicts of sin, of righteousness, and of judgment to come. There are prophets in the church today who are seers who God has given gift to foresee future blessings or catastrophic events, which is, of course, biblical, but the Word of God, the Bible, must measure that prophet or seers and if what he or she says comes to pass is of God, if what they speak fails to come to pass they are false, in some cases that person might be saved but what they prophesied is false.

Diverse kinds of tongues were languages of supernatural utterance through the power of the Holy Spirit in a person to give the word from God to the Church. The Holy Spirit energizes the tongue to edify believers through language and music and the preaching of the Gospel of our Lord! Diverse tongues are the most misunderstood and dynamic gift. It is not necessarily your prayer language (speaking in tongues), but it can surface through intercession, conference, or through the individual in time of prayer, and it has often surfaced in me in time of prayer or at times of great struggle and adversity. Tongues are uttered in languages not known to the speaker; these languages may be existent in the world, revived from some past culture, or "unknown" in the sense that they are a means of communication inspired by the Holy Spirit.

For with stammering lips and another tongue will he speak to this people.

— Isaiah 28:11

And they were all filled with the Holy Ghost, and began to speak with other tongues, as the Spirit gave them utterance.

— Acts 2:4

To another the working of miracles; to another prophecy; to another discerning of spirits; to another divers kinds of tongues; to another the interpretation of tongues.

— 1 Corinthians 12:1

The spiritual gift involving the ability to speak in foreign languages was not previously studied or to respond to experience of the Holy Spirit by uttering sounds that those without the gift of interpretation could not understand. In Corinth, some members of the church uttered sounds the rest of the congregation did not understand; this led to controversy and division.

The apostle Paul tried to unite the church, assuring the church that there are different gifts but one Spirit. When the apostles were baptized in the Holy Spirit, these are the words recorded in Bible: "Now when this was noised abroad, the multitude came together, and was confounded, because that every man heard them speak in his own language" Acts 2:6.

The people visiting Jerusalem during the Feast of Pentecost were from different places and spoke different languages. They heard the disciples speaking in different languages, which some of them recognized as their native tongue. The phenomenon of tongues allowed those early Christians who possessed this ability to gain the hearer's attention and impress upon the hearer that something supernatural was present.

Interpretation of tongues. Not all hearers in an audience could always understand a language; hence, the need for miraculous interpretation. Speaking in another language was of no use; the speaker had to be understood so the meaning could instruct and benefit specific instruction given to the church at Corinth regarding tongues. "If any man speaks in an unknown tongue, let it be by two, or at the most by three, and that by course, and let one interpret," Paul wrote. But if there be no interpreter, let him keep silence in the church, or more simply said, let them and be silent. It is important to note that "interpretation" of tongues is not the same thing as a foreign language translation. For example, the message in tongues may be long and the interpretation short because the interpretation only gives the meaning. On the other hand, one may speak a short time in tongues and then be given a lengthy interpretation. Yet still, at other times, the interpretation is almost word for word. If someone speaks in tongues, you can ask God to move through you to give the interpretation so others will understand, but you can also do this in your private prayers for your own personal benefit.

In the Church, praying in tongues can be of great spiritual benefit to every believer in Jesus Christ. For instance, Americans speak American English; there is a different accent spoken by their people in every State. The people of Britain speak English with an English accent, and Canadians speak with a different accent, but whatever type of English you speak, and this, of course, is applied to believers in Christ Jesus, especially full Gospel people, when you pray in English, there comes a time in your praying seems like the English language you are praying in seems inadequate. This is where praying in tongues, the language of the baptism of the Holy Spirit, comes in. This means the Holy Spirit is interceding through you. The Holy Ghost language pierces deep into a different godly spiritual realm as your praying intensifies and brings you into a realm where you are closer to God, where you can have a breakthrough within your spirit and your prayers answered.

So often, it was noticed that when an individual is being used of God in the gifts of the Holy Spirit, the man or woman becomes prideful and wants to draw attention to them. But the gift that is being manifested should lead people to Jesus and not to individual; this also should benefit the Body of Christ and bring restoration, healing, and deliverance.

Please remember that the Holy Spirit cannot be led by you; instead, He leads you as you yield yourself to Him for God's service in meeting the needs of the people, such as a timely word for the Church or someone in need of healing or a miracle.

As a matter of fact, the Holy Spirit cannot be manipulated by anyone. When an individual submits him or herself to the Holy Spirit, then the gift or gifts of the Holy Spirit can flow through them. Generally speaking, the gifts of the Holy Spirit are given to the Church to glorify God, edify the Church, and meet the needs of hurting humanity.

CHAPTER 6
The Fruit of the Holy Spirit

The fruit of the Holy Spirit is a must and so desperately needed in the Body of Christ. This subject obviously is like the icing on the cake that crowns the ministry gifts and the gifts of the Holy Spirit. The fruit of the spirit is like looking at a crown of gold on a king's head with some of the finest diamonds, rubies, and emeralds, multicolored sapphires perched and lined on that crown which enhances the crown. It is the same way the fruit of the spirit completes, enhances, and exemplifies the ministry gifts and the gifts of the spirit. The apostle Paul, whom God used to reveal the ministry gifts, the gifts of the spirit, now tops it all off with fruit of the spirit. This, of course, is an eye-opener, a soul searcher, and a revelation, of course, which can cause one greatest move of God before the second return of Jesus Christ.

Apostles, prophets, evangelists, pastors, teachers, helps—all of these are God-ordained ministries within the Church of Jesus Christ. Within the past years, there have been some of the greatest moves of God, such as the Welsh Revival and Azusa Street, and in the 1940s–1970s, there was such an outpouring of the Holy Spirit during this time, God raised up some of the greatest men and women and gave them ministries that shook America and the world, this, of course, was followed by some of the greatest supernatural miracles signs and wonders which of course caused billions of souls to be saved. Thank God for what He is doing today; we have seen an unprecedented wave of evangelism where certain ministers and ministries are attracting crowds of millions, and millions are being saved with miracles and signs following.

But we are yet to witness a move of God like unto the ministry of Jesus Christ and the apostles recorded in *Matthew*, *Mark*, *Luke*, *John*, and the book of *Acts*. But if this is going to happen, there must be a change in attitude and a higher standard of biblical principles that must be adhered to, along with a deep conviction of right and wrong. We are living in times where we have had a spasmodic outpouring of the Holy Spirit in certain places, but then it lasts for a while and then fizzles out like Alka-Seltzer! Why? No fruit of the Holy Spirit.

There is a reason for this, a wave of worldliness, ungodly living, and fleshy lust; why? Most ministers are preaching a compromising Gospel. While some of them have the audacity, without shame and embarrassment, to endorse homosexuality (God loves these souls but not their sins) and other sins of the flesh. What do you expect of the people they minister to? Like leader, like people! Worst of all, some of them are twisting the word of God to support their modern-day life, lust, and iniquity as the divorce rate is skyrocketing even among church folks; before going any further, here are the words of the apostle Paul:

> *Now the works of the flesh are manifest, which are these; Adultery, fornication, uncleanness, lasciviousness, idolatry, witchcraft, hatred, variance, emulations, wrath, strife, seditions, heresies, envyings, murders, drunkenness, revellings, and such like: of which I tell you before, as I have also told you in time past, that they which do such things shall not inherit the kingdom of God.*
> — Galatians 5:19–21

For revival to occur, as an example, the ministry of Jesus recorded in Matthew, Mark, Luke, and John, and the apostles in the book of Acts, the leaders of the church need to put away or get rid of the sins of the flesh and start living like Jesus and the apostles, then we would have a real revival. All through this book, the author has repeated the statement a revival like Jesus and the apostles; this is not meant for repetitiveness' sake, but so that the readers and church would get the point.

When the apostles died, most of the church went into apostasy, which ushered in an apostate church or major religion that had its origination from a conflagration of other religions, made it resemble some of the priests from Old Testament practices, with a mixture of some Hinduism, Buddhism, etc., combined with its "okay to do as you like, sin like you want to." At a certain time of the year, they invented lent, which after you can go to priest and sprinkle away all the sins that people committed throughout the year, they do and practice year after year, sad to say. Still, the church, in general, got into the same kind of rut of sinning and repenting; this kind of living and lifestyle could never suffice and cause revival.

The moment you are saved and baptized with the Holy Spirit, you become a son or daughter of God, but this does not mean to say that you are going to remain in a baby state or stage. From the moment you become a Christian, you will read your Bible, pray (that is, personal daily devotion and corporate prayer or praying with other Christians in the local congregation), attend church, tithing, do something in the local church (like teaching a Sunday school class, etc.), witnessing or becoming involved in the church outreach or soul-winning program (if they have one) helping people in need, giving for missions and reaching lost souls in particular people that have never heard the gospel. Most of all, you will want to live a holy and clean life; this is called sanctification; please note that sanctification is immediate and progressive. It is of utmost importance that you live a sanctified or holy and clean life; this means if you do, God will use and manifest His power through you, and you will be ready for the second return of Jesus Christ.

Speaking in tongues is the initial and *one* of the pieces of evidence of the baptism of the Holy Spirit. This statement coming from a full gospel preacher might be shocking and, obviously, get your attention. Which certainly is meant to be? Hang on to your seats. There is more to come. Anyone who claims that they are baptized with the Holy Spirit and do not have and manifest the fruit of the Holy Spirit needs to get back to the altar and let the blood of Jesus cleanse you or them and get a refreshing of the Holy Ghost, hit the refresh button and start all over, this means manifesting the fruit of the Spirit. Most naturally speaking, when there is fruit on a fruit tree, the fruit tree is seen and not heard; this means a Christians does not conjure up or show out to get noticed or attention, but if they are really are baptized with the Holy Spirit, they will have and manifest the fruit of the Spirit most of all seen and not heard. I am a humorous person with a sense of humor; watching TV is not something I do much; some news, documentaries, and shows of people and other countries I like; sometimes some clean comedy shows I like a bit. "Does the show *Sanford and Son* ring a bell with you?" Yes, it does; well, one of the characters in that show is a guy called Grady. Well, what gets me with him is when he says, "If you got it, you got it," well! If you got the fruit of the Spirit, you got it, and people will see it. This in itself is a great witness of who you are and, of course, the Gospel of Jesus Christ.

Forget what some of these grace preachers are preaching and teaching (even though we know what grace is all about). Biblical revival will never come about with so many living like they like, doing what they want, the church in the morning and the club at night, living after the pattern of worldly people, fleshly lusts, which means often divorcing, shacking up, or living in adultery, hate, jealousy, pride, prejudice, homosexuality, fornication (sex out of marriage) messing with witchcraft, voodoo, church one day and the world next day, and expect God to send revival.

Our actions determine if we are walking with God or not. Common sense will tell you if the Holy Spirit is in a person, they will live like Jesus and not like the devil. Again, hold on to your seats to clarify this statement "speaking in tongues is not the *only* evidence of the baptism of the Holy Spirit; it is *one* of the pieces of evidence." But when an individual receives the baptism of the Holy Spirit, they will speak in tongues like the apostles did in the Upper Room (Acts, chapter 2). Christians should take into consideration the words of the apostle Paul wrote to the church of Galatia; we accept everything else from the Bible, we must read, study, examine, and if an individual professes that they are baptized with the Holy Spirit according to the book of Acts 2:1–2, what goes along with speaking in unknown or other tongues, obviously is the fruit of the spirit.

> *But the fruit of the Spirit is love, joy, peace, longsuffering, gentleness, goodness, faith,*
> *Meekness, temperance: against such there is no law.*
> *And they that are Christ's have crucified the flesh with the affections and lusts.*
> *If we live in the Spirit, let us also walk in the Spirit.*
> *Let us not be desirous of vain glory, provoking one another, envying one another.*
> — Galatians 5:22–26

The above words of the apostle Paul demand a second look, especially in relation to the baptism of the Holy Spirit, because according to the inspired words of the apostle Paul, combined with the ministry gifts, apostles, prophets, evangelists, pastors, teachers, *helps*, the Gifts of the Spirit, and now the fruit of the Spirit, attest the fact that there are more pieces of evidence of and with the baptism of the Holy Spirit, which is the fruit of the Spirit, which exemplifies a Christ-like life through us. After people become saved, according to John, chapter 3, and baptized with the Holy Spirit, according to Mark, chapter 16, Acts, chapter 2, Acts, chapter 16, they could, should, and would speak in other tongues. Speaking in other tongues is one of the signs and evidence that an individual is baptized with the Holy Spirit. But there are other pieces of evidence of the baptism of the Holy Spirit, and the first one is love, along with the other fruit of the spirit; therefore, if you are baptized with the Holy Spirit, and you speak in tongues and do not have the joy, peace, longsuffering (patience) gentleness, goodness, faith, meekness, temperance, love (save for last) for God, love for your brothers and sisters in Christ and fellow human beings (regardless of race and doctrinal differences), and a love for lost souls here and especially in other and poorer countries of the world. If you do not love to reach lost souls and help feed and clothe them, your tongues and Christian life are vain.

> *If we live in the Spirit, let us also walk in the Spirit. Let us not be desirous of vain glory,*
> *provoking one another, envying one another, envying one another.*
> — Galatians 5:25–26

An orange tree does not bear apples, and an apple tree neither bears oranges nor produces thorns; a tree is known by its fruit. Something is radically wrong if someone says they are Christians, especially a minister, and the life he, she, or they are living is attested with:

> *Now the works of the flesh are manifest, which are these;*
> *Adultery, fornication, uncleanness, lasciviousness,*

> *Idolatry, witchcraft, hatred, variance, emulations, wrath, strife, seditions, heresies, Envyings, murders, drunkenness, revellings, and such like: of which I tell you before, as I have also told you in time past, that they which do such things shall not inherit the kingdom of God.*
>
> — Galatians 5:19–21

The fruit of the Spirit is continual and indispensable in the work of God and towards one another. It affects our spiritual growth and development in God. We need the fruit of the Spirit as a true witness of Jesus Christ so we can effectively and graciously relate to others around us.

The pivotal point of this chapter is wrapped up in these words, which is one of the greatest inspired chapters of the Bible that every human being should read over and over; here it is,

> *Though I speak with the tongues of men and of angels, and have not charity, I am become as sounding brass, or a tinkling cymbal.*
>
> *And though I have the gift of prophecy, and understand all mysteries, and all knowledge;*
>
> *And though I have all faith, so that I could remove mountains, and have not charity, I am nothing.*
>
> *And though I bestow all my goods to feed the poor, and though I give my body to be burned, and have not charity, it profiteth me nothing.*
>
> *Charity suffereth long, and is kind; charity envieth not; charity vaunteth not itself, is not puffed up,*
>
> *Doth not behave itself unseemly, seeketh not her own, is not easily provoked, thinketh no evil;*
>
> *Rejoiceth not in iniquity, but rejoiceth in the truth;*
>
> *Beareth all things, believeth all things, hopeth all things, endureth all things.*
>
> *Charity never faileth: but whether there be prophecies, they shall fail; whether there be tongues, they shalcease; whether there be knowledge, it shall vanish away.*
>
> *For we know in part, and we prophesy in part.*
>
> *But when that which is perfect is come, then that which is in part shall be done away.*
>
> *When I was a child, I spake as a child, I understood as a child, I thought as a child: but when I became a man, I put away childish things.*
>
> *For now we see through a glass, darkly; but then face to face: now I know in part; but then shall I know even as also I am known.*
>
> — 1 Corinthians 13:1–12

CHAPTER 7

In the Image of God

When God made Adam and Eve, He made them threefold beings; this means He made them with a body, spirit, and soul. After He made them, He bestowed upon them the ability to bring forth another human being like themselves. This is called procreation. Every human being born of Adam and Eve to the present time possesses a *body*. The word body comes from the Greek word "*Soma*," which means an instrument of life; the Hebrew word for body is "*Gewiyah*," which means a human body that conveys the idea by some a house for the spirit and soul to live in. Another Hebrew word for body is "*Basar*," which means human flesh lasting for a certain period of time.

The body, of course, is important, and it houses the two most important things—*the spirit and soul*. In continuing the study of the body, spirit, and soul, there has always been a bit of controversy, especially in the study of identifying the spirit and the soul. The body, spirit, and soul are distinctively different. Here is a scripture to support this:

> *For the word of God is quick [living], and powerful, and sharper than any two-edged sword, […] dividing asunder the soul and the spirit, and of joints and marrow [body construction], and is a discerner of the thoughts and intents of the heart.*
>
> — Hebrews 4:12

Then there are times in the Bible when the spirit and soul are similarly meant to be the same, this is the reason the author chooses to deal with the spirit first, and the soul lasts for a specific reason.

> *And the* Lord *God formed man out of the dust of the ground and breathe into his nostrils the breath of life [put a spirit in man]; and man became a living soul.*
>
> — Genesis 2:7

The word spirit comes from the Hebrew word "*Puema*," which means breathe of life. This is the part of a human being that is immaterial and alive; God placed a spirit in every human being so that God can communicate with and dwell in mankind by His Spirit. The human spirit is the part of ourselves where we can worship, praise, pray, and most of all, communicate with God. It is our inner-most being. When something gets down into your heart or human spirit, you know that most of all, you are a son or daughter of God. Most of all, the spirit that God breathes into you can communicate, know, understand, and receive, which are godly spiritual things.

It is of utmost importance that these inspired words of the Bible be interjected here,

> *But as it is written, Eye hath not seen, nor ear heard, neither have entered into the heart of man, the things which God hath prepared for them that love him.*
>
> *But God hath revealed them unto us by his Spirit: for the Spirit searcheth all things, yea, the deep things of God.*
>
> *For what man knoweth the things of a man, save the spirit of man which is in him? even so the things of God knoweth no man, but the Spirit of God.*
>
> *Now we have received, not the spirit of the world, but the spirit which is of God; that we might know the things that are freely given to us of God.*
>
> *Which things also we speak, not in the words which man's wisdom teacheth, but which the Holy Ghost teacheth; comparing spiritual things with spiritual.*

But the natural man receiveth not the things of the Spirit of God: for they are foolishness unto him: neither can he know them, because they are spiritually discerned.

But he that is spiritual judgeth all things, yet he himself is judged of no man.

For who hath known the mind of the Lord, that he may instruct him? but we have the mind of Christ.

— 1 Corinthians 2:9–16

God placed a spirit within mankind that when he or she is born again, according to the Gospel of John, chapter 3, and gets baptized with the Holy Spirit (Acts, chapter 4), the Holy Spirit comes in and dwells in mankind's spirit, or, to put it plainly, God placed a spirit within mankind to accommodate God's Spirit.

The Greek word for *body* is "*soma,*" and the Hebrew word for *body*—"*gewiyah*" were created by God to house our *spirit*—"*puema*" and "*nepesh*" or "*phyche*"—Hebrew for *soul*, meaning the real person or you. When the Bible says we were made in the image of God, it means we were made to live forever (this means our spirit or soul).

So God created man in his own image, in the image of God created he him; male and female created he them.

— Genesis 1:27

The soul is the seat of your life, which means your will, expression, and sensitivity to feelings by which a person reflects and feels his mind and his emotions.

The soul is the center of your life. From the depth of the soul, an individual expresses what is within their being. The soul is the inner person. The soul has the God-given potential to live forever, believe this or not, but according to biblical studies, the soul of a human being has the potential to live eternally like God. This is the main reason why Jesus came and died on the cross so He could redeem the souls of mankind from the fall of mankind's sin and the relationship they had with God from the beginning. This is the reason Moses recorded in the book of Genesis.

And the LORD God formed man out of the dust of the ground, and breathed into his nostrils the breath of life [spirit]; and man became a living soul.

— Genesis 2:7

A person's soul lives on forever, and if a soul will go to heaven and shun hell, this depends on the person or people's belief in Jesus Christ and their Lord and Savior and the written Word of God, the Bible. Here lies the reason for an individual or people; if they go to heaven, they have to believe and go to a gathering (church), believe and accept the teachings of Jesus recorded in the Gospel of John 3 and 4, and of course, the book of Acts 2.

The above paragraph is written with the intent of bringing the reader, ministers, the church in general to a sobering fact as to what is the most important responsibility of the Church of Jesus Christ. The responsibility of the Church is not buildings (church building has its place and necessity), but when Jesus Christ returns, He is not coming back for the church building or buildings, but He is coming back for your *soul* and the *souls* we have won in this lifetime to Jesus Christ. The Church building should not be our priority.

Why should this be when we have a new generation of people, of which 49 percent have never heard the Gospel of Jesus Christ? The author personally and firmly believes that millions of dollars spent on some buildings and other programs have caused the Church of Jesus Christ to be sidetracked and lose focus of the sole purpose of what the Church of Jesus Christ should be doing. And that is *winning lost souls here in America, especially people who have never heard the Gospel of Jesus Christ.*

Call me old-fashioned, if you will, but my old-fashioned beliefs are singled out and based on the Bible. Please excuse me, but words like a burden for souls, compassion for lost and dying people, interceding and weeping for lost souls to be saved, and standing in the gap for the lost souls going off into a Christless eternity, this type of language is seldom heard within the church world today. And believe me, if you do have this kind of concern for lost souls, talk about lost souls, preach about lost souls, put out a magazine about souls, show films about lost souls, 90 percent of the church world are not interested. As an individual minister who loves God with all my heart, soul, and spirit and winning lost souls, if asked to minister and start preaching about lost souls (of course, I preach messages of faith, healing, and deliverance and do everything to build that particular church), some pastors and people look at me with a puzzled expression on their faces and seemingly thinking I am not in sync or trending, most of them look at me like I am crazy or lost my mind, talk, preach, or teach about lost souls. Some do not know what I am talking about. By the way, the main reason Jesus died on the cross was for lost souls.

Before Jesus died on the cross, His foremost message was about the *souls of human beings.* Why did He tell the story of the rich man and Lazarus? I cannot remember in this day and time when last I heard a sermon, message, or word on the rich man and Lazarus! Anyone studying this detailed account preached by Jesus and recorded in Luke, chapter 16,

> *There was a certain rich man, which was clothed in purple and fine linen, and fared sumptuously every day:*
>
> *And there was a certain beggar named Lazarus, which was laid at his gate, full of sores,*
>
> *And desiring to be fed with the crumbs which fell from the rich man's table: moreover the dogs came and licked his sores.*
>
> *And it came to pass, that the beggar died, and was carried by the angels into Abraham's bosom: the rich man also died, and was buried;*
>
> *And in hell he lift up his eyes, being in torments, and seeth Abraham afar off, and Lazarus in his bosom.*
>
> *And he cried and said, Father Abraham, have mercy on me, and send Lazarus that he may dip the tip of his finger in water, and cool my tongue; for I am tormented in this flame.*
>
> *But Abraham said, Son, remember that thou in thy lifetime receivedst thy good things, and likewise Lazarus evil things: but now he is comforted, and thou art tormented.*
>
> *And beside all this, between us and you there is a great gulf fixed: so that they which would pass from hence to you cannot; neither can they pass to us, that would come from thence.*
>
> *Then he said, I pray thee therefore, father, that thou wouldest send him to my father's house:*
>
> *For I have five brethren; that he may testify unto them, lest they also come into this place of torment.*
>
> *Abraham saith unto him, They have Moses and the prophets; let them hear them.*

And he said, Nay, father Abraham: but if one went unto them from the dead, they will repent. And he said unto him, If they hear not Moses and the prophets, neither will they be persuaded, though one rose from the dead.

— Luke 16:19–31

Studying the above Scripture, Jesus emphasized heaven, hell, and life after death. Jesus constantly emphasized eternity in His daily teachings and preaching. There are approximately four hundred thirty-five references about the souls of mankind recorded in the Bible. Jesus referred to the souls of human beings more than anything; these are His words recorded in Matthew, "For what is a man profited, if he shall gain the whole world, and lose his own soul? or what shall a man give in exchange for his soul?" Matthew 16:26

Jesus, Himself, knew us from the beginning. Just think for a while: Jesus is telling in the recorded word that *one soul* is worth more than the entire world's good, money, gold, silver, diamonds, rubies, emeralds, and other precious gemstones.

Jesus did set a perfect example in soul-winning: This statement might surprise you, but Jesus spent more time outside the Church building except for the time of prayer and worshiping and studying and teaching the word of God on the Sabbath. Jesus spent more of His time preaching the kingdom of God to lost souls in the market places, the streets, the hills, mountains, valleys, and the riverside; as a matter of fact, some of His greatest miracles of salvation, transformation, physical healing, and miracles occurred outside the church buildings and the apostles took over exactly where He left off. After His resurrection and Jesus went back to heaven, the apostles centered their preaching of the Gospel solely in Jerusalem. Persecution arose, which caused the apostles to be scattered throughout the then known world.

The apostle Thomas found his way to South India, where he preached the Gospel of Jesus Christ with miracles, signs, and wonders following. He was martyred by the Hindus, but the seed he sowed of the Gospel of Jesus Christ produced the greatest results. After His martyrdom, His blood cried out, and millions of Hindus turned to Jesus Christ. Now there are millions of Christians serving Jesus Christ as they gather each year in South India to celebrate the apostle Thomas going to India preaching the Gospel of Jesus Christ. While the other apostles and disciples went to others places preaching the Gospel with signs and wonders following. God raised up the apostle Paul and sent him out with great power and anointing as thousands of souls turned to Jesus Christ under his ministry, especially the Gentile people. What is it that drove Jesus and the apostles to go? Was it a deep realization of the worth of a soul or souls?

When Jesus died on the cross, He died for us humans to experience sins forgiveness through the blood of Jesus Christ, which in turn will cause those who believe to be born again, and in turn, we humans will experience peace, joy, real happiness, contentment, a personal relationship with God, assurance of eternity with the hope and joy of eternal life.

When Jesus died on the cross, He did not die for you alone but for your loved ones, family, friends, and the people of your neighborhood, community, towns, city, state, or states, and of course, the entire world. There should be a God-driven compelling desire in every Christian to tell others and the entire world about Jesus. From the birth of the Church on the day of Pentecost recorded in the book of Acts, chapter 2, to the present time, the Church of Jesus Christ has grown immensely, with unprecedented waves of evangelism with an emphasis on winning lost souls we have witnessed billions of souls ushered into the kingdom of God. This is commendable, but shockingly, if the author may use the word the American

Church, it is only 15 percent of the American Church is directly involved and active in missions, frontline evangelism, and soul-winning at this present time.

Yours truly, the author entered a full Gospel Church at the age of five; a seed of the Gospel of Jesus Christ was sown in my heart; growing up and moving from one city to another, I stayed in church but did not make a full commitment to God. Just as I turned sixteen in the year 1959, prior to several visitations from God with dreams that really had me thinking, I was genuinely converted, born again, saved, and baptized with the power of the Holy Spirit. This deep experience with God was a total transformation of my life as I knew the call of God to enter into the ministry. While preparing for the ministry, I was immediately exposed to and admired some of the greatest men of God whose ministries exemplified soul-winning attested with the power of God followed by miracles, signs, and wonders to win these souls. I would like to mention some of these names, but because of the modern-day trend of thinking in the minds of some modern-day church members, ministers and ministries, I do not dare to mention some of these names because of fear of being branded, stigmatized, ostracized for life. But I will take the liberty to mention one of these names, and he is T. L. Osborn.

Everything about this man of God was about winning souls. I remember confiscating him and some other deliverance magazines from the Bible college library I attended because the teachers did not want us to be exposed to this kind of material of what they called far out (now, to me, how true). But after I graduated, I obtained all of the soul-winning tools that he offered freely; most of all, I obtained all of his books, tapes, and material, which are in my library today, because every single one of them was about winning lost souls, which intensified the compassion for lost souls that was placed within me at my conversion. With hardly any television exposure, God blessed my wife, Sherry, and me; we pastored for a while, then, with three children, we entered the evangelistic field, may I say full-time soul winning, with no church or ministry to support us, just faith in God. By God's help, He blessed us, and we have ministered the Gospel of Jesus Christ in fifty-five countries.

I have stood on many crude platforms; stood and ministered to crowds estimated at approximately five hundred thousand or more, with healings, miracles, and signs following. Thank God we are still going, now doing missionary work in Brazil and ministering in other countries. What puzzles this preacher is the fact that with all of the millions of professing Christians that American preachers boast about (which is going to bring us to the point of this chapter), why has 49 percent of the world not been evangelized with the Gospel of Jesus Christ?

Most of the Church world is looking for a new revelation; some are looking for dreams and visions with the idea of being deep with the intention of blowing people's minds; at this present time, people do not need preachers to blow people's minds. They have thousands of problems that are blowing their minds. What the people of the world need right now is the simple Gospel of Jesus Christ that will deliver them from the clutches of sin and its results. Plus, they need the Gospel of Jesus Christ to preach to them that will bring them peace, joy, contentment, real happiness, and a hope for the future, plus eternal life. Where are the ministers, ministries, and people of God who will preach a simple Gospel and just get people saved, healed, and delivered? Here are some sobering words from the apostle Paul: "I am not ashamed of the Gospel of Jesus Christ, for it is the power of God unto salvation" Romans 1:16a.

Chapter 7: In the Image of God

Jesus said, "[…] for the son of man has come to seek and to save that which was lost."

— Luke 19:9–10, NKJV

But if our gospel be hid, it is hid to them that are lost [and to save that which was lost].

— 2 Corinthians 4:3

Most of Christendom does not like to face facts and would just like to go to church where they can be entertained and go back home to continue a lifestyle of status quo with the routine of their daily life and do nothing for God. Worst of all, never give to win a soul or never win a soul to Jesus Christ. But if most of the church world would buckle down and face up to some truthful Godly facts about lost souls, millions and more would be reached with the Gospel of Jesus Christ. Thank God for the ministers and Christians who are doing something to win the lost and the millions of souls that have been reached with the Gospel of Jesus, but there are billions of lost souls that must be reached before Jesus can return. Thank God for prophecy, preachers, and teachers, but personally speaking, I would like to see all of them talk or make an altar call for lost souls, but they seldom do.

But he that shall endure unto the end, the same [your soul] shall be saved. And this gospel of the kingdom shall be preached in all the world for a witness unto all nations; and then shall the end come.

— Matthew 24:13–14

The Hebrew word for *witness* is "ud," which means to testify, admonish, warn, to be assured because of evidence. Thank God there are more Christian TV and radio stations, as individual TV ministries filled the airways with their individual style of ministry and preaching of the Word of God. There are more translations of the Bible than at any other time in history; the internet is saturated with biblical studies of every type of biblical subject; there are more Christian books, magazines, and other literature being printed and distributed in this day and time like never before. Again, forgive my repetitiveness; thank God for the lives that are being touched by these modern-day communications, but research shows that the Gospel of Jesus Christ is definitely more effective by personal contact, personal witnessing, and frontline mass evangelism and crusades.

Forty-nine percent of the world population has never heard of Jesus and does not understand the salvation message. Seventy percent of Americans belong to some kind of religion, and within this percentage, most of them claim that they are Christians but ask them if they are really saved and going to heaven; they are not sure. It will surprise you to see the lack of understanding that Americans have concerning the Gospel of Jesus Christ. Many of them will be able to talk the familiar statements such as "Jesus died for our sins" or "You have accepted Jesus as your Savior." Some confess that they are born again. Yet, if asked to explain how Jesus dying on a cross could save them from their sins, few could explain. Moreover, if questioned further, many of the people surveyed will add, "I live a good life, keep the Ten Commandments, and go to church." Thus, just because a person knows about Jesus Christ and Christianity does not mean he has a clear understanding of the gospel and what it means to be saved.

Being aware that Jesus Christ existed and died on a cross is not enough to save anyone. People in America are saturated with the gospel message, yet it is still often misunderstood. Many people remain unreached due to barriers in language, geographic location, or technical deficiencies. Others are happy with their religion and do not feel it necessary to listen to differing ideas. Take yourself, for example; can you truly say you have taken the time to carefully examine the other major religions? If you haven't, how can you expect the rest of the world to carefully examine and accept Christianity?

If the command given by Jesus is to make disciples of all nations or ethnic groups, then common sense would tell us that our job is to find those nations that have not been reached or taught to be followers of Christ. People desiring to fulfill the great commission need to know where these unreached groups of people are so that our efforts in completing the task will not just be busy but productive.

People need to be reached with the Gospel of Jesus Christ everywhere because there are lost souls in every country and every area of these countries. But the vast majority of these unreached people live in an area of the world nicknamed the "10/40 window." The 10/40 window is simply a term used to describe a region of the world within ten and forty degrees latitude from Western Africa to Eastern Asia. If you were to draw it on a map, the top would go from Portugal through Japan, and the bottom would go from Guinea through the bottom tip of India all the way to the Philippines. This is an important region to think about because most of the people who have not had an opportunity to hear the gospel live here. The thirty-one least reached countries in the world are in this "window." The people who are lost in the 10/40 window are not "more lost" than your neighbor or family member who does not know Christ. But, they are "unreached" in the sense that they have not had an opportunity to hear the Gospel. The issue here is that they are lost. People can be unevangelized without being reached with the Gospel. There are people in some places in the United States that are ignorant of the Gospel of Jesus Christ.

Most people living in the 10/40 window couldn't find out about Jesus, even if they wanted to! These are unreached people who do not have access to the gospel. There are over 3.6 billion unreached people in the world today. Of those 3.6 billion people, 88 percent live in or near the 10/40 window. Only 2.17 percent of these unreached people live in North and South America combined! This area of the world is so unreached for several reasons. First, these people do not live in a spiritual vacuum. The world's major religions began in this part of the world and are firmly entrenched there. In the 10/40 window, there are 724 million Muslims, 787 million Hindus, and 240 million Buddhists; there might be a sprinkle there, but the other unreached people belong to some type or kind of religion. Many of these are oppressive to Christianity, but serious praying, compassion, and love for these *souls* can be reached with the Gospel of Jesus Christ.

Jesus spoke these words, which should cause every Christian to avoid the sin of omission and procrastination,

> *Say not ye, There are yet four months, and then cometh the harvest [winning lost souls]? […] lift up your eyes, and look unto the fields; for they are white already to harvest.*
> *And he that reapeth receiveth wages, and gathereth fruit unto life eternal: that both he that soweth and he that reapeth may rejoice together.*
>
> — John 4:35–36

Both verses are important, but please note verse 36, "*He that reapeth receiveth wages,*" giving a thousand dollars (for what) Jesus is emphasizing here, "*He that reapeth receiveth wages.*" We are living in a day and time where most of the emphasis is on prosperity and blessing, and if you give, you will be blessed. It is true that giving is a blessing, but what Jesus is emphasizing here (I pray that God will open your eyes to see this) is that we do not have to fall for all types of gimmicks, tricks, or schemes; all we have to do is to *put souls first and win souls to Jesus*, if you make soul winning your priority, God will bless you in every way. Someone might ask or say, "Well! I have to work and make a living and care for my family." True this is: but just to make a point; why spend 3,000,00 dollars for a plasma TV to fit the adjacent wall of your bedroom or living room, when you can get a cheaper TV, with the excuse I can see the news (that is between you and God) and give the balance of the money to *win souls*. This is what Jesus is emphasizing, "*He that reapeth receiveth wages*"—KJV version. My version—"*If you put souls first, you will be blessed.*"

The biggest reason this part of the world is so unreached is that there is a lack of Christians willing to go to these places. It is estimated that only 4 percent of foreign missionaries today are working to reach these unreached people. The other 96 percent are working in evangelized but not unreached areas. Ninety-seven percent of preachers (this means all of the fivefold ministries) in the Church are preaching to 98 percent of people that are hearing the Gospel of Jesus Christ over and over and over and over (hope you get the point), while 49 percent of the world's population has never heard of Jesus. According to the World Christian Encyclopedia, of all the money designated for "missions" in the US, only 5.4 percent is used for foreign missions. Of that 5.4 percent, only 0.37 percent is used to take the gospel to unreached people who don't have access to the gospel. That's about two cents out of every one-hundred dollars given to missions! The rest goes towards ministry operations. Why not cut down the fancy offices and unnecessary buildings and staff and spend that money to win lost souls.

With all of the above-mentioned facts, it all boils down to this fact one hundred or more people die each second; 6,000 people or more die every minute; 36,000 people or more die every hour; 864,000 people or more die in one day or every twenty-four hours; 6,048,000 people or more die each week; 181,440,000 or more people die every month; 2,177,280,000 people or more die each year.

These facts and figures should have every Christian giving and running to get people saved and baptized with the Holy Spirit and praying that they will make it to heaven.

It is true that in our day and time, it has become very difficult to send evangelists and missionaries and conduct mass crusades or what we would term front line evangelism in certain countries; God is using the media ministries such as Christian television and radio to penetrate into some of these countries with the Gospel of Jesus Christ, to some of these looking and listening to these Christian programs, that's all they have for their soul salvation. But in comparison, there are more countries open for the preaching of the Gospel of Jesus Christ, and now is the time to get up from our blessed assurance and *go*.

While there are few ministries and churches (if I may use the word "churches") that are evangelizing like what are considered biblical examples of real evangelism, most ministries are ministering to Christians over and over or shining the coins. There are few from a biblical point of view that can be singled out that are really winning souls. Most of the meetings that are held these days are for Christians; praise God, which meets the needs of *some* people; *some* souls are saved, *some* lives are changed; the author certainly understands that money is needed to finance the preaching of the Gospel, but most of the time the impression is created in the minds of the public that money is the sole purpose in some of these meetings. These meetings come and go without the city or town being impacted. What is really needed in this modern-day time is meetings with *soul winning in mind*.

The name T. L. Osborn was mentioned above; everything about this man of God's ministry was about soul winning. The author, yours truly, recalls one particular meeting that I was involved in; this man of God and all of his representatives mobilized all pastors and their congregation. The city was chosen as an open park as the site for the meetings; gospel literature and tracts (hardly anyone knows what gospel tracts are today) were passed out with an emphasis on personal witnessing and soul winning (there is one ministry that I know of that does this today). Most of all, prayer meetings were organized and continued night and day for these meetings. The time came; and driving to these meetings, the power and presence of God were felt from about twenty to thirty miles before getting to the park or field where the meeting was being held, walking, which is common, or driving to these meetings, there was the awesome power and presence of God that charged the atmosphere as there was an aura of expectancy in the people for miracles.

In this particular meeting with T. L Osborn, the worship leaders had one thing in mind to lead about two hundred thousand people to worship and praise God until the presence of God filled the field and elevated the people in an atmosphere to receive from God (there was no show here). After a short time of worship, this man of God took the microphone, prayed, and began to preach a simple salvation faith message. When the altar call was given, it seemed like every hand went up to receive Jesus Christ as Savior because there was no room for people for the altar call; thousands upon thousands were saved, the people were properly instructed about their soul salvation and given literature with a step-by-step instruction how to follow and live for Jesus.

After the altar call, step-by-step instructions were given to the sick people on how to receive healing or a miracle because, in these meetings, there were multitudes of sick people; as the man of God prayed, healings and miracles began to occur everywhere among the hundreds of thousands of people, as people stormed the platform to testify of God's healing power. What really caught my attention was the emphasis on souls being saved, and by the way, in every church in that city, new converts flooded the churches ready to live for God.

Jesus preached two of His greatest messages to two individuals, one of them was Nicodemus, and the other was the woman of Samaria. The words that Jesus preached to these two individuals are mentioned and preached from that time to the present because these words of Jesus recorded in the Gospel of John, chapters 3 and 4, are the central point of individual salvation. Two of the greatest word or messages preached by Jesus were not in a swanky plush office or in a five thousand people church stained glass padded pews and more church buildings (nothing wrong with this), but Jesus did not hide in an exclusive office with every type of convenience, or behind a TV camera or in a plush mansion in a hidden mountainside (no criticism meant here). Jesus' main motive was for lost souls, which brings us to the point where the church or Body of Christ needs to return to *personal evangelism or soul winning.*

The ministry of winning souls and frontline evangelism are completely gone from the church of today. Remember these words "a burden for souls," these words are foreign to most of the Body of Christ. The reason there is a lack of compassion for souls in this day and time is that most TV preachers hardly take the time to preach, teach and talk about lost souls; most of the time, it seems like most of these preachers create the idea that Jesus died for money and not for lost souls, yes! I know money is needed in every area of ministry, in particular for winning souls, but *souls* should always come first, start winning souls and watch God bless and confirm His Word with His blessings upon your life.

The author always makes this statement in his revival meetings: *"If you do not care about your own soul, you will not care for the souls of others."*

This business of personal soul winning is about dead from ministries and churches today. There was a time that Christians had such love for lost souls that after worship meeting or bible study, a pastor who had a love and burden for souls used to see to it that a rack, shelf, or table with about seven to ten different types of tracts (some do not know what I am talking about) with some of the most powerful salvation messages. On their way out, the members of the church used to stop by and grab some of them like it was a matter of life and death and go out of the church building with the intention of winning lost souls. This was emphasized by the pastor to pick up some tracts about salvation and go out with the intention of winning lost souls. I cannot remember when last I saw a rack or shelf at the inside entrance or exit door of a church building; if I missed it, forgive me if there was one.

Here are the words of the apostle Paul:

> *For there is no difference between the Jew and the Greek: for the same Lord over all is rich unto all that call upon him.*
>
> *For whosoever shall call upon the name of the Lord shall be saved.*
>
> *How then shall they call on him in whom they have not believed? And how shall they believe in him of whom they have not heard? and how shall they hear without a preacher?*
>
> — Romans 10:12–14

The love for lost souls is so imbedded within the author's being; when I am not on the mission fields or ministering here in the US in different meetings in between, I am always on the lookout to win a soul or souls to Jesus. I recall so vividly that many years ago, my wife, three children, and I were conducting some revival meetings in New Orleans, Louisiana. During the evening hours, I will pray and take time to study and prepare for the night's meeting. In the morning hours, I will take my wife and children to walk the shopping malls, visit different places, and spend some time with them outdoors. Even though it was many years ago, I recall so vividly I decided to take them to or by the Lake Pontchartrain in New Orleans.

While the children were playing in the park close to this lake, my wife and I were sitting with our feet hanging over the water, I saw a young lady about twenty feet away from us doing the very same thing, but she looked distraught and very troubled. The Spirit of God spoke to me to witness to her. I, being a man, thought it wiser to ask my wife to go and tell her about Jesus and pray with her or even win her soul to Jesus. Sherry, my wife, went to her, sat down where she was, and started talking and witnessing to her. I could not hear the conversation because of the waves lashing against the concrete wall that held back the water, but after about half an hour, I saw my wife with her hands on her shoulders praying for her, then they both stood up, hugged each other (total stranger), then she left; to remind you, this young lady was about thirty years old.

Sherry came back to where I was, and I asked her to tell me what had happened. She explained that God really spoke to her about witnessing to that young lady. She said as she told her about Jesus and what He can do for her, she told her about Jesus dying on the cross, the resurrection, and now He is sitting at the right hand of the Father or God, waiting for her to pray, and if she accepted Him as Lord and Savior of her life, He would give her peace, real joy, happiness, most of all how she can have a daily relationship with God and eternal life.

This young lady told her that she and her husband had a quarrel and fight, which was quite intense, and then this young lady told her that she was waiting for us to leave, after which she was going to throw herself into the deeper part of the water and take her own life or commit suicide. What caused this young lady to change her mind, turn around, and not take her own life or commit suicide? It's all because someone cared for her and the power of the Gospel of Jesus Christ to save, change her life, heal, and deliver.

CHAPTER 8

What Jesus and the Apostles Taught

Jesus knew everything from beginning to end, even as a little boy growing up in Nazareth, His knowledge of the scriptures confounded the priests, scribes, rulers of the synagogues, Pharisees, Sadducees and Herodians, and of course, all other religious leaders of that day. Jesus knew the scriptures, and as God, He saw everything that transpired from Genesis to Malachi. Then being God in the flesh as He walked the streets of Jerusalem and surrounding areas when it was necessary, He quoted from the Law, Psalms, Proverbs, and Prophets but in His own unique, astounding, assertive, and faith-building words with power and miracles introduced a new kind of (if the author would use the word religion because religion is man-made and mankind's search for God) religion. Jesus, in particular, His words or teachings, including His ministry in general, superseded the teachings of all religions of that day.

Jesus' ministry produced amazing results; His supernatural ministry caught the religious leaders of that day with surprise and amazement. This is the reason He was always opposed, and whenever God sends a man or woman with the Gospel of truth backed up with a ministry, messages and miracles, the devil and his crowd, even religious people and they will not leave him alone, especially in this day and age. Most of the church world is mesmerized with a spirit of confusion as everyone is teaching something different than the other with no power and miracles to back up what they are teaching and preaching.

Mathew, the apostle, introduced Jesus' ministry in this manner:

> *From that time Jesus began to preach, and to say, "Repent, for the kingdom of heaven is at hand."*
>
> *And Jesus, walking by the Sea of Galilee, saw two brothers, Simon called Peter, and Andrew his brother, casting a net into the sea; for they were fishermen. Then He said to them, "Follow Me, and I will make you fishers of men." They immediately left their nets and followed Him.*
>
> *Going on from there, He saw two other brothers, James the son of Zebedee, and John his brother, in the boat with Zebedee their father, mending their nets. He called them, and immediately they left the boat and their father, and followed Him.*
>
> *And Jesus went about all Galilee, teaching in their synagogues, preaching the gospel of the kingdom, and healing all kinds of sickness and all kinds of disease among the people. Then His fame went throughout all Syria; and they brought to Him all sick people who were afflicted with various diseases and torments, and those who were demon-possessed, epileptics, and paralytics; and He healed them.*
>
> *Great multitudes followed Him—from Galilee, and from Decapolis, Jerusalem, Judea, and beyond the Jordan.*
>
> — Matthew 4:17–25, NKJV

The apostle Luke introduced the book of Acts, which he wrote in this manner,

> *The former treatise have I made, O Theophilus, of all that Jesus began both to do and teach,*
>
> *Until the day in which he was taken up, after that he through the Holy Ghost had given commandments unto the apostles whom he had chosen:*
>
> *To whom also he shewed himself alive after his passion by many infallible proofs, being seen of them forty days, and speaking of the things pertaining to the kingdom of God:*
>
> *And, being assembled together with them, commanded them that they should not depart from Jerusalem, but wait for the promise of the Father, which, saith he, ye have heard of me.*

> *For John truly baptized with water; but ye shall be baptized with the Holy Ghost not many days hence.*
>
> — Acts 1:1–5

> *And there are also many other things which Jesus did, the which, if they should be written every one, I suppose that even the world itself could not contain the books that should be written. Amen.*
>
> — John 21:25

Matthew, Mark, Luke, and John—these four apostles were inspired by the Holy Spirit—recorded the life, teachings, works or healings, and miracles that Jesus did. Luke wrote about the Acts of the Holy Spirit through the lives of the apostles. It was impossible to write about everything that Jesus and the apostles taught and did, but what is written is comprehensible and should be an example for us to follow and teach. Why should anyone want to teach other than what Jesus and the apostles taught and did? In this day and time, the teachings of the apostate church have replaced teachings, works, and ministry of Jesus Christ; you must have already understood the purpose of this book is to restore what Jesus and the apostles taught. The purpose of this book, in particular this chapter, is to encourage the church of Jesus Christ to get back to the basics of Christianity or the foundational principles of Christianity. If done faithfully with clean and honest hearts with the purpose of glorifying God and reaching the world with the Gospel of Jesus Christ, we will experience what Jesus and the apostle experienced in Matthew, Mark, Luke, and the book of Acts.

In reading this book, you will realize that the author wants the reader or the Church of Jesus to comprehend that while being faithful in living for Jesus, honoring and serving Jesus by and practicing (not practicing in the sense of going through the motion), but striving to perfection while it's being done (the basics) the Church of Jesus Christ can experience the supernatural power of God like in the Bible where the people experience God with supernatural visitations, angelic encounters with miracles and signs following. In plain language, we do not have to go around like zombies just looking for supernatural visitations for people to show off or exalting themselves but to bring glory to God.

In observing the basics of Christianity, you will also discover the Jesus' teachings on the Beatitudes (which means having the right attitudes towards God and man); what murder, adultery, divorce, marriage between a man and woman, making an oath (your word) forgiveness, restitution, real love, the Lord's Prayer, fasting, wealth, prayer, and how to get results in praying is. Truth and false teachings, knowing who and what is right and wrong, the fruit of the Spirit flowing from the lives of those who confess to Christianity. Faith in God combined with a solid foundation in God, your attitude concerning money and material things, the way to heaven and to escape hell, and obviously much more that is all recorded in the Gospels. The miracles He did, turning water into wine, opening blind eyes, unstopping deaf ears, making the lame walk, multiplying the loaves and fishes, raising the dead, casting out demons, cursing of the fig tree, walking on water, and much more. The basics of Christianity are also knowing where we are at in prophesying the fulfillment of the Church ages and how to live and be in readiness for the second return of Jesus Christ.

What are the basics teaching of Jesus and the apostles that will bring about a change and a spiritual climate within the church today, which will produce the supernatural and, of course, revival? The ministry of Jesus obviously was not a profession; neither was His ministry an indication of a name, fortune, and fame. He shunned the glamour and glitter of being in public, except for ministering and meeting the needs of people who had no hope, and healing the sick and suffering, casting out the demons from people who were possessed (in this day and age, some denominations, organizations, and independents call demon-possessed people mentally deranged and send them to a mental asylum); why? They do not have the power to cast out devils.

Here is another brief summary of Jesus' ministry as described by Luke, the medical doctor and apostle:

> *And he came to Nazareth, where he had been brought up: and, as his custom was, he went into the synagogue on the sabbath day, and stood up for to read.*
>
> *And there was delivered unto him the book of the prophet Esaias. And when he had opened the book, he found the place where it was written,*
>
> *The Spirit of the Lord is upon me, because he hath anointed me to preach the gospel to the poor; he hath sent me to heal the, to preach deliverance to the captives, and recovering of sight to the blind, to set at liberty them that are bruised,*
>
> *To preach the acceptable year of the Lord.*
>
> *And he closed the book, and he gave it again to the minister, and sat down. And the eyes of all them that were in the synagogue were fastened on him.*
>
> *And he began to say unto them, This day is this scripture fulfilled in your ears.*
>
> — Luke 4:16–21

The above Scripture was the focal point of Jesus' ministry, which is recorded in the Gospel of John; anyone reading their Bible would and should realize that Jesus is coming to earth, and His ministry was all about meeting the needs of humanity and the local people. Jesus taught on subjects that the religious leaders and religions of that time never taught. Most of all, Jesus keyed in on the basics of Christianity, applicable from that time to the present. All of Jesus' teachings must be applied to our lives and is important to our everyday living, salvation, and relationship to God while we live here on earth. The author realizes that the customs, culture, tradition, clothing, and living conditions would be different to suit our day and time. It is of utmost importance for the reader of this book to read the four Gospels, *Matthew*, *Mark*, *Luke*, and *John*, which are about the life of Jesus, His teachings, if believed, would bring peace of mind, heart, and contentment, real and lasting happiness, purpose in life, hope for the future, and most of all, your soul salvation, life beyond the grave and throughout eternity. Here are some focal points on the preaching and teaching of Jesus Christ and the apostles,

BORN AGAIN

Two thousand years ago, the basic and fundamentals principles of the Christian faith had their origination when a ruler of the Jews, named Nicodemus, came to Jesus by night; here is the conversation recorded in the Bible:

> *There was a man of the Pharisees, named Nicodemus, a ruler of the Jews:*

The same came to Jesus by night, and said unto him, Rabbi, we know that thou art a teacher come from God: for no man can do these miracles that thou doest, except God be with him.

Jesus answered and said unto him, Verily, verily, I say unto thee, Except a man be born again, he cannot see the kingdom of God.

Nicodemus saith unto him, How can a man be born when he is old? can he enter the second time into his mother's womb, and be born?

Jesus answered, Verily, verily, I say unto thee, Except a man be born of water and of the Spirit, he cannot enter into the kingdom of God.

That which is born of the flesh is flesh; and that which is born of the Spirit is spirit. Marvel not that I said unto thee, Ye must be born again.

The wind bloweth where it listeth, and thou hearest the sound thereof, but canst not tell whence it cometh, and whither it goeth: so is every one that is born of the Spirit. Nicodemus answered and said unto him, How can these things be?

Jesus answered and said unto him, Art thou a master of Israel, and knowest not these things?

Verily, verily, I say unto thee, we speak that we do know, and testify that we have seen; and ye receive not our witness.

If I have told you earthly things, and ye believe not, how shall ye believe, if I tell you of heavenly things?

And no man hath ascended up to heaven, but he that came down from heaven, even the Son of man which is in heaven.

And as Moses lifted up the serpent in the wilderness, even so must the Son of man be lifted up:

That whosoever believeth in him should not perish, but have eternal life.

For God so loved the world, that he gave his only begotten Son, that whosoever believeth in him should not perish, but have everlasting life.

For God sent not his Son into the world to condemn the world; but that the world through him might be saved.

— John 3:1–17

John 3:1–17 is the Gospel of Jesus Christ in a nutshell.

Seventeen of the most powerful verses in the Bible hold the eternal destiny of every human being on the face of the earth if they believe.

After ministering to thousands of people in the marketplace, mountainsides, hills, and valleys, very late in the evening, Jesus seemingly wanted to be alone; this moment was short-lived when suddenly, He heard the crackling of leaves of someone approaching; Jesus had seen this leader of the Jews before in some of His meetings. Nicodemus must have known of the area or place where Jesus prayed as he broke the silence of late evening approached and said to Jesus, "The same came to Jesus by night and said unto him, Rabbi, we know that thou art a teacher come from God: for no man can do these miracles that thou doest, except God be with him" John 3:2. He did not allow Nicodemus to say another word but zeroed deep down within his spirit as Jesus did not mince words or compromise; Jesus was direct and to the point, as He said unto him. "Jesus answered and said unto him, Verily, verily, I say unto thee, Except a man be born again, he cannot see the kingdom of God" John 3:3.

Which was followed by these words from Jesus?

> *Jesus answered, Verily, verily, I say unto thee, Except a man be born of water and of the Spirit, he cannot enter into the kingdom of God.*
>
> *That which is born of the flesh is flesh; and that which is born of the Spirit is spirit. Marvel not that I said unto thee, Ye must be born again.*
>
> *The wind bloweth where it listeth, and thou hearest the sound thereof, but canst not tell whence it cometh, and whither it goeth: so is every one that is born of the Spirit.*
>
> — John 3:5–8

Being a ruler of the synagogue, he was puzzled as he said, "Nicodemus answered and said unto him, How can these things be?" John 3:9

What does it mean to be *born again*? Since the fall of Adam and Eve in the Garden of Eden, the entire human race, from then to the present time, inherited a sinful nature. You do not have to look very far to realize this; (besides those trying to live for God) the human race had broken every commandment of God and had gone beyond this by living and doing things contrary to God's nature, righteousness, and word. The only way that the nature of sin can be destroyed in human flesh is by the born-again experience. Please notice what the author is emphasizing—"*born again experience*"—because it is an experience with God.

To be born again means to be saved. When you were born from your mother, you were born with the nature of sin, but now that you have grown and are at the age of accountability, spiritually speaking, you have to be born again. How can this be? Recognize what Jesus did for you on the cross; He died and shed His precious blood for you, all you have to do is sincerely repent of your sins and ask Jesus to come into your heart and receive Him as your Lord and Savior, and you will be born again. You are born once, you die twice, this means if you are not born again when you die, you will die in your sinful nature, and you will be separated from God throughout eternity.

You are born twice; you die once. When an individual is born of their mother, this means they were born in sin, but when an individual accepts Jesus Christ as Lord and Savior of their life, the Spirit of God hooks up with your Spirit and crucifies the flesh; you become a child of God; this is what it means to be born again. Being born again, you will experience the peace of God, happiness, real love, joy, a relationship with God, and eternal life, and you will make it to heaven. By the way, if you die without being born again, you will die and go to hell, and absolutely no one has the power to pray you out of hell to get to heaven.

Even though Jesus preached the above scriptures to an individual, this was and is the Gospel of Jesus Christ for people of the entire world throughout all generations. Nicodemus received the answer from Jesus he did not expect. The answer Jesus gave introduced us to the basics of Christianity which is so desperately needed to be taught in the church of today and is an absolute for the strength and advancement of Christianity. By the way, I cannot remember when last I heard a solid good salvation message preached; this would be one of the greatest salvation messages that can be delivered by any preacher, Christian worker, or even Christians. Someone might come to a conclusion this is elementary and not deep; personally speaking, I am weary of hearing of deepness and souls are going to hell; what could be more significant, greater, deeper, and profound than soul or souls to be born again and on their way to heaven. Are we deeper than Jesus? *"Ye must be born again…"*

Jesus died on the cross for your sins, peace, sicknesses, problems, needs, situations, circumstances, and most of all, eternal life. Every single need that you have was already paid for, most of all, your salvation. The Hebrew word for salvation that is written in the Old Testament is "*yeshuwah,*" which means literally "something saved" and abstractly "*deliverance.*" The Greek word for salvation that is written in the New Testament is "*soteria,*" and means literally the act of "*physcial and moral rescue*" was paid for, since Jesus already paid for your sins on the cross as a human being, when you hear someone preach, teach the Gospel of Jesus Christ, in church, TV, radio, internet, street corner, gospel tract, some kind of religious literature, reading your Bible, the mission fields, especially if they preach about Jesus dying on the cross, the Holy Spirit convicts you of your sin as you humble yourself and respond to the leading of the Holy Spirit by an altar call or some other way, and with faith in God you pray, say, speak, confess these words: "Jesus, I thank You for dying on the cross, thank You for shedding Your blood for me, I accept You into my heart as Lord and Savior, cleanse me and wash away all my sins, make me a son or daughter of God"; this is where the Holy Spirit moves and changes your life, this is where God's spirit hooks up with your spirit (because you tried everything else and were never satisfied), now that you receive Jesus Christ into your heart, a change takes place. You have an experience with God; this is what it means to be born again. A born-again person is a changed person; the words of the apostle meant the same thing they did when he wrote them two thousand years ago.

BAPTISM WITH THE HOLY SPIRIT

Concerning baptism, Jesus gave the greatest illustration and example of what the baptism of the Holy Spirit is all about. The disciples had gone to purchase food, and while they were gone, Jesus wanted to teach the disciples an important lesson. He deliberately waited at Jacob's well; here comes a woman of Samaria; her life was so messed up and tarnished by living an adulteress life, and the man she was living with was not her husband. Besides this, she had four men in life that she lived with, and the man in her life was the fifth one and not her husband. But Jesus knew His purpose at the well and went about his business cool, calm, and collective because He had a purpose being at the well. Jesus, Himself, said one soul is worth more than all the world's good. This means one soul is worth more than all the gold, diamonds, rubies, and gemstones, even more than all the material things of this world. Sometimes people read their Bible but do not really realize what they are reading, especially when it comes to lost souls.

Jesus, being God and also man, read this woman like a book, and He revealed her past, present, and now going into her future. Jesus did not look at her race, color, or creed. All He was concerned about was her *soul*. He did not look at her nationality, culture, or custom, and her filthy life made no difference to Him. He looked at her as a human being who was made in the image of God and had a soul like everyone else who needed help. What is the message that Jesus preached to this woman that changed her life? He did not load her down with a bunch of rules, regulations, creeds, dogmas, directions from the head of the church or the head office, bishop, superintendent, etc., but it was Jesus who had so much love and compassion that changed her life. He was concerned about her soul.

Jesus preached one of the greatest words to the woman of Samaria; even though this woman and her adulteress life condemned her, her relative's family, friends, neighbors, society, and worst of all, the religions of that day already had condemned and sent her to hell. Jesus knew this woman was tormented all her life; no priest, no scribe, no Pharisee, no religious leader gave her hope, peace, forgiveness, and joy. Phillip, the evangelist, is mentioned in the book of *Acts* as having one of the greatest revivals in Samaria. Little is said about the woman of Samaria whom Jesus witnessed to. She ran to her village and told everyone, "Come see a man who told me all things."

This was the seed of God, and for God, Jesus sowed in the Samaritan woman by leading her to God that changed her life, then the woman of Samaria, in turn, sowed the seed of revival in the hearts of the people of Samaria, then Phillip a deacon, mind you! Came after her and reaped a harvest of souls. Here is how the apostle John records this divine appointment and revelation from the Holy Scriptures.

He left Judaea, and departed again into Galilee.

And he must needs go through Samaria.

Then cometh he to a city of Samaria, which is called Sychar, near to the parcel of ground that Jacob gave to his son Joseph.

Now Jacob's well was there. Jesus therefore, being wearied with his journey, sat thus on the well: and it was about the sixth hour.

There cometh a woman of Samaria to draw water: Jesus saith unto her, Give me to drink. (For his disciples were gone away unto the city to buy meat.)

Then saith the woman of Samaria unto him, How is it that thou, being a Jew, askest drink of me, which am a woman of Samaria? for the Jews have no dealings with the Samaritans.

Jesus answered and said unto her, If thou knewest the gift of God, and who it is that saith to thee, Give me to drink; thou wouldest have asked of him, and he would have given thee living water.

The woman saith unto him, Sir, thou hast nothing to draw with, and the well is deep: from whence then hast thou that living water?

Art thou greater than our father Jacob, which gave us the well, and drank thereof himself, and his children, and his cattle?

Jesus answered and said unto her, Whosoever drinketh of this water shall thirst again:

But whosoever drinketh of the water that I shall give him shall never thirst; but the water that I shall give him shall be in him a well of water springing up into everlasting life.

The woman saith unto him, Sir, give me this water, that I thirst not, neither come hither to draw.

Jesus saith unto her, Go, call thy husband, and come hither. The woman answered and said, I have no husband. Jesus said unto her, Thou hast well said, I have no husband:

For thou hast had five husbands; and he whom thou now hast is not thy husband: in that saidst thou truly.

The woman saith unto him, Sir, I perceive that thou art a prophet.

Our fathers worshipped in this mountain; and ye say, that in Jerusalem is the place where men ought to worship.

Jesus saith unto her, Woman, believe me, the hour cometh, when ye shall neither in this mountain, nor yet at Jerusalem, worship the Father.

Ye worship ye know not what: we know what we worship: for salvation is of the Jews.

But the hour cometh, and now is, when the true worshippers shall worship the Father in spirit and in truth: for the Father seeketh such to worship him.

God is a Spirit: and they that worship him must worship him in spirit and in truth.

The woman saith unto him, I know that Messias cometh, which is called Christ: when he is come, he will tell us all things.

Jesus saith unto her, I that speak unto thee am he.

And upon this came his disciples, and marvelled that he talked with the woman: yet no man said, What seekest thou? or, Why talkest thou with her?

The woman then left her waterpot, and went her way into the city, and saith to the men,

Come, see a man, which told me all things that ever I did: is not this the Christ?

—John 4:3–29

These words that Jesus spoke to the woman of Samaria were and are concerning the born-again experience, the joy of salvation, and the baptism of the Holy Spirit. The words of Jesus above emphasize being born again and being baptized with the Holy Spirit.

"But whosoever drinketh of the water that I shall give him shall never thirst; but the water that I shall give him shall be in him a well of water springing up into everlasting life" John 4:14.

The entire account of Jesus expressing the depth of salvation and the baptism with the Holy Spirit is stated in the above verse; "whosoever drinks of the water or salvation that I shall give him" (means men or women) will be content, satisfied, with God's salvation (to be free from the condemnation of sin) combined with the baptism of the Holy Spirit which is *God's life* flowing within the human *soul* and *spirit* with the assurance that guarantees eternal life. Most human beings nurse or carry the desire for life beyond the grave, well! Here is the answer Jesus has it all. Being saved and the baptism with the Holy Spirit is not a conflagration of a bunch of man-made rules and a watered-down whopping and hacking sermon or a twenty-minute lecture or some type of fast beat music that you have to conjure up to bring people into hype and height of emotion so that when they leave church, they do not know if they are saved or not. This does not mean people should be lifeless, dead, and in order (order is in the cemetery). What Jesus offered to her and to every human being was an experience with God, that change of life, her life, and this is what can change your life, your family, the church, and the world.

The baptism of the Holy Spirit is like running living water within your being. There are some who teach that when you become born again, you receive the Holy Spirit, and there are some who teach that you can receive the Holy Spirit after you are born again. But what the Bible does say is written in the book of Acts:

And it came to pass, that, while Apollos was at Corinth, Paul having passed through the upper coasts came to Ephesus: and finding certain disciples,

He said unto them, Have ye received the Holy Ghost since ye believed? And they said unto him, We have not so much as heard whether there be any Holy Ghost.

And he said unto them, Unto what then were ye baptized? And they said, Unto John's baptism [repentance].

Then said Paul, John verily baptized with the baptism of repentance, saying unto the people, that they should believe on him which should come after him, that is, on Christ Jesus.

When they heard this, they were baptized in the name of the Lord Jesus.

And when Paul had laid his hands upon them, the Holy Ghost came on them; and they spake with tongues, and prophesied.

And all the men were about twelve.

— Acts 19:1–7

The above Scripture is self-explanatory, clear as crystal, and really does not need any interpretation or explanation. Therefore, after an individual is saved, he or she is cleansed by the blood of Jesus Christ. The Holy Spirit moves upon and within that individual and commences the work of God for salvation within the inward and outward being in human life; this is called *justification*—this is an act of God, in which He pronounces an individual righteous in the eyes of God. The Hebrew word for *justification* is "*tsaddag*," which means you are righteous in the sight of God as long as you stay saved and live for God.

But to him that worketh not, but believeth on him that justifieth the ungodly, his faith is counted for righteousness.

— Romans 4:5

Sanctification—this word means when a person is saved, they are washed in the blood of Jesus (receiving what Jesus did on the cross), cleansed, purified, and separated unto God. The Hebrew word for *sanctification* is "*hagios*," which means to be made clean (same for holiness), which is immediate and progressive as an individual continues to live for Jesus.

And the very God of peace sanctify you wholly; and I pray God your whole spirit and soul and body be preserved blameless unto the coming of our Lord Jesus Christ.

— 1 Thessalonians 5:23

Glorification means to live above the power and consequences of sin; the Hebrew word for *glorification* is "*kavod*." This Hebrew word, in particular, does not refer to God's glory. Still, from a human point of view, whom that is saved, you live above the reproach that sin causes; since the Bible was translated from Aramaic and Greek, the word *glorification* comes from Greek—"*doxa*," meaning you are celebrated because you can live above sin.

Moreover whom he did predestinate, them he also called: and whom he called, them he also justified: and whom he justified, them he also glorified.

— Romans 8:30

Who does all of this work, the Holy Spirit in the life of believers in Christ? Now in plain everyday language, a believer or believers receive the Holy Spirit after they believe; this Scripture is worth printing again,

> *And it came to pass, that, while Apollos was at Corinth, Paul having passed through the upper coasts came to Ephesus: and finding certain disciples,*
>
> *He said unto them, Have ye received the Holy Ghost since ye believed? And they said unto him, We have not so much as heard whether there be any Holy Ghost.*
>
> *And he said unto them, Unto what then were ye baptized? And they said, Unto John's baptism.*
>
> *Then said Paul, John verily baptized with the baptism of repentance, saying unto the people, that they should believe on him which should come after him, that is, on Christ Jesus.*
>
> *When they heard this, they were baptized in the name of the Lord Jesus.*
>
> *And when Paul had laid his hands upon them, the Holy Ghost came on them; and they spake with tongues, and prophesied.*
>
> *And all the men were about twelve.*
>
> — Acts 19:1–7

After a person is saved, it is important that you be baptized with the Holy Spirit; you do not have to continue your Christian life dead, lifeless, dry, and powerless. Going back to what Jesus said in John 4:10–14:

> *Jesus answered her, "If you knew the gift of God and who it is that asks you for a drink, you would have asked him and he would have given you living water."*
>
> *"Sir," the woman said, "you have nothing to draw with and the well is deep. Where can you get this living water?*
>
> *Are you greater than our father Jacob, who gave us the well and drank from it himself, as did also his sons and his livestock?"*
>
> *Jesus answered, "Everyone who drinks this water will be thirsty again,*
>
> *but whoever drinks the water I give them will never thirst. Indeed, the water I give them will become in them a spring of water welling up to eternal life."*
>
> — John 4:10–14, NIV

The Holy Spirit is a must in the lives of every Christian to strengthen every Christian to fight against the onslaught of the power of the world, the flesh, and the devil that is raging against this day and age.

Some churches, denominations, and organizations spend millions of dollars in conferences, seminars, and meetings, arguing and criticizing the people who believe in the teachings of Jesus and the apostles' teachings on the miracles, signs, the supernatural, healings, miracles, the gifts of the Holy Spirit, speaking in tongues that comes with the baptism of the Holy Spirit (no hocus-pocus, snake handlers, etc.). But if you read the scriptures, they enjoyed these blessings more than trying to explain them and fight them. Instead of receiving the baptism of the Holy Spirit and enjoying the benefits of God sending the Holy Spirit, millions of people and, of course, some so-called Christians are drinking, smoking, partying, visiting physiatrists, popping pills by the billions, turning to the religions of the east, mysticism, and cults, wasting money in unnecessary trips, vacation, cruises, to alleviate their deep spiritual yearning and desire within their being. But the power of the Holy Spirit can help you overcome all of these things.

The answer is found right there in your Bible, lying on the coffee table, maybe with dust on it; all an individual has to do is pick the Bible and read the Gospel of John. And after reading the account of Jesus' death on the cross, His resurrection, and His priestly office where He is sitting at the right hand of the Father God, waiting for you to come to Him and pray and tell Him all about what you are going through, you will find relief. Most of all, God sent the Holy Ghost to help in every area of your life, problems, needs, and situations. So many people are hurting that they are trying to live the Christian life all by themselves and not rely on the Holy Spirit's power. These are the words of Jesus written in the Gospel of John 14:16–18:

> *And I will pray the Father, and he shall give you another Comforter, that he may abide with you for ever;*
>
> *Even the Spirit of truth; whom the world cannot receive, because it seeth him not, neither knoweth him: but ye know him; for he dwelleth with you, and shall be in you.*
>
> *I will not leave you comfortless: I will come to you.*
>
> — John 14:16–18

Jesus knew He was going to die for the sins of the people of the world. He knew that He was only one man in the flesh, so after His resurrection, He said, "I will send someone who is the Holy Spirit, and He will satisfy, comfort, lead, and guide you…"

> *Howbeit when he, the Spirit of truth, is come, he will guide you into all truth: for he shall not speak of himself; but whatsoever he shall hear, that shall he speak: and he will shew you things to come.*
>
> *He shall glorify me: for he shall receive of mine, and shall shew it unto you.*
>
> — John 16:13–14

The Holy Spirit is called the Spirit of Truth, and He will also guide and lead you to know and receive the truth, which is the teaching and life of Jesus.

> *Nevertheless I tell you the truth; It is expedient for you that I go away: for if I go not away, the Comforter will not come unto you; but if I depart, I will send him unto you. And when he is come, he will reprove the world of sin, and of righteousness, and of judgment:*
>
> *Of sin, because they believe not on me.*
>
> *Of righteousness, because I go to my Father, and ye see me no more;*
>
> *Of judgment, because the prince of this world is judged.*
>
> — John 16:7–11

The Holy Spirit will also show you right from wrong, how to live a godly life, and most of all, the Holy Spirit will give you power over sin, sickness, the flesh, and power over the evil spirits, demons, and the devil.

WATER BAPTISM

Water baptism was instituted by Jesus Christ Himself and should be observed and done in the manner of how He was baptized. Baptism in itself does not save anyone, but baptism is an act of obedience that should be done in response when a person believes and accepts Jesus Christ as Lord and Savior. Baptism in water is one of the rites that must be done exactly like Jesus was baptized by John the Baptist in the River Jordan; how did John baptize Jesus? It was done by John the Baptist by immersing Jesus under the water and then bringing Him up again from under the water.

I have seen some documentary and religious films of Jesus being baptized and could not help but chuckle and become a bit adamant about how they portrayed John the Baptist baptizing the so-called Jesus by taking a handful of water and pouring it on the head of the acting Jesus. Some of them, I have seen the priest or whosoever was acting as John the Baptist, sprinkled the water of the head of the so-called Jesus. But all of this is not true; even though some of them mean well, this is not the way Jesus was baptized in water. John immersed Jesus into the water a brought him up from under the water in rapid succession; if you do not understand this statement, John the Baptist ducked Jesus under the water and quickly brought Him up from under the water. A minister performing the act of water baptism immerses the person being baptized under the water and quickly brings them up from under the water. This is biblical and a real baptism in water, which is called "water baptism." To affirm water baptism, here is the biblical record of Jesus being baptized by John,

> *And this is the record of John, when the Jews sent priests and Levites from Jerusalem to ask him, Who art thou?*
>
> *And he confessed, and denied not; but confessed, I am not the Christ.*
>
> *And they asked him, What then? Art thou Elias? And he saith, I am not. Art thou that prophet? And he answered, No.*
>
> *Then said they unto him, Who art thou? That we may give an answer to them that sent us. What sayest thou of thyself?*
>
> *He said, I am the voice of one crying in the wilderness, Make straight the way of the Lord, as said the prophet Esaias.*
>
> *And they which were sent were of the Pharisees.*
>
> *And they asked him, and said unto him, Why baptizest thou then, if thou be not that Christ, nor Elias, neither that prophet?*
>
> *John answered them, saying, I baptize with water: but there standeth one among you, whom ye know not;*
>
> *He it is, who coming after me is preferred before me, whose shoe's latchet I am not worthy to unloose.*
>
> *These things were done in Bethabara beyond Jordan, where John was baptizing.*
>
> *The next day John seeth Jesus coming unto him, and saith, Behold the Lamb of God, which taketh away the sin of the world.*
>
> *This is he of whom I said, After me cometh a man which is preferred before me: for he was before me.*
>
> *And I knew him not: but that he should be made manifest to Israel, therefore am I come baptizing with water.*
>
> *And John bare record, saying, I saw the Spirit descending from heaven like a dove, and it abode upon him.*

And I knew him not: but he that sent me to baptize with water, the same said unto me, Upon whom thou shalt see the Spirit descending, and remaining on him, the same is he which baptizeth with the Holy Ghost.

And I saw, and bare record that this is the Son of God.

— John 1:19–34

And he said unto them, "Go ye into all the world, and preach the gospel to every creature. He that believeth and is baptized shall be saved; but he that believeth not shall be damned."

— Mark 16:15–16

When a person hears the Gospel of Jesus Christ and is convicted of their sinful nature or realizes they are living in sin, repents (means to turn around) and makes the confession with their mouth and words, "Lord, I realize I am a sinner, I now repent of all my sins, forgive me, wash me in the blood of Jesus Christ; wash away all my sins and save me, make me a child of God," in Jesus' name, that person is saved or born again. This entire act of repentance also means like Jesus was crucified, your sinful nature was crucified; just like Jesus resurrected from the grave, you were raised from the grave.

"Therefore we are buried with him by baptism into death: that like as Christ was raised up from the dead by the glory of the Father, even so we also should walk in newness of life."

— Romans 6:4

The death, burial, and resurrection of Jesus are represented in every baptismal ceremony; the minister or the person officiating stands in a pool of water, river or seashore, or other baptismal means, holds the person's hands, and immerses them into or under the water, saying, "Upon the confession of your faith in Jesus Christ, through the Father, Son, and the Holy Spirit, I now baptize you in the name of the Lord Jesus Christ."

The baptismal service or ceremony also represents the death and resurrection of Jesus Christ. It must be noted and emphasized that in all water baptism ceremonies, the person being baptized must be immersed and brought up from under the water quickly. A sense of humor is always good for the soul, but every time I, the author, teach or preach about people being baptized in water, I especially mention, in particular, these days there are people who do not intend to live for Jesus, or they are not serious about being baptized in water, I usually say or feel like holding them under the water for a while (remember having some fun) and ask them if they intend to straighten up or not!

ASSEMBLING TOGETHER

For those of you reading this book, you will be surprised to know of the millions of people that do not believe in gathering together for worship or attending Church. Gathering together for worship is God's plan for a believer to grow, glow, and go. You cannot be faithful to Christ and don't have any desire to be in the house of God. Gathering with other believers in a place of worship is uplifting, encouraging, motivating, and from a social point of view, to fellowship with other believers. Believers in Jesus Christ must not be separated from the local church or assembly. A true believer should have a desire to attend the house of

God, and the believer's first intention should be to worship and praise God individually and with other believers.

Not forsaking the assembling of ourselves together as the manner of some of them is, but exhorting one another: and so much the more, as ye see the day approaching.

— Hebrews 10:25

Going to a born again, baptized with the Holy Spirit, Church or, to be correct, assembly or gathering, where the Word of God, the Bible, is taught and preached, you will be exhorted, encouraged, there are times the word of God will be rebuked, corrected, and your faith would be lifted and strengthen to live the Christian life so you can make it to heaven. Attending Church is beneficial for the entire family, in particular if you have children and grandchildren. Just dropping off the children and grandchildren at Church, or let's say Sunday school is spiritually detrimental to your family, especially your children. Don't drop them off at Sunday school; take them or lead them to the house of God. I saw some pictures of the middle east of a four and five-year-old, even older, carrying guns, shooting one another, even strapping, even allowing adults to strap them with self-made bombs to kill other people and take their own lives, yet we drop off our children to church and go partying. While this book is being written, young people are marching the streets of America with a socialistic and Marxist (his name does not warranty a capital letter) doctrine on their diluted minds indoctrinated by socialistic professors and universities, and Americans are wondering, "What has gone wrong?"

Thank God for the families, fathers, and mothers in America who have the boldness and courage to take or lead their children to church, but what is happening in our schools at the present time? Nobody should like this except for persons with demented minds and perverted spirits. To a greater extent, some Americans have sown a wind and now reaping a whirlwind. In our elementary schools, high schools, and universities, the Bible was taken out, prayer is exempt, and God or Jesus Christ or the Holy Spirit cannot be mentioned if anyone has the courage to mention God, Jesus, or the Holy Spirit, they become a laughing stock, hated and at times expelled. The Ten Commandments have been chiseled out or torn down; no wonder most of the kids in school today are carrying knives, explosives, and guns, and most Americans are trying to figure out what went wrong. I'll tell you where most Americans went wrong! It's all because God and the Bible were booted out, but God and the Bible cannot be booted out because He is alive, and God has a way of letting us humans realize we cannot do without Him.

Most of all, going to church should be an incentive to get involved in the ministry of the church, the missionary program, and a desire to win souls here in America and especially those who have never heard the Gospel of Jesus Christ in other countries of the world. Believe the author: there is nothing else that stirs your soul, lifts your spirit, or gives you added joy like giving to and winning lost souls; this is within the outreach program of the local church and its foreign missions program. By the way, it has been proven by the physiatrists and scientists that the pleasure points in your brains light up when you do something good for someone else and in particular when you give to and win lost souls. All the meetings in a local church gathering are important, but Bible study and prayer are most important (which most Christians do not seem interested in); but this meeting proves who the real Christians are; these are the ones who will survive the onslaught of persecution, trials, and testing that has begun in America. Prayer, which is God's life, is infused into your soul and spirit; the Bible, the Word of God, will minister to your soul and spirit; these two will give you the strength to endure to the end.

But he that shall endure unto the end, the same shall be saved.
— Matthew 24:13

The greatest feeling about going to church is the fact that knowing you have a family to fellowship with (there can be no fellowship if there are no fellows on the ship), people who know how to pray for you and your family when you are in need, to be motivated and encourage you, by the way, if I were an ordinary church member, I would look for a church that teachers the basics or the fundamental principles of Christianity.

PRAYER

Excuse the negativism before the positive; in most areas within the Body of Christ, prayer is a forgotten word. Jesus was grieved when He walked into the temple or the house of God and saw what was going on. Here are His words recorded in Matthew 21:12–13:

And Jesus went into the temple of God, and cast out all them that sold and bought in the temple, and overthrew the tables of the moneychangers, and the seats of them that sold doves,
And said unto them, It is written, My house shall be called the house of prayer; but ye have made it a den of thieves.
— Matthew 21:12–13

Religious merchandising, profiteering, commercializing, and agricultural and animal trading in the house of God did not sit well with Jesus. As a matter of fact, what Jesus did, in this day and age, He would have been a prime target for one of the biggest lawsuits by religious people of our day. I wonder what would happen if He should walk in some of the so-called houses of God today. The above scriptures brought out the righteous indignation in Jesus, which caused Him to take a whip and chase out the money changers, traders, and those that were literally charging exorbitant fees for religious services. Even though some of this was being carried out outside the temple court, but inside, where the religious leaders of that day were involved in arguments about the law, which they should condemn or not, how to nitpick the words of Jesus and His disciples, most of all how to kill Jesus (within the temple, how religious!). While all of this was going on, He was outside, busy chasing out all of the money changers, etc., but what was His main message to all of them outside and inside the temple? Here is it again: *"And said unto them, It is written, My house shall be called the house of prayer; but ye have made it a den of thieves."*

Call the author old-fashioned, if you want to, and if I am old-fashioned, then blame this on Jesus; if you think I am a fanatic, then blame this on Jesus; you might think I am one track-minded, blame this on Jesus because He is the one that said, "My House shall be called a House of Prayer." Even though this statement can be referred to different aspects of worship, it is a rare thing today to walk into a church building today and see people down by the altar or in the church sanctuary praying, and if you do have some that are desirous of praying they will be ushered into a room away from the sanctuary because some pastors do not want some their members who might be sports personalities, Hollywood stars, dignitaries to be disturbed by prayer or praying.

I hear someone saying that prayer should be in the closet; true, this might be to a certain extent, but I still hear the resounding echo of Jesus' words ringing through the corridors of time to this present hour, *"My House shall be called a House of Prayer."* Thank God for the necessary conveniences to make the house of God conducive for worship, but some people are more prone to an air-conditioned building than a prayer-conditioned building.

This is not a book about prayer, it is not a book on how to pray, it is not how you can pray successfully, and there are too many books on prayer. Reading about prayer, hearing about prayer, and preaching about prayer is commendable; all of this is no substitute for real praying. There is nothing that stirs the soul of this preacher like when I walk in a church building to minister and see and hear people (this might be a strange language to some people) crying out to God in prayer. The source of every blessing, the move of God, miracles, signs, wonders, supernatural visitations, revival in the church (not a day's meeting with a popular evangelist), a soul-saving revival that would stir communities, towns, cities, states, countries—all of this is birth in prayer.

Prayer is a two-way communication; you talk to God, and He talks to you. Just think about this for a moment, you might not be able to meet the President of America or some celebrity or leader of another country, but prayer is having a one-to-one meeting with the Almighty God; prayer is spending time with and in the presence of God. This is the reason the devil fights a praying church and a praying people or a praying minister or individual. Eating a meal when not fasting gives you physical strength. When you pray, you receive spiritual strength; prayer is drawing life from God to suffice your life; it is true that prayer is bringing all your problems, needs, and petitions to God:

> *Be careful for nothing; but in every thing by prayer and supplication with thanksgiving let your requests be made known unto God.*
>
> — Philippians 4:6

But please understand that prayer is also drawing life, power, strength, comfort, direction, leadership, wisdom, and much more from God; also, you can survive the onslaught of a demonic-influenced world. And find solace and satisfaction being with the Almighty God. Jesus, Himself, spoke of the perilous times in which we are living; if you will survive till the end and make it to heaven, here are some sobering words from the mouth of Jesus.

> *Watch ye therefore, and pray always, that ye may be accounted worthy to escape all these things that shall come to pass, and to stand before the Son of man.*
>
> — Luke 21:36

FASTING

Thank God for the members of the Body of Christ who have learned the secret of fasting and praying, but generally speaking, the trend of our day in most churches (just the term that is generally used today referring to different denominations, etc.) is feasting, not fasting. Like prayer, how come people would read about Jesus prayed and fasted, and it seems like this means nothing to them. It's all because people do not know the truth and realize the benefits, effects, and the power of fasting. Fasting once in a while is beneficial for an individual health-wise and spiritually; nothing can break the spiritual drought in your life and the church like fasting. Fasting will also break the power of wickedness, witchcraft, and demonic influences, also crucify, curtail fleshly lust, and cause an individual to overcome the world, demons, and the devil. Most of all, fasting causes you closer to God, and if you are a minister, you can experience a greater anointing and manifestation of the power of God throughout your life.

Concerning fasting, it is not a command but an option that can produce supernatural results for the individual who chooses to fast. There are several different types of fast that the author will briefly mention at this point of this book: (1) a day of fasting can be done without food and water (water if an individual chooses); this type of fasting starts in the morning and goes through the night till sunrise the next day; (2) a three-day fast with only water, some individual might choose some type of warm drink (optional), but it is advisable to drink water only. (3) A seven-day fast with water (which is so much better when fasting), but I know of individuals who cannot do without some type of liquid drink; this is a matter of choice if there are health reasons involved. (4) A twenty-one-day fast is the same pattern of a seven-day fast. (5) A forty-day fast, there are two people mentioned in the Bible that fasted for forty days without water; they were Moses and Jesus. From all biblical accounts, during Jesus' and Moses' fast, they did without water, but after Jesus fasted for forty days, according to the biblical record, He hungered. In an attempt to fast, for instance, for seven days, after three days, an individual who fasts loses desire for food, but if the desire for food is not imminent, then follow your lack of desire for food and continue fasting for as long as you can go; obviously, you can drink water. No one should attempt a forty-day fast until they are certain that God spoke to them.

There are yet three other fasts which are referred to as the Daniel's Fast, which the prophet Daniel did himself; each of these fasts lasted for twenty-one days. These fasts are called (1) the bread and water fast, and this is exactly what it reads like, just bread and water. Daniel did another twenty-one-day fast, which he, himself, called "pulse." Pulse is translated to mean early translations of the Bible refer to "pulse," which, translated, means "foods grown from seeds," according to Daniel fast. Based on this, Daniel's diet includes fruits, vegetables, and whole grains. Another fast mentioned in the Bible is called the Ezekiel bread fast; this bread is made from grains and four beans. Typically this bread contained wheat, spelled or rye, barley, millet, lentils, great northern beans, kidney beans, and pinto beans.

The specific mixture of grains and beans has been tested by food experts and scientists and was found to be wholesome and nutritious. All of these above-mentioned fasts can be done according to your body's capability of handling these facts; wisdom is the principal thing here.

HOLINESS

In this day and age, there are myriads of interpretations pertaining to the word "holiness." So far, the author has avoided too much of the Greek and Hebrew language from which the Bible was translated. From the original language, which was Aramaic, into English, for the first printing of the King James Version of the Bible. In interpreting the word "holy" or "holiness," it is imperative that the Hebrew word must be used here in interpreting the word "holiness." Jesus and the apostles taught and lived holy lives; it must be said of Jesus and the apostles that holiness was more lived than taught. Like prayer, the word holiness is like the bad word in most of the Body of Christ. Mention the word "holiness," and immediately, you will get a leprous-like look from some pastors and people in this day and time. Then, within some denominations, independents, and holiness folks, this word is interpreted by some of them to mean we are better than every other Christian organization; to add insult to injury, this attitude goes much further with a pessimistic view, we are the only ones going to heaven because we are dressing differently from all other Christian groups. I warn you, the next few paragraphs will be shocking.

First of all, God is Holy, Jesus is Holy, the Ghost is Holy, and the Bible is called the Holy Bible. Certain denominations, organizations, independents, and some religions basically understand holiness as being separate from worldly influences. We see in extreme examples that some of the men in the Catholic religion become priests and practice celibacy. Some become monks and live in monasteries, while some of the women become nuns and live in convents separate from the rest of the world. In Eastern religions, we have seen that the concept of holiness also entails separation from everyday life and convenes in an environment that promotes peace and tranquility. In every religious group, the concept of holiness entails a separation from everyday living, marriage, and family life. For the church world to comprehend the word "holy" or "holiness," first of all, we must understand that God is a Holy God.

You are to be holy because I am holy.

— Leviticus 21:8

But as he which hath called you is holy, so be ye holy in all manner of conversation; Because it is written, Be ye holy; for I am [God] holy.

— 1 Peter 1:15–16.

The word "*holy*" or "*holiness*" comes from the Hebrew word "*kodesh.*" This word is applied to God, and we are to be like Him, which means separated, clean, pure, to make separate. This word also means if we are going to approach God, we have to endeavor or try everything possible clean; this means in spirit, soul, and body to be like Him. This Scripture should not be taken lightly and be brushed over: "*Without holiness no man can see God*" Hebrews 12:14.

Which does not mean literally seeing God face to face? It means that people will never have results like answered prayer (just His mercy if He answers) results and revival.

In His Holiness, God wants us to come to Him clean in spirit and body. God made the way through Calvary for us to approach God and come to him; God is not like some man-made religion or organization that has set up a particular man that very few people can approach that man, and if you do have to approach that man you have to walk forward and kiss the ground, then His ring talk and then walk backwards.

The root meaning of the Hebrew noun "*godesh*" means holiness; the objective here is the adjective to practice holiness, which should be the common goal of every Christian to be holy or set apart to God and for the service of God. This means that we should be like God through Jesus Christ in every way; this also means our talk or conversation, even in our dressing, we should be modest. Right here, the author is going to interject his personal thoughts, I know I would be getting a lot of emails because of this statement, but

I certainly believe that holiness in a Christian man or woman emanates what's inside the individual than what is on the outside. If the inside of a person is holy, this will reflect on the outside. I firmly believe that Christians, especially those who have the responsibility, especially if ministering in some way to people, their code of dress should be properly attired and not revealing, in particular women.

In the Koine Greek of the New Testament, the idea of holiness is most commonly a translation of the word "*hagios.*" This word also has the basic idea of "to cut off from" or "make separate." The Greek word for Holiness is "*Hagios,*" of which the original meaning indicated an individual who worships and ministers in the service of God. This includes born-again people who ought to be separated from the sins of the flesh, worldly pleasures, unclean living, and be consecrated unto God. The translation of these two words, Hebrew "*kodesh*" and Greek "*hagios*" are consistent with the idea to be cut off from or to be separated from. It must be understood here that as Christians, obviously, we live in a world with other people, and we do not have to cut ourselves off from those around us, but we do not have to practice their sinful ways, but live if I may use the words, live a Jesus life so you can win them to God and save a soul. These thoughts are consistent with the words of Jesus.

"You are in this world but not of this world."

— John 15:10

In fifty-five years of ministry, I have had the opportunity to minister in every denomination, organization, and independent Christian church. I have been exposed to every kind of doctrine and belief; whenever I have the opportunity to minister, by God's help, I shy away from preaching about dress codes, long hair, short hair, dress lengths, etc., and respect them if they do. But I have met people in some churches and ministries who were resentful of other people who did not dress like them or vice versa; every time I meet someone who does not dress according to my standard, I love them anyhow. Holiness is, in fact, goes a little further; it goes to the heart of men and women (especially Christians). By no means we shouldn't have any prejudiced feelings against any human being because of their dress code, race, culture, or creed.

Even though a certain race of people does not worship or praise God as you do (referring to born again people), this does not mean that there should be resentful towards that group of people, but an effort should be made to appreciate each other and learn to worship God in spirit and in truth, this is also holiness. Believe it or not, living holy lives can birth one of the greatest revivals. Why? Someone might ask! Because God is looking for sanctified and holy people, He can work through.

"Blessed are the pure in heart (this is holiness) for they shall see God."

— Matthew 5:8

GIVING

America is the greatest country in the world; seventy-five percent of Americans have a spirit of giving. Generally speaking, whenever there is a crisis such as earthquakes, tsunamis, hurricanes, tornadoes, wars, floods, etc. Americans are the first to respond. God bless some of our entertainers who will share their gifts and talents to raise monies for the victims of different catastrophes when they occur in a certain part of the world. The population in America is approximately 326.897, 184 as of July 23, 2018; the professing Christian population of the United States is approximately 240 million, 37 percent of these professes to be full gospel or evangelical Christians. Out of these professing full gospel Christians, approximately 19 percent obeys the great commission and gives for the propagation of the Gospel of Jesus Christ. Seemingly 19 percent seems rather small. Still, more Christians should be involved in the propagation of the Gospel of Jesus Christ. Still, taking into consideration the United States is foremost in giving and the propagation of the Gospel of Jesus Christ in the World.

Giving originated with God, who instilled giving in the heart of man. Sacrificing and giving an offering, whatever it might be, is an act of worship and thankfulness to God. Who is it taught Abel to offer up a sacrifice unto God? Deep down within Abel's spirit, there was a deep desire and yearning to be thankful to God the Supreme Being. He wanted to show his thankfulness and love to God by offering the best sheep of his flock as a sacrifice unto God.

What did God say about Abel's Sacrifice?

> *And in process of time it came to pass, that Cain brought of the fruit of the ground an offering unto the* LORD.
> *And Abel, he also brought of the firstlings of his flock and of the fat thereof. And the* LORD *had respect unto Abel and to his offering.*
>
> — Genesis 4:3–4

After rescuing his nephew, Abraham, returning from a fierce battle, was the first person to pay tithes to the priest and king of Salem and honored God by paying his "tithes." There are some ministers and people who do not support tithing and are adamant with corresponding statements that tithing is not for today, but why would the apostle Paul (whom I believe is the author of the book of Hebrews) mention tithing in the New Testament.

> *And Melchizedek king of Salem brought forth bread and wine: and he was the priest of the most high God.*
> *And he blessed him, and said, Blessed be Abram of the most high God, possessor of heaven and earth:*
> *And blessed be the most high God, which hath delivered thine enemies into thy hand. And he gave him tithes of all.*
>
> — Genesis 14:18–20

> *And Solomon went up thither to the brazen altar before the* LORD, *which was at the tabernacle of the congregation, and offered a thousand burnt offerings upon it.*
> *In that night did God appear unto Solomon, and said unto him, ask what I shall give thee.*
>
> — 2 Chronicles 1:6–7

God visited Solomon because of his liberality. What kind of attitude did the Old Testament people, including leaders, prophets, and kings, have about giving? What about Jesus and the apostles and the people in the New Testament? What kind of spirit did they give? We are about to find out. After God had given instructions to build the Tabernacle in the wilderness, God gave Moses to take up an offering in the wilderness (some modern-day people would have said, "Take up an offering in the wilderness, there is no money in this wilderness"); well, here is the record in the Bible.

> *And the L*ORD *spake unto Moses, saying,*
> *Speak unto the children of Israel, that they bring me an offering: of every man that giveth it willingly with his heart ye shall take my offering.*
> *And this is the offering which ye shall take of them; gold, and silver, and brass,*
> *And blue, and purple, and scarlet, and fine linen, and goats' hair,*
> *And rams' skins dyed red, and badgers' skins, and shittim wood,*
> *Oil for the light, spices for anointing oil, and for sweet incense,*
> *Onyx stones, and stones to be set in the ephod, and in the breastplate.*
> — Exodus 25:1–7

The children of Israel responded by giving everything they could give, but the notable thing about this the people who gave with a willing heart.

> *And they received from Moses all the offering which the children of Israel had brought for the work of the service of making the sanctuary. So they continued bringing to him freewill offerings every morning. Then all the craftsmen who were doing all the work of the sanctuary came, each from the work he was doing, and they spoke to Moses, saying, "The people bring much more than enough for the service of the work which the Lord commanded us to do." So Moses gave a commandment, and they caused it to be proclaimed throughout the camp, saying, "Let neither man nor woman do any more work for the offering of the sanctuary." And the people were restrained from bringing, for the material they had was sufficient for all the work to be done.*
> — Exodus 36:3–7, NKJV

Have you ever heard in this day and time people where church members gave so much, and if this was so today, do you think that ministers would stop the people from giving?

Amazing is the word for the last Old Testament book, the book of Malachi was written about 515 BC, decades after the Hebrew people returned from captivity under Ezra's leadership, they built and dedicated the temple or the house of God. After this, the people had become unconcerned, relaxed, or lackadaisical. They neglected the house of God, neglected and disrespected the priestly office. Some of the priests misused the priestly office; they did not honor God like they should on the Sabbath, corruption and loose living prevailed in a society that was supposed to uphold godly standards and principles, and most of all those they were not honoring God with the first fruits or 10 percent of what they earned.

God raised up the prophet Malachi to correct the lax religious and social behavior of the Israelites. The prophet Malachi delivered his prophecy; what was the word from God?

> *For I am the L*ORD*, I change not; therefore ye sons of Jacob are not consumed.*
> *Even from the days of your fathers ye are gone away from mine ordinances, and have not kept them. Return unto me, and I will return unto you, saith the L*ORD *of hosts. But ye said, Wherein shall we return?*

Chapter 8: What Jesus and the Apostles Taught

> *Will a man rob God? Yet ye have robbed me. But ye say, Wherein have we robbed thee? In tithes and offerings.*
>
> *Ye are cursed with a curse: for ye have robbed me, even this whole nation.*
>
> *Bring ye all the tithes into the storehouse, that there may be meat in mine house, and prove me now herewith, saith the Lord of hosts, if I will not open you the windows of heaven, and pour you out a blessing, that there shall not be room enough to receive it.*
>
> *And I will rebuke the devourer for your sakes, and he shall not destroy the fruits of your ground; neither shall your vine cast her fruit before the time in the field, saith the Lord.*
>
> — Malachi 3:6–11

God raised up the prophet Malachi to correct the lax religious and social behavior of the Israelites. The prophet Malachi delivered his prophecy. What was the word from God? *"Return Unto Me,"* God was speaking through the Prophet Malachi. To *"Return unto God"* at this point, you would think God used the prophet to call people back to repentance and prayer; this obviously they did, but please note in what area in the people's lives God was trying to zero into their hearts, their pockets, their money, let's read Malachi 3:6: "For I am the Lord, I change not."

There are some ministers and church members who constantly reiterate that tithing is not for today but the word of God to the prophet, "I am the Lord I change not," is a rebuke to those who make this statement because God and His word don't change. He is the same yesterday, today, and forever. Paul the apostle, whom I believe wrote the book of Hebrews, emphasized tithing.

> *This Melchizedek was king of Salem and priest of God Most High. He met Abraham returning from the defeat of the kings and blessed him, and Abraham gave him a tenth of everything. First, the name Melchizedek means "king of righteousness"; then also, "king of Salem" means "king of peace." Without father or mother, without genealogy, without beginning of days or end of life, resembling the Son of God, he remains a priest forever.*
>
> *Just think how great he was: Even the patriarch Abraham gave him a tenth of the plunder! Now the law requires the descendants of Levi who become priests to collect a tenth from the people that is, from their fellow Israelites even though they also are descended from Abraham. This man, however, did not trace his descent from Levi, yet he collected a tenth from Abraham and blessed him who had the promises. And without doubt the lesser is blessed by the greater. In the one case, the tenth is collected by people who die; but in the other case, by him who is declared to be living. One might even say that Levi, who collects the tenth, paid the tenth through Abraham.*
>
> — Hebrews 7:1–9, NIV

From the patriarchs, prophets, kings, Jesus, and the apostles, tithing was emphasized and practiced; even the Pharisees, Sadducees, and Scribes tithe, and Jesus said so. This statement will seem blunt, bold, and bewildering, and this is for non-Christians and Christians alike, "You can know an individual by the kind of attitude they have about giving" when someone has a spirit to give, it shows who they are towards God. The prophet Malachi had a message for the people back then and now, and it was, "Return unto me [God], and I will return unto you" Malachi 3:7.

The keyword here is "Return unto Me [God] I will Return unto You." Well! The question is, how can we return to God?

Here comes the answer, "In tithes and offerings." The tithes are 10 percent of everything that you own. In particular, this has to do with your monies or, in other words, your income; 10 percent belongs to God. The question here is honor? One notable fact is that everyone should find someone to honor. Honoring God is foremost in our lives; how do we honor God by the first fruits, and this includes our tithes. Then we should honor our parents, and this should always be honoring God's servants, that is, his true servants who are carrying out God's program of preaching the Gospel of Jesus Christ

When you honor God with the 10 percent, you are actually showing and saying God thank you for all your blessings. When individuals, people, the church, and our nation honors God with the *tithes*, the word of God says He will open up the windows of heaven and pour you out a blessing. How can a nation, people, and ministers get blessed when they rob God? The meaning of the word "*tithes*" originated from the Hebrew word "*Aser*," which is translated as ten (10) the "*ma'aser*" or *tithe*, which means the tenth part. The "*tithes*" is the act of worship. Paying the tithes is honoring God in obedience to what He says; this, in turn, would open up the heavens, "*heavens*" have you never taken the time to study the meaning "*open up the heavens and pour you out a blessing.*"

Look at the heavens; it is so huge that you cannot measure it, and anywhere and everywhere you go under the heavens, you will be blessed. The practice of tithing was not limited to God's people; this was a widespread practice among other religions and cultures outside Israel and the Semitic people. Jesus and the apostles taught and practiced giving; Jesus did not limit giving by just the tithing; the tithes and tithing were expected, but here comes another shocker. Jesus taught giving beyond the tithes; He taught giving all you can give. Shocked! Yes, He did. Most of all, Jesus *watched* those who gave and did not give. He stood and *watched* what the people gave. This is how He knew the woman gave all she had.

> *And Jesus sat over against the treasury, and beheld how the people cast money into the treasury: and many that were rich cast in much.*
>
> *And there came a certain poor widow, and she threw in two mites, which make a farthing.*
>
> *And he called unto him his disciples, and saith unto them, Verily I say unto you, That this poor widow hath cast more in, than all they which have cast into the treasury: For all they did cast in of their abundance; but she of her want did cast in all that she had, even all her living.*
>
> — Mark 12:41–44

Jesus sat right by the synagogue treasury box where everyone in the congregation walked up and gave their offering by putting it in the synagogue treasury box (He did not pick up collection in a small silver or gold-colored plate); the people brought their offering and this they did as an act of worship. The rich people were casting large sums of money in the treasury box, but they held back most of their money. Jesus saw this poor and lonely widow placed a small coin, which was called the lepton, this was the smallest Jewish copper coin, and it was worth an eighth of a cent. She was the poorest of the poor, and what she gave it was all she had. It was all her living. In other words, that was all she had to buy something to eat, but she gave it; there was nothing else at the moment upon which to depend. She had no one to support her, no banking account, no social security, no IRA, no 401Ks, the only money she possessed, but she gave it all.

Please remember Jesus was sitting in a position so He could see who was giving. He was concerned with the amount they gave, but Jesus was looking at their attitude of their soul. He was observing their spirit of giving. The rich people were holding back 90 percent of their money in their homes, doing nothing when they could have given more to help to finance the kingdom of God. Jesus knew they had to live, purchase food, buy clothing and pay their bills, but most of what they had hidden was doing nothing. Look at Jesus' attitude in giving, which is recorded in Luke 6:36: "Give and it shall be given you, pressed down shaken together and running over, shall men give unto your bosom."

The apostles in the book of Acts taught and had the same attitude that Jesus had about giving, the apostles continued exactly where Jesus left off in His teaching of the word, togetherness, united, and daily they had fellowship with one another, praying, fasting, winning lost souls, backing up what they preached by healing the sick, casting out demons, as miracles, signs, and wonders were following their ministry. Angels visited and assisted them so often in delivering them from their persecutors. Lawsuits were unheard of because they had a spirit of forgiveness and helped each other. As a matter of fact, the early church supported and helped one another; none of them lacked. Anyone reading the book of Acts would realize that the book of Acts church, which included the apostles and disciples, was a different kind of church of today. In no way the author is insinuating intruding in the privacy of an individual, ministers, and people's life and ministry, but the general trend today is to walk in with an entourage, preach and minister, pick up an offering, and then out the back door with their entourage and after that "don't bother me" attitude.

The reason why they had a move of God is that they had fellowship with one another, helped one another, and, most of all, they had a spirit to give. According to the Word of God from the Old Testament to the New Testament, they paid tithes, but they went beyond the tithes in their giving; as the early church people or the book of Acts Christians went beyond the tithing and gave not to make ministers multi-millionaires but to minister and help others. God can and will make ministers multimillionaires invest back in God's program of winning lost souls and helping those that are in need here and in poorer countries of the world. This is the reason the book of Acts Christians—none of them lacked or suffered financially and materially. Lands, gold, and silver…they were just sitting there doing nothing; they gave to the apostles so they could have used the money to finance the Gospel of Jesus Christ and help those people in need.

> *But a certain man named Ananias, with Sapphira his wife, sold a possession.*
>
> *And he kept back part of the proceeds, his wife also being aware of it, and brought a certain part and laid it at the apostles' feet.*
>
> *But Peter said, "Ananias, why has Satan filled your heart to lie to the Holy Spirit and keep back part of the price of the land for yourself?*
>
> *While it remained, was it not your own? And after it was sold, was it not in your own control? Why have you conceived this thing in your heart? You have not lied to men but to God."*
>
> *Then Ananias, hearing these words, fell down and breathed his last. So great fear came upon all those who heard these things. ⁶ And the young men arose and wrapped him up, carried him out, and buried him.*
>
> *Now it was about three hours later when his wife came in, not knowing what had happened.*

And Peter answered her, "Tell me whether you sold the land for so much?" She said, "Yes, for so much."

Then Peter said to her, "How is it that you have agreed together to test the Spirit of the Lord? Look, the feet of those who have buried your husband are at the door, and they will carry you out."

Then immediately she fell down at his feet and breathed her last. And the young men came in and found her dead, and carrying her out, buried her by her husband.

So great fear came upon all the church and upon all who heard these things.

— Acts 5:1–11, NKJV

The above biblical account generated a fear of God throughout the early church; why? Because they lied in the presence of God and grieved the Holy Spirit. The Spirit of God was moving, souls were being saved, the sick were being healed, supernatural miracles were taking place, the gifts of the spirit were being manifested, demons were being cast out, lives were being changed, and most of all, people began experiencing the love of God, like never before, and one of the signs of a true revival and a move of God is the spirit of giving. This is what was happening in the book of acts; the love of God hit Ananias and Sapphira they wanted to give.

But they had a piece of land that was not in use and did not need; they decided to sell it and gave the money to the apostles so they could minister to the needs of the people, support the apostles most of all, finance the preaching of the Gospel of Jesus Christ. Ananias and Sapphira meant well as they realized it takes money to win lost souls, but when they sold the land, the money that they received for the price of the land looked so good that they decided to keep back part of it; originally, they had decided to give it all, but greed got in the way as they held back part of the money and they went to the Holy Ghost revival to give the money they received from the sale of land the Holy Ghost showed to Peter what they had done, as they held back part of the money. Well, it was their money, to begin with, but what was the problem, they held back part of the money and lied about it, and of course, they died.

Thank God for the faithful people that are giving to finance the Gospel of Jesus Christ, but how many liars do we have in the pews and behind the pulpit today? It is not what you give, but it's what people are holding back; this is the reason why multitudes of souls are dying and going to hell; why? It's because millions of dollars are being held back. One of the things that touch the heart of God and move Him to move for you is a spirit to give and an offering. In this day and age, it does not have to be an offering of a sheep heifer or bullock, but giving can be in the form of lands not in use, gold, silver, gemstones, diamonds, or jewelry; there are times that an offering can be a car, motorbike, or anything of value. But most of all, an offering in this day and age is in the form of money for which an individual can pay their tithes and give an offering, special gifts, or missions. Generally speaking, the tithes should go to the local church or assembly, offerings are a special gift given to the church or ministry, and there are times that a local church or ministry gives a special offering to a visiting minister, speaker, or a special invitee who has been invited to conduct some kind of special meetings.

There are times in a church when a pastor invites a guest speaker; it is the responsibility of the local pastor and church to care for all of the expenses of the visiting minister and, of course, honor the visiting with a special love or appreciation offering. Suppose the visiting missionary, an evangelist, is involved in a mission program in the US or overseas and is in need of financial support. In that case, they should discuss it with the pastor they are conducting the meeting for before endeavoring to solicit or, in simple language, ask the congregation for an offering to help or support their ministry.

But there are times people from the local church would come up to the visiting minister or evangelist, and they would slip a special love offering into the visiting speaker's hand; this is quite normal, and none of the pastors, board, or local financial committee's business, in some cases if it's a substantial amount of money if the missionary, evangelist or visiting minister senses that he needs inform the pastor he or she is conducting the meeting for, this obviously is feasible, but a broadminded or a pastor who really is broadminded and not struggling (excuse the language) will praise God that someone was able to give the visiting speaker an offering. Generally speaking, in megachurches, this might not be a problem because financial arrangements should be made before the special meeting. There are some pastors who can become very adamant or apoplectic about their members giving visiting speakers an offering personally; this has caused many problems between pastors and visiting ministers. There are some pastors who try to control this type of giving with an iron fist or hand, but this is just plain old witchcraft (rebellion) and stinginess.

A pastor who will go out of his way to stop or hinder this kind of giving obviously shows who he really is, again, stingy. The visiting minister or evangelist should be courteous enough to inform the pastor that some of the members put an offering in his hands, but this depends on the pastor's spirit or attitude. If the pastor asks how much that's fine, be honest and tell him, but there are some pastors who are broadminded, and they just leave it alone; then again, there are some pastors who do not like their members putting offerings in the visiting minister's hand and after the visiting ministers leave the members who put an offering in the visiting minister's hand gets chewed out or fussed at by the pastor for an offering that amounts to practically nothing. Just plain old fashion talk here. Sometimes just leave it alone, say nothing, or keep your mouth shut. Proper financial arrangements should be made between the pastor and the visiting minister.

Yours truly always maintain a sense of humor, and these other few lines either would make you laugh or cry or both at the same time. I remember a true story of one of my minister friends, who used to be a police detective; God saved him and filled him with the Holy Spirit, and then God called him into the ministry. He was in the ministry for many years as he did the work of an evangelist. God used him in a mighty way, he called a certain pastor, and he and the pastor made arrangements for one week of revival meetings; both the pastor and my friend, the evangelist, made arrangements that the offerings that came in would be shared, the church would get 40 percent plus the tithes and my friend, the evangelist, would get 60 percent, God blessed the revival meeting as souls were saved, healed, and delivered. People were also healed as great things happened during the revival meeting. At the end of the revival, the pastor called my friend, the evangelist, into his office before he left and handed him a check for $200.00. He knew they had raised $15,000 besides tithes. The evangelist did not say a word as he told the pastor, "Excuse me for a minute," as he went back into the car, got his 45, or revolver, came back into the office, pointed it to the pastor as he said, "Now gimme (give me) my money." Guess what the pastor did? Tore up the $200.00 check and wrote him a check for the amount that was due to him. Ask my friend, the evangelist, if he was serious about hurting the pastor? Nope! He said, "I was only bluffing, but my 45 pointing in his face was the only language he understood." You be the judge!

The current USA population is over 311 million people (311,800,000 in mid-2011), so the United States has the world's third-largest population in the world. Our American populace, 11 percent of the Christian population responsible for spreading the Gospel of Jesus Christ here and especially around the world. Here is another shocking figure—97 percent of the monies collected in Christian denominations, organizations, and independents; it is an indisputable fact that 90 percent of these monies go for overhead expenses. Even though certain ministries, organizations, denominations, God blessed television ministries, and Christian television stations are doing their best to reach the world with the Gospel of Jesus Christ. Thank God for the 59 percent of the world has been reached with the Gospel of Jesus Christ, but what about the 49 percent which needs to reach with the Gospel of Jesus Christ. If the church world, in general, would realize winning lost souls is God's priority and the most important job right now is the saving of a soul, Haiti, India, Africa, the Amazon (where yours truly is working to reach these people), and other needy countries of the world, most of the world could have been reached with the Gospel.

If preachers would give of their time, monies, and gifts and work together to reach the country of Haiti as an example, this country would have been better off and evangelized by now. But most, if I may use the word top of the line, preachers are not going to Haiti or some other poor countries of the world. It's because there are no offerings there. It is true that when going into these poor countries, souls should be the first motive. Still, there are always expenses; believe me, it takes money for everything. Some believers think it does not take money to reach lost souls. Still, it does. How about traveling, hotels, setting up the meetings, caring for and assisting the local pastors to travel back and forth to the meetings, sound systems, music, which is important, plus other expenses, rests on the evangelist, missionary, or whosoever is the main speaker. But here is the point, even though there is hardly any money (the people, I mean) in some of these countries again, souls are what this is all about. So what's the point? It rests upon the speaker or evangelist to teach the people to give whatever they can to help financially, teaching them to give with no pressure on them to give. God will bless the people and the country. It must be reiterated, even though the people are poor and are of a different nationality, race, or color than you; please remember that red blood runs through their veins, and their skin is a fraction of pigmentation or color, but let this sink in your spirit; they are made in the image of God, and it is the same red blood running through their veins, no amount of money is worth their soul.

No true Christian minister or Christian should be embarrassed about the word money because Jesus was never ashamed talking about money and giving. There are some ministries, organizations, denominations, and independents where a minister who can minister is not allowed and cannot say anything about money. Because some of them are afraid that their people would leave the church, their names would be tarnished or branded as money grabbers. There are some ministers who will not lift up an offering, but they do have someone else in their board or associate who would come up to the platform and give a half an hour lecture about the tithes and offering before lifting the tithes and offering. This they do in every meeting; to me, this is personally boring but occasionally acceptable. There are ministries and pastors who will not allow a visiting minister to mention anything about money but do know how to take care of a visiting minister. Then there are some who do know how to take care of a visiting minister, and the visiting minister dare not mention money because some pastors are afraid that their people will be extravagant and give the visiting minister more than they deserve or their monies will go somewhere else. Some of them have the attitude like a dog in the manger; the dog will not eat the hay and will not allow the cow to eat it.

This is because they were never taught in the first place about giving or just plain stingy. The reason for giving (even though the money situation and giving have gotten out of control in some areas), but the main reason for giving is for churches and ministries to finance their ministry operations. The purpose of receiving tithes and offerings is for the overhead expenses; this is to care for the pastor, leaders, workers, recurring bills, course maintenance, and, of course, visiting ministers. But the primary purpose for receiving monies is to conduct outreaches in ministering to the needs of the people and win lost souls here and in America, especially people overseas who have never heard of the Gospel of Jesus Christ.

I personally know of pastors and churches that never once given to missions or for a soul-winning project and would spend thousands upon thousands which amount to millions of dollars, generally speaking, for trips, cruises, banquets, entertainment, then give to win the lost, and if they do give, it would be two or three hundred dollars to help (thank God). Still, it takes more than two or three hundred dollars to evangelize the world or win souls. I remember, as a little boy in church, the leaders of our church used to ask the congregation if we were going to pick up a missionary offering, all I used to hear dropping in the collection plates was pennies, nickels, dimes, and quarters (believe me, this was about the only time I heard some noise in the church), pennies, nickels, dimes and quarters (thank God), but if you are really thinking straight and as a Christian you really believe that every human being that does not know Jesus Christ as Lord and Savoir and is going to hell, you will wake up and think, say and give. Folks wake up; it takes billions of dollars to finance the preaching of the Gospel of Jesus Christ around the world.

THE DEATH AND RESURRECTION OF JESUS CHRIST

The death and resurrection of Jesus Christ were the focal point of the apostles' teaching and preaching. They constantly and consistently preached Jesus died on the cross and His resurrection. Preaching and teaching Jesus died on the cross kept them close together, broken, bended, and humbled and in unity and fellowship one with another. Most of all, the preaching of the death and resurrection of Jesus Christ resulted in thousands upon thousands being saved, healed, and delivered.

Jesus died on the cross, and His resurrection laid a foundation for supernatural results in the books of *Acts* which was a pattern and foundation for the ongoing church to the present time. Philosophy, psychology, physiology, the good life, prosperity (which is all good), but prosperity without God is no prosperity. Seven points to a successful financial life and marriage, prophesy about end-times events dominates the airways while so many just listen and do nothing. But preaching and teaching about Jesus who died on the Cross does not appeal to the modern-day lifestyle because it zero's into a lifestyle of self-denial to follow Jesus. The majority of people in the church today want to be entertained, but they do not want to shed a tear over the Son of God who suffered, shed His blood, and died for their sins and the sins of the entire world. No cross, no crown, no pain, no gain. Within the church, there must be the preaching and teaching of crucifixion before the resurrection of Jesus Christ. If there is going to be life, there must be death. Excuse me, please; what I am talking about is spiritual death, the death of the flesh, which will birth the life of Christ within an individual.

> *Verily, verily, I say unto you, Except a corn of wheat fall into the ground and die, it abideth alone: but if it die, it bringeth forth much fruit. He that loveth his life shall lose it; and he that hateth his life in this world shall keep it unto life eternal.*
>
> — John 12:24–25

The early church, which is the book of *Acts* church, we do have to admit the results that they had were astounding, vindicated by signs, wonders, and miracles. The book of Acts church can be termed the Acts of the Holy Spirit; this church witnessed one supernatural miracle or act of God one after another. What was the reason? They constantly and insistently preached Jesus Christ and Him crucified and the power of His resurrection.

> *Ye men of Israel, hear these words; Jesus of Nazareth, a man approved of God among you by miracles and wonders and signs, which God did by him in the midst of you, as ye yourselves also know:*
>
> *Him, being delivered by the determinate counsel and foreknowledge of God, ye have taken, and by wicked hands have crucified and slain:*
>
> *Whom God hath raised up, having loosed the pains of death:*
>
> — Acts 2:22–24a

> *Be it known unto you all, and to all the people of Israel, that by the name of Jesus Christ of Nazareth, whom ye crucified, whom God raised from the dead, even by him doth this man stand here before you whole.*
>
> — Acts 4:10

> *He that spared not his own Son, but delivered him up for us all, how shall he not with him also freely give us all things?*
>
> *Who shall lay any thing to the charge of God's elect? It is God that justifieth.*
>
> *Who is he that condemneth? It is Christ that died, yea rather, that is risen again, who is even at the right hand of God, who also maketh intercession for us.*
>
> — Romans 8:32–34

Before revealing the spiritual benefits of Jesus dying on the cross and His resurrection, here are two scriptural accounts from the Gospel of Luke and the Gospel of John,

> *And it was about the sixth hour, and there was a darkness over all the earth until the ninth hour.*
>
> *And the sun was darkened, and the veil of the temple was rent in the midst.*
>
> *And when Jesus had cried with a loud voice, he said, Father, into thy hands I commend my spirit: and having said thus, he gave up the ghost.*
>
> *Now when the centurion saw what was done, he glorified God, saying, Certainly this was a righteous man.*
>
> — Luke 23:44–47

"When Jesus therefore had received the vinegar, he said, It is finished: and he bowed his head, and gave up the ghost" John 19:30. When Adam and Eve sinned in the Garden of Eden, they plunged the entire earth with its vegetation, animals, fruit trees, and everything else. Most of all, everything was affected by the curse of sin; the earth was so affected by the curse of sin it brought forth thorns and thistles. This obviously would bring us to the point that Adam and Eve inherited a sinful nature; this means that every human being that was born through Adam and Eve inherited a sinful nature. The author is aware that Christian people would be reading this book, but we must take into consideration that this book is written with the understanding and intention that there is a possibility that non-Christians would be reading this book; this is the reason the author had to interject the Bible's record of the beginning of sin.

Now the serpent was more subtil than any beast of the field which the Lord God had made. And he said unto the woman, Yea, hath God said, Ye shall not eat of every tree of the garden?

And the woman said unto the serpent, We may eat of the fruit of the trees of the garden:

But of the fruit of the tree which is in the midst of the garden, God hath said, Ye shall not eat of it, neither shall ye touch it, lest ye die.

And the serpent said unto the woman, Ye shall not surely die: For God doth know that in the day ye eat thereof, then your eyes shall be opened, and ye shall be as gods, knowing good and evil.

And when the woman saw that the tree was good for food, and that it was pleasant to the eyes, and a tree to be desired to make one wise, she took of the fruit thereof, and did eat, and gave also unto her husband with her; and he did eat.

And the eyes of them both were opened, and they knew that they were naked; and they sewed fig leaves together, and made themselves aprons.

And they heard the voice of the Lord God walking in the garden in the cool of the day: and Adam and his wife hid themselves from the presence of the Lord God amongst the trees of the garden.

And the Lord God called unto Adam, and said unto him, Where art thou?

And he said, I heard thy voice in the garden, and I was afraid, because I was naked; and I hid myself.

And he said, Who told thee that thou wast naked? Hast thou eaten of the tree, whereof I commanded thee that thou shouldest not eat?

And the man said, The woman whom thou gavest to be with me, she gave me of the tree, and I did eat.

And the Lord God said unto the woman, What is this that thou hast done? And the woman said, The serpent beguiled me, and I did eat.

And the Lord God said unto the serpent, Because thou hast done this, thou art cursed above all cattle, and above every beast of the field; upon thy belly shalt thou go, and dust shalt thou eat all the days of thy life:

And I will put enmity between thee and the woman, and between thy seed and her seed; it shall bruise thy head, and thou shalt bruise his heel.

Unto the woman he said, I will greatly multiply thy sorrow and thy conception; in sorrow thou shalt bring forth children; and thy desire shall be to thy husband, and he shall rule over thee.

And unto Adam he said, Because thou hast hearkened unto the voice of thy wife, and hast eaten of the tree, of which I commanded thee, saying, Thou shalt not eat of it: cursed is the ground for thy sake; in sorrow shalt thou eat of it all the days of thy life;

Thorns also and thistles shall it bring forth to thee; and thou shalt eat the herb of the field; In the sweat of thy face shalt thou eat bread, till thou return unto the ground; for out of it wast thou taken: for dust thou art, and unto dust shalt thou return.

And Adam called his wife's name Eve; because she was the mother of all living.

Unto Adam also and to his wife did the Lord God make coats of skins, and clothed them.

And the Lord God said, Behold, the man is become as one of us, to know good and evil: and now, lest he put forth his hand, and take also of the tree of life, and eat, and live for ever:

Therefore the Lord God sent him forth from the garden of Eden, to till the ground from whence he was taken.

Therefore the Lord God sent him forth from the garden of Eden, to till the ground from whence he was taken.

So he drove out the man; and he placed at the east of the garden of Eden Cherubims, and a flaming sword which turned every way, to keep the way of the tree of life.

— Genesis 3:1–24

And about the ninth hour Jesus cried with a loud voice, saying, Eli, Eli, lama sabachthani? that is to say, My God, my God, why hast thou forsaken me?

Some of them that stood there, when they heard that, said, This man calleth for Elias.

And straightway one of them ran, and took a spunge, and filled it with vinegar, and put it on a reed, and gave him to drink.

The rest said, Let be, let us see whether Elias will come to save him.

Jesus, when he had cried again with a loud voice, yielded up the ghost.

And, behold, the veil of the temple was rent in twain from the top to the bottom; and the earth did quake, and the rocks rent;

And the graves were opened; and many bodies of the saints which slept arose,

And came out of the graves after his resurrection, and went into the holy city, and appeared unto many.

Now when the centurion, and they that were with him, watching Jesus, saw the earthquake, and those things that were done, they feared greatly, saying, truly this was the Son of God.

— Matthew 27:46–54

At the very hour Jesus died on the cross, there was total darkness throughout the known world, which lasted from noon to 3:00 p.m. At the moment of Christ's death, the light departed from the sun, and the land was darkened at noonday, which was a wonder recorded in the annals of history and is preserved in archives unto this day. The Greek writer Phlegon, writing in AD 137, reported, "What does this mean? This darkness represented God's judgment on Jesus for the sins of humanity, which Jesus took upon Himself." The darkness also represents that God could not for that time look at the sins of mankind, which Jesus took upon Him. So in plain everyday language, Jesus died for our sins.

Here are other reasons why Jesus died on the cross, including the whipping that He received at the whipping post opposite Pilate's Judgment Hall. This whipping was particularly taught and done by one roman soldier. Could you imagine trained to whip criminals now turned to their animosity on Jesus? The whip that they whipped Jesus with was made up of leather about two feet long. At the tip of this whip, these leather tongs combined a sharp hook-like lead or pieces of bones; when Jesus was whipped, the Roman soldier was trained to lash the body of Jesus and at the same time drag the whip across Jesus' body, pulling the flesh to cause severe pain at the same time exposing some bones. But what benefit was the whipping that Jesus took for us! Here are the words of the prophet Isaiah, called the messianic prophet,

> *Who hath believed our report? and to whom is the arm of the LORD revealed?*
>
> *For he shall grow up before him as a tender plant, and as a root out of a dry ground: he hath no form nor comeliness; and when we shall see him, there is no beauty that we should desire him.*
>
> *He is despised and rejected of men; a man of sorrows, and acquainted with grief: and we hid as it were our faces from him; he was despised, and we esteemed him not.*
>
> *Surely he hath borne our griefs, and carried our sorrows: yet we did esteem him stricken, smitten of God, and afflicted.*
>
> *But he was wounded for our transgressions, he was bruised for our iniquities: the chastisement of our peace was upon him; and with his stripes we are healed.*
>
> *All we like sheep have gone astray; we have turned every one to his own way; and the LORD hath laid on him the iniquity of us all.*
>
> *He was oppressed, and he was afflicted, yet he opened not his mouth: he is brought as a lamb to the slaughter, and as a sheep before her shearers is dumb, so he openeth not his mouth.*
>
> — Isaiah 53:1–7

The prophet Isaiah is telling us that the whipping that Jesus did was for our healing, which was later consummated by His death on the cross. When Jesus died on the cross, He died for your sins, forgiveness of sins, salvation (to be free from sin), healing from all sicknesses, diseases, problems, oppression, depression, to deliver you from witchcraft, voodoo, demons, evil spirits, and the devil. When he died on the cross, He died to experience (note the word peace) this is inner peace, real joy, happiness, contentment, and satisfaction. Everlasting or eternal life was the main reason why Jesus died on the cross.

Secrets are an age-old tactic that, when kept, then revealed either by word, deed, or action, can either cause an element of surprise to affect good or evil, lose or win, experience victory or defeat, or bring joy or sadness, elevate or suppress. Even though the death of Jesus Christ was written about in types and shadows, seen in visions, and prophesied by prophets, there was a secret kept between God and Jesus that the devil and his demons had no clue about, and that was the death of Jesus on the cross.

The devil thought he had Jesus cornered, beat, and whopped. The Scribes, Pharisees with the devil's inspired compromise to crucify Jesus, thought Jesus would be done for, but the very crucifixion of Jesus on the cross turned out to be the devil's nightmare. Even in death, Jesus whopped the devil. Jesus overcame the devil by shedding His blood; just mention the words "the blood of Jesus," and demons tremble and flee.

When Jesus died on the cross, the lighting, the thunder, the rain represented the cleansing of the heavens and the earth by the blood of Jesus; the earthquake that occurred was the purification from sin and, at the same time, opened up the earth and released the Old Testament saints from Abraham's bosom (which was paradise) to above or to heaven. All of the above benefits of Jesus dying on the cross obviously are of utmost importance, but hold on to your seats; here is the front door key of why Jesus died on the cross. He opened up the way for every human being to approach God for themselves. The moment an individual or people repent of their sins and accept Jesus Christ as Lord and Savior and ask Him to wash and cleanse, you and others do the same, and an act of God occurs in you or their lives. This means you become born again, and from this point on, you begin to develop a relationship with the Almighty God.

> *Jesus, when he had cried again with a loud voice, yielded up the ghost.*
>
> *And, behold, the veil of the temple was rent in twain from the top to the bottom; and the earth did quake, and the rocks rent;*
>
> — Matthew 27:50–51

Really! What does the above Scripture mean? Please remember that when Adam and Eve were first made by God and were residents in their first home, Eden, God used to come down in the cool of the day. Now please be mindful of this the Creator God Himself used to come down and spend time with them; this means God used to fellowship, talk, commune, or communicate with Adam and Eve. But after they sinned, they were driven from the presence of God, and from that time, everyone that was born after Adam and Eve God singled out certain people and spoke to them. Moses had a deep yearning for God, and God manifested Himself to Moses in the burning bush. This is the reason when he saw the fire on the bush, instead of dismissing this sight, his curiosity, hunger, and thirst for God drove him up the mountain to find out why the bush was burning with fire and not burnt.

> *Now Moses kept the flock of Jethro his father in law, the priest of Midian: and he led the flock to the backside of the desert, and came to the mountain of God, even to Horeb.*
>
> *And the angel of the Lord appeared unto him in a flame of fire out of the midst of a bush: and he looked, and, behold, the bush burned with fire, and the bush was not consumed.*
>
> *And Moses said, I will now turn aside, and see this great sight, why the bush is not burnt.*
>
> *And when the Lord saw that he turned aside to see, God called unto him out of the midst of the bush, and said, Moses, Moses. And he said, Here am I.*
>
> *And he said, Draw not nigh hither: put off thy shoes from off thy feet, for the place whereon thou standest is holy ground.*
>
> *Moreover he said, I am the God of thy father, the God of Abraham, the God of Isaac, and the God of Jacob. And Moses hid his face; for he was afraid to look upon God.*
>
> *And the Lord said, I have surely seen the affliction of my people which are in Egypt, and have heard their cry by reason of their taskmasters; for I know their sorrows;*
>
> *And I am come down to deliver them out of the hand of the Egyptians, and to bring them up out of that land unto a good land and a large, unto a land flowing with milk and honey; unto the place of the Canaanites, and the Hittites, and the Amorites, and the Perizzites, and the Hivites, and the Jebusites.*

> *Now therefore, behold, the cry of the children of Israel is come unto me: and I have also seen the oppression wherewith the Egyptians oppress them. Now therefore, and I will send thee unto Pharaoh, that thou mayest bring forth my people the children of Israel out of Egypt.*
>
> *And Moses said unto God, Who am I, that I should go unto Pharaoh, and that I should bring forth the children of Israel out of Egypt?*
>
> *And he said, Certainly I will be with thee; and this shall be a token unto thee, that I have sent thee: When thou hast brought forth the people out of Egypt, ye shall serve God upon this mountain.*
>
> *And Moses said unto God, Behold, when I come unto the children of Israel, and shall say unto them, The God of your fathers hath sent me unto you; and they shall say to me, What is his name? what shall I say unto them?*
>
> *And God said unto Moses, i am that i am: and he said, Thus shalt thou say unto the children of Israel, I AM hath sent me unto you.*
>
> *And God said moreover unto Moses, Thus shalt thou say unto the children of Israel, The Lord God of your fathers, the God of Abraham, the God of Isaac, and the God of Jacob, hath sent me unto you: this is my name for ever, and this is my memorial unto all generations.*
>
> *Go, and gather the elders of Israel together, and say unto them, The Lord God of your fathers, the God of Abraham, of Isaac, and of Jacob, appeared unto me, saying, I have surely visited you, and seen that which is done to you in Egypt:*
>
> *And I have said, I will bring you up out of the affliction of Egypt unto the land of the Canaanites, and the Hittites, and the Amorites, and the Perizzites, and the Hivites, and the Jebusites, unto a land flowing with milk and honey.*
>
> *And they shall hearken to thy voice: and thou shalt come, thou and the elders of Israel, unto the king of Egypt, and ye shall say unto him, The Lord God of the Hebrews hath met with us: and now let us go, we beseech thee, three days' journey into the wilderness, that we may sacrifice to the Lord our God. And I am sure that the king of Egypt will not let you go, no, not by a mighty hand.*
>
> *And I will stretch out my hand, and smite Egypt with all my wonders which I will do in the midst thereof: and after that he will let you go.*
>
> *And I will give this people favour in the sight of the Egyptians: and it shall come to pass, that, when ye go, ye shall not go empty:*
>
> *But every woman shall borrow of her neighbour, and of her that sojourneth in her house, jewels of silver, and jewels of gold, and raiment: and ye shall put them upon your sons, and upon your daughters; and ye shall spoil the Egyptians.*
>
> — Exodus 3:1–22

The fire on the bush brought him face to face with God; this experience changed his life, and God placed the responsibility on him to go to Egypt to deliver and lead the children of Israel out of bondage from Egypt into the Promised Land.

During their wilderness journey, God wanted to communicate Himself to the children of Israel through Moses; most of all, He wanted them to see who He was and witness His power and glory. God gave Moses the instruction of erecting a Tabernacle; please read Exodus, chapter 25.

First, there was the outer curtain which formed the Tabernacle or Sanctuary with one front door as an entrance, then was the gate, the brazen altar and the tabernacle of sacrifices, the laver (big basin), menorah (lampstand), table of showbread, the golden altar of incense in the holy place, the holy of holies with the Ark of the Covenant. Between the holy place and the holy of holies was a curtain that separated the Holy Place and the Holy of Holies. This temple curtain was no ordinary curtain; it was sixty feet long, thirty feet high, and about four inches thick; composed of seventy-two squares sewn together; so heavy that it required three hundred men to lift it. For it to be torn suddenly from top to bottom (rather than gradually fraying from bottom to top) would indeed be a noteworthy event, especially for Jewish people.

This curtain was between the Holy Place and the Holy of Holies. From the Holy Place to the Holy of Holies, only the High Priest alone could have entered the Holy of Holies with a rope tied to himself if he had entered into the Holy of Holies with sin in his life after a period of time if he did not come out and the other priests waiting outside they knew he had died and they had to drag him out. But please get this—only one man could have gone into the Holy of Holies to represent God to the people and the people to God. Even though God used to speak to certain people, prophets, kings, and individuals as they communicated with the people what God said and required, generally speaking, hardly anyone really had the privilege of going to God for themselves, but when Jesus died on the cross and the Bible, the Word of God, says Jesus, when He had cried again with a loud voice, yielded up the ghost. And, behold, the veil of the temple was rent in twain from top to bottom. When Jesus died on the cross, spiritually speaking, the curtain that separated mankind from God was literally torn from top to bottom, and the way was opened for all mankind. This means whosoever and wherever to come to God through Jesus Christ's sacrificial death on the cross.

> *And as Moses lifted up the serpent in the wilderness, even so must the Son of Man be lifted up,*
> *That whoever believes in Him should not perish but have eternal life.*
> *For God so loved the world that He gave His only begotten Son, that whoever believes in Him should not perish but have everlasting life.*
> *For God did not send His Son into the world to condemn the world, but that the world through Him might be saved.*
>
> —John 3:14–17

"And I, if I be lifted up from the earth, will draw all men unto me" John 12:32. The apostles always preached Jesus died on the cross but always combined this with the resurrection of Jesus and the outpouring of the Holy Spirit.

The resurrection of Jesus is important for several reasons. First, it witnesses the immense power of God Himself. To believe in the resurrection is to believe in God. The resurrection proves that God exists, and if He created the universe, He has power over it. He has power to raise the dead. If He does not have such power, He is not a God worthy of our faith and worship. Only He who created life can resurrect it after death; only He can reverse the hideousness that is death itself, and only He can remove the sting that is death and the victory that is the grave. In resurrecting Jesus from the grave, God reminds us of His absolute sovereignty over life and death. Second, the resurrection of Jesus is a testimony to the resurrection of human beings, which is a basic tenet of the Christian faith. Unlike all other religions, Christianity alone possesses a Founder who transcends death and who promises that His followers will do the same. All other religions were founded by men and prophets whose end was the grave. As Christians, we take comfort in the fact that our God became man, died for our sins, and was resurrected on the third day. The grave could not hold Him. He lives, and He sits today at the right hand of God the Father in heaven.

Paul explains in detail the importance of the resurrection of Christ. Some in Corinth did not believe in the resurrection of the dead, and in this chapter, Paul gives six disastrous consequences: if there were no resurrection—preaching Christ would be senseless. The author, yours truly, had to interject this entire chapter at this point because it is one of the most important chapters in the Bible pertaining to the resurrection.

> *Moreover, brethren, I declare unto you the gospel which I preached unto you, which also ye have received, and wherein ye stand;*
>
> *By which also ye are saved, if ye keep in memory what I preached unto you, unless ye have believed in vain.*
>
> *For I delivered unto you first of all that which I also received, how that Christ died for our sins according to the scriptures;*
>
> *And that he was buried, and that he rose again the third day according to the scriptures:*
>
> *And that he was seen of Cephas, then of the twelve:*
>
> *After that, he was seen of above five hundred brethren at once; of whom the greater part remain unto this present, but some are fallen asleep.*
>
> *After that, he was seen of James; then of all the apostles.*
>
> *And last of all he was seen of me also, as of one born out of due time.*
>
> *For I am the least of the apostles, that am not meet to be called an apostle, because I persecuted the church of God.*
>
> *But by the grace of God I am what I am: and his grace which was bestowed upon me was not in vain; but I laboured more abundantly than they all: yet not I, but the grace of God which was with me.*
>
> *Therefore whether it were I or they, so we preach, and so ye believed.*
>
> *Now if Christ be preached that he rose from the dead, how say some among you that there is no resurrection of the dead?*
>
> *But if there be no resurrection of the dead, then is Christ not risen:*
>
> *And if Christ be not risen, then is our preaching vain, and your faith is also vain.*
>
> *Yea, and we are found false witnesses of God; because we have testified of God that he raised up Christ: whom he raised not up, if so be that the dead rise not.*
>
> *For if the dead rise not, then is not Christ raised:*
>
> *And if Christ be not raised, your faith is vain; ye are yet in your sins.*
>
> *Then they also which are fallen asleep in Christ are perished.*
>
> *If in this life only we have hope in Christ, we are of all men most miserable.*

But now is Christ risen from the dead, and become the firstfruits of them that slept.

For since by man came death, by man came also the resurrection of the dead.

For as in Adam all die, even so in Christ shall all be made alive.

But every man in his own order: Christ the firstfruits; afterward they that are Christ's at his coming.

Then cometh the end, when he shall have delivered up the kingdom to God, even the Father; when he shall have put down all rule and all authority and power.

For he must reign, till he hath put all enemies under his feet.

The last enemy that shall be destroyed is death.

For he hath put all things under his feet. But when he saith all things are put under him, it is manifest that he is excepted, which did put all things under him.

And when all things shall be subdued unto him, then shall the Son also himself be subject unto him that put all things under him, that God may be all in all.

Else what shall they do which are baptized for the dead, if the dead rise not at all? why are they then baptized for the dead?

And why stand we in jeopardy every hour?

I protest by your rejoicing which I have in Christ Jesus our Lord, I die daily.

If after the manner of men I have fought with beasts at Ephesus, what advantageth it me, if the dead rise not? let us eat and drink; for to morrow we die. Be not deceived: evil communications corrupt good manners.

Awake to righteousness, and sin not; for some have not the knowledge of God: I speak this to your shame.

But some man will say, How are the dead raised up? and with what body do they come?

Thou fool, that which thou sowest is not quickened, except it die:

And that which thou sowest, thou sowest not that body that shall be, but bare grain, it may chance of wheat, or of some other grain:

But God giveth it a body as it hath pleased him, and to every seed his own body.

All flesh is not the same flesh: but there is one kind of flesh of men, another flesh of beasts, another of fishes, and another of birds.

There are also celestial bodies, and bodies terrestrial: but the glory of the celestial is one, and the glory of the terrestrial is another.

There is one glory of the sun, and another glory of the moon, and another glory of the stars: for one star differeth from another star in glory.

So also is the resurrection of the dead. It is sown in corruption; it is raised in incorruption:

It is sown in dishonour; it is raised in glory: it is sown in weakness; it is raised in power:

It is sown a natural body; it is raised a spiritual body. There is a natural body, and there is a spiritual body.

And so it is written, The first man Adam was made a living soul; the last Adam was made a quickening spirit.

Howbeit that was not first which is spiritual, but that which is natural; and afterward that which is spiritual.

The first man is of the earth, earthy: the second man is the Lord from heaven.

As is the earthy, such are they also that are earthy: and as is the heavenly, such are they also that are heavenly.

And as we have borne the image of the earthy, we shall also bear the image of the heavenly. Now this I say, brethren, that flesh and blood cannot inherit the kingdom of God; neither doth corruption inherit incorruption.

Behold, I shew you a mystery; We shall not all sleep, but we shall all be changed,

In a moment, in the twinkling of an eye, at the last trump: for the trumpet shall sound, and the dead shall be raised incorruptible, and we shall be changed.

For this corruptible must put on incorruption, and this mortal must put on immortality.

So when this corruptible shall have put on incorruption, and this mortal shall have put on immortality, then shall be brought to pass the saying that is written, Death is swallowed up in victory.

O death, where is thy sting? O grave, where is thy victory?

The sting of death is sin; and the strength of sin is the law.

But thanks be to God, which giveth us the victory through our Lord Jesus Christ.

Therefore, my beloved brethren, be ye stedfast, unmoveable, always abounding in the work of the Lord, forasmuch as ye know that your labour is not in vain in the Lord.

— 1 Corinthians 15:1–58

One of the biggest arguments against the Christian faith is that the resurrection story is a myth that developed over as much as a century after Jesus was crucified on a Roman cross. It was originally thought that the gospel accounts were written as much as one hundred years after Jesus walked the earth. Recent scholarship in manuscript reliability and textual criticism now places the gospels at thirty to fifty years after Jesus. Why is the above passage so important? Because biblical scholars, using the historical records of Paul and his early travels to Damascus and Jerusalem, place the above scripture at about AD 35; this is dramatic because those same scholars would hold that this basic creed for the Christian faith developed far too quickly for a myth to develop and distort the historical record of the resurrection. Since the foundation of the Christian faith is Jesus Christ and His resurrection, then the historical veracity of His life, death, and resurrection are tantamount.

For as Paul declared later in his letter to the Corinthians:

And if Christ be not risen, then is our preaching vain, and your faith is also vain.

Yea, and we are found false witnesses of God; because we have testified of God that he raised up Christ: whom he raised not up, if so be that the dead rise not. For if the dead rise not, then is not Christ raised:

And if Christ be not raised, your faith is vain; ye are yet in your sins.

— 1 Corinthians 15:14–17

The apostles in the book of Acts often reiterated that the souls that were being saved, the healings, miracles, signs, and supernatural things that were happening as they preached the word under the unction of the power of the Holy Spirit were attested to the fact that Jesus was alive. The priestly work of Jesus Christ, answered prayer, supernatural occurrences, results, miracles, healings, the power of God manifesting while the word of God is being preached, the souls that are saved, and more attest to the fact that Jesus is alive and working through the power of the Holy Spirit in His followers.

> *Be it known unto you all, and to all the people of Israel, that by the name of Jesus Christ of Nazareth, whom ye crucified, whom God raised from the dead, even by him doth this man stand here before you whole.*
>
> — Acts 4:10

The message of the early Christians and the focal point of the New Testament were stated in this simple truth by the apostle Paul—this is the central truth of the Christian faith. The importance of the resurrection of Jesus Christ cannot be overemphasized. Without the resurrection, there is no Christianity. The resurrection was central to the teaching and preaching of the apostles. It was the subject of every sermon we find in the book of Acts. "Therefore let all Israel be assured of this: God has made this Jesus, whom you crucified, both Lord and Christ" Acts 2:36, NIV.

Without the resurrection, Christianity has no meaning for humanity—its founder would have been a liar and a failure, and its followers would have no hope. Thus the importance of the resurrection to the Christian faith cannot be overestimated. There are those who say that even without the resurrection, Christianity has significance. They hold that Christ's teachings provide ethical guidelines for humanity. The New Testament, however, testifies that this is not the case. Without the resurrection, there is no meaningful Christianity.

> *Now if Christ is preached that He has been raised from the dead, how do some among you say that there is no resurrection of the dead?*
>
> *But if there is no resurrection of the dead, then Christ is not risen.*
>
> *And if Christ is not risen, then our preaching is empty and your faith is also empty.*
>
> *Yes, and we are found false witnesses of God, because we have testified of God that He raised up Christ, whom He did not raise up—if in fact the dead do not rise.*
>
> *For if the dead do not rise, then Christ is not risen.*
>
> *And if Christ is not risen, your faith is futile; you are still in your sins!*
>
> *Then also those who have fallen asleep in Christ have perished.*
>
> *If in this life only we have hope in Christ, we are of all men the most pitiable.*
>
> — 1 Corinthians 15:12–19

Then those also who have fallen asleep in Christ have perished. If we have hoped in Christ in this life only, we are of all people most to be pitied; we add further areas of importance of Christ's resurrection. It is important to Jesus' identity, to His true character, to His ministry, and to His message. The resurrection of Jesus Christ is unique to the Christian faith; no other religious figure has ever predicted his own resurrection and then accomplished it. Other entire world religions are based on a founder who lived in the past and whose religion is his only legacy. Mohammed died at age sixty-one on June 8, AD 632, in Medina. He is still dead. Confucius died, and Buddha also died. They also remain dead.

Jesus Christ is alive; Paul said that Christian preaching is empty if Jesus did not come back from the dead. The faith of the believer is worthless if Christ is not raised because He is the object of the faith. In addition, Christ is not who He said He was. He would have been a liar. The apostles are also liars for testifying to a resurrection that did not occur. Furthermore, there is no forgiveness for anybody's sin.

Those who have died believing in Christ have no hope. If hope in Christ is limited to this life, Christians are to be pitied above all people. The resurrection is also important to the identity and mission of Jesus. First, the resurrection is important to His identity. The resurrection is the demonstration that Jesus indeed is the Son of God. The resurrection is also important to His character. Jesus would not have been a true prophet had He not come back from the dead as He predicted that He would. It is important to Jesus' ministry. If He did not come back from the dead, then His ministry would have ended in defeat. Finally, it is important to His message. The centrality of the Christian message is that Jesus died and then came back from the dead. If He did not come back from the dead, then there is no Christianity. Consequently, we see that the resurrection of Jesus Christ is absolutely crucial and of utmost importance to the Christian faith.

HELL

Jesus and the apostles obviously did teach and preach about heaven and hell. A minister who preaches about heaven or hell in this day and time is considered out of touch, rational, and does not fit in modern times is out of touch with society.

Heaven and hell were the subjects of a good Sunday night evangelistic healing meetings with songs like "Let the healing waters flow," "When we all get to heaven," or "Running for my life" used to be sung with fervor and meaning with foot-stomping and hands clapping, after which the pastors used preach like he or she is really going to heaven and running from hell. Well! Those days are over now; the Sunday night evangelistic meeting died a natural and spiritual death many years ago, and because some pastors and church members killed it, so is the preaching of *heaven and hell*.

This, of course, was substituted by a huge plasma TV screen to view the latest sporting event or movie; while some would either hit the clubs, beach, or movie theater, then most church members wonder why sinners do not attend church in some areas. Praise God for the pastors and people whose courage is not and will not be intimidated by those who have killed or are killing the Sunday night meeting. Two reasons for this can be explained in this way laziness or worldliness.

The meaning of or the definition of the word "hell" of which there are three words from the Greek language that defines the word hell; they are *Tartaroo, Hades*, and *Gehenna*. Let us look at their meanings in the KJV of the Bible. The term *hell* is used fifty-four times, thirty-one times in the Old Testament, and twenty-three times in the New Testament. What is the meaning of the word *hell* in the Bible? In the Old Testament, it is translated from one word, *Sheol*. In the New Testament, "*hell*" is translated from Greek *Tartaroo* New Testament. *Hell* is translated only one time from Tartaroo, which is from the root *Tartaros*, which means the deepest abyss of *Hades*.

Peter was writing about a place of flames and torments, "For God did not spare even the angels who sinned, but threw them into hell, chained in gloomy caves and darkness until the judgment day" 2 Peter 2:4.

Sheol—Hebrew Old Testament; *Hades*—Greek New Testament. What is the meaning of the word *hell* in the Old Testament? *Hell* is always translated from the Hebrew word *Sheol* which is used sixty-five times in the Old Testament and means simply *hell* or *Sheol*—is where the wicked go. The Greek Septuagint, which our Lord used when he read or quoted from the Old Testament, gives *Hades* as the exact equivalent of the Hebrew *Sheol*, and when the Savior, or His apostles, used the word, they meant the same as is meant in the Old Testament. Thus, the New Testament usage agrees exactly with the Old Testament. Literally, *Hades* means *hell* and is the same as *Hades*; it is used eleven times in the New Testament. It is translated ten times as "hell." Hades means "the place or state of departed souls." Hell is translated twelve times from *Gehenna* or, as it is sometimes transliterated, *Geenna*.

This is the Greek equivalent of the Hebrew word *Hinnom*, which is the name of a valley outside Jerusalem where garbage and the carcasses of animals were cast into and consumed by fire constantly, kept burning. Thus, *Gehenna* is the only one of those words translated as *hell* in the Bible that has any idea of fire or torment resident in it. Look at Matthew 5:22,

> *But I say unto you, That whosoever is angry with his brother without a cause shall be in danger of the judgment: and whosoever shall say to his brother, Raca, shall be in danger of the council: but whosoever shall say, Thou fool, shall be in danger of hell fire.*
>
> — Matthew 5:22

"And if thine eye offend thee, pluck it out, and cast it from thee: it is better for thee to enter into life with one eye, rather than having two eyes to be cast into hell fire" Matthew 18:9. *Gehenna* is also used in Luke 12:5, "But I will forewarn you whom ye shall fear: Fear him, which after he hath killed hath power to cast into hell; yea, I say unto you, Fear him."

Matthew 8:12; 13:42 clearly states an example of "eternal" fire. This is the same Greek word that is used for "everlasting fire" punishment, "But the children of the kingdom shall be cast out into outer darkness: there shall be weeping and gnashing of teeth" Matthew 8:12. "And shall cast them into a furnace of fire: there shall be wailing and gnashing of teeth" Matthew 13:42.

Hell is "everlasting punishment." The Bible plainly teaches that hell is on this earth; so far as we can tell from Scripture, the present *hell* is somewhere in the heart of the earth itself. It is also called the pit.

> *Then shall he say also unto them on the left hand, Depart from me, ye cursed, into everlasting fire, prepared for the devil and his angels:*
> *For I was an hungred, and ye gave me no meat: I was thirsty, and ye gave me no drink:*
> *I was a stranger, and ye took me not in: naked, and ye clothed me not: sick, and in prison, and ye visited me not.*
> *Then shall they also answer him, saying, Lord, when saw we thee an hungred, or athirst, or a stranger, or naked, or sick, or in prison, and did not minister unto thee?*
> *Then shall he answer them, saying, Verily I say unto you, Inasmuch as ye did it not to one of the least of these, ye did it not to me.*

And these shall go away into everlasting punishment: but the righteous into life eternal.
— Matthew 25:41–46

Isaiah 14:9, 15 and Ezekiel 32:18–21 make reference to an abyss, "Hell from beneath is moved for thee to meet thee at thy coming: it stirreth up the dead for thee, even all the chief ones of the earth; it hath raised up from their thrones all the kings of the nations" Isaiah 14:9.

And he opened the bottomless pit; and there arose a smoke out of the pit, as the smoke of a great furnace; and the sun and the air were darkened by reason of the smoke of the pit.
— Revelation 9:2

The author certainly believes there is a hell to be real and geographically *beneath* the earth's surface. To say this is not scientific is to assume science knows much more about the earth's interior than is actually the case. The great pit (hell) would only need to be about one hundred miles or less in diameter to contain, with much room to spare, all the forty billion or so people who have ever lived, assuming their spiritual bodies are the same sizes their physical bodies. The earth's inner core has a temperature of over 12,000 degrees Fahrenheit. You have seen pictures of a volcano erupting, spewing ponds of fire from inside the earth consuming everything within its pathway from its heat. There were reports when Mount Saint Helens in Washington State erupted on May 18th, 1980; reporters described the scene as hell open its mouth.

Jesus Christ gives a frightening picture of hell in Luke, chapter 16, and a must printing these verses in this book,

There was a certain rich man, which was clothe in purple and fine linen and fared sumptuously every day,

And there was a certain beggar named Lazarus full of sores,

And it came to pass the rich man also died, and was buried;

And in hell he lift up his eyes, being in torments, and seeth Abraham afar off, and Lazarus in his bosom.

And he cried and said, Father Abraham, have mercy on me, and send Lazarus, that he may dip the tip of his finger in water, and cool my tongue; for I am tormented in this flame.

But Abraham said, Son, remember that thou in thy lifetime receivedst thy good things, and likewise Lazarus evil things: but now he is comforted, and thou art tormented.

And beside all this, between us and you there is a great gulf fixed: so that they which would pass from hence to you cannot; neither can they pass to us, that would come from thence.

Then he said, I pray thee therefore, father, that thou wouldest send him to my father's house:

For I have five brethren; that he may testify unto them, lest they also come into this place of torment.

Abraham saith unto him they have Moses and the prophets, let them hear them,

And he said, Nay, father Abraham: but if one went unto them, they will repent

And he said unto him, if they hear not Moses and the prophets, neither will they be persuaded if one rose from the dead.
— Luke 16:19–31

Hell is a place of fire. The rich man that Luke 16:24 spoke about said, "I am tormented in this flame."

Jesus says, "And shall cast them into a furnace of fire there shall be wailing and gnashing of teeth" Matthew 13:42.

In Matthew 25:41, Jesus says, "[…] Depart from me, ye cursed, into everlasting fire […]."

Revelation 20:15 says, "And whosoever was not found written in the book of life was cast into the lake of fire."

The Bible gives the location of hell. When Jesus Christ died on the cross, He descended into hell; Peter made reference to this, "He seeing this before spake of the resurrection of Christ, that his soul was not left in hell, neither his flesh did see corruption" Acts 2:31.

And in Matthew 12:40, Jesus Christ says, "For as Jonas was three days and three nights in the whale's belly: so shall the Son of man be three days and three nights in the heart of the earth."

The Bible gives the account of people falling into hell alive!

> *And the earth opened her mouth, and swallowed them up, and their houses, and all the men that appertained unto Korah, and all their goods.*
>
> *They, and all that appertained to them, went down alive into the pit, and the earth closed upon them: and they perished from among the congregation.*
>
> — Numbers 16:32–33

They went down alive into the pit, and the earth closed upon them. Jesus Christ says about hell, "Where their worm dieth not, and the fire is not quenched" Mark 9:46. Jesus said plainly, "Their worm dieth not."

Everyone should read this Scripture because this is where it sets the record straight about hell; this entire chapter is of utmost importance in particular. Again, here is a must that this Scripture must be printed about hell,

> *And I saw a great white throne, and him that sat on it, from whose face the earth and the heaven fled away; and there was found no place for them.*
>
> *And I saw the dead, small and great, stand before God; and the books were opened: and another book was opened, which is the book of life: and the dead were judged out of those things which were written in the books, according to their works.*
>
> *And the sea gave up the dead who were in it; and death and hell delivered up the dead which were in them: and they were judged every man according to their works.*
>
> *And death and hell were cast into the lake of fire. This is the second death. And whosoever was not found written in the book of life was cast into the lake of fire.*
>
> — Revelation 20:11–15

Anyone reading the Bible, especially Jesus teaching on the subject of hell, should come to a somber, solemn realization that He was God Himself in the flesh. What He preached and taught about hell should cause us, and, in particular, you, reader, that hell is real. Advocates of the modernist movement and other modernistic movements, so call religious teachers, communist, atheistic advocates, and countries who believe the same, even in our country, the US right now is experiencing a wave of socialistic advocates, plus our universities, millennia's at the present time with certain individuals running for president, some of them are obsessed with the fact that there is no God. Homosexuality, lesbianism, same-sex marriage, abortion to the point of when a baby or babies are born to kill the baby after birth and some of these mothers allowing the same with no heart, feelings, or compassion for these babies who are gifts from God. What will you do on Judgment Day?

God does not send anyone to hell! If anyone goes to hell, it is because they choose to go there; why? Because God gave everyone human the power of choice, did you ever realize that God cannot choose for us, but humans have the power to choose God or the devil, heaven or hell? Therefore, if anyone goes to hell, it is not God to be blamed; He already did what He had to do? This is the reason He sent Jesus Christ to die on the cross, yes! Mankind will be judged for their evil deeds, but most of all, mankind will be judged by refusing God's way to escape hell, and this is by accepting what Jesus did for the human race on the Cross.

> *The Lord is not slack concerning his promise, as some men count slackness; but is longsuffering to us-ward, not willing that any should perish, but that all should come to repentance. [This is the only way an individual can escape hell.]*
>
> — 2 Peter 3:9

HEAVEN

Heaven, surprisingly so, according to a poll conducted by a leading TV network reported that nine out of ten people (9 out of 10) in the United States believe there's a heaven. God imbedded deep within every human a hope of the afterlife. This hope of the afterlife is expressed by most religious people who believe in reincarnation or some sort of life after death and beyond the grave. Here are some comments that the author has heard in fifty-five years of ministry, "Energy never vanishes; it will take another form—a soul. If you believe there is a soul, then it can not be left unnoticed; after death, the so-called soul becomes another form of energy; it may be another soul, and believe me, energy cannot be destroyed."

There are many religions that believe in life after death and expect to depart to a good place; it just depends on what religion you are asking about because different religions have different points of view of what happens when you die, then the spirit goes to some kind of paradise. Most Eastern religions (Buddhism, Hinduism, etc.) believe you get reincarnated as someone, something else after death, according to your Karma, the good or the bad things you've done.

Christianity defines heaven as being in the presence of God with places prepared for the faithful by Jesus and is viewed as eternal bliss beyond that which can currently be known. Those who are allowed into heaven are given new bodies that do not decay, and death will be gone. Marriage is not a part of heaven. It is also possible there are different levels of heaven. According to the apostle Paul, who describes his journey to the third heaven, the conditions to enter heaven in Christianity are defined by Jesus in the Gospel, where He commands everyone to follow His laws and commandments to enter heaven and escape hell.

According to the Bible and the apostle Paul, the whole person survives. Even the body is raised again so that if it is no longer flesh and blood. "Now this I say, brethren, that flesh and blood cannot inherit the kingdom of God; neither does corruption inherit incorruption" 1 Corinthians 15:50.

It, nevertheless, has continuity with the present body, sameness in form, if not in material element,

So then they that are in the flesh cannot please God.

But ye are not in the flesh, but in the Spirit, if so be that the Spirit of God dwell in you. Now if any man have not the Spirit of Christ, he is none of his.

— Romans 8:8–9

In heaven, the redeemed will be in the immediate presence of God. And will forever live from the glory and presence of God, beholding the glory of Jesus' face. Though there is much conjecture about what heaven is like, its central core is that we will be with Jesus Himself. He has entered back into the presence of the Father and has conveyed to us that the redeemed of the Lord will likewise be with Him where He is. Paradise may be to heaven as the foyer may be to the inner room of a great mansion.

Without a doubt, Jesus responded to the penitent thief on the cross who was turning to Him and said, "[…] Lord, remember me when thou comest into thy kingdom. And Jesus said unto him, Verily I say unto thee, Today shalt thou be with me in paradise" Luke 23:42–43. He also said, "[…] where I am, there you may be also" John 14:3, NKJV. And speaking of the time that we will be in the presence of Jesus, John the apostle says, "[…] we shall be like Him, for we shall see Him as He is" 1 John 3:2b, NKJV. "[…] eye hath not seen, nor ear heard, neither have entered into the heart of man, the things which God hath prepared for them that love him" 1 Corinthians 2:9.

With regard to what heaven actually looks like, our human mind is limited, but certain is that the reality of heaven is beyond earthly comprehension, as we can acknowledge from Paul, when he speaks to the Corinthians, saying, "They truly signify Christ, who is glorified in them. They make manifest the cloud of witnesses who continue to participate in the salvation of the world and to whom we are united, above all in sacramental celebrations."

The essential joy of heaven is called the beatific vision, which is derived from the vision of God's essence. The soul rests perfectly in God and does not or cannot desire anything else than God. After the Last Judgment, when the soul is reunited with its body, the body participates in the happiness of the soul. It becomes incorruptible, glorious, and perfect. Any physical defects the body may have labored under are erased. Heaven is also equated with paradise in some cases.

The characteristics of the new creation tell us that it will be vastly different from what we are used to on earth. Probably the most noticeable difference will be the lack of gravity. The New Jerusalem is described as a 1,500-mile cube. Structures of this size would automatically become a sphere in this universe because of gravity. Therefore gravity will either be absent or significantly reduced in the new creation. There will be no Sun or Moon. This makes sense since there will be little or no gravity. Without gravity, the new creation would not be bound to its source of heat and light. The lack of the Sun is not a problem for the new creation since the Bible tells us that the glory of God Himself will provide illumination. The illumination provided by God is probably not the same kind of electromagnetic radiation (photons) that we call light.

The illumination provided by God certainly involves the wisdom and knowledge that He possesses with this kind of light; there would be no need to visually see things since this would severely restrict our ability to see everything as God sees them. There will be no oceans, which means that there will be no water cycle. It would be difficult for a water cycle to operate without gravity. There will be the river of the water of life, which flows from the throne of God.

The Bible tells us that there will be no heat. In this universe, the second law of thermodynamics controls virtually everything that happens. The law states that heat flows from hot bodies to cold bodies. Stars cannot shine, animals cannot consume food to produce energy to move, and chemical reactions cannot occur since all these processes require the exchange of heat. This law is also called the law of entropy or decay since the ultimate result of heat flow is that the universe continues to become more and more disordered. Science tells us that the universe, as we see it now, is temporary. It has a moment of creation and, without God's intervention, will eventually expand to produce a collection of cold, lifeless matter.

Obviously, such a universe would not be acceptable for housing eternal beings, such as those described in the new creation. As discussed previously, the processes requiring heat flow seem to be absent from the new creation. These include the Sun, the sea, the water cycle, and growing old and dying. Although there is described a tree (the tree of life) that bears fruit in heaven, it doesn't seem to be there for eating. In fact, the Bible says the leaves of the tree are for the healing of the nations; given all the violence and genocide that has been perpetrated on the earth over the centuries, there will be a need for healing among all the people groups. The lack of eating in heaven goes along with the idea that thermodynamics will be absent there. Finally, the Bible says the creation itself also will be set free from its slavery to corruption, suggesting a release from the laws of thermodynamics.

The record and description of heaven are of utmost importance; this is the reason the author decided to interject and print the Word of God, the Bible, when needed in this book; here is apostle John's interpretation and vision of heaven while he was imprisoned on the Isle of Pathos.

> *And I saw a new heaven and a new earth: for the first heaven and the first earth were passed away; and there was no more sea.*
>
> *And I John saw the holy city, new Jerusalem, coming down from God out of heaven, prepared as a bride adorned for her husband.*
>
> *And I heard a great voice out of heaven saying, Behold, the tabernacle of God is with men, and he will dwell with them, and they shall be his people, and God himself shall be with them, and be their God.*
>
> *And God shall wipe away all tears from their eyes; and there shall be no more death, neither sorrow, nor crying, neither shall there be any more pain: for the former things are passed away.*
>
> *And he that sat upon the throne said, Behold, I make all things new. And he said unto me, Write: for these words are true and faithful.*
>
> *And he said unto me, It is done. I am Alpha and Omega, the beginning and the end. I will give unto him that is athirst of the fountain of the water of life freely.*
>
> *He that overcometh shall inherit all things; and I will be his God, and he shall be my son.*
>
> *But the fearful, and unbelieving, and the abominable, and murderers, and whoremongers, and sorcerers, and idolaters, and all liars, shall have their part in the lake which burneth with fire and brimstone: which is the second death.*
>
> *And there came unto me one of the seven angels which had the seven vials full of the seven last plagues, and talked with me, saying, Come hither, I will shew thee the bride, the Lamb's wife.*

And he carried me away in the spirit to a great and high mountain, and shewed me that great city, the holy Jerusalem, descending out of heaven from God,

like unto a stone most precious, even like a jasper stone, clear as crystal;

And had a wall great and high, and had twelve gates, and at the gates twelve angels, and names written thereon, which are the names of the twelve tribes of the children of Israel:

On the east three gates; on the north three gates; on the south three gates; and on the west three gates.

And the wall of the city had twelve foundations, and in them the names of the twelve apostles of the Lamb.

And he that talked with me had a golden reed to measure the city, and the gates thereof, and the wall thereof.

And the city lieth foursquare, and the length is as large as the breadth: and he measured the city with the reed, twelve thousand furlongs. The length and the breadth and the height of it are equal.

And he measured the wall thereof, an hundred and forty and four cubits, according to the measure of a man, that is, of the angel.

And the building of the wall of it was of jasper: and the city was pure gold, like unto clear glass.

And the foundations of the wall of the city were garnished with all manner of precious stones. The first foundation was jasper; the second, sapphire; the third, a chalcedony; the fourth, an emerald;

The fifth, sardonyx; the sixth, sardius; the seventh, chrysolite; the eighth, beryl; the ninth, a topaz; the tenth, a chrysoprasus; the eleventh, a jacinth; the twelfth, an amethyst.

And the twelve gates were twelve pearls; every several gate was of one pearl: and the street of the city was pure gold, as it were transparent glass.

And I saw no temple therein: for the Lord God Almighty and the Lamb are the temple of it.

And the city had no need of the sun, neither of the moon, to shine in it: for the glory of God did lighten it, and the Lamb is the light thereof.

And the nations of them which are saved shall walk in the light of it: and the kings of the earth do bring their glory and honour into it.

And the gates of it shall not be shut at all by day: for there shall be no night there.

And they shall bring the glory and honour of the nations into it.

And there shall in no wise enter into it any thing that defileth, neither whatsoever worketh abomination, or maketh a lie: but they which are written in the Lamb's book of life.

— Revelation 21:16–27

They cite the great wedding feast of the Lamb. Is this meant to be taken literally? Of course, the most important part of the wedding is not the feast, but the marriage. Are we going to be married in a literal physical marriage to Jesus Christ? Obviously no! This will be a spiritual wedding. We will be with our Savior and our Father in heaven and see Him face to face. I believe that the Jewish wedding was chosen to represent the celebration that will happen in heaven since it was a most joyous and lengthy event known to the people for whom the message was given. One can be certain it will be a great celebration, whether or not we actually eat food.

The new creation will be a place of awesome beauty and is described in terms of precious jewels and metals. Although the description (may not) represent literal earthly jewels, it is intended to represent the amazing beauty of its appearance, as John, the apostle, saw it. For a preview of the description, heaven's timelessness exists outside the dimensions of both space and time.

Once the choices have been made, there is no longer a need for time to exist at all. So, when the Bible says God destroys the present universe and time, in fact, it does not matter when you die; you will end up in heaven with all the other people you know who went to be in heaven. This includes your saved ancestors and descendants. Since we are not restricted by time in heaven, could you look back at your life on earth and watch it happen? Probably not since the Bible says that the former things will not be remembered or come to mind (Isaiah 65:17).

When God destroys the present universe, it will have been as if it had never existed. No one would have access to it.

How do things happen in the absence of time?

Good question! Obviously instantly! There will be no more waiting for anything. Everybody will be able to talk to Jesus for an infinite amount of time, all simultaneously. Of course, there would be a new language that all would understand.

Where is heaven?

Asking where heaven exists is a little like asking where the center of the universe is. In fact, the universe doesn't have a center since everything is moving away from every other thing. The Bible indicates that heaven does not exist in this universe but is God's abode. In fact, the Bible indicates that even the highest heavens of this universe cannot contain God. Since we, human beings, are restricted to the space-time dimensions of this universe, we can never go into a spaceship and find heaven since it is not any place to which we can travel. However, there is a way to get there, but by being saved and born again and having the nature of Christ, born again or saved people will be recognizable in heaven, as a matter of fact, if you have families who have gone on before to heaven, you will be able to recognize them only much younger because they will have the same physical resemblance but a glorified body.

CHAPTER 9

The Church May Ice in the Summer

A season is the division of the year, marked by changes in the weather, ecology, and hours of daylight. The four seasons are winter, spring, autumn or fall, and summer. Most people obviously like spring and summertime. Summertime is the time that people plan and follow through for travel, holiday, beach parties, overseas trips and vacation, summer camps, fishing trips, outside grilling, cookouts, sporting events, sailing on boats, yard sales, and flea markets. As a matter of fact, people are more relaxed and loosed in the summer. People do more traveling than any time within the year. The author was inspired by the Holy Spirit to write this book while driving and conducting revival meetings in the US during the wintertime. While driving, you obviously will come to some bridges, where there are signs that read like this as you approach these bridges "Bridge may ice in the winter." This is where the thought hit the author who produced this book—*The Church May Ice in the Summer*. Now, notice it says—"*may ice in the summer.*" Negativism obviously is not the purpose of this book but to bring us back to the point of restoration, revival, and a move of the Holy Spirit like unto the ministry of the prophets, Jesus, and the apostles, even greater as Jesus stated.

While conducting some revival meetings in New York, a prominent pastor friend decided to introduce me to another minister who has a church or congregation in New Jersey. We drove for about two hours, and after arriving at our destination, we parked on the church compounds with the intention of meeting the pastor. To our disappointment, there was a sign on the door which read "closed for the summer." We were very disappointed, but the thought did cross my mind how could a church be closed (a week or so, okay) but for the entire summer? Remember the song by Sam Cooke, "Summertime," and the living is easy, well! These words express the sentiment of summertime. Realizing people work hard most of the year when summertime arrives, they deserve some rest, relaxation, and recuperation. Generally speaking, summertime is a time people tend to be more at ease; there are more activities, less work (some do) during the summer; kids are away from school, and parents use this opportunity to travel and take vacations. During the summer month's ministries, pastors are susceptible to dwindling attendance and financial problems. It's a time of ease, pleasure, and getting away from certain commitments and responsibilities.

Summer is the warmest season of the year and starts at the summer solstice and runs till the autumnal equinox. The word summer derives from Old Norse "*sumar*" but ultimately is from Proto-Germanic. By the late 1500s to early 1600s, it locked into its current spelling, summer. The term summer actually refers to the day of the summer solstice as well as the "middle of summer." Its formation was patterned on words like midday, midnight, and midwinter. Bonfire comes from the words bone and fire, referring to an open-air burning of bones or funeral pyre during the summertime. The Oxford English Dictionary describes the practice in Scotland of *ritual bane-fire* and also the annual midsummer rite *banefire* or *bonfire* in the burgh of Hawick, for which bones were collected and stored regularly until around 1800. Lighting bone-fires (bonfires) was one of the most universal of ancient midsummer rites and one that still survives in some northern European countries. The solstice bone-fires were believed to prevent cattle disease and were also associated with human courtship and fertility. Observances of the summer solstice are rare; there were celebrations in ancient times in Europe, the British Isles, China, Egypt, North Africa, and Scandinavia.

After reading the above paragraphs, it's beginning to dawn on you, the reader, why such a title was chosen for this book, *The Church May Ice in the Summer*. Naturally speaking, it's impossible for anything to freeze or ice in the summer. But spiritually speaking, the Church may ice in the summer. The word summer came from the word "sumar" and had its origin from Proto-Germanic; by the late 1500s to 1600s, it was locked into its present-day spelling—summer.

Within the years from the 1400s to 1800s, the people used to have bonfires; during this time, at midnight, they used to gather a collection of human bones and conduct what they called bone-fires, now translated as bonfire. According to history, this rite started at midnight and continued throughout the morning, culminating in illicit sex and husbands and wives swapping. The burning of bones was also a ceremony to prevent cattle disease and to encourage human courtship and fertility. *Sumar*—now *summer*—is summarized as vacation; this word comes from Latin vacation "*vacatio*," from *vacare*—"to be free, empty; to be at leisure." "Don't care attitude," "it's my time, let me do as I please," "relax," "lackadaisical," "I don't care," 'leave me alone," "I don't want to be bothered," "adios amigos."

The church world has taken a vacation, some a leave of absence, some left and never came back, and of course, neglected the teachings of the prophets, Jesus Christ, and the apostles. Apostasy is obvious; hunger and thirst for God are notoriously absent from a generation who seemingly wants to be free from any type of (spiritually speaking) conviction that curtails or crucifies the flesh and brings it in line with the obedience to the word of God to be subjected to the will, plan, and God's program. Some just want to be entertained in the disguise of what is religiously perforated and called praise and worship. Praise and worship are very important when it is designated to God, letting Him know we love Him, which is expressed in a manner at times with our hands uplifted, "Jesus, I love You," "God, I adore You," "Praise the Lord," "Hallelujah," "Thank You, Jesus," "Thank You, Jesus, for dying on the cross for me," "Thank You for sending the Holy Spirit in my life," "Holy Spirit, I recognize You for who You are," as people would offer a crescendo of praise and worship to God with all of their body, spirit, and soul. There are times that praise and worship are combined with prayer when an individual chooses to be alone with God just to love, worship, and praise God.

Today praise and worship are, all day or night, of concerts, Christian rock, and other gospels bands getting together in a meeting to perform and entertain others. But call an all-night prayer for souls to be saved, healed, and delivered, and for God to send revival that would shake America and the world, you could hardly find people attending. Seeking after God and His kingdom is a thing supposedly only meant for the older folks. The lack of hunger, thirst, and a desire for God and His foundational truths, and the practice, upkeep, and observance of biblical foundational principles and basics of Christianity have been pushed aside with so-called Christian rock bands with music and lyrics that have no anointing, no God, Jesus, or Holy Spirit in it; which sounds no different from the music of some hard rock musical bands. A certain minister friend who is a well-respected man of God with miracles, supernatural signs, and healings following his ministry said or spoke these words forty years ago, "When Jesus is about to return, it would be somewhat difficult to tell the difference between the music of the world and the music of the church in some places of worship." We have to adapt but not be persuaded to compromise the word and shut out his anointing and power of bringing the Holy Ghost conviction, which will cause people to come to Jesus Christ and His saving grace.

Those who live a Christ-like life and have a desire for God and His truths with a desire to win lost souls, with the power of God being manifested and a deep yearning for a move of God and revival are being labeled as out of touch, old fogies with the advice this is a modern-day we have to adapt if we are going to go with the flow. Large-screen TV and alcoholic drinks are now being brought into some church buildings and sanctuaries for certain sporting events, while the prayer room has been substituted with elaborate banquet facilities so church folks can eat, drink, and be entertained.

When Jesus walked this earth two thousand years ago, He said, "My house shall be called the house of prayer; but ye have made it a den of thieves" Matthew 21:13.

Jesus and the apostles prophesied about this happening in our day, "And because iniquity shall abound, the love of many shall wax cold" Matthew 24:12. "Now the Spirit speaketh expressly, that in the latter times some shall depart from the faith" 1 Timothy 4:1a.

> *This know also, that in the last days perilous times shall come. For men shall be lovers of their own selves, covetous, boasters, proud, blasphemers, disobedient to parents, unthankful, unholy,*
> *Without natural affection, trucebreakers, false accusers, incontinent, fierce, despisers of those that are good,*
> *Traitors, heady, highminded, lovers of pleasures more than lovers of God;*
> *Having a form of godliness, but denying the power thereof: from such turn away.*
> — 2 Timothy 3:1–5

> *Love not the world, neither the things that are in the world.*
> *If any man love the world, the love of the Father is not in him. For all that is in the world, the lust of the flesh, and the lust of the eyes, and the pride of life, is not of the Father, but is of the world.*
> *And the world passeth away, and the lust thereof: but he that doeth the will of God abideth for ever.*
> — 1 John 2:15–17

Instead of bonfires (bone-fires), which were a religious rite with traditional ritualistic insignias year after year, the church of Jesus Christ should be experiencing the fullness of the baptism of the Holy Spirit with revival fires that would affect the US and world, which will surely prepare us for the second return of Jesus Christ.

The church may ice or freeze in the summer is definitely caused by one day in, one day out Christianity. *We do not need truth on ice; we need truth on fire.* Departure from the word of God and its truths and the basics of Christianity is spiritual death.

The apostle Paul wrote, "But she that liveth in pleasure is dead while she liveth" 1 Timothy 5:6, this, of course, meaning the Church.

There are people in America and other parts of the world that are doing everything possible to please God but generally speaking, what the apostle is saying in the above, a majority of the church world is dead, again spiritually dead. The apostle Peter reminded the church that we should be alive and not dead, "Ye also, as lively stones, are built up a spiritual house, an holy priesthood, to offer up spiritual sacrifices, acceptable to God by Jesus Christ" 1 Peter 2:5.

There are Bible-believing Christians that are longing to see a biblical revival, like recorded in the four Gospels—*Matthew, Mark, Luke, John, the book of Acts,* and what's recorded in the epistles of Paul's ministry. Like Nero, he was singing and strumming on his harp while Rome burned, the same way we have a majority of Christians strumming their guitar, playing their instruments, and singing their songs while America and the world burn. (Yes, the author likes beautiful music.) But how can we be comfortable when we are witnessing with our own eyes almost every prophecy that the prophets, Jesus, and the apostles prophesied being fulfilled at this moment. Prayer, the Bible, and of course, the Ten Commandments have already been outlawed and torn down from our schools and public places, while more than ever, the Nativity Scene is challenged and adamantly requested by atheistic groups in America to be removed in public places.

While all of this is going on, we have a former administration and their leader seemingly with no godly conviction and is in favor of condoning homosexuality, lesbianism, and, worst of all; same-sex marriage is being signed into law in so many States. Telling the difference between a man and a woman is becoming very difficult, and if the previous president had one more year in office, it might have been very difficult to differentiate who is a man or woman. A percentage of our society would be in a quagmire of transgender signed into law by a previous president that men could go into women's bathroom and women could go into men's bathroom, same for kids in school.

When God made man and woman in the beginning, He made Adam and Eve. Adam was the male; Eve was the female; from then on, as the human race began to populate, everyone knew who was a man and who was a woman. But the devil and his followers wanted to pervert and ruin God's creation. In Noah's day, God had to wipe out the human race because that generation was a generation of evil-doers who produced a type of men and women who were not like how God made them in the Garden of Eden. The same is happening today; the devil and his crowd are pushing for the same thing today, wanting to pervert God's original creation.

Abortion has reached the point that when a woman becomes pregnant, she can carry the baby for nine months, then at the point of birth, the baby lays on the table, and the mother can decide to kill the baby, and then a murderous doctor can take the baby's life. This is nothing but murder and, of course, the agenda of a certain party. Sixty million abortions were performed in one year, while baby parts and organs are being sold for money, the root of all evil, and this is done while you are reading this book. The sad and deceitful things about this are those who are performing the act of abortion and murdering these babies and selling baby parts with their leaders and some government lawmakers. The courts sanctioning this have to conviction or heart because their conscience is seared or hardened.

There was a time when gays (this word had a different meaning back forty or more years ago) used to hide in the closet, but now they came out in the open and parading the streets with no shame or respect and fear for God. While ninety percent of the news media are allowing and insinuating TV shows that this is a normal way of life, and millions of viewers are condoning this with the motto "if it feels good, do it." Hollywood, which 99 percent is a cesspool of hell, who are making movies with some of the hideous creatures, who condone homosexuality and lesbianism, a transgender lifestyle along with scenes of sex acts, murders, and crimes are now being peddled in millions of homes in America and other countries and some people sit down and watch these filthy, demonic, devil acts, and some people sit and watch with no godly conviction.

Video games are now being filled with the occult and witchcraft and murder scenes where children and adults are absorbing its content into their minds and are now being played out in our nation by hundreds being killed ever so often. Don't blame the present administration, but blame where the blame belongs; it is all in these filthy, devil conjured games and movies.

The demon of murder is rampant as even certain sports personalities are making news headlines of these hideous crimes. Human lives have been cheapened as thousands of people are being slaughtered by certain religious groups, fulfilling the words of Jesus; they would kill in the name of God to consummate their blood-thirsty hell-bound souls. To make the present situation past gross and appalling, members of a certain party continue to carry out the gruesome action of aborting babies during a woman or women's term of pregnancy in its early and late-developing stages, and now they have signed into law the doctor can terminate the life of a newborn baby or babies after he or she is born.

There are leaders of some denominations and organizations that openly support homosexuality, lesbianism, and the gay lifestyle and even perform wedding ceremonies for same-sex couples to add insult to injury. Their ministers are doing the same. God in His Word, the Bible, condemns this and calls it an abomination to God. Some of them are not reading the same Bible I am reading. Pornography of every sort is now being peddled into millions of people's homes and hotel rooms by cable and satellite companies with the excuse people want it. Most of our young people are consuming more intoxicated and alcoholic drinks than at any other time in history.

Hard drugs such as cocaine, crack (a form of cocaine, smokeable), depressant fentanyl, GHB (Gamma-hydroxybutyric acid), heroin, inhalants, ketamine, LSD (Lysergic acid diethylamide), marijuana, MDMA (Methylenedioxy-methamphetamine), mescaline, methamphetamine, methcathinone, opium, PCP (Phencyclidine), psilocybin/psilocin, Ritalin, Rohypnol, steroids have found its way not just to the street people but to some students in colleges and universities.

Doctors, physiatrist, physiologist, and other social organizations are scratching their heads and are in a dilemma of what next to do, but the fact is, this is not a social problem but a spiritual one. When God made Adam and Eve in the Garden of Eden, He made them a threefold being. He made them with a body, and the word "*body*" comes from the Greek word "*Soma*," which means your body is temporal and is not going to last forever. The other part of mankind is his or her spirit; the word "*spirit*" comes from the Hebrew word "*Pheuma*," which means *God breathes*, and in other words, God breathes into you or every human the spirit of life. Now please get this, your spirit was given to you by God to receive or accommodate God's Spirit. How is this done?

God sent His Son, Jesus Christ, as Savior of humankind, and when you repent of your sins and receive Jesus Christ as your Lord and Savior, God renews your Spirit, or God's Spirit hooks up with or unites with your spirit, and you become a son or daughter of God. The other part of a human being is the *soul*. The soul is the real you, the seat of your life, your will, your emotion; the word soul comes from the Hebrew word "*Nephesh*," which means something that will last forever. This means if you are saved and have the Spirit of God, you will go to heaven, and if you are not saved and have not the spirit of God, you will spend eternity with the devil and his angels.

"But as many as receive Him, [Jesus Christ] to them give he power to become a child of God" John 1:12. *Please read the entire Gospel of John, chapter 3.*

To remind you of the above three chapters of this page, yours truly wrote about the sins of the flesh also different types of hard drugs that millions of people are getting hooked on; this is the point that the author wants to get across to you, a Christian, and if you are not a Christian, here is the fact of why people go after or run down the pleasures of life and go after drugs. God made every human being and gave them a spirit to receive or accommodate God's Spirit in their spirit, and when God's Spirit is not within your spirit, there is emptiness or vacuum within every human being that does not know God; this means people without God will try everything, the pleasures of this life, illicit sex, drugs and more to fill up and satisfy the emptiness inside of them, but not until they come to God through Jesus Christ and accept Him as the Lord and Savior into their lives, they will never be satisfied.

Here is a must-read from the Bible, the apostle Paul, through the inspiration of the Holy Spirit, wrote these words,

> *For I am not ashamed of the gospel of Christ: for it is the power of God unto salvation to every one that believeth; to the Jew first, and also to the Greek.*
>
> *For therein is the righteousness of God revealed from faith to faith: as it is written, The just shall live by faith.*
>
> *For the wrath of God is revealed from heaven against all ungodliness and unrighteousness of men, who hold the truth in unrighteousness;*
>
> *Because that which may be known of God is manifest in them; for God hath shewed it unto them.*
>
> *For the invisible things of him from the creation of the world are clearly seen, being understood by the things that are made, even his eternal power and Godhead; so that they are without excuse:*
>
> *Because that, when they knew God, they glorified him not as God, neither were thankful; but became vain in their imaginations, and their foolish heart was darkened.*
>
> *Professing themselves to be wise, they became fools,*
>
> *And changed the glory of the uncorruptible God into an image made like to corruptible man, and to birds, and fourfooted beasts, and creeping things.*
>
> *Wherefore God also gave them up to uncleanness through the lusts of their own hearts, to dishonour their own bodies between themselves:*
>
> *Who changed the truth of God into a lie, and worshipped and served the creature more than the Creator, who is blessed for ever. Amen.*
>
> *For this cause God gave them up unto vile affections: for even their women did change the natural use into that which is against nature:*
>
> *And likewise also the men, leaving the natural use of the woman, burned in their lust one toward another; men with men working that which is unseemly, and receiving in themselves that recompence of their error which was meet.*
>
> *And even as they did not like to retain God in their knowledge, God gave them over to a reprobate mind, to do those things which are not convenient;*
>
> *Being filled with all unrighteousness, fornication, wickedness, covetousness, maliciousness; full of envy, murder, debate, deceit, malignity; whisperers,*
>
> *Backbiters, haters of God, despiteful, proud, boasters, inventors of evil things, disobedient to parents,*

Without understanding, covenantbreakers, without natural affection, implacable, unmerciful:

Who knowing the judgment of God, that they which commit such things are worthy of death, not only do the same, but have pleasure in them that do them.

— Romans 1:16–32

Jesus began His ministry two thousand years ago; when Jesus came, His life, teachings, ministry, and mission, plus His love and compassion for people, were opposed to the teachings of the religious leaders and religions of that day. He recruited twelve men; of course, one of them betrayed Him. Then God saved and ordained the apostle Paul; the eleven disciples, including the apostle Paul, lived, preached, and taught exactly what Jesus taught as they exemplified in miracles, signs, and wonders exactly as Jesus did. But to get to the point, the apostles taught, ministered, and did exactly what Jesus did in *Matthew, Mark, Luke,* and *John*, which is recorded in the book of *Acts*.

It is of the author's opinion that most people reading this book have some knowledge of God and are Christians, but if this is not so, just that no one misunderstands what is going to be mentioned about a certain organizational church, which within this organization are some wonderful human beings and this church organization has and is spending billions of dollars assisting and helping humanity socially (families and educational programs), financially, physically (caring for the sick, hospitals, etc.), materially (food programs, etc.); of course this is commendable. But sometimes, their educational and charitable programs are with a catch, to join their religion just like others do.

In the Bible, which is the original King James Version, we have to stand by its truth and godly principles and teachings. What is going to be mentioned in the next paragraph or two is coming from a heart of love for the leaders and people of this particular church organization, whom some of their people are now beginning to realize are unbiblical and are now beginning to accept the truth and teachings of Jesus Christ and the apostles.

After Jesus completed His three years of ministry, then after His death and resurrection, the apostles took over where He left off and continued the teachings and ministry of Jesus. They continued with fervor and power exactly what Jesus taught, preached, and did. Anyone reading the Gospels and the book of Acts has enough godly sense to discern that after the last apostle, who is John (who gave us the book of Revelation), after his death, probably prior to that, apostasy started setting in or had its origin.

Soon after, Jesus died and was raised again and went back to heaven; for about twenty years or more, in the book of Acts, Christians believed as Jesus did, and it became clear that an individual could be a Christian without being a Jew. This was clearly decided at the so-called Council of Jerusalem in AD 49 to 50; there, the first leaders of the Jesus kind of Christianity, Peter, James, John, and Paul, agreed that the Gentiles for whom Jesus also died could become the heir of salvation through the grace of God.

For Scriptural reference, please read the entire chapter of Acts, chapter 15, and Galatians 2:1–10.

Even though Jesus and the apostles' Christianity was faith in Jesus Christ and their lives were different, Roman officials often linked the Jews and Gentile Christians together. Monotheistic faith (one God) was foreign to Greco-Roman polytheism (many gods). Judaism, a mixture sometimes of the Law of Moses and the teaching of Jesus and the apostles, was a permitted religion known as *religio-licta* (religious freedom), which the Roman government offered some protection and freedom of worship as long as the Jews paid taxes (could you imagine—in their own land!) and did not revolt. The Jesus kind of Christianity did not have the same privilege and did not have a structured life of its own. Most of these Christians had to borrow from their Jewish roots with some rabbis and elders who strayed away from the original teachings of Jesus Christ and the apostles. This amalgamation of old Jewish laws and Jesus and apostles type Christianity built a stage for a type of Christianity that was adaptable to anyone, including those who served other gods, idols, and images.

By the year of AD 100, the Roman government persecuted, suppressed, fed to lions, and burnt to the stakes the true followers of Jesus Christ. Some of them were killed by gladiators (some gladiators were forced to kill their own families). Prior to this, the remnant of the true church of Jesus Christ had gone into hiding; if found, they were burnt to the stakes, fed to lions, or killed by Nero and other Roman emperors and soldiers. During this time, people's faith in God began to wane, and anything that resembled Christianity, the religious people of that time were willing to be part of. This was a golden opportunity for the devil to use certain religious kings, emperors, and leaders to be inspired by Satan to introduce the religion of Babylon with Roman idol worship and worshipers. History does not pinpoint the exact time for the beginning of the Roman Catholic Church. The Roman Catholic Church was ushered in, and the people of that day went for this type of religion because it appealed to their ways and lifestyle; in other words, they could have said and done what they wanted to and then be part of the Roman Catholic Church with added protection from the Roman government.

The turning point for the formation of the Roman Catholic Church in the Roman Empire was 313 CE, the date of Emperor Constantine's so-called conversion to "Christianity." How did this conversion come about? In 306 CE, Constantine succeeded his father and eventually, with Licinius, became co-ruler of the Roman Empire. He was influenced by his mother's devotion to Christianity and his own belief in divine protection. Before he went to fight a battle near Rome at the Milvian Bridge in 312 CE, he claimed that he was told in a dream to paint the "Christian" monogram—the Greek letters *khi* and *rho*, the first two letters of Christ's name in Greek on his soldier's shields. With this sacred talisman, Constantine's forces defeated his enemy Maxentius shortly after winning the battle. Constantine claimed that he had become a believer, although he was not baptized until just prior to his death some twenty-four years later. He went on to obtain the support of the professed Christians in his empire by his adoption of the Greek letters *Chi-Rho* artwork as his emblem. However, the *Chi-Rho* had already been used as a ligature joining of letters in both pagan and Christian contexts.

As a result, the foundation of the Roman Catholic Church was laid. This so-called type of Christianity began with Emperor Constantine, with Constantine's support; Christendom's religion became the official state religion of Rome. Why was Constantine's "conversion" so significant? Because as emperor, he had a powerful influence in the affairs of the doctrinally divided "Christian" church, and he wanted unity in his empire.

As a result, the new teachings were developed as a fusion of Christianity and paganism, which taught "twisted doctrines." For example, they taught people to worship the state and to sacrifice their lives for it in warfare. Thus, so-called Christians participated in the Crusades and slaughtered people whom they considered to be nonbelievers. They also went to war and killed their own "brothers" of the same religion. They certainly did not practice Christian neutrality and love of neighbor.

Leaders of the Roman Catholic Church claim that their church originated from the Scripture Matthew 16:18, when Christ supposedly appointed Peter as the first pope. However, the honest and objective student of the Scriptures and history soon discovers that the foundation of the Roman church is none other than the pagan mystery religion of ancient Babylon. While enduring the early persecutions of the Roman government, AD 65 to 300, most professing Christianity went through a gradual departure from New Testament doctrine concerning church government, worship, and practice. Local churches ceased to be autonomous by giving way to the control of "bishops" ruling over hierarchies.

The simple form of worship from the heart was replaced with the rituals and splendor of paganism. Ministers became "priests," and pagans became "Christians" by simply being sprinkled with water. This tolerance of an unregenerate membership only made things worse. *Sprinkled paganism* is the best definition of Roman Catholicism. The Roman Emperor Constantine established himself as the head of the church around AD 313, which made this new Christianity the official religion of the Roman Empire. The first actual Pope in Rome was probably Leo I, AD 440 to 461, although some claim that Gregory I was the first pope, AD 590 to 604. This ungodly system eventually ushered in the darkest period of history known to man, properly known as the "Dark Ages," AD 500 to 1500.

Through popes, bishops, and priests, Satan ruled Europe as the Roman Catholic Church instituted the papal system, with the idea that the pope was infallible and as pope, he must reign forever. As time went by, the Roman Catholic Church conjured up hundreds of unscriptural teachings such as the Worship of Many (as was said earlier in this book, when someone is sick, we do not need the doctor's mother, they need the doctor), Mass (their main worship in which Mary's name is invoked during their Mass over and over. Confession of sins was allotted to the priest, as a parishioner could confess their sins to a man (the priest). Purgatory, which is one of this church's main doctrines, that after a member of the Roman Catholic Church dies, they would be able to pay a certain amount of money to the church or priest to pray to retrieve or bring their loved one out of hell.

The richer the family, this ritual or service became more costly; image worship became a daily routine within this church. As salvation was obtained by works, without a doubt, this particular church, especially in its earlier stages, was deeply involved in witchcraft and, at certain times of the year, introduced, which allowed their members and now entire nations to be involved in a two, three, or one week of revelry, which is called Carnival, where the revelers can parade the streets some practically naked, such as the New Orleans Mardi Gra, Brazil, and Trinidad, and other parts of the world where Roman Catholic religion is predominant. They could commit any kind of sin, and then on Ash Day, the day after Carnival or Mardi Grad, the revelers can go to this church and have some ashes sprinkled on them, and their sins can be forgiven; how convenient?

Biblical Christianity became illegal in most of Europe and some other countries of the world, but through all of this, however, there remained individual groups of true Christians, such as the Waldenses and the Anabaptists, who would not conform to the Roman system. From the Roman Catholic Church came the Church of England, then the Methodist, Episcopalians, Greek Orthodox, Anglicans, Lutherans, Presbyterians, etc. Then there were splits and splinters and a group here and a group there, each one in their own corner with their own beliefs with no biblical teaching.

There are thirty-three plus denominations, organizations, and major religions, including independents today in this world; thankful is the word for those who held on to the Bible, which is the Word of God, and are experiencing the blessings of God and a spasmodic move of the Holy Spirit. Still, each of these organizations, denominations, Independents, and Full Gospel people differ in doctrinal beliefs, and some are condoning a lifestyle that is of the world, the flesh, and the devil.

> *Love not the world, neither the things that are in the world.*
> *If any man loves the world, the love of the Father is not in him.*
> *For all that is in the world, the lust of the flesh, and the lust of the eyes, and the pride of life, is not of the Father, but is of the world.*
> *And the world passeth away, and the lust thereof: but he that doeth the will of God abideth for ever.*
> — 1 John 2:15–17

The majority of these denominations, organizations, and independents have taken a holiday, vacation, leave of absence, and (as was mentioned earlier) some never came back, but most of them have forsaken the teachings of Jesus and the apostles. There were great men and women raised up and ordained by God within the past centuries and years with miracles, signs, wonders, and the supernatural power following their ministry. These revivals produced outstanding results, but they always seemed to want to organize the Holy Spirit (which you cannot); some just wanted to build a name for themselves along with a multi-billion-dollar building as their own kingdom. They died, and their organization died spiritually; some of them are existing, but they are dead: no power, no life, no flow of the spirit of God, and we wonder why there is no biblical revival or move of the Holy Spirit in our day like Jesus and the apostles recorded in Mathew, Mark, Luke, and John. This obviously would include the book of Acts and the ministry of the apostle Paul. Is there any hope for the Church of our day, yes?

Not very much attention is given to the parable about the Ten Virgins, and if anyone mentions, teaches, or preaches, there are always so many different interpretations with the intention of applying to suit themselves and their organization so they can get a name and the glory for themselves. No Scripture is of any private interpretation.

> *Study, to show thyself unto God rightly dividing the word truth.*
> — 2 Timothy 2:15

Was Paul's admonition to Timothy? With the help of the Holy Spirit, this Scripture will be correctly interpreted. The words of Jesus must not be taken lightly; He is God Himself speaking to us. Here are some sobering words that every Christian should read over and over and think, then pray always and be ready for the second return of Jesus Christ.

> *Then shall the kingdom of heaven be likened unto ten virgins, which took their lamps, and went forth to meet the bridegroom.*
> *And five of them were wise, and five were foolish.*
> *They that were foolish took their lamps, and took no oil with them: But the wise took oil in their vessels with their lamps.*

Now while the bridegroom tarried, they all slumbered and slept.

And at midnight there was a cry made, Behold, the bridegroom cometh; go ye out to meet him. Then all those virgins arose, and trimmed their lamps.

And the foolish said unto the wise, give us of your oil; for our lamps are gone out.

But the wise answered, saying, not so; lest there be not enough for us and you: but go ye rather to them that sell, and buy for yourselves.

And while they went to buy, the bridegroom came; and they that were ready went in with him to the marriage: and the door was shut.

Afterward came also the other virgins, saying, Lord, Lord, open unto us.

But he answered, verily, verily I say unto you I know you not

Watch therefore, for ye know neither the day nor the hour wherein the Son of man cometh.

— Matthew 25:1–13

The kingdom of God is likened unto Ten Virgins; it did not say like (but liken, resembled, looked like) these Ten Virgins represent the entire church world who believes in God with good intentions, sincerity, and morals; all of these Virgins had some spiritual insight or light (that's what a lamp is for light). All of the Virgins have an expectation of going to be with Jesus when He returns the second time. Five of these Virgins were wise, and five were foolish (foolish, no knowledge of what it takes to go to be with Jesus); all they wanted to do was gather together and have what you call a good time. Ask them about what the preacher preached or taught about; the answer is "I don't know." You can never make it to heaven with that type of Christianity.

The foolish Virgins enjoyed whatever spiritual light that they had, but they did not have the Holy Spirit. But the wise lived and had the Spirit of Jesus, who is the Holy Spirit, and walked in righteousness and holiness, and they did not just talk about the second return of Jesus. But they took time often in prayer and fasting, studying the Word of God, going to church, doing something for Jesus. Most of all, they were involved in the outreach program of their church and helping the ministries like missionaries win lost souls overseas, especially those who did know Jesus as Lord and Savior.

By doing this, they realized this would keep them involved to stay in church, which will strengthen and prepare them for the second return of Jesus Christ. And anyone who is saved, baptized with the Holy Spirit, will automatically want or desire to do something for God, such as giving of monies and material things to reach their community, town, or city with the Gospel of Jesus Christ, especially the people overseas who have never heard of Jesus. They would love for their brethren and do something for those in need, feeding the hungry, clothing the naked, sheltering the homeless, and of course, other outreach ministries as we wait for the second return of Jesus.

Here is the point about the five foolish virgins; while the bridegroom tarried, they all slumbered and slept; this is the spirit of our day, slumbering and sleeping. This is the reason why the Church could possibly *"ice in the summer"* and all other times. There have been many cases reported of certain people dreaming and getting out of bed and walking; some would do certain chores until they were awakened by a family member. In some cases, this type of sleepwalking was and has proven to be detrimental. There are millions of activities going on in the church world today, but generally speaking, most of the Church world is asleep. These are not the words of an individual or the author, but these are the words of Jesus.

> *And at midnight there was a cry made [shout], "Behold, the bridegroom cometh; go ye out to meet him"*
>
> — Matthew 25:6

At this present time, it is the midnight hour, and a cry is being made, preaching, teaching, and warning is being heard on TV, radio, from the pulpits, from dedicated Jesus living pastors, evangelists, missionaries, teachers, leaders, church members, books, videos, DVDs, etc. Behold, the bridegroom cometh. As this cry is made, *"Behold, the bridegroom cometh, go ye out to meet him,"* then all the virgins arose and trimmed their lamps. They shook themselves and said, "We are ready," but at that moment, when they thought they were ready, the foolish virgins realized that they had no oil, again, which is the Holy Spirit.

> *And the foolish said unto the wise, Give us of your oil; for our lamps are gone out. [We thought we were ready, but we are not; what was the reason they were not ready? They had no oil.]*
> *But the wise answered, saying, Not so; lest there be not enough for us and you: but go ye rather to them that sell, and buy for yourselves.*
>
> — Matthew 25:8–9

This is a perfect type of the Bride and the Church. Notice what is being said by the *Bride* and the *Church*. The people that are expecting Jesus to return will prepare for the second return of Jesus, and they will be ready; why? It's because they are baptized with the Holy Spirit, and these are the people that will be caught up to be with Jesus in the first resurrection (the author will explore and explain this in another chapter). Right here solves the problem of the saints who will go to be with Jesus in the first resurrection, which everyone calls the Rapture, which means the catching away of the Bride of Christ and the Christians who will be left behind, whom reference is made to as the Tribulation Saints, who missed the first resurrection.

And when they went to buy, the Bridegroom came, and they that were ready went in with him to the marriage: "[…] and the door was shut. Afterward came also the other virgins, saying, Lord, Lord, open unto us. But he answered and said, Verily I say unto you, I know you not" Matthew 25:10b–12. The big question here is: if the five foolish virgins were part of the church, why were they left behind? First of all, when the Bridegroom tarried, they were asleep; no dedication, no prayer or fasting, no word (just entertainment); the name Christian but in church one day, the next day—partaking of the world (ungodly things of the world), flesh (adultery, etc.), and the devil (witchcraft, etc.).

Some Christians must realize that being a member of a church, denomination, organization, or some type of religion, going through some traditional creeds, dogmas, washing in rivers, trips to so call-ed holy sites, climbing stairs on their knees chanting some traditional prayers, and more does not guarantee them going to heaven (thank God they have some kind of desire for God), but this is not God's way. Then there are people that are more concerned about going to Jerusalem several times within the year, but there are concerns that they will make it to the New Jerusalem or heaven.

The five foolish virgins were left behind because they had no oil; oil here represents the fullness of the baptism of the Holy Spirit. Please note what was mentioned the fullness of the Holy Spirit. This means to be born again, repentance, and being washed inside and out by the blood of Jesus Christ but to the filled with the fullness of the Holy Spirit. Why were the foolish virgins left out?

They had to oil! Oil represents being ready at all times. Oil means that you are always lighting and again being ready for the second return of Jesus Christ.

The Hebrew word for *"Oil"* is *"Shaman,"* which means to shine. God instructs Moses to speak to the Hebrews, one of the instructions was to use the oil that was made for cleansing, purification, being ready for service, preparation, and anointing to go at the Lord's command. Oil is for light; being saved and baptized with the Holy Spirit spiritually and naturally speaking opens up your eyes to see where you are going.

Oil for the light.

— Exodus 25:6a

And thou shalt sanctify them, that they may be most holy: whatsoever toucheth them shall be holy.

And thou shalt anoint Aaron and his sons, and consecrate them, that they may minister unto me in the priest's office.

And thou shalt speak unto the children of Israel, saying, This shall be an holy anointing oil unto me throughout your generations.

— Exodus 30:29–31

Their main source of light came from oil. That anointing oil will bring forth the diversities of the illumination. It may bring forth light, revelation, insight, wisdom, healing, and miracles, anything we desire. The anointing not only speaks of separation and sanctification, but it brings the presence of His person that reveals who He is. Going as far back to Genesis to the New Testament, Eastern custom, especially in relation to a marriage ceremony, was to anoint the bride for one week, sometimes more, with different types of herbs and spices and, in particular, just the day before the marriage, they used to anoint the bride with special types of perfumes and oils. This represents cleansing, purification and sanctification, and readiness to meet the bridegroom. This is the reason Jesus used this particular parable in relation to His second return.

Besides oil representing the Holy Spirit in a believer's life, oil also represents cleansing, purification, sanctification, and readiness to meet the bridegroom. This means the church of Jesus Christ must be ready to meet Jesus Christ when He returns; the Bride of Christ must be ready.

There is a Scripture in the Bible that seemingly has been overlooked by hundreds of thousands of Christians, but this is a Scripture that must be emphasized by ministries, pastors, and missionaries to their congregation in every Christian gathering and meeting with the intention of reminding of the importance of being filled with the Holy Spirit. Here it is:

Let no corrupt communication proceed out of your mouth, but that which is good to the use of edifying, that it may minister grace unto the hearers,

And grieve not the Holy Spirit of God, whereby ye are sealed unto the day of redemption.

Let all bitterness, and wrath, and anger, and clamor, and evil speaking, be put away from you, with all malice:

And be ye kind one to another, tenderhearted, forgiving one another, even as God for Christ's sake hath forgiven you.

[Please note verse 30] And grieve not the Holy Spirit of God whereby ye are sealed unto the day of redemption.

— Ephesians 4:29–32

God be praised for an unprecedented move of God in evangelism and soul-winning where certain men and women of God were used of God in leading millions of souls to Jesus Christ. There were spasmodic outpourings of the Holy Spirit, of which we are thankful. We have witnessed some outstanding miracles through the ministry of some dedicated men and women of God, but generally speaking, the Church of Jesus Christ is at a crossroads, living in a fantasy of revival but never experiencing a revival. It's all because of a summer-like spirit in us, Americans, and some other countries of the world. Yes! Most of the church has had its summer-like vacation. Some went away on a long vacation and never came back; prayerfully, some would awaken to the fact that we have taken a long vacation, away from the O.T saints, prophets, kings, Jesus, and the apostles' ministry. But now, some are awakening to the truth and are longing to see a revival (forgive the repetition of this statement) like unto Jesus' ministry, as recorded in the Gospel of *Matthew*, *Mark*, *Luke*, and *John*, the apostles in the books of *Acts*.

CHAPTER 10
Prophecy: Where We At!

While this book is being written, the Middle East countries are in turmoil. The civil war in Syria continues as hundreds of thousands of people have been killed and being killed. Sad to say, hundreds of thousands of innocent children are being murdered every day in the US. Since September 11th, 2001, the continuous, constant threat by Al-Qaeda to destroy America and Americans makes the headlines almost daily, while so many Americans are killed overseas ever so often. These threats are of constant rhetoric and are a daily routine by other militant groups. ISIS, one of the most feared militant groups, now an army, suddenly popped up out of nowhere with no regard for human lives. The sad thing about this is they are doing what they want as America and the world look on and do nothing until President Donald Trump was sworn into office.

The nation of Israel (like never before) at this present time is surrounded and threatened with the intention of annihilation by almost every Moslem nation, especially Iran. The threat of nuclear attack is closer than ever before, while there are some internal wars going on in so many African countries, including Sudan, as starvation and famine are killing hundreds of thousands in these countries. The devastating earthquake in Haiti before this and to the present time there is constant unrest in that country. Every European country is experiencing daily financial problems as its economy is being rattled with the uncertainty of its financial future. The open arms, open-door attitude by its leaders is now beginning to rattle these European countries. Japan made the news of the year when one of the worst tsunamis caused its land to look like an ocean with ships in parking lots and cars and buses piling up on each other everywhere.

China, while its economy might be better off than the rest of the world, its cry for religious freedom is heard daily by some of its citizens, as they struggle with a younger generation leaning to the West for an easier lifestyle, Pakistan, India, and most of those Asian countries are seething with to dissatisfaction as religion has no answer for the people who are empty, void and are looking for something spiritual satisfaction. Venezuela and other South American countries are in constant threat by socialistic and communist neighboring ally Cuba. Worst of all, there is a new wave of socialistic movement in America, waving banners and leading marches for a socialistic government in America. By the way, most of these socialistic movements are instigated by young women with godless agendas who should be home learning how to cook and care for their children if they care to have any. Like the Bible says, they are without natural affection; as a matter of fact, they would rather care for a poodle dog than a child.

Thousands of our soldiers are fighting a war with mixed feelings as so many of them are losing their lives and a war that seemingly might not end, with a price tag that has helped cripple the US economy. Iraqi and Afghanistan police and soldiers that our army personnel has trained and are training are turning on our soldiers and killing our soldiers as America continues to send billions of dollars in aid to other countries that are of no benefit to the United States; in any way!

Mexico's drug war has taken the lives of thousands, and it seems like there is no end in sight as lives are being lost daily. South and Central America, including Brazil, are doing everything possible to stabilize their economy while millions still live in poverty and are threatened by socialism and communism. With every country of the world facing some type of internal conflict, the United Nations leaders in New York are scratching their heads and biting their nails; they have no answer to solve the world's problems.

Something is going to be written about here that the author wants the reader to understand that his responsibility is to pray for anyone that God allows to be elected as president and support him in every way possible, but the election of President Trump, who convincingly won the 2016 election, his election triggered and exposed a sector of our society with an open display of vehement hate, jealousy, with murderous and destructive denunciation and disrespect for the office of the president that is ever being witnessed in America. Under this president's leadership, America is experiencing an economic revival and a host of other improvements in every facet of our society; so what is the problem? *God*…God is the problem; we have a president who is not ashamed and afraid to mention the word "*God.*" This present president leadership 2017–2019 is not the problem, and then what really is the part of the problem? To mention the name God and standing up for righteousness!

The movies and television shows are filled with violence, porn, and raw sex; while homosexuality is being portrayed as normal, same-sex marriage is now placed into law in so many of these United States, and righteous living people dare not speak against it; why? Because we now have authorities and individuals who are implementing laws to stop anyone who speaks against this type of unbiblical lifestyle. Certain networks and TV stations and their officials condone this type of lifestyle with the idea that it's normal, and their programming on TV consists of violence, pornography, homosexuality, and violence. Some sports personalities, with all their fame and the millions of dollars that they are making, are often making the headlines of extreme alcoholism, drug abuse, murder, and suicide. All because they are looking for something besides God to satisfy the emptiness they are experiencing inside of them.

With all of the above, someone might ask, "Where are we; what's next, and what's going to happen? Are we at the end of time? When will all of this end?" Believe this or not, we were not placed on this earth to live forever. Most of all, God has a time frame for mankind; as a matter, we were placed here by God to worship and praise Him, most of all to fulfill His plan and purpose to use our time, talent, and monies to preach the Gospel of Jesus Christ and reach those who have never heard of Jesus and the love of God. But everything else is being done but reaching the people who have never heard of Jesus. Some people might adamantly reiterate over and over what this has to do with us. The thought here should be, "What have I done for God before the end comes."

Talking about the end, we do not have to look very far; the unusual occurrences that are taking place daily, sinner or saint can tell we are close to the end of time; this, itself, is an indication that we are at the end of time. The author does not profess that he is an austere student of prophecy in particular but has enough biblical knowledge to explore the fact that we are at the end of time. For the benefit of those who have never read the Bible, some prophecies are being fulfilled that would be reiterated, but the author will show you some biblical teachings which point to the end that probably no one has ever explored and revealed before.

The Bible records prophetical events, some of them happening now, some of them will occur in the near future, which points to the greatest event that is going to take place, that is, the second return of Jesus Christ. Jesus said the generation that witnesses all of these prophesy being fulfilled (and this is a sobering fact), the second return of Jesus will happen in our generation. What are some of the prophecies that point to the Second Return of Jesus Christ? They are a spirit of deception, lawlessness, disrespect for governments and authorities, disrespect and the cheapening of human lives, wars, violence, famine, drought, catastrophes, earthquakes, epidemics, and diseases. HIV, Aids continue to take the lives of millions; emboli, cancer, and other sicknesses are claiming the lives of thousands each year. With the rise of mysticism and other religions of the east, Americans by the hundreds of thousands are deceived and are becoming part of them. Worst of all, there are people with an attitude in America that they made God and have an attitude towards God; who are You, God? But the fact is that God does not need us; we need Him because the very air we breathe comes and depends on God.

The rise of a European Union that will seek global control, a powerful religious figure who will lead all denominations, organizations, and religions back to the Roman Catholic Church or organization, also leaders of the governments and political systems of which both of these will give power to the Antichrist. The gospel of Jesus Christ will be preached to all nations, and persecutions and destructions of Christians as faith in Jesus Christ will become a matter and life and death. Constant attacks on Jerusalem until the battle of Armageddon, the abomination of desolations, the collapse of the American economy, signs in the heavens, the great tribulation, the sun would be darkened; the moon would turn into blood, the seven plagues, the seven churches of Asia Minor—will be explained in the next few paragraphs.

> *And at the time of the end shall the king of the south push at him: and the king of the north shall come against him like a whirlwind, with chariots, and with horsemen, and with many ships; and he shall enter into the countries, and shall overflow and pass over.*
>
> *He shall stretch forth his hand also upon the countries: and the land of Egypt shall not escape.*
>
> *But he shall have power over the treasures of gold and of silver, and over all the precious things of Egypt: and the Libyans and the Ethiopians shall be at his steps.*
>
> — Daniel 11:40, 42–43

> *For, behold, in those days, and in that time, when I shall bring again the captivity of Judah and Jerusalem,*
>
> *I will also gather all nations, and will bring them down into the valley of Jehoshaphat, and will plead with them there for my people and for my heritage Israel, whom they have scattered among the nations, and parted my land.*
>
> *And they have cast lots for my people; and have given a boy for an harlot, and sold a girl for wine, that they might drink.*
>
> — Joel 3:1–3

> *Behold, the day of the* LORD *cometh, and thy spoil shall be divided in the midst of thee.*
>
> *For I will gather all nations against Jerusalem to battle; and the city shall be taken, and the houses rifled, and the women ravished; and half of the city shall go forth into captivity, and the residue of the people shall not be cut off from the city.*
>
> — Zechariah 14:1–2

> *Behold, I will make Jerusalem a cup of trembling unto all the people round about, when they shall be in the siege both against Judah and against Jerusalem.*
>
> — Zechariah 12:2

> *Alas! for that day is great, so that none is like it: it is even the time of Jacob's trouble; but he shall be saved out of it.*
>
> — Jeremiah 30:7

Chapter 10: Prophecy: Where We At!

Note for the reader. Please read from your Bible: Matthew chapter 24, Mark chapter 13, and Luke chapter 21.

> *Now we beseech you, brethren, by the coming of our Lord Jesus Christ, and by our gathering together unto him,*
>
> *That ye be not soon shaken in mind, or be troubled, neither by spirit, nor by word, nor by letter as from us, as that the day of Christ is at hand.*
>
> *Let no man deceive you by any means: for that day shall not come, except there come a falling away first, and that man of sin be revealed, the son of perdition.*
>
> — 2 Thessalonians 2:1–3

> *And I beheld, and heard an angel flying through the midst of heaven, saying with a loud voice, Woe, woe, woe, to the inhabiters of the earth by reason of the other voices of the trumpet of the three angels, which are yet to sound!*
>
> — Revelation 8:13

The Seven Church Ages recorded in the Bible in the book of Revelation are hardly mentioned, taught, or preached about. Israel is God's people, and if you want to know where we are at in prophesying, watch "Israel." Israel is God's time clock for the world, the "Seven Church Ages" is God's time clock for the Church. If you are going to understand where we are at, the Church needs a revelation (revelation of the Word, the Bible). Revelation certainly does not mean some way out spooky interpretation of the word of God, but revelation must line up with the Bible, the Word of God, and shed light or illuminate the scripture itself, especially the prophetic books and, in particular, the book of Revelation.

The year was AD 30, Emperor Nero, whose twisted Jekyll and Mr. Hyde demonic mind, unleashed the worst and severest murderous persecution against followers of Jesus Christ. Before and during Nero's reign, most of the apostles were martyred and killed by gruesome deaths, Christians were fed to lions and eaten alive, gladiators deliberately killed some, and Roman soldiers ravished, raped, and killed with the sword, some even with babies, some were strapped in clothes size leather and thrown in the sun and heat until they were baked to death. In contrast, others were thrown from high buildings to their death. In contrast, a hardened seared, conscience Roman citizens laughed. Most of them were executed, or their heads chopped, surrounded by gleeful laughing crowds. Some were shut up in dark jails like dungeons until they died, and much more such as murderous acts against the followers of Jesus Christ.

The apostle John, the beloved apostle of Jesus Christ, who by God's divine guidance and protection divinely survived Emperor Nero's Holocaust or persecution against the early church, was banished on the Isle of Patmos. This was God's master plan for giving us one of the greatest books of the Bible, the book of Revelation, the last book of the Bible. This was one of the darkest hours of the apostle John's life but subsequently turned out to be of immense benefit spiritually speaking to the Church of Jesus Christ.

Please remember we are dealing with the subject of "Prophecy: Where We at!" What is written about here, most of the church world does not know and has innocently or deliberately overlooked the most important aspect of the Church and its relation to the second return of Jesus Christ. The author has taken the time to bring you a brief study of the Church Ages to bring you to the point of where we are at. To do this, let us read from the book of Revelation,

> *The Revelation of Jesus Christ, which God gave unto him, to shew unto his servants things which must shortly come to pass; and he sent and signified it by his angel unto his servant John:*
>
> *Who bare record of the word of God, and of the testimony of Jesus Christ, and of all things that he saw.*
>
> *Blessed is he that readeth, and they that hear the words of this prophecy, and keep those things which are written therein: for the time is at hand.*
>
> *John to the seven churches which are in Asia: Grace be unto you, and peace, from him which is, and which was, and which is to come; and from the seven Spirits which are before his throne;*
>
> *And from Jesus Christ, who is the faithful witness, and the first begotten of the dead, and the prince of the kings of the earth. Unto him that loved us, and washed us from our sins in his own blood,*
>
> *And hath made us kings and priests unto God and his Father; to him be glory and dominion for ever and ever. Amen.*
>
> *Behold, he cometh with clouds; and every eye shall see him, and they also which pierced him: and all kindreds of the earth shall wail because of him. Even so, Amen.*
>
> *I am Alpha and Omega, the beginning and the ending, saith the Lord, which is, and which was, and which is to come, the Almighty.*
>
> *I John, who also am your brother, and companion in tribulation, and in the kingdom and patience of Jesus Christ, was in the isle that is called Patmos, for the word of God, and for the testimony of Jesus Christ.*
>
> *I was in the Spirit on the Lord's day, and heard behind me a great voice, as of a trumpet,*
>
> *Saying, I am Alpha and Omega, the first and the last: and, What thou seest, write in a book, and send it unto the seven churches which are in Asia; unto Ephesus, and unto Smyrna, and unto Pergamos, and unto Thyatira, and unto Sardis, and unto Philadelphia, and unto Laodicea.*
>
> *And I turned to see the voice that spake with me. And being turned, I saw seven golden candlesticks;*
>
> *And in the midst of the seven candlesticks one like unto the Son of man, clothed with a garment down to the foot, and girt about the paps with a golden girdle.*
>
> *His head and his hairs were white like wool, as white as snow; and his eyes were as a flame of fire;*
>
> *And his feet like unto fine brass, as if they burned in a furnace; and his voice as the sound of many waters.*
>
> *And he had in his right hand seven stars: and out of his mouth went a sharp twoedged sword: and his countenance was as the sun shineth in his strength.*
>
> — Revelation 1:1–16

The above Scriptures explicitly mention the names of the Seven Churches; there were seven different congregations located in different cities of Asia Minor. Jesus visited John on the Isle of Patmos and gave him a word or message for each of these churches. These messages spoken through Jesus came as a warning, rebuke, admonition, correction, and of course, encouragement. These messages were directed to each congregation or church located in different cities scattered throughout Asia Minor, and each of these messages was addressed to a particular congregation of those particular congregation which message or word was addressed and applicable to the church ages from that time up to the present time.

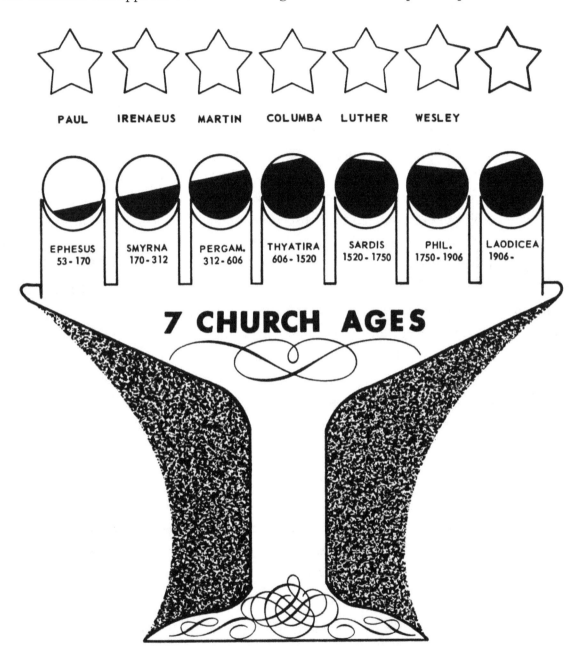

The first thing that must be drawn to the reader's attention is the fact that there are only seven (7) church ages; mind you, only seven, there will be no more. Seven is God's divine number; seven church ages, each in a given time and their spiritual condition. Seven angels mean prophets or leaders in each age; seven golden candlesticks—spiritual light for each age; seven churches, which were from the early book of Acts church to the church of our present time.

The church ages are:

- Ephesus, AD 53–170
- Smyrna, 170–312
- Pergamos, 312–606
- Thyatira, 606–1520
- Sardis, 1520–1750
- Philadelphia, 1750–1906
- Laodicea, 1906–to the present time

All of the church ages are very important, but more significant is the Church of Laodicea. There will not be another Church age which is an indication we are close to the end. From the chart above, please notice within the circles of the chart, the lighter color represents the amount of spiritual light and the revival spirit of that particular age. The darker color represents the amount of spiritual darkness there was in that particular age. For instance, in the church of *Ephesus*, which is the book of Acts Church, there was a move of the Holy Spirit of God through the apostles and other great men and women of God. May I repeat, they took over exactly Jesus left off. It also can be noticed from the chart as the ages progressed, the spiritual light gradually disappeared, and it became, spiritually speaking, darker and darker. The church of *Laodicea* has the least amount of light. What God is saying about our church age would be taught and dealt with explicitly in another later chapter. It will be dealt with in a manner to emphasize a point that would prepare us for revival and to be ready for the second return of Jesus Christ.

Every book in the Bible, especially the prophets and prophetic books, pointed to our day and time; this is the age where our generation will witness prophecies that the prophets, Jesus, and the apostles spoke about. One of our earlier presidents spoke these words and said, "Our generation has a date with destiny" Franklin D. Roosevelt. He was so right. From the day Israel became a nation, May 15th, 1948, this was the fulfillment of the fig tree budding of which Jesus spoke about in Matthew 24:32–35.

> *Now learn a parable of the fig tree; When his branch is yet tender, and putteth forth leaves, ye know that summer is nigh:*
> *So likewise ye, when ye shall see all these things, know that it is near, even at the doors.*
> *Verily I say unto you, This generation shall not pass, till all these things be fulfilled.*
> *Heaven and earth shall pass away, but my words shall not pass away.*
>
> — Matthew 24:32–35

The church age of *Laodicea* started in 1906 to the present time. This is the generation of the last days that will witness, experience catastrophes, signs, wonders, apostasy, ungodliness, lawlessness, people with no rule for law and taking of human life would mean nothing to ruthless killers, trafficking of young people for the sex trade, homosexuals and lesbianism, abortion and the sale of baby parts and human organs and such atrocities which is too gruesome to describe. Hard-heartedness and seared conscience among the ungodly, also persecution against Christians worldwide, but the Church can experience a move of God like never before; like no other generation has seen. The Antichrist is alive and well at this present time; he is a young man being educated at the present time in every aspect of business, social, economic, financial, industrial, technological, and religious life. He is also being acquainted with the population of the entire world and its culture, and he will have knowledge that will supersede any human being on earth and, at the present time, looking to all world events. In due time the nations of the world will want him as a world leader to solve their problems. He certainly will because at this time, the devil will possess him, and like the Bible says, he will do signs and wonders as he will deceive all people of the world, and they will wonder and go after him.

Believe it or not, the Mark of the Beast (whether it's the real Mark of the Beast) people who are injecting a chip on their forehead or forehead in California and other States in America can walk to a bank door and stand at the teller's desk or counter with no teller in attendance, a transaction from the account is already processed and within a few seconds, they can walk out their bank.

Here are some sobering words of the prophet Daniel and the apostle Paul,

> *[That a willful king will arise] And in his estate shall stand up a vile person, to whom they shall not give the honor of the kingdom;*
>
> *But he shall come in peaceably, and obtain the kingdom by flatteries [through ten kings or world rulers].*
>
> — Daniel 11:21

> *And the king shall do according to his will; and he shall exalt himself, and magnify himself above every god, and shall speak marvellous things against the God of gods.*
>
> — Daniel 11:36a

> *Now we beseech you, brethren, by the coming of our Lord Jesus Christ, and by our gathering together unto him,*
>
> *That ye be not soon shaken in mind, or be troubled, neither by spirit, nor by word, nor by letter as from us, as that is the day of Christ at hand.*
>
> *Let no man deceive you by any means: for that day shall not come, except there come a falling away first, and that man of sin be revealed, the son of perdition;*
>
> *Who opposeth and exalteth himself above all that is called God, or that is worshipped; so that he as God sitteth in the temple of God, shewing himself that he is God.*
>
> *Who opposeth and exalteth himself above all that is called God, or that is worshipped; so that he as God sitteth in the temple of God, shewing himself that he is God.*
>
> *Remember ye not, that, when I was yet with you, I told you these things? And now ye know what withholdeth that he might be revealed in his time. For the mystery of iniquity doth already work: only he who now letteth will let, until he be taken out of the way.*
>
> *And then shall that Wicked be revealed, whom the Lord shall consume with the spirit of his mouth, and shall destroy with the brightness of his coming: Even him, whose coming is after the working of Satan with all power and signs and lying wonders,*
>
> *And with all deceivableness of unrighteousness in them that perish; because they received not the love of the truth, that they might be saved.*
>
> *And for this cause God shall send them strong delusion, that they should believe a lie:*

> *That they all might be damned who believed not the truth, but had pleasure in unrighteousness.*
>
> — 2 Thessalonians 2:1–12

The apostle warns in the above Scripture that Christians should not be afraid of the world-shaking events that would be occurring at this present time. He speaks about Jesus' words the love (love for God) of many shall wax (become) cold (they would lose faith in Jesus Christ). The Antichrist would reign on earth as millions would be deceived and turn to the Antichrist because of his deceptive lying signs and wonders; billions of people of every nation, of course, would worship him as a god.

The first resurrection of which the Bible refers to and the "catching away of the bride of Christ" who is the true Church, those who are saved, baptized with the Holy Spirit and living clean and holy lives, praying and fasting once in a while, involved in doing something for God, winning lost souls (note, the author did not say hidden pastors, prophets, evangelists hidden in a mountain or valley somewhere doing nothing). Most of all know they are saved, according to John, chapter 3, baptized with the Holy Ghost (John, chapter 4, Acts, chapter 2), prepared and preparing for the second return of Jesus Christ.

The apostle Titus spoke these words as a warning to Christians:

> *Looking for that blessed hope, and the glorious appearing of the great God and our Savior Jesus Christ.*
>
> — Titus 2:13

These people are the ones who will go with Jesus when He returns. Too much emphasis is spent on the subject of when the rapture (which really is the catching away of the true church) will occur, for example, before the tribulation, during the tribulation, or after the tribulation. The point here is just being ready when Jesus returns.

> *In a moment, in the twinkling of an eye, at the last trump: for the trumpet shall sound, and the dead shall be raised incorruptible, and we shall be changed.*
>
> — 1 Corinthians 15:52

> *And he carried me away in the spirit to a great and high mountain, and shewed me that great city, the holy Jerusalem, descending out of heaven from God,*
>
> *Having the glory of God: and her light was like unto a stone most precious, even like a jasper stone, clear as crystal;*
>
> — Revelation 21:10–11

> *But I would not have you to be ignorant, brethren, concerning them which are asleep, that ye sorrow not, even as others which have no hope.*
>
> *For if we believe that Jesus died and rose again, even so them also which sleep in Jesus will God bring with him. For this we say unto you by the word of the Lord, that we which are alive and remain unto the coming of the Lord shall not prevent them which are asleep.*
>
> *For the Lord himself shall descend from heaven with a shout, with the voice of the archangel, and with the trump of God: and the dead in Christ shall rise first:*

Then we which are alive and remain shall be caught up together with them in the clouds, to meet the Lord in the air: and so shall we ever be with the Lord.

Wherefore comfort one another with these words.

— 1 Thessalonians 4:13–18

CHAPTER 11

Revival Is Not!

The author of this book does not intend to create the idea that he is critical of some words, actions, or manifestations that occur in the church of Christian meetings; they mean good and have the right motive, and they want to honor God in every way. This chapter, in particular, which is relatively short, is just a brief review to bring us to the understanding of what really is—"revival." Some ministers, ministries, and people can only operate, move and walk in the amount of spiritual knowledge or light that they have.

Going through a dark tunnel, the brighter the light—the father you see; without proper light, you can stumble, trip, and fall, even hurt yourself. Spiritually speaking, you can only speak, move, function, and operate by the amount of knowledge or spiritual light that you have. Now that you understand, we can proceed with this chapter and comprehend where the author is coming from.

Revival; recognized this word revival; it is the most misused word in the church today, also one of the most popular words in the Church of Jesus Christ today. The word revival is constantly reiterated over and over again and again, especially in full gospel churches. Whenever pastors and board members are planning a meeting, the first word that is flouted from their vocabulary is—"we need revival" or "we need an evangelist to conduct a revival." The signboards and the flashing neon signs in front of the church building illuminate the word revival with the name of the evangelist with dates and time. Every time the church doors are open, you can hear the word revival being uttered from the preacher's mouth to the evangelist; the word revival is most mentioned. The word revival is seldom left out from the church bulletin, invitation cards, and flyers, while TV and radio advertisements have popularized the word revival as listeners wait eagerly to run down another meeting for a word or prophecy concerning their lives and, more so, their materialistic benefits.

A one-night stand with a popular minister visiting a city, a few nights of services in a megachurch, or an evangelist conducting a three nights or weeks meeting is considered a revival. How about certain young people, gathering with different artists performing on stage, are now considered revival while some popular TV preacher coming to town with packed auditoriums, with advertisements announcements on a specific subject on the great life, the good life, seven steps to success, wealth and riches in promised to the hearers (cannot remember a sermon on the crucified life). The does realize that some good is done, souls are saved (which is most important) some people are healed, but believe it or not, this is not revival.

How to be a successful businessman or woman, life in the fast lane, healing campaigns, and crusades are being held year after year throughout the US, while at some meetings with placards, name tags, badges, pins, and WWJD shirts, ties create the impression that this is revival. Within the past years, we have witnessed Toronto, Pensacola, Brownsville, and Lake City. Of course, these meetings produced some outstanding results of souls being saved, people being healed, unusual happenings, miracles, and healings (thank God), but all of these meetings were labeled revival.

This statement might come as a shock to some readers, but all of the mentioned church activities might be considered the basics of Christianity, but this is not revival. The author is not trying to create a dialogue for discussion in creating an issue, but the word revival is not found in the New Testament but in the Old Testament,

Wilt thou not revive us again: that thy people may rejoice in thee?

— Psalm 85:6

This is one of the most powerful scripture suited and needed in the modern-day Church. Jesus and the apostles and the book of Acts saints never needed revival, and they did not need the programs, rituals, hypes, and all of the above to keep them revived (this would be explained in the next chapter), but what was their secret to the power of God that shook the world.

Revival is not an emotion; you can feel very spiritual, dance, jump up and down, kick your feet like the New York Rockets in a Broadway Play, fall to the floor, shake and weep hysterically, cry aloud—this in itself is not revival. Yours truly has witnessed over and over again, even hundreds of times, ministers announced on TV, radio, newspapers, flyers, internet, etc., that revival is coming to town.

Most religious activity does not come close to revival; revival is not when the top blows off but rather when the bottom falls out. In simple language, revival is not when all the celebrities, sports personalities assumed Christian and worldly millionaires gather together for a meeting on television. Imitation and showmanship are cheap and are definitely not revival. Thousands of times, entertainers convey the idea that when they gather together and the crowds go into a frenzy by waving hands, swaying from one side to another with uplifted hands is revival, but it is not. We schedule popular speakers and the best musicians and set aside a week for special meetings, these meetings are of certain spiritual benefits, but it's not revival; most of the time, these are set up by organizers, not agonizes. Again the author would reiterate this will do some good, but the sober-minded fact is this is not revival.

Revival is not heaven on earth, but earth-minded people are concerned about going to heaven. Peter, James, and John were the most privileged apostles who experienced the glory of God on the Mount of Transfiguration; these three apostles witnessed Jesus in His true Glory talking to Moses and Elijah, what they felt no other human being experienced and felt God's glory and awesome presence of God like they did. This supernatural experience as they exclaimed, "Master, it's good for us to be here." (Notice, it's good for us to be here.) No harm in experiencing God's power and supernatural experiences, plus the gifts of the Spirit in operation, miracles, healings, signs, and wonders, any of the other apostles would have traded places with Peter, James, and John.

Jesus wanted Peter, James, and John to see Him for whom He really is, this experience of witnessing His transfiguration on the mountain was what Jesus wanted them to witness so they could come down from the mountains and tell the other apostles, their wives, families, people they minister to that He is God in the flesh and that He is not to be taken for granted. Most of all, He wanted them to be effective in ministry, word, power, and most of all, to meet the needs of people, like healing their sickness and diseases. This experience was beneficial for their spiritual lives, but their priority should be to reach the lost tribes of Israel or win souls when they came down from the mountain.

The problem is they wanted to stay on the mountain; worst of all, they wanted to build three Tabernacles, one for Moses, Elijah, and Jesus; awesome! This sounded great, impressive, even super-spiritual, and the megachurch mentality (not that the author has anything against megachurches of our day).

What is the point here? With all the revival or what is often said as moves or working of the Holy Spirit in the past or in our day and time, most leaders or men and women of God have never learned the lesson that God wanted to learn, *first of all*, you cannot organize the Holy Spirit or God. *Secondly*, revival and again moves of the Holy Spirit cannot be organized into organizations, denominations, into independents groups with leaders or heads of organizations like popes, cardinals, archbishops, bishops, and other hierarchy, names and positions, even independents movements who experience some kind of revival but they fell into the same trap of organizing with heads and positions. Organizations, denominations, and independent movements have had this very same spirit which has produced men who have failed to give the glory to God, megachurches, self-seeking avarice preachers who have taken their eyes of Jesus and have centered or fixed their eyes on money, fame, and fortune.

Someone reading this book might have the inclination that the author is against church administration, which must be done decently and in order by capable representatives and leaders to fill, administer and execute important positions, but this is not so. A dictatorial spirit within the church is not what God intended, and this kind of spirit should not be termed revival.

Jesus did not encourage or condone building three tabernacles on the Mount of transfiguration, but He told the apostles, "Let us descend from the mountain because the needs of the people must be met, we must get souls saved and deliver people from sin, sickness, oppression, depression, and the power of the devil; most of all, preach to them the hope of eternal life." Again! Is it wrong to have a megachurch building if it's needed? No! But let's get the souls of mankind saved first and if the buildings are needed to house the souls of men, then let them be built for lost souls of mankind but not entertainment; entertaining people definitely is not revival.

Revival is not individualism; no one man or woman gets the glory from revival; it is not man-planned, man-timed, man-determined, and man controlling (this is the reason pastors, in particular, are afraid of revival; revival would interfere with their extravagant lifestyle, traditional ritualistic and program within the local Church). Revival is not planned and organized; it is not entertainment; we are living in a day and time church services have become so mechanized; the so-called revival begins with a quick traditional prayer, then the choir sings, a solo or two is rendered, the pastor preachers a sermonet to the "christian-nets." During this time, some within the congregation just sit there and are entertained, and while being entertained, so many cannot seem to get their eyes off their watches or church clock with the idea that the sermon is too long or the music is too loud or the church band sounds like a Mardi Gras parade or the downtown May Day parade, with the attitude, "I am going to miss the ball game or restaurant buffet." How could this be a revival?

Revival is not heaven on earth but God's perfect will, plan, and program being fulfilled on earth; this is the reason Jesus prayed, "Thy will be done on earth as in heaven." These words are worth reiterating, programs, seminars, and huge campaigns, some for namesake, have replaced the true born again experience with myriads of activity as denominational and organizational leaders sit in their plush offices with every modern convenience, and from their swivel chairs, they call, emails, text, twitter their political instructions of who should go where, who pastor they should move, which one is better to compromise with them in the larger churches so they can bolster their head office operations with the support of church members and widows who pay their tithes and offering. This is not revival.

Revival is not death; the author does not like church buildings in cemeteries; it resembles what's inside the church building, death. Death in the pulpit and the platform means death in the congregation. We have a generation of preachers who earns every degree that is there to obtain, but they are dead (spiritually dead). Universities offer all of these degrees as pastors and leaders enhance the beginning and ending of their names with degrees that stretch across town. Still, they are dead, as they whine and complain that this is a modern-day while they openly support a lifestyle that is unbiblical and ungodly. At the same time, they intentionally, deliberately, and maliciously actually hate those that believe that marriage is God-ordained and solely between a man and a woman.

This is a generation of Christians, most of the so-called Christians who have twisted the Scriptures, especially the teachings of Moses in the first books of the Bible, the prophets, Jesus' words written in the Gospels and the writings of the apostle Paul, plus the writings of all the other apostles. These Scriptures they have twisted to suit their own lifestyle, and if true Christians (there are true Christians in America and the world) believe otherwise, they are branded as fanatics, but the above writings are nothing compared to the words of Jesus as He preached two thousand years ago, here are the words of Jesus—Matthew 23:1–33.

Revival is not men increasing and Jesus decreasing! Revival cannot be birth by hindering the Holy Spirit for man's ideas and programs; the bulletin and the program guide are so populated with so many participants doing their thing not even the Holy Spirit can get in! And if the Holy Spirit does move on an individual who is spirit-filled with the Holy Spirit to worship, praise God, and pray aloud, they are ushered in a room by a dead usher, deacon, and now security officers in the Church congregation. Revival is not going through the motion, tradition, ritual, or formality; there is not a relationship with God; revival is not how much money a quest speaker can raise; if you cannot raise x amount of dollars, you are not considered a popular speaker.

Revival is not whipping up the crowd into a frenzy, emotionalism, and then there are preachers and people who go through the mechanics of a Sunday morning service this means from preacher to people and then walk out of the church building, and right after church manifest funny and ungodly spirits, bad attitudes, unforgiving hearts. Revival is not having hate, jealousy, pride, or being selfish; revival is not harboring an ungodly lifestyle such as being unfaithful to your wife or husband, and most of all, revival is not an individual professing he or she is a Christian and condone and practices same-sex marriage, might be right to some so-called Christians but totally wrong according to the Bible and most of all wrong in the God's sight.

There is a false revival, and there is a true revival. Later in this book, the subject of revival will be dealt with in its entirety; readers and members of the Body of Christ or the Church, in general, are those who are truly born again and have experienced the transformation through salvation through Jesus Christ must be aware that there is a false revival and a true revival. This false revival inevitably has nothing that is biblical and the teachings of Jesus and the apostles, but it's a modern-day revival that Protestants are not Protestants anymore.

The Ecumenical Movement is one of the most popular subjects at this present time. What is the Ecumenical Movement? The word "ecumenical" comes from the Greek word "*oikoumene*," which basically means "this inhabited world." At present, there are two great bodies—the World Council of Churches and the National Council of Churches. The main aim of the Ecumenical Movement is to bring churches of all denominations and cults, and ultimately, all other religious organizations together as One Ecumenical Church or World Church. At the first Ecumenical Assembly held in Amsterdam in 1948, the motto "one church-one world" was adopted.

It is agreed that one of the major issues for the WCC to tackle is the relations between the churches and the organizations of all the other religions and ideologies. With regards to this issue, dialogues are being held among the different religions of the world. The Bible prophecy of a super Church is now being fulfilled. Present, there are two great bodies; there are the relations between the churches and the held among the different religions of the world. The Bible prophecy of a super Church is now being fulfilled.

The courtship between the World Council of Churches and the Roman Catholics has progressed rapidly over the years gone by; Roman Catholic bishops from around the world met at the Vatican from 1962 to 1968, which now has a name—The Ecumenical Council. They revised the Catholic liturgy and have updated the church in several areas in an effort to bring the Protestants back into the fold. In the higher echelons of Catholicism, Protestants are no longer called "heretics" but are referred to as "separated brethren." It should be noted that this procedure has not reached the grassroots level in some areas. Booklets are being distributed to Catholic laymen on "ecumenical etiquette" Each year, millions of leaflets, "Week of Prayer for Christian Unity," are distributed. Catholics and Protestants have joint communion services. They undertake joint projects for social activities and even have joint folk singing programs. One of the biggest drives toward unity is the amalgamation of Catholic and Protestant seminaries. For the first time in history, Roman Catholic churches are joining the city church council. The Archbishop of Canterbury was the first Anglican primate to visit a pope in four hundred years. Official Roman Catholic documents are beginning to use the term "church" to describe Protestant churches. It must be mentioned that at the time this book is being written, there is a movement that is rapidly growing, which is sanctioned by so many religious organizations called *Chrislam*. This marriage between so-called Christianity and some Muslims is another movement that would automatically end up in the World Council of Churches and the Ecumenical Movement.

Some full gospels organizations, denominations, and religions, other religious organizations call this movement one of the greatest religious movements that they have labeled "revival," hundreds of thousands of religious leaders of different organizations and religions are blindly heading into this so-called revival. Some of them are labeling this movement as the greatest movement since in the year of October 31st, 1517.

In the year of October 31, 1517, when Martin Luther nailed his 95 Thesis on the church door of the Cathedral Whittenburg, Germany, of which he was the leading priest and pastor, this started the great reformation from that time most every religious organization came out from the Roman Catholic Church. Some of them were called Protestants because they, and rightfully so, had something to protest about, but now they are not protesting anymore. They are blindly going back into a church system that has blinded the eyes of millions of people over the centuries gone by, but what is happening now is prophesy being fulfilled. The leader of a one-world government and the leader of the one church organization will finally designate their authority and leadership power to the "antichrist," which will lead them to the Mark of the Beast and the short reign of "The Antichrist" (Revelation, chapter 13).

CHAPTER 12

Revival: What Is It?

Did Jesus, the apostles, the apostle Paul, and the book of Acts saints need *revival*? Before answering this question positively and constructively, "it must be understood that revival is a personal thing" with ongoing results; revival is a "co-cooperative thing," then "a city-wide thing," then "a State thing," then "a National thing," then "a worldwide thing." The word revival is so often reiterated again and again in Christian circles, whether it is a church meeting, conference seminars, or other gatherings; to some, the word revival is a pass time word, but at least it shows a sense of concern, but those who are mentioning the word revival and are praying for the same, most of them do not realize what they are asking for.

To answer the question, did Jesus, the apostles, the apostle Paul, and the book of Acts saints need revival? The answer is *no*. Jesus was revival all by Himself; while Jesus was on earth, anywhere He went, His ministry brought about a spiritual change in individuals, homes, villages, towns, and cities. His primary message was "God in you," which was backed up with healings, miracles, and supernatural signs and wonders. How anyone could read Matthew, Mark, Luke, and John and deny the message that Jesus preached was a different message than the Scribes, Pharisees, Sadducees, and other religious sects of that day.

Jesus' word was also backed up by the supernatural power of God; again, His message was "God in you, the Kingdom of God is within you." Is there scripture to back up this statement? Yes!

> *Neither shall they say, Lo here! or, lo there! for, behold, the kingdom of God is within you.*
> — Luke 17:21.

Jesus is not talking about that He is a King and has lords, knights, and people within a kingdom (some writers might have a different view and written books about this), who are subject to Him. What is Jesus speaking about? He is telling us that He came to make it possible for God to dwell in you and be with you always! And this would be possible by Him dying on the cross, opening the way for all human beings to approach God for themselves after they believe, and then He will send the Holy Ghost (God, to dwell in human beings) to live in us. This means God living in human beings; this is what it means by the kingdom of God shall be in you.

God living in us is a revelation; this is the reason Jesus, the apostles, Paul, and the book of Acts saints always had a revival. The majority of Christians live a backslidden state of life ninety percent of the time, always wanting someone or something to stir them up some of them into a frenzy, and when the frenzy is over after they get home and after a few weeks, the so-called revival they had fizzled out like Alka-Seltzer, then they continue searching for another someone or something to pump them up again, and this has been an ongoing thing for ages within most of the Church World or Body of Christ. Is it wrong to have evangelists, guest speakers, TV evangelists, and celebrities coming to a church and having special meetings? No.

But in some churches, it seems like some pastors and churches are more interested in celebrities and popular artists, but some of them are not saved and baptized with the Holy Spirit. The author is making a statement here, and this is with the love of God and respect and honor for every ministry gift and people of God in the Body of Christ. If the Church or Body of Christ realizes this revelation of God wanting to dwell in us by His Spirit, this is going to put a lot of so-called professional preachers, ministers, evangelists, speakers, gospel singers, and entertainers out of business.

The Gospel of Jesus Christ has become so commercialized that there is hardly anyone preaching "God Living in you and me." Revival is God dwelling in us, with us and through us edifying the Body of Christ, strengthening them to endure to the end, or helping them prepare for the second return of Jesus Christ, and most of all reaching out to a lost around the world that does not Jesus as Lord and Savior, especially those that have never heard of Jesus.

The ministry of Jesus never ceases to amaze me; there was never a dull moment in the life and ministry of Jesus. Talk about revival; He had a real revival going from the moment He began His ministry, from recruiting twelve disciples, then being baptized by John the Baptist in the River Jordan (He was not sprinkled with water, but He was immersed into the water) to forty days of fasting, then turning water into wine, preaching a different word—the beatitudes (having the right attitude), loving your enemies (how many people do you see loving their enemies). Then He healed a leper, the centurion moved Jesus by his faith as Jesus spoke the word, and the centurion's servant was healed from many miles away. Jesus healed Peter's mother in law of a fever, quieted a storm while riding on a boat, cast out a thousand demons from a man dwelling in a cemetery (some preachers would have run from him), healed a paralyzed and dumb man, cursed a tree, and it dried down, then the miracle was—He raised Lazarus from the dead, and this miracle raised the devil in the Scribes, Pharisees, and other religions of that day. This trend of ministry continued in this fashion throughout Jesus' ministry until His death and resurrection. What was Jesus' secret? God was working through Him. All you have to do is read Matthew, Mark, Luke, and John. This is what you term real *revival*. Jesus is revival.

The book of Acts is God working through the apostles by the power of the Holy Spirit. After the resurrection of Jesus, He spent forty days with the eleven apostles reminding, refreshing re-schooling them of the things He had taught them during the three years He had been with them. Then before ascending to heaven, He gave them specific instructions, recorded in the book of Luke.

"And, behold, I send the promise of my Father upon you: but tarry ye in the city of Jerusalem, until ye be endued with power from on high."

— Luke 24:49

One hundred and twenty disciples…this is including the eleven apostles obeyed, and this is what happened, which is recorded in the book of Acts.

And when the day of Pentecost was fully come, they were all with one accord in one place. And suddenly there came a sound from heaven as of a rushing mighty wind, and it filled all the house where they were sitting.
And there appeared unto them cloven tongues like as of fire, and it sat upon each of them.
And they were all filled with the Holy Ghost, and began to speak with other tongues, as the Spirit gave them utterance.

— Acts 2:1–4

We are still on the subject of revival, so please pay particular attention to what happened in the next paragraph.

Immediately after they received the Baptism of the Holy Ghost or Holy Spirit (God in the Apostles), Jehovah God manifested Himself as the Father in the Old Testament. He manifested in Jesus, His Son, in Matthew, Mark, Luke, and John. In the book of Acts, God is manifesting Himself through the eleven apostles, including the apostle Paul who made up the twelve apostles, in the power of the Holy Spirit. This means that God was in them, working through ministry gifts (fivefold ministry in the church). Gifts of the Holy Spirit through the apostles operating and manifesting His power in souls being saved, healings, miracles, signs, and wonders. What happened after they were baptized with the Holy Spirit in the Upper Room? Peter (who denied Jesus was a changed man) got up and preached and prophesied and made reference to the prophet Joel (this is that which was spoken by the prophet Joel). Yes, Peter and the others, after receiving the Holy Spirit and speaking in tongues, please note! They did not remain in the upper room just waiting on some sensations, shaking, prophesying to each other; immediately after Peter preached and prophesied (please catch this), three thousand souls got saved and received the Holy Spirit.

Right after three thousand souls got saved, they continued in the Apostles Doctrine, going house to house, places or buildings where they could worship freely, including synagogues when they were allowed to, studying the Word, fellowship, communion, and prayer. Then the fear of God came upon every soul, and many signs and wonders were done by the apostles. They were of one heart, one soul, and one mind. Those who had lands, houses, gold, silver, and other material things sold it and brought it and laid it at the apostle's feet to evangelize and preach the Gospel of Jesus Christ. During this revival, a man and his wife named Ananias and Sapphira sold a piece of land but held back some of the money and lied about the price they sold the land for; guess what happened? They died.

Peter and John went to the temple to pray, and a certain man lame from birth was begging alms, who saw Peter and John going in to pray to ask them for some money. Peter told him, "Look on us." Now notice they were going to pray; could you imagine what could have happened after they prayed? Then Peter with John said, "Look on us"; not to look to the building or "let's go in the temple, we will call a service. We will sing three songs and let the choir render a few selections; we would have sister Peter sing a special. Then John would read the scriptures, we would pick up an offering, then Peter would preach, I would make the altar call, then we would call everyone to the altar to sing a few blood songs, everybody would get in hype, and then we would lay hands on you. We do not know if you will get healed or not, but we will try." None of this was said and done.

After Peter and John said, "Look on us," the lame man was expecting to receive some money, but Peter and John said unto him, "Silver and gold have we none but in the name of Jesus rise up and walk" Acts 3:6. then Peter lifted him up, and he started to run all over the place perfectly healed. We are living in a day and time when most of the church world has silver and gold but no power to heal and deliver people. After the lame man got healed, Peter preached another great word, and five thousand souls got saved. Persecution arose from every direction after this miracle of the lame man walking, they did not have the favor of the governor or the mayor, and they did not invite Peter and John to have a banquet; what happened? They beat them with sticks and sent them to jail. But God delivered them, and they were right back preaching, healing the sick, casting out demons, and getting souls saved.

Deacons were appointed by the leading of the Holy Spirit, and those that were chosen as deacons were full of the Holy Ghost and power. After the deacons were elected, the power of God was so eminent; the anointing was so strong, the moving of the Holy Spirit moved in such an unusual manner which caused a move of God or a revival to break out, which caused thousands of souls to be saved, healed with supernatural visitations of God. This also brought about persecution. (real revival causes persecution) Stephen, a deacon filled with the Holy Spirit, preached with such fervor, power, and anointing that the Scribes, Pharisees, and other religious Sects were so jealous and infuriated that their followers were turning to Jesus; they became so hateful and antagonist that they killed Stephen. Saul, who became Paul, initiated the death of Stephen. This same Saul received permission from the high priest with letters from the Roman government to kill all Christians. On his way to Damascus, he was smitten from his horse by a bright light, who was Jesus. Then after he was saved and baptized and became one of the greatest apostles, from here the book of Acts Christians was flowing in the waves of God's glory in revival with a move of the Holy Spirit combined with unprecedented supernatural results.

The modern-day trend of thinking among 90 percent of Christians is that serving and living for God is a life filled with blessings, prosperity, fame, and fortune. Is anything wrong with this? No! But reading the book of Acts and as time progressed, and then throughout the dark ages and to the present time, persecution against true Christians was an ongoing thing. Persecution is expected, especially during a revival, such as was the case in the book of Acts. No true Christian deliberately goes around looking for persecution; a perfect example of the mentality of an individual who called himself a Christian approached the author, yours truly, and addressed me with these words, "Hey, Pastor Seebran, I heard you do not believe in the Tribulation anymore." Having an idea of these individual beliefs, my reply to him was, "I believe in Jesus and His grace and strength to help me through my Christian life." But deliberate, presumptuous, self-provocative self invitee persecution because of my bad attitude towards people who do not believe like I do causes and inflicts persecution to my family, neighbors, community, certain religious sects, the State, or Nation. But persecution will come the moment you confess Jesus Christ as your Lord and Savior.

As revival continued in the book of Acts, Saul (now Paul), with letters from all of the religious sects and the Roman government, was creating havoc persecuting the true Christians, but revival prevailed and continued. Phillip, one of the elected deacons, not a bishop, pastor, evangelist, prophet, apostle, teacher, but a deacon filled with the Holy Ghost, went to Samaria, a people whom the Jews did not regard as a people; Phillip had one of the greatest revivals, here is the record in Scripture,

> *Then Philip went down to the city of Samaria, and preached Christ unto them.*
> *And the people with one accord gave heed unto those things which Philip spake, hearing and seeing the miracles which he did.*
> *For unclean spirits, crying with loud voice, came out of many that were possessed with them: and many taken with palsies, and that were lame, were healed.*
> *And there was great joy in that city.*
> *But there was a certain man, called Simon, which beforetime in the same city used sorcery, and bewitched the people of Samaria, giving out that himself was some great one:*
> *To whom they all gave heed, from the least to the greatest, saying, This man is the great power of God.*
> *And to him they had regard, because that of long time he had bewitched them with sorceries.*
> *But when they believed Philip preaching the things concerning the kingdom of God, and the name of Jesus Christ, they were baptized, both men and women.*
> — Acts 8:5–12

The book of Acts is a perfect example of what revival is all about; the above record is a perfect example of the same. Revival is not a show, but revival is about a dedicated vessel like Phillip going to a city and preaching the Gospel of Jesus Christ, with results as is recorded above. Phillip was so dedicated and given over to the Holy Spirit; even the angel of God spoke to him about an Ethiopian man of great authority who was under the Queen Candace of Ethiopia. Phillip listened to the angel of God and went to the desert by a river in Gaza. There he saw this Ethiopian man who was sitting in his chariot reading the book of Isaiah, and he went and sat with him and asked him if he understood what he read; the Ethiopian reply was,

> *And he said, How can I, except some man should guide me? And he desired Philip that he would come up and sit with him.*
>
> *The place of the scripture which he read was this, He was led as a sheep to the slaughter; and like a lamb dumb before his shearer, so opened he not his mouth:*
>
> *In his humiliation his judgment was taken away: and who shall declare his generation? for his life is taken from the earth.*
>
> *And the eunuch answered Philip, and said, I pray thee, of whom speaketh the prophet this? of himself, or of some other man?*
>
> *Then Philip opened his mouth, and began at the same scripture, and preached unto him Jesus.*
>
> — Acts 8:31–35

Because of this, the Ethiopians received the Gospel of Jesus Christ. Revival is not a hit-and-miss thing, with myriads of spasmodic unintelligible manifestations, and after its over no results, it is true that when the Holy Spirit moves, there would be people who would react to the moving of the Holy Spirit in different ways. Some would cry, shout, laugh, jump, run, scream, or speak in tongues, but when there is revival and a move of God among people, revival will reach all types of people regardless of race, color, or creed and will produce results like Phillip and the Ethiopian which, in turn, would affect a town, city, nation, country, and people.

Revival produces the supernatural and supernatural results; revival is so needed at this time, especially so close to the second return of Jesus. It is imperative that we have revival and a supernatural (beyond the norm) move of God and so needed to break down the word supernatural. First known use of this word was in the fifteenth century, su-per-nat-u-ral (adjective), su-per-nat-che-rel. Middle English, from Medieval Latin—"supernaturalis," from Latin super + natura (natural); this means relating to an order or existence beyond the visible observable universe, especially of or relating to the Supreme Being Almighty God.

Supernatural also means departing from what is usual, normal, status quo, traditional, ritualistic, and formality. Also means to transcend from the laws of nature, such as the opening of the Red Sea for the children of Israel to pass through on their way to the Promised Land; manna from heaven, water from rock, quails appearing in the skies, and falling to earth for the children to eat. Supernatural also means, like when Solomon dedicated the temple, the priests could not minister because the glory of God (like a thick mist or fog) filled the temple so that the priest could not minister. Also means that when Jesus started recruiting the twelve apostles, He told Phillip, "When you were under the fig tree, I saw the discernment and the word of knowledge. Jesus was turning water into wine, unstopping deaf ears, making the blind see, lame walk, cursing a tree, and it dried from the roots, raising Lazarus from the dead plus a few others. The record in Acts, chapter 2, of the baptism of the Holy Spirit, three thousand, five thousand people being saved after and receiving the Holy Spirit. Peter was delivered from prison by an angel of God, and Paul and Silas were freed from Jail after an earthquake; these are very few biblical examples of the supernatural. These supernatural occurrences can happen if the church, in general, desires and hunger after God and pray towards this effect. This type of result would usher in a move of God or real revival, and billions of souls would be saved and filled with the Holy Spirit, which would advance God's plan and program and hasten the coming of the Lord Jesus Christ.

All over the world and right here in America, people gather to worship God, some during the week, some on Saturday, and most on Sunday. Is this wrong? Certainly not; typical worship service begins with songs of praise, worship, and special music, then probably a welcome for the visitors and a scanty and brief mention or introduction of visiting ministers. Then the tithes and offering with music combine, a rendition of special from the choir. After this, the pastor or guest speaker stands and proceeds to the podium and begins to teach or preach a half an hour sermon with a percentage of people looking at their watches, maybe an altar call (by the way, an altar call is a thing of the past in most churches).

By the way, in some churches, if an altar call is given, a percentage of the people is already gone out the front or side door of the church building to catch a ball game, restaurant, or some TV show. I recall there was a time when the altar call was given; some church members would be praying and interceding (a strange word to some). God save some souls, deliver these people. Thank God for the few who stay and pray through these souls into the kingdom of God. But a percentage of the people just sit down with eyes wide open while some are chewing gum. It is the prayer of some ministers of God and people for churchy to get a hunger for God and for the supernatural power of God and to have the results of supernatural miracles of some of the Old Testament saints, Jesus, and the apostles.

Revival is pleading or praying to God for His divine intervention in restoring the Church to its original roots, which means to be infused with the teachings, life, and demonstrative miracle healing power of Jesus Christ. A typical example of Jesus was demonstrated through the life of the apostle Paul as revival continued in the book of Acts. As a matter of fact, after all of the apostles and those who were in the Upper Room received the baptism with the Holy Spirit, they demonstrated a Christ-like life with power to reach their generation. Interjecting this thought right here is of utmost importance. The reason so many revivals in the past reached a standstill and fizzled off like Alka-Seltzer is that there were too much sensationalism, emotionalism, man's exaltation, organizationalism, religionism, and all other "isms."

Driving through Virginia and Washington, DC, many years ago, the winter months were quite severe; every tree along the interstates and highways looked dead and lifeless and created the idea that they would be done for and never come back to life again. But comes springtime, every shrub and tree would begin to turn green, then spring forth leaves and every type of greenery and blooms. Living in British Colombia, Canada, for several years in the Okanogan Valley, its winter months is the severest; you can feel the cold going through your bones, but when springtime arrives, the apples, plums, cherry, grapes, pears, and so many different types of fruit trees begin to put forth its leaves and in particular, begin to blooms, it is one of the most awesome and best smelling places in the world. The reason for this is that there was life imbedded deep down in the roots and in the middle of every tree trunk and shrub. But it takes springtime, the sunshine, warmer winds, warmer climate, running water, warmer raindrops, and moisture, and all of this is occurring outside of these trees and shrubs, which affects or warms up the root that triggers the life that was dormant in the winter months.

When springtime hits with sunshine, warmer winds, warmer climate, running water, warmer raindrops, the right moisture suddenly there is a burst of greenery from the tress with beautiful leaves protruding from the branches and twigs, as some of the shrubs with its multicolor leaves and blooms gracing the landscape. Alas! Everyone breathes a sigh of relief; spring is here. This is what revival is all about. By the way, some of these trees and shrubs never survived the winter and died; the only way you could have verified that they died is in the springtime and the heat of the summer months; why? They did not spring forth leaves, blooms, fruits, or flowers; this is the way it is with some Christians, they did not spring forth in the springtime, and death was seen in the summer. Yes! The Church may ice in the summer.

The general term for revival is "to bring back to life that which was once alive but is now dead." It must be clearly understood that we are dealing with the natural and the spiritual; naturally speaking, when something or someone is dead, it is impossible for it or an individual to come back to life unless it is an act of God, divine intervention, or a supernatural miracle. Because, naturally speaking, death does not respond. It has nothing to respond to! Because it's dead, but life responds to life; spiritually speaking, life can respond to life because God is life. Ever since the beginning of this chapter on revival, yours truly has been longing to write these words, "To have and experience what Jesus and the apostles had, this example of revival should be the desire the righteous actions of Christians." God is always waiting and ready to respond to our desire for Him and our righteous actions. Here are some words or synonyms relevant to revival, reanimate, recharge, regenerate, rejuvenate, rekindle, renew, resurrect, resuscitate, revitalize, revivify, reawake, reawaken, restore, restoration, rekindle, refresh, refreshing.

There is only one word close to the word "revival" that is found in the Bible, "Wilt thou not revive again that thy people may rejoice in thee" Psalm 85:6.

Little did we realize in our day that this one word would have such a wide and immense impact, especially our generation who needs so desperately a revival like unto the ministry of Jesus and the apostles? This is a Psalm of thankfulness and praise to God for bringing them out of captivity, forgiveness of sins, and his bestowing upon them the abundant blessings of God. This is exactly what revival does, it brings us out of our natural and spiritual captivity, and it puts exaltation, praise, and worship to God and the abundance of God's blessings. Revival changes the atmosphere within the local church and, of course, the Body of Christ. When people turn to God in Spirit and in truth, He sends revival, and it changes the carnal church to a spiritual church which affects the community, town, city, state, and nation. Revival affects and changes the immoral condition of a people and nation and can stop the tide of sin, immorality, murders, and other crimes.

When people become hard, callous, and are heading to reprobate minds, revival leads them back to the foot of the cross where Jesus shed His blood; as they ask God to wash them afresh in the blood of Jesus, their hearts become mellow and soft again. Revival causes the love of God to flow for one another (not just the mention of the word I love you with no feelings or meaning), but in real revival, there can be such godly love for other people; some will even love their enemies. Of course, this is what Jesus said, "Love your enemies," and when this happens, then it is genuine revival.

In times of revival, preachers will not be consumed and controlled by their name, fame, and fortune; the spirit of my name is Jimmy; all I want is for you to gi-me, gi-mi (give me, give me); they will want to share financially and materially with their fellow ministers to work together to bring in the end-time harvest of souls. During the revival, ministers and ministries certainly will not want to do ministry by and for themselves just for fame, name, and glory, but they would be willing to help other ministers financially, materially, and otherwise to bring in or reap in thousands of souls who will be saved. God will always get the glory, even though He can use one man, but one man does have a monopoly on God. Revival is unity working together, praying together, winning souls together so that God will be glorified, and the Church is perfected to bring in a harvest of souls prepared for the second return of Jesus.

The apostle Paul was one of the highest educated men, but worst of all, he was one of the most religious men before God got a hold of him. On the road to Damascus to kill and persecute real Christians, he had an encounter with God; here is a brief Scriptural reference from the book of Acts,

> *And as he journeyed, he came near Damascus: and suddenly there shined round about him a light from heaven:*
>
> *And he fell to the earth, and heard a voice saying unto him, Saul, Saul, why persecutest thou me?*
>
> *And he said, Who art thou, Lord? And the Lord said, I am Jesus whom thou persecutest: it is hard for thee to kick against the pricks.*
>
> *And he trembling and astonished said, Lord, what wilt thou have me to do? And the Lord said unto him, Arise, and go into the city, and it shall be told thee what thou must do.*
>
> — Acts 9:3–6

When the apostle Paul had his encounter and experience with God, what were the first words that he spoke or said, "And he trembling and astonished said, Lord, what wilt thou have me to do? And the Lord said unto him, Arise, and go into the city, and it shall be told thee what thou must do" Acts 9:6.

"*What will thou have me to do?*" ask most people or individuals after getting saved because some of the preachings that they have heard, they want fame, fortune, a name, some wants a Rolls Royce and to be rich, famous, and popular. But what did Paul say? "*What will thou have me to do?*" True revival will produce a type of Christians that will answer the call of God to go and win the lost at any cost instead of settling for some whimsical sensation and just asking God for the material things of this life. Nothing is wrong with prosperity, but again, it must be reiterated money is needed to reach lost souls, but prosperity for prosperity's sake and settling for some whimsical sensation and just asking God for the material things of this life and not doing something for God is not revival.

The ministry and life of the apostle, now Paul, through the power of the Holy Spirit, dominated the book of Acts as revival fires burn night and day, which produced results of souls being saved, healed, and delivered by signs, wonders, miracles, and supernatural visitations of God. By this time, the apostle Peter realized that God raised up the apostle Paul (one who had seen Jesus and was sent by Him) to be the apostle to the Gentiles; God confirmed this to Peter, who at first had nothing to do with the Gentiles.

The revival started with the Jews; now, revival breaks out among the Gentiles, recorded in the book of Acts, chapter 10. This is one of the most inspiring magnificent writings in Scriptures, which is able to open the eyes of ministers as well as church members, as we read the book of Acts, chapter 10, a perfect example of the revival of God working and manifesting Himself through dreams, visions, and revelations (which the majority of the church has rejected), which projected a Roman centurion who led a thousand soldiers by the name of Cornelius who was proselyte Jew of which the Bible tells us he was faithful to God and Church, prayed night and day, attended church regularly and gave much alms (offerings to the church) to help the ministry and care for the poor and needy (he never once asked for a Mansion, Cadillac, Bentley, or Lincoln), but he was faithful to God and church, prayed night and day, love the brethren, and gave to the ministry, poor, and needy. Here come the results of Cornelius' overall faithfulness; he had a visitation from God in a dream or vision. The author felt it necessary to insert the record about Cornelius from the book of Acts.

> *There was a certain man in Caesarea called Cornelius, a centurion of the band called the Italian band,*
>
> *A devout man, and one that feared God with all his house, which gave much alms to the people, and prayed to God alway.*
>
> *He saw in a vision evidently about the ninth hour of the day an angel of God coming in to him, and saying unto him, Cornelius.*
>
> *And when he looked on him, he was afraid, and said, What is it, Lord? And he said unto him, Thy prayers and thine alms are come up for a memorial before God.*
>
> *And now send men to Joppa, and call for one Simon, whose surname is Peter:*
>
> *He lodgeth with one Simon a tanner, whose house is by the sea side: he shall tell thee what thou oughtest to do.*
>
> *And when the angel which spake unto Cornelius was departed, he called two of his household servants, and a devout soldier of them that waited on him continually;*
>
> *And when he had declared all these things unto them, he sent them to Joppa.*
>
> *On the morrow, as they went on their journey, and drew nigh unto the city, Peter went up upon the housetop to pray about the sixth hour:*
>
> *And he became very hungry, and would have eaten: but while they made ready, he fell into a trance,*
>
> *And saw heaven opened, and a certain vessel descending upon him, as it had been a great sheet knit at the four corners, and let down to the earth:*
>
> *Wherein were all manner of fourfooted beasts of the earth, and wild beasts, and creeping things, and fowls of the air.*
>
> *And there came a voice to him, Rise, Peter; kill, and eat.*
>
> *But Peter said, Not so, Lord; for I have never eaten any thing that is common or unclean.*
>
> *And the voice spake unto him again the second time, What God hath cleansed, that call not thou common.*
>
> *This was done thrice: and the vessel was received up again into heaven.*
>
> *Now while Peter doubted in himself what this vision which he had seen should mean, behold, the men which were sent from Cornelius had made enquiry for Simon's house, and stood before the gate,*

And called, and asked whether Simon, which was surnamed Peter, were lodged there.

While Peter thought on the vision, the Spirit said unto him, Behold, three men seek thee.

Arise therefore, and get thee down, and go with them, doubting nothing: for I have sent them.

Then Peter went down to the men which were sent unto him from Cornelius; and said, Behold, I am he whom ye seek: what is the cause wherefore ye are come?

And they said, Cornelius the centurion, a just man, and one that feareth God, and of good report among all the nation of the Jews, was warned from God by an holy angel to send for thee into his house, and to hear words of thee.

Then called he them in, and lodged them. And on the morrow Peter went away with them, and certain brethren from Joppa accompanied him.

And the morrow after they entered into Caesarea. And Cornelius waited for them, and he had called together his kinsmen and near friends.

And as Peter was coming in, Cornelius met him, and fell down at his feet, and worshipped him.

But Peter took him up, saying, Stand up; I myself also am a man.

And as he talked with him, he went in, and found many that were come together.

And he said unto them, Ye know how that it is an unlawful thing for a man that is a Jew to keep company, or come unto one of another nation; but God hath shewed me that I should not call any man common or unclean.

Therefore came I unto you without gainsaying, as soon as I was sent for: I ask therefore for what intent ye have sent for me?

And Cornelius said, Four days ago I was fasting until this hour; and at the ninth hour I prayed in my house, and, behold, a man stood before me in bright clothing,

And said, Cornelius, thy prayer is heard, and thine alms are had in remembrance in the sight of God.

Send therefore to Joppa, and call hither Simon, whose surname is Peter; he is lodged in the house of one Simon a tanner by the sea side: who, when he cometh, shall speak unto thee.

Immediately therefore I sent to thee; and thou hast well done that thou art come. Now therefore are we all here present before God, to hear all things that are commanded thee of God.

Then Peter opened his mouth, and said, Of a truth I perceive that God is no respecter of persons:

But in every nation he that feareth him, and worketh righteousness, is accepted with him.

The word which God sent unto the children of Israel, preaching peace by Jesus Christ: (he is Lord of all:)

That word, I say, ye know, which was published throughout all Judaea, and began from Galilee, after the baptism which John preached;

How God anointed Jesus of Nazareth with the Holy Ghost and with power: who went about doing good, and healing all that were oppressed of the devil; for God was with him.

And we are witnesses of all things which he did both in the land of the Jews, and in Jerusalem; whom they slew and hanged on a tree:

Him God raised up the third day, and shewed him openly;

Not to all the people, but unto witnesses chosen before God, even to us, who did eat and drink with him after he rose from the dead.

And he commanded us to preach unto the people, and to testify that it is he which was ordained of God to be the Judge of quick and dead.

To him give all the prophets witness, that through his name whosoever believeth in him shall receive remission of sins.

While Peter yet spake these words, the Holy Ghost fell on all them which heard the word.

And they of the circumcision which believed were astonished, as many as came with Peter, because that on the Gentiles also was poured out the gift of the Holy Ghost.

For they heard them speak with tongues, and magnify God. Then answered Peter,

Can any man forbid water, that these should not be baptized, which have received the Holy Ghost as well as we?

And he commanded them to be baptized in the name of the Lord. Then prayed they him to tarry certain days.

— Acts 10:1–48

While all these supernatural visitations were occurring in Cornelius' life, God visited the apostle Peter and redeemed him from his deep, imbedded, biased and prejudiced spirit and thinking, then reminded him that all humans are equal in the eyes of God. The work of the Holy Spirit continued through and in the lives of the apostles, in particular Peter.

Thank God there are people in America and the world that believe in the supernatural, but a majority of church folks do not believe in such supernatural happenings and, most of all, reject those who believe the Bible like it should be believed. The Church of Jesus Christ is built on the revelation of who Jesus is, Matthew 16:18–19 (not just a baby born in a manger), and His power that can change lives and faith in God to experience His manifested power in the supernatural of visions, dreams, revelations, the gifts and fruits of the Holy Spirit bringing healing, miracles, signs, and wonders to sick humanity who needs deliverance at this very hour.

Ritual, formality, traditions, and man-made programs cannot deliver sick, bound-up humanity; it takes the supernatural power of God. After Cornelius' visitation from God, Peter was staying with a Christian family in a city called Joppa, a house that was by the sea; of course, his hosts and the family that housed and cared for him obviously understood that the apostle Peter being a leader in the early church as he excused himself and went on the housetop to pray. About the same time, the Holy Spirit, who was speaking and moving in and for Cornelius, had a dream vision. Peter was on the housetop praying; he went into a trance (vision or dream). To the people who criticize visions or dreams and doubt such supernatural occurrences, you must understand Peter was not asleep but walking on the housetop about 3:00 p.m., praying in broad daylight, and of course, he was not losing his mind. The trend of thinking pertaining to revival in our day is so different from what transpired through Jesus' ministry recorded in Matthew, Mark, Luke, and John and the apostles' ministry in the book of Acts. To be specific, this was not just entertainment, hype, and sensation.

The book of Acts revival continued as Herod (who was called great) persecuted the church, and as the Bible puts it, *he harassed the church and killed the apostle James*; this pleased the religious people of that day, especially the Jews. Herod, recognizing this, wanted to kill Peter the following day. It is a fact that biblical revival always brings persecution. Herod had Peter jailed, but the Church of that day, recognizing he was going to kill Peter also, gathered in one of the saints' houses (there was no multi-million dollar church building open back then, but these saints knew how to pray). They gathered and prayed all night; one of the most wonderful feelings is to know that someone or church members are praying for you; if I was a church member, I would be looking for a church that prays.

While these saints were praying, God could not find one human being to help Peter, so He called an angel and sent him to the jail where Peter was locked up. The angel supernaturally went into the prison, tapped Peter on his shoulder, woke him up, broke the chains from his feet, walked through the walls of the first and second prison. Then the angel led him outside of the prison to the street. Peter, now realizing what had happened, walked straight to the house where the saints were praying. There were their prayers standing, knocking on the door; a young lady named Rhoda, recognizing Peter, ran back to the room where they were praying and told them Peter was knocking on the door. They did not believe until they came to the door and saw Peter. God answers prayer, but we have to pray first before there can be answers. This entire account is recorded in the book of Acts.

> *Now about that time Herod the king stretched forth his hands to vex certain of the church.*
>
> *And he killed James the brother of John with the sword.*
>
> *And because he saw it pleased the Jews, he proceeded further to take Peter also. (Then were the days of unleavened bread.)*
>
> *And when he had apprehended him, he put him in prison, and delivered him to four quaternions of soldiers to keep him; intending after Easter to bring him forth to the people.*
>
> *Peter therefore was kept in prison: but prayer was made without ceasing of the church unto God for him.*
>
> *And when Herod would have brought him forth, the same night Peter was sleeping between two soldiers, bound with two chains: and the keepers before the door kept the prison.*
>
> *And, behold, the angel of the Lord came upon him, and a light shined in the prison: and he smote Peter on the side, and raised him up, saying, Arise up quickly. And his chains fell off from his hands.*
>
> *And the angel said unto him, Gird thyself, and bind on thy sandals. And so he did. And he saith unto him, Cast thy garment about thee, and follow me.*
>
> *And he went out, and followed him; and wist not that it was true which was done by the angel; but thought he saw a vision.*
>
> *When they were past the first and the second ward, they came unto the iron gate that leadeth unto the city; which opened to them of his own accord: and they went out, and passed on through one street; and forthwith the angel departed from him.*

And when Peter was come to himself, he said, Now I know of a surety, that the Lord hath sent his angel, and hath delivered me out of the hand of Herod, and from all the expectation of the people of the Jews.

And when he had considered the thing, he came to the house of Mary the mother of John, whose surname was Mark; where many were gathered together praying.

And as Peter knocked at the door of the gate, a damsel came to hearken, named Rhoda.

And when she knew Peter's voice, she opened not the gate for gladness, but ran in, and told how Peter stood before the gate.

And they said unto her, Thou art mad. But she constantly affirmed that it was even so. Then said they, It is his angel.

But Peter continued knocking: and when they had opened the door, and saw him, they were astonished.

But he, beckoning unto them with the hand to hold their peace, declared unto them how the Lord had brought him out of the prison. And he said, Go shew these things unto James, and to the brethren. And he departed, and went into another place.

— Acts 12:1–17

These are some of the supernatural things that can happen during the revival, and these supernatural visitations do not necessarily occur in one location, but during the revival, these supernatural happenings can happen anywhere to work out God's plan and purposes. These supernatural happenings recorded in the book of Acts were allowed by God to be placed in the New Testament by inspiration of the Holy Spirit as a cryptic inspiration for us of today to read and seek the same from God for this modern-day church to experience if a church or people would be confronted with similar situations.

Forget about some false professional teachers and preachers who constantly and vehemently affirm and spend more time disbelieving than believing, which goes around telling people that these things are not for our day. But it is written in Hebrews.

"Jesus Christ is the same yesterday, today and forever" Hebrews 13:8. This should be an everyday reminder that God does not change. If we are going to experience this type of revival, we must get back to the standards, life, and godly principles that these early Christians adhered to; this is one of the foremost reasons why this kind of biblical revival is absent from the present-day Church; it's all because of the fact we are talking it but not living it.

It must be understood that God is looking for *pure human vessels to work through*. The words of Jesus should echo through the corridors and centuries of time in the ears and hearts of the present-day church; why? Because we have Bibles everywhere in America, hundreds of different translations; now, even more Bibles are on iPads, iPhones, and more, do not allow the spirit of blindness to hinder you but let the words of Jesus, the book of Acts, including the epistles, sink deep down within your spirit, and we will experience the same results Jesus and the apostles had.

Hunger is the word for Biblical Revival.

"Blessed are the pure in heart for they shall see God."

— Matthew 5:8

The ministry of the apostle Paul dominated the latter half of the book of Acts, whose ministry then shook the Gentile world. Peter was used of God mightily as recorded in the book of Acts, the example of revival; he was used of God in raising a dead woman by the name of Tabitha and many outstanding miracles. Most of all, by this time, his eyes were opened to the fact that God was no respecter of persons, and the work of the grace of God was evident in his life as he wholeheartedly supported the preaching of the Gospel by the apostle Paul to the Gentiles. Peter did not stay in Jerusalem, but he found his way to some of the scattered Tribes of Israel throughout the areas of the Black Sea; according to history, he came as far to Britain, and God used him as revival broke out there.

The other apostles, such as Andrew, James, Bartholomew, Matthew, Luke, Mark, spearheaded revival throughout Europe, Africa, and Ethiopia, Islands of the Seas, but the seed of the Gospel of Jesus Christ and revival was sown throughout the world. The apostle Thomas found his way to South India, and thank God he preached to the Indian people there with miracles and signs following. The ministry of Thomas brought about a climate of revival in the hearts of the Indian people of South India as they turned from idols to Jesus Christ.

History tells us that the apostle Thomas caught the attention of the Indian people by preaching the death of Jesus on the cross as multitudes came to Jesus Christ and accepted Him as Lord and Savior. Sadly the life of the apostle Thomas came to an abrupt end by a spear trusted into his body, where he died in India. But the seed of the Gospel of Jesus Christ was already sown; each year, millions of Indian people gather at his shrine or tomb, thanking God for sending the apostle Thomas to India. Amazingly revival broke out throughout the entire then known world, and the apostles did it without all the modern-day conveniences that we have today.

CHAPTER 13

Revival! Returning to Your First Love

Most of the apostles who returned to Jerusalem sealed their faith by martyrdom; this was, of course, orchestrated by organized vindictive, jealous religious Jews and the oppressive Roman government. The only apostle who survived the gruesome death of martyrdom was the apostle John. He was tried and tested severely for his faith in Jesus. History states Domitian tried to kill John by putting him in a cauldron of boiling oil, but God had a supernatural plan for John. He did not allow John to die. Then the Jews and the Roman government banished him on the Isle of Patmos. Approximately AD 95–96, after all the apostles and most of the Christians in the book of Acts had died, few of them remained alive, but most of the churches of that time were in a backslidden state, as a remnant of the book of Acts held on to their faith in Jesus Christ and the teachings of the apostles.

God's divine plan, purpose, and His infinite mercy showed up as He visited the apostle John on the Isle of Patmos, giving him the natural and spiritual condition of this era. Also, what is to transpire prophetically speaking of the political and spiritual future of the true church, the false church, and the final destiny of Church of Jesus Christ and ungodly people.

Absolutely we are continuing on the subject of what is revival, with the understanding from the preceding chapters "Revival Is Not," "What Is Revival," and now a surprising revelation of the word revival in its true original meaning "your first love is revival." To further understand revival, let God's word reveal itself from the message of Jesus Christ to the first Church, the Ephesians Church, from the year of AD 53–170.

> *Unto the angel of the church of Ephesus write; These things saith he that holdeth the seven stars in his right hand, who walketh in the midst of the seven golden candlesticks;*
>
> *I know thy works, and thy labour, and thy patience, and how thou canst not bear them which are evil: and thou hast tried them which say they are apostles, and are not, and hast found them liars:*
>
> *And hast borne, and hast patience, and for my name's sake hast labored, and hast not fainted.*
>
> *Nevertheless I have somewhat against thee, because thou hast left thy first love.*
>
> *Remember therefore from whence thou art fallen, and repent, and do the first works; or else I will come unto thee quickly, and will remove thy candlestick out of his place, except thou repent.*
>
> — Revelation 2:1–5

When an individual or people recognize the sacrificial atoning work of Jesus Christ by the shedding of the His blood on Calvary and accept Jesus as Lord and Savior into their hearts, they confess and renounce their ungodly life and sins. The blood of Jesus Christ cleanses that individual or people, this act of cleansing by the blood of Jesus is implemented by the work of the Holy Spirit. If they are genuinely saved and baptized with the Holy Spirit, obviously, they will experience a change in their life. This means their life or lives would and will be transformed by the power of God; they become a new person in Christ Jesus.

At the same time, they will experience joy, peace, contentment, real happiness, and assurance of going to heaven, and then they will develop a relationship with God and have a daily walk with Him. In order to keep a relationship with God, it is necessary to read and study the word of God, the Bible, pray daily, attend church regularly, where you can be inspired to worship and praise God, then be motivated to do or willingly do something in the kingdom of God. Pay their tithing and support for the propagation of the

Gospel of Jesus Christ here in America and especially in other countries of the world. These individuals would have such a love for God that they will endeavor to do something for God by working through a local assembly. Someone might ask, "Can anyone do something for God as an individual besides belonging to a local assembly or church?" Yes, they can.

Excitement, exuberance, zeal, and a total commitment to God through Jesus Christ are what you would describe as *first love*. Nothing means more to a person who is experiencing their first love; all they want to do is love, praise, and worship God. Most of all, they will want to do anything in the service of God and for their brethren in Christ. If you love someone, you will want to spend time with them; when you experience your first love for Jesus, you will want to spend time with Him (for example, pray, etc.). How could anyone say they love Jesus or God and do not want to spend time with Him and do something for Him? *Revival is keeping your first love for God*; no revival is losing your first love; this is the reason Jesus and the apostles did not need revival; they maintained a love for God and a relationship with Him all the time. But after they left the scene, people began to lose their first love for God, and apostasy set in; this is the reason why Jesus told John to tell the Ephesians Church you have left your first love.

Jesus' visitation to John as He delivered a stern message first with commendations, encouragement, and to know the truth and to discern what is false. The Ephesians Church did not mix truth and false at the same time like we see what is happening in a certain sector of the so-called church in this day and time. For example, the World Council of Churches and Chrislam which is a mixture of Christianity and Islam.

> *I know thy works, and thy labour, and thy patience, and how thou canst not bear them which are evil: and thou hast tried them which say they are apostles, and are not, and hast found them liars:*
>
> *And hast borne, and hast patience, and for my name's sake hast laboured, and hast not fainted*
>
> — Revelation 2:2–3

Someone might exclaim, "What a Church!" The Ephesians Church, whose works were caring for people in every way, was consistent in the good they were doing. Men who came around professing that they were apostles were quick to discern that they were false prophets and liars. They did endure all types of trials and testing; most of all, they exemplified in the fruits of the Spirit, in particular patience. They worked harder than anyone else in every way, working for Jesus; most of all, they did not give up. What a Church! God surely would reward them for all of this, but there was one spot in their garments, the most important thing was left out, and that was *first love*, which meant they were going through the mechanics (like going to church with all the traditions, formality, rituals but had no relationship with God). What Jesus was actually telling the church of Ephesus, "God bless and reward you for everything you are doing, but in everything you are doing, there is a possibility you can do all of it and have no personal devotion or relationship with me, Jesus, there is a possibility you can lose your soul."

First love is primarily an unceasingly devoted relationship to and for Jesus Christ. What is first love? The answer is obvious. It is the love you felt for Jesus when you first came to know Him. It is that wonderful sense of discovery that He loved you, and you love Him unceasingly. He freed you from your sins. Your heart went out to him in gratitude and thanksgiving; you had eyes for no one but him. Watch a couple who has fallen in love and note how they have eyes only for each other. Talk to them; they do not even hear you; they are only thinking of themselves. So it is with a Christian when he or she first comes to Christ, their heart is filled with gratitude and love for God. What an amazing experience that he or she has their sins forgiven! This is why new Christians often break down and cry when giving a testimony of their newfound faith in Jesus Christ.

The commendable love stern warning message to the Ephesians Church was not without warning: recede, remember, and recall the time you started to lose your relationship and love for Jesus, repent and do thy first works. There were choices the Ephesians Church had to make; this was to recede, remember, and recall the time you began to lose your love and relation with God. Repent was the first choice; choice is an affirmative word here because it's a fact God cannot choose for us; we have to initiate and do our own choosing. And repent was the other choice they had to make. Repent! The Church, yes! If the world is going to repent, the church has to do some repenting.

This is where revival has its beginning. Repentance, as some might think, is for the worldly people, but the sins of the world have crept into certain of the Church. When the Church repents, the world repents, negative some might reiterate but think for a moment the word repentance is as positive as positive can be because it produces positive results, revival. Revival has its origination when the Church repents. This is the first word that was uttered out of the mouth of John the Baptist that preceded the first appearance of Jesus from birth, growth, ministry, death, resurrection, and ascension of Jesus was repent.

Look at frown puzzled look on some church members' faces when a preacher tells them to repent. Some of them even look like they were hit with a ton of bricks or a baseball bat; why? They would insist, "I am already a Christian." Please tell that to Jesus because He is the one that is addressing the fatal spiritual death of an individual Christian or congregation by going through the mechanics and no personal relationship with God. Returning to your first love, this was God's prerogative?

Do you recall when God first made Adam and Eve? He used to come down in the cool of the day (even God-like air condition) and have fellowship and share His secrets with Adam and Eve. What makes us think that in this highly sophisticated technological, philosophized educated age, He does not want to have fellowship with His creation? Yes! He longs to have fellowship with His creation called mankind? When mankind fell, surely God was not in a dilemma, but man's dilemma became God's plan for mankind to return to God. He did this by preparing the Hebrew people who would prepare the way for the Messiah, Jesus Christ, who died on the cross to open the way for all mankind so that mankind could retain that relationship with God they had from the beginning.

Serving God and revival is not a quagmire of running and ripping, raving and ramping mechanical, emotional hip-hop all night long partying like the world (in Church); what about an all-night prayer for a change. Mention the word pray to some ministers and church folks; you hear some of the lamest excuses, and these same folks, when they hear the word prayer, they run like rats into their rat holes when the light is turned on. The key to revival is getting ready to go to heaven. Your first love is a consistent relationship with God. I always wonder about the times when God used to come down in the Garden of Eden and talk, communicate, and fellowship with Adam and Eve, but think of this, the same privilege is allowed to us today. This is what revival is. The choice is yours, brothers and sisters in Christ. God is not to be blamed;

He did what He wanted to do for us by sending Jesus Christ out of love; please, let's give Him back our love which is your first love. This is what revival is all about.

"Repent and do thy first works." In the first instance, Jesus told John, "I know thy works." Then He said to John, "Repent and do thy first works." I know thy works are referring to the fact I know what you stand for, patience, sound doctrine, truth, discerning who is right and wrong, labor (in the sense of believing and working hard for the truth), but now Jesus is telling John, to the leader of the Ephesians Church, to warn the members of the Body of Christ of that day, "to repent and do thy first works." There is no conflict here but God's revelation and interpretation of this word. "Repent and do thy first works" actually means to get back to your first love, and that is to get back to your relationship with God and out of love for God, worship, praise, glorify, and pray as you spend time with God, go to the house of God, worship, praise, and glorify God with the other saints, study the Word, express your love to Him, and He, in turn, will love you.

Then out of love, yes! Stand for righteousness, holiness, and sound doctrine but out of love, feed the hungry, clothe the naked, help the poor and needy by your prayers and financial support, care for the widows and orphans, and most of all, care for and support the apostles so that they can go and preach the Gospel to those that have never heard of Jesus, amen. Is this first love or what! What was Jesus telling the Ephesians Church? I am tired of the mechanics; get back to the dynamics and, with love and devotion to Jesus, do what's really needed to be done instead of, like in modern terminology, stop running and ripping, fighting over who is right and wrong, fighting over whose denomination, organization is going to heaven and who is not, please go back to loving on Jesus with all your heart, soul, and mind and do something worthwhile for Jesus. If this is not revival, nothing else is. Or else I will come quickly and remove your candlestick out of its place.

The Ephesians Church was presented with an opportunity for God's best. Then became lackadaisical, relaxed, and unconcerned about its spiritual condition, which was losing the most important need of returning to its first love. To enhance its commendations from God, Himself, but refusing this serious and last warning, repent or else I will come quickly and remove your candlestick out of his place; this causes them to lose the greatest privilege of spearheading a revival that could have shaken Ephesus and surrounding areas but ended in complete ruin. Returning to your first love is one of the most important aspects of the Christian life; losing your first love should never come about and occur because Jesus and the apostles never had this problem, especially Jesus. His life and constant relation with the Father never fluctuated or waned, and the apostles followed their Master's footsteps as they carried on where he left off. The Ephesians Church failed to heed a warning that could have stopped the beginning of apostasy. Their refusal opened up the floodgate of spiritual apathy in forthcoming years. Instead of revival, there was a ruin.

Thank God for the ministers and Christians in America who have unflinching faith in Jesus Christ! We are witnessing some levels of persecution here in America; I often wonder what would happen if severe persecution occurring in other countries should happen here in America. Daily reports are being heard on Christian media of persecution against Christians in other countries, such as in the Middle East, Sudan, certain places in Africa, India, Pakistan, China, and other countries. But what it is that keeps these precious saints faithful to Jesus Christ even unto death. It is their unflinching, unwavering love and faith in Jesus Christ. First love should be a continuous love for God through Jesus Christ, and this is of utmost importance. This love for God that is being written about is an individual Christian love for God that nothing else matters.

"And thou shalt love the Lord thy God with all thine heart, and with all thy soul, and with all thy might" Deuteronomy 6:5. Jesus repeated this in the Gospel of Luke, "[…] Thou shalt love the Lord thy God with all thy heart, and with all thy soul, and with all thy strength, and with all thy mind; and thy neighbour as thyself" Luke 10:27.

I heard and read a report of a Chinese Christian who spent twenty-six years in a tiny cell in prison for his faith in Jesus Christ. When he was released from prison, he was interviewed by certain Christian news media and leaders of the Christian faith in China. He was asked the question, "How did you handle your faith in Jesus Christ while in confinement?" His answer shook the media, Christian leaders, people in China and other countries. He said that his imprisonment was like a honeymoon with Jesus.

Why are so many other nations experiencing a real revival, and we are not? It's all because they never lost their first love or their love for God through Jesus Christ. There are many activities within church circles of this day that are being implemented; they are doing everything to attract people to their meetings and other church activities. Why is this? It is because there is no love and personal relationship with God. No pastor should have to plead with their people about attending the house of God, praying (spend time with God), reading their Bible, doing something for Jesus in the local congregation, tithing, and giving of their income for the propagation of the Gospel of Jesus Christ. Win a soul or souls to Jesus, love and help one another, and praise and worship God without reservation; this and more should be done out of love for God.

As a missionary-evangelist, I have had the opportunity of preaching the Gospel of Jesus in fifty countries of the world. I, by God's help, have conducted revival meetings in almost every State of this Union. I recall being in some of these churches; mind you, these were supposed to be revival meetings, but each time I did conduct these meetings, I would hear the pastor pleading with people, "Please pray, please attend the revival, invite someone to the meetings, please support the revival, please give, give someone a ride to church, be in time to catch the bus to church, etc." But when people have a love for God, in particular the first love, no one, not even the pastor, should have to beg or please ask anyone to do anything. Revival or the first is automatic; you really don't have to beg, please, or ask anyone to do anything for God; it should already be in you.

CHAPTER 14

How to Keep Your First Love

Christianity is based on faith in Jesus Christ and what Jesus has done for us. God had a plan in sending Jesus Christ. Jesus came and fulfilled God's plan; first of all, Jesus set a precedent and an example in teaching, preaching, and how to have and keep a daily relationship with God. This, of course, would be initiated through the born-again experience, baptism in water, and baptism with the Holy Spirit.

> *There was a man of the Pharisees, named Nicodemus, a ruler of the Jews:*
>
> *The same came to Jesus by night, and said unto him, Rabbi, we know that thou art a teacher come from God: for no man can do these miracles that thou doest, except God be with him.*
>
> *Jesus answered and said unto him, Verily, verily, I say unto thee, except a man be born again, he cannot see the kingdom of God.*
>
> *Nicodemus saith unto him, How can a man be born when he is old? can he enter the second time into his mother's womb, and be born?*
>
> *Jesus answered, Verily, verily, I say unto thee, Except a man be born of water and of the Spirit, he cannot enter into the kingdom of God.*
>
> *That which is born of the flesh is flesh; and that which is born of the Spirit is spirit.*
>
> *Marvel not that I said unto thee, Ye must be born again.*
>
> *The wind bloweth where it listeth, and thou hearest the sound thereof, but canst not tell whence it cometh, and whither it goeth: so is every one that is born of the Spirit.*
>
> *Nicodemus answered and said unto him, How can these things be?*
>
> *Jesus answered and said unto him, Art thou a master of Israel, and knowest not these things?*
>
> *Verily, verily, I say unto thee, We speak that we do know, and testify that we have seen; and ye receive not our witness.*
>
> *If I have told you earthly things, and ye believe not, how shall ye believe, if I tell you of heavenly things?*
>
> — John 3:1–12

> *And when the day of Pentecost was fully come, they were all with one accord in one place.*
>
> *And suddenly there came a sound from heaven as of a rushing mighty wind, and it filled all the house where they were sitting.*
>
> *And there appeared unto them cloven tongues like as of fire, and it sat upon each of them.*
>
> *And they were all filled with the Holy Ghost, and began to speak with other tongues, as the Spirit gave them utterance.*
>
> *And there were dwelling at Jerusalem Jews, devout men, out of every nation under heaven.*
>
> — Acts 2:1–5

Jesus' words were backed up with miracles, signs, and wonders; the Gospels clearly state that He had compassion on the multitudes as He healed the sick and performed every imaginable miracle. The individual who needed healing, He healed them. He even spoke the word and stopped the adverse course of nature, spoke fishes into existence and a fish with a piece of gold in its mouth, and of course, He raised the dead. All through this book, yours truly has been appealing to the readers "read the Gospels, Matthew, Mark, Luke, and the book of Acts," read it over and over; it will leave an indelible, lasting impression on your mind and prayer. God, I long for this in our day, Jesus said we would do greater works, and He is not talking about buildings, etc. He is talking about the miracles He did to meet the needs of the people of that day, such as the miracles of healing on the people of that day, "He that believeth on me, the works that I do shall he do also; and greater works than these shall he [you] do; because I go unto my Father" John 14:11–12b.

The main reason why Jesus came was to die on the cross. This, of course, was God's perfect plan in implementing mankind's redemption and bringing the human race back to God. Besides, the redemptive work of Jesus Christ in providing salvation, healing, peace, joy, contentment, and real happiness, opening the way for us to come to God for ourselves and, of course, eternal life. What was the first instruction or command that Jesus gave His disciples after his resurrection? Was it to build church buildings and implement programs to keep people occupied in these church buildings? What is it that causes people to maintain their first love and stay revived?

Before proceeding, it must be realized that the author is not ignorant of the fact that buildings are necessary for those who need them to accommodate the huge crowds or congregation that they pastor. There are pastors and congregations who must be commended for their godly Holy Spirit leadership and plans in keeping the congregation together whom God had set them over. Some of them ought to be commended for their outreach and missions program in reaching lost souls. But, generally speaking, what a price some of these leaders have to pay to hold their people together. Millions of bulletins, agendas combined with neon signs flashing announcements of services and other church activities, and millions of dollars worth of computers, projectors, and sometimes hundreds of plasma screens and large screens. Except in a few cases where this might be needed, I reserve my opinion for when we stand before Jesus on Judgment Day!

Now back to the three questions in the previous chapter above. Jesus' first instruction and command to the church was to go into all the world and preach the Gospel. Priority as far as God is concerned is to reach humanity with the Gospel of Jesus Christ or, in layman's everyday language, *win lost souls*. Even though, as was mentioned earlier, building a church building to house God's people where it's needed is understandably so, building magnificent edifices just for namesake and people hardly enter them to pray in the midweek prayer meeting is a sin in the eyes of God. What is it that causes people to maintain their first love and stay revived? The answer is simple and, in most cases, overlooked by pastors and people. The author did not get sidetracked or forget that he is writing about first love coherent to revival, first love, and how to keep your first love burning for Jesus Christ.

But here is a revelation of the word which the church world should never forget, and this includes yours truly. Revival, missions, soul-winning or winning lost souls, with miracles, signs, and wonders is revival, as recorded in the Gospels and the books of Acts is revival. But most of the modern-day systemized church does not want anything to do with this kind of revival because it interrupts their plans and programs.

> *And he said unto them, Go ye into all the world, and preach the gospel to every creature.*
> *He that believeth and is baptized shall be saved; but he that believeth not shall be damned.*
> *And these signs shall follow them that believe; In my name shall they cast out devils; they shall speak with new tongues; [...] they shall lay hands on the sick and they shall recover.*
> — Mark 16:15–18b

And when the day of Pentecost was fully come, they were all with one accord in one place.

And suddenly there came a sound from heaven as of a rushing mighty wind, and it filled all the house where they were sitting.

And there appeared unto them cloven tongues like as of fire, and it sat upon each of them.

And they were all filled with the Holy Ghost, and began to speak with other tongues, as the Spirit gave them utterance.

— Acts 2:1–4

Just a thought from the author, which is worth mentioning, the Scripture's verses mentioned in this book are of utmost importance because this book is to emphasize what God's words say, and the thoughts of the author must be backed up by the Word of God. As a matter of fact, the Scriptures mentioned so often in this book were not to create more pages because the Word of God must be printed to solidify the message of this book. The author is recognizing the validity of reinforcing the fact of how an individual can keep and maintain their first love and stay revived. These words of Jesus are of utmost importance, obviously so, and must be printed here in this book. With that said, every minister and believer in Jesus Christ should read, study, meditate, and put into practice the Gospel of John. Please recall we are dealing with the subject of how to keep your first love or stay revived. Here is a brief verse by verse study from John, chapter 15, "I am the true vine, and my Father is the husbandman" John 15:1.

Naturally speaking, a husbandman is a person who owns and governs the entire field or orchard, which means that God is in charge of this entire world. Jesus came directly from the Father God. "Every branch in me that beareth not fruit he taketh away: and every branch that beareth fruit, he purgeth it, that it may bring forth more fruit" John 15:2.

Every believer in Jesus Christ who is not producing or not bearing fruit, or not winning souls, becomes dry and lifeless, and spiritually speaking, they die; yours truly has pastored many congregations, and over fifty-five years of ministry, I have noticed members who were lazy, laxidacical, and unconcerned about their own soul and souls of men, women, young people, and children; they died, spiritually speaking. But those who were going to church, reading the Word, praying, fasting once in a while, tithing, giving to missions, doing some for Jesus in the local congregation, and most of all *winning lost souls*, were always alive on the inside, which showed on the outside in every way.

"Now ye are clean through the word which I have spoken unto you" John 15:3. The more you do something for Jesus, God cleanses you by the power of the word and uses you for His glory.

Abide in me, and I in you. As the branch cannot bear fruit of itself, except it abide in the vine; no more can ye, except ye abide in me.

I am the vine, ye are the branches: He that abideth in me, and I in him, the same bringeth forth much fruit: for without me ye can do nothing.

If a man abides not in me, he is cast forth as a branch, and is withered; and men gather them, and cast them into the fire, and they are burned.

— John 15:4–6

The above three verses are the key to keeping your first love for Jesus and staying revived, and that is *abiding in Jesus Christ*. God cannot use anyone who has the tendency to be in and out, or one day you are with Jesus, and the next day you are out in a backslidden condition. The old English word for *"abiding"* is to stay with, dwell, remain, and endure. The Hebrew word for abiding, which I like very much, is *"Yashab,"* which means to remain with all the time. It must be noted that abiding in Jesus Christ rests upon the individual Christian or all Christians. God has already done His part, and that is sending Jesus to die on the cross, and when Jesus died on the cross, He died for every single problem that you are going through; yes! He is willing to keep you, but choice and abiding in Christ remains up to you, especially if you want to be used of God. "If ye abide in me, and my words abide in you, ye shall ask what ye will, and it shall be done unto you" John 15:7.

Here are the benefits of abiding in Jesus Christ; it is so simple. God will use you, and your prayers will be answered. While ministering in different places, so many people approach and want to speak with me and ask questions, one of the questions more often asked—"Why are my prayers not being answered?" I would ask them, "Are you abiding in Jesus Christ?" "Pastor," they would exclaim, "are there Scriptures to back this up?" There are many scriptures to back this up, but this one, in particular, tells us why.

First of all, abiding in Jesus Christ is positive and not negative. When you abide in Jesus Christ and keep your relationship with God, Jesus, Himself, said if your prayers will be answered, but if you are not abiding in Jesus and don't have a relationship with God, your prayers will not be answered, except you develop a relationship with God, a relationship with God begins with genuine repentance and turning to God. This is through the born-again experience Jesus spoke about in John's Gospel, chapter 3.

"Herein is my Father glorified, that ye bear much fruit; so shall ye be my disciples" John 15:8. God is glorified when we are bringing forth fruits or doing something for him, such as feeding the hungry, clothing the naked, shelter for the homeless, visiting those in prison, etc., especially *winning lost souls*. Please note the last sentence here! When we are doing these things, then and only then we are his disciples.

> *As the Father hath loved me, so have I loved you: continue ye in my love.*
>
> *If ye keep my commandments, ye shall abide in my love; even as I have kept my Father's commandments, and abide in his love.*
>
> — John 15:9–10

Real love is continuous when you love someone or the brethren in Jesus Christ, family members, friends, neighbors, or lost souls. Love is all the time, love in charity this means you do not love and do good one time, but all the time, love is not to love one someone or doing something today and drop them or it like a hot potato tomorrow because love is always. "These things have I spoken unto you, that my joy might remain in you, and that your joy might be full" John 15:11.

One of the benefits of accepting Jesus Christ as Lord and Savior is that He gives you joy or real happiness. God's joy through Jesus Christ is not temporary, but it is now and forever; yes, you might be hated, or persecuted, but God gives you joy through all of it. "This is my commandment, That ye love one another, as I have loved you" John 15:12. "Greater love hath no man than this that a man lay down his life for his friends" John 15:13.

Jesus' command is for us to love each other as He has loved us; when we love one another, we will sacrifice for one another as He sacrificed for us. Really, what Jesus is stating here is that love is not just words, but if you really love God and love your brothers and sisters in Christ, you will prove your love by sacrificing for one another like He sacrificed His life on Calvary? In essence, this does not mean dying on a cross, but going the extra mile would indicate that you love one another.

CHAPTER 15
Staying Revived

With a pure heart, the right motive, and a desire to fulfill their calling, hundreds of thousands of pastors faithfully prepare their sermons, plus the pressure of introducing new plans, programs, and methods plus thousands of others in the name of the Lord's activities with the intention their members, followers, adherents would cling to the church they pastor. This, of course, is done with the idea of attracting new people.

The Christian music industry has risen from obscurity. The Christian artists who are the main attraction have pinnacled into a multi-billion dollar business; celebrities, concerts, and other means of Christian entertainment will fill up the church and other buildings where these main attractions are held. (May I say this with respect to my Lord but poor Jesus—He is not the main attraction anymore.) Millions of people will jam-pack these events, but they will not darken (dark all right) the church door for the mid-week prayer meetings.

Suppose there is the scarce commodity of new plans, programs, methods, or some type of gala entertainment to suit the modern-day Christian crowd fancy they will not attend. Yes! I have heard the lame excuse this is a modern-day! But have we become so modern that we cannot get down on bended knees to keep our relationship with God. It scares me when I attend a church, and the worship leaders do all the worship, the choir does all the singing, the band does all the playing, the soloist does the singing, and the preacher does the preaching with no communication with the worshipers. The benediction is suddenly pronounced, and then most of the worshippers walk out of the meeting place without their souls being wet (that is, if this kind of language is understood). Hundreds of thousands of Christian artists and concerts are held each week, luring millions of young people and adults into rock'n'roll type music with hardly any anointing, hardly any emphasis on a relationship with God; no peace and satisfaction.

Thank God for the pastors who are baptized with the Holy Spirit and have the anointing of God upon their lives and members of their congregation who are spirit-filled and by their prayers, Bible reading, church attendance, tithing, fitting in the church program of ministering to the sick and shut-in (and sometimes the shut-ins needs to get out and go to church) hospitals, prisons, outreach, etc. This, of course, and more would always cause a church to stay revived. But think for a moment the hundreds of thousands of pastors who are heartbroken because of the hundreds of thousands who will not attend church if there is a lack of something new. Think for a moment the millions of church members while in their local congregation are always on the run looking for ministries with something new with the intention of obtaining a blessing. The same can be applied to millions of young people running from concert to concert, looking for something that would bring them peace and satisfaction.

Here are a few Scriptures from the Word of God, the Bible. If believers in Jesus Christ would read, study, and take them seriously and live accordingly (I don't like the word practice), it would put a lot of preachers out of business. By making this statement, it is not meant that men of God who are called by God to the ministry and fulfilling God's purpose and winning the lost to Jesus Christ are desperately needed, especially today. What is meant by putting a lot of preachers out of business is the fact that ministers and preachers who are in the ministry as a profession? Not called and compromising about abortion, homosexuality, lesbianism, transgender, the world, the flesh, and the devil, they would have to quit because people are living a pleasing life to God according to the Word of God.

Chapter 15: Staying Revived

The story is told of the Welsh Revival, which occurred under the leadership of Evans Roberts in the year 1904. People attended this revival from everywhere, and obviously, some Americans attended this revival; when they arrived at the city where the revival was happening, they saw a policeman who was quite exuberant, singing and praising God. And they asked him, "My good man, can you please tell us where is the building where the revival is taking place under the leadership of Evans Roberts?" The policeman replied, "You are looking at the Welsh Revival." The policeman gave them the answer he did because he was trying to tell them the revival was not in the building but in him.

For revival to begin, it must begin in you. Conventions, conferences, seminars, and lectures on seven principles or points for revival and prosperity are commendable, but none of these means anything; revival must begin and continues with you. Revival within an individual can be habituated from the true born again experience, baptism with the Holy Spirit, sanctification, prayer, studying the word, a burden, and compassion for lost souls and to win them to Jesus Christ. A deep-down yearning hunger and thirst for God, and a desire to have the results that Jesus and the apostles had in the Gospels and the book of Acts.

Wilt thou not revive us again: that thy people may rejoice in thee?

— Psalm 85:6

For thus saith the high and lofty One that inhabiteth eternity, whose name is Holy; I dwell in the nigh and holy place, with him also that is of a contrite and humble spirit, to revive the spirit of the humble, and to revive the heart of the contrite ones.

— Isaiah 57:15

Wherefore be ye not unwise, but understanding what the will of the Lord is.
And be not drunk with wine, wherein is excess; but be filled with the Spirit;
Speaking to yourselves in psalms and hymns and spiritual songs, singing and making melody in your heart to the Lord;
Giving thanks always for all things unto God and the Father in the name of our Lord Jesus Christ;

— Ephesians 5:17–20

Wherefore he saith, Awake thou that sleepest, and arise from the dead [spiritually dead], and Christ shall give thee light.

— Ephesians 5:14

Draw nigh to God, and he will draw nigh to you.

—James 4:8a

There are hundreds of thousands of ministers, godly men who are respected and, of course, have a heart for lost souls and hungers to see and experience a true revival. Most of all, these men and women desire to help people in every way (and then if you don't want to help people stay out of the ministry) because ministry is people. But there are also hundreds of ministers who use their ministry and gifts for selfish monetary gain and other purposes, who pry and take advantage of multitudes of people. Then there are thousands of people, who are sick, suffering, and in need. God has honored their faith as they are being saved, healed, and blessed. But there are millions of people who will seek out a minister just for the purpose of being called up or want to be prophesied over about being prosperous, successful, or rich. In no way would the author criticize a minister who is used of God in the gifts of Spirit in giving someone a word of prophecies, etc. But some of these people would never settle down in a local church and be taught the basics of Christianity, do something for God in the local church, win souls, and prepare their souls for the second return of Jesus Christ.

Herein lies the key to personal revival; every Christian should read these words of the apostle Paul from the book of Ephesians.

> *I therefore, the prisoner of the Lord, beseech you that ye walk worthy of the vocation wherewith ye are called,*
>
> > *With all lowliness and meekness, with longsuffering, forbearing one another in love;*
> >
> > *Endeavouring to keep the unity of the Spirit in the bond of peace.*
> >
> > *There is one body, and one Spirit, even as ye are called in one hope of your calling;*
> >
> > *One Lord, one faith, one baptism,*
> >
> > *One God and Father of all, who is above all, and through all, and in you all.*
> >
> > *But unto every one of us is given grace according to the measure of the gift of Christ.*
> >
> > *Wherefore he saith, When he ascended up on high, he led captivity captive, and gave gifts unto men.*
> >
> > *(Now that he ascended, what is it but that he also descended first into the lower parts of the earth?*
> >
> > *He that descended is the same also that ascended up far above all heavens, that he might fill all things.)*
> >
> > *And he gave some, apostles; and some, prophets; and some, evangelists; and some, pastors and teachers;*
> >
> > *For the perfecting of the saints, for the work of the ministry, for the edifying of the body of Christ:*
> >
> > *Till we all come in the unity of the faith, and of the knowledge of the Son of God, unto a perfect man, unto the measure of the stature of the fulness of Christ:*
> >
> > *That we henceforth be no more children, tossed to and fro, and carried about with every wind of doctrine, by the sleight of men, and cunning craftiness, whereby they lie in wait to deceive;*
> >
> > *But speaking the truth in love, may grow up into him in all things, which is the head, even Christ:*
> >
> > *From whom the whole body fitly joined together and compacted by that which every joint supplieth, according to the effectual working in the measure of every part, maketh increase of the body unto the edifying of itself in love.*
> >
> > *This I say therefore, and testify in the Lord, that ye henceforth walk not as other Gentiles walk, in the vanity of their mind,*
> >
> > *Having the understanding darkened, being alienated from the life of God through the ignorance that is in them, because of the blindness of their heart:*

Who being past feeling have given themselves over unto lasciviousness, to work all uncleanness with greediness.

But ye have not so learned Christ;

If so be that ye have heard him, and have been taught by him, as the truth is in Jesus:

That ye put off concerning the former conversation the old man, which is corrupt according to the deceitful lusts;

And be renewed in the spirit of your mind;

And that ye put on the new man, which after God is created in righteousness and true holiness.

Wherefore putting away lying, speak every man truth with his neighbour: for we are members one of another.

Be ye angry, and sin not: let not the sun go down upon your wrath:

Neither give place to the devil.

Let him that stole steal no more: but rather let him labour, working with his hands the thing which is good, that he may have to give to him that needeth.

Let no corrupt communication proceed out of your mouth, but that which is good to the use of edifying, that it may minister grace unto the hearers.

And grieve not the holy Spirit of God, whereby ye are sealed unto the day of redemption.

Let all bitterness, and wrath, and anger, and clamour, and evil speaking, be put away from you, with all malice:

And be ye kind one to another, tenderhearted, forgiving one another, even as God for Christ's sake hath forgiven you.

— Ephesians 4:1–32

CHAPTER 16

When the Price Is Right

Jesus dying on the cross was the ultimate price for humanity. When Jesus died on the cross, He paid the price for every single problem that humanity faced. The death of Jesus on the cross was, in fact, God manifesting His love to us humans to experience God's love to its fullest. But the worst excuse that I have heard from some church folks, sinners, or ungodly people is that they go through life with the attitude since Jesus did it all, we don't have to do anything. The excuse is that God is a God of grace and mercy (this, of course, is a fact), but this does not mean people will deliberately constantly sin against God, with the thought in mind that Jesus already died on the cross, all we have to do is just sit down be lazy and do nothing. As a matter of fact, most of this lazy, do-nothing attitude comes from some (the author always mentions the word some) modernistic preachers with an upsurge of preaching on the subject of prosperity and now grace (the author do believe in prosperity and grace), which millions of Christians have misinterpreted with the lame excuse of being lazy and laxidacical.

The greatest Scripture in the Bible is the Gospel of Jesus Christ, "For God *so loved* the world, that *he gave* his only begotten Son, that whosoever *believeth* [believes] in him should not perish, but have everlasting life" John 3:16.

God loves us humans unreservedably that He gave; God saw the entire human race plunged into sin by our first parents, Adam and Eve. He did something about it; He gave His Son, Jesus Christ, then His Son, Jesus Christ, gave Himself as Jesus paid the ultimate price by sacrificing Himself. He suffered pain like no human being suffered, and by the way, He did not stop in Gethsemane, neither Pilate's judgment hall nor at the whipping post nor did He go half the way climbing up to Calvary's Hill with the cross on His back. Jesus willingly, graciously, sacrificially went all the way to Calvary's Hill, where the cruel Roman soldiers mercilessly drove the nails in His hands and His feet and lifted Him and jerked His entire body into the ground as the weight of His body with excruciating pain once again tear into His nail-pierced hands and feet as the cross with His body on it, sunk into the hole that was made for the cross. There is scorn, ridicule, reproach, and shame hung the Son of God in front of His disciples as the Roman soldiers and the religious world spew insults while Jesus lay dying on the cross.

No Christian deliberately chooses to suffer like Jesus, He already sacrificed His life for us, but persecution does occur when you are a real Christian. The apostles realized the price they had to pay to follow their Lord and Savior, but then they paid a price for God's miracle-working power.

The apostles realized the price they had to pay to follow their Lord and Savior, but then they paid a price for God's miracle-working power. We have a majority of Christians today who know nothing about the supernatural working power of God, all because some preachers are preaching that God is a God of grace; we don't have to do anything because it's already done. All we got to do is sit back, relax, enjoy being prosperous for prosperity's sake, and just cruise our way to heaven. "For God so loved the world that he gave his only begotten Son, that whosoever believeth [believes] in him should not perish, but have everlasting life" John 3:16.

From the greatest Scripture in the Bible derives these two words, *gave* and *believe*. These two words mean that we have to do something to experience God's working power in our lives and experience revival like the ministry of Jesus and the apostles, as recorded in the Gospels and the book of Acts. "Howbeit this kind goeth not out but by prayer and fasting" Matthew 17:21.

> *And now, Lord, behold their threatenings: and grant unto thy servants, that with all boldness they may speak thy word,*
>
> *By stretching forth thine hand to heal; and that signs and wonders may be done by the name of thy holy child Jesus.*
>
> *And when they had prayed, the place was shaken where they were assembled together; and they were all filled with the Holy Ghost, and they spake the word of God with boldness.*
> — Acts 4:29–31

> *And by the hands of the apostles were many signs and wonders wrought among the people; (and they were all with one accord in Solomon's porch.*
>
> *And of the rest durst no man join himself to them: but the people magnified them.*
>
> *And believers were the more added to the Lord, multitudes both of men and women.)*
>
> *Insomuch that they brought forth the sick into the streets, and laid them on beds and couches, that at the least the shadow of Peter passing by might overshadow some of them.*
>
> *Insomuch that they brought forth the sick into the streets, and laid them on beds and couches, that at the least the shadow of Peter passing by might overshadow some of them.*
> — Acts 5:12–15

With their first love and their relationship for God intact and a continuous revival within their spirit, the above Scriptures are what can be referred to as nothing short but real revival. The apostles did not rely on and the grace alone do nothing syndrome, but they put into action what they believed that Jesus Christ was alive by and through the power of His resurrection, *prayed* and *fasted*, after which signs and wonders followed because they paid a price for the miracle-working power of Jesus Christ.

The word "believe" comes from the Hebrew word "*aman*," which means to have faith (not just to isolate the word faith), but to have *faith in God* is to do something. To put your faith in God is to have assurance and confidence to rely upon. To believe is putting your faith into action. For an individual to be saved, they have to believe. But believing does not stop by just believing (passive) but by being active; for people to be saved, they must recognize what Jesus did for them on the cross and believe He was raised from the dead and is now sitting at the right hand of God making intercession for us.

> *Seeing then that we have a great high priest, that is passed into the heavens, Jesus the Son of God, let us hold fast our profession.*
>
> *For we have not an high priest which cannot be touched with the feeling of our infirmities; but was in all points tempted like as we are, yet without sin.*
>
> *Let us therefore come boldly unto the throne of grace that we may obtain mercy, and find grace to help in time of need.*
> — Hebrews 4:14–16

We have to accept Jesus into their hearts as Lord and Savior; this can be done by an individual or people. After believing, any individual or people has to put their faith into action, then confess with their mouth and say these words, "God, I thank You for sending Jesus Christ to die on the cross for my sins, wash away all my sins by the blood of Jesus that was shed on Calvary, I receive Jesus into my heart as Lord and Savior, save my soul now, I ask You for peace, joy, love, and happiness into my heart and life. I give You my life; use me in Your service in Jesus' name. Amen." Here is confirmation that the prayer you prayed is biblically sound doctrine, "That if thou shalt confess with thy mouth, the Lord Jesus, and believe in thine heart that God hath raised Jesus from the dead, thou shalt be saved" Romans 10:9.

There is a reason for the above-written paragraph, and of course, this is not to criticize teachers of grace. Yes! God is a God of grace, but the grace of God does not give license for laziness. Faith and believing are doing something about what Jesus has done on Calvary, and this is putting your faith and belief into action and doing something about the Gospel of Jesus Christ. God's love and grace must be responded from us human beings with action. Grace demands action, and then grace would be initiated, validated, and be efficacious in our lives and in His kingdom. This same principle is applicable in relation to healing, deliverance, prosperity, success, and revival.

We have a generation of Christians who want to sit on the pews of a church building and be entertained, be at ease in a comfort zone, settle for the status quo and expect God to send revivals like Jesus, the apostles, and our church fathers who experienced the manifestation of God's power in a usual way.

Here is God's recommendation for revival—our lives must be governed by the inspired word of God, especially the teachings of Jesus and the apostles, backed up by a dedicated life and the basics of Christianity; if some people did not get it, the author would not hesitate to reiterate. The basics of Christianity are the born again experience, baptism with the Holy Spirit, being baptized in water by immersion, Bible study, church attendance, holiness (holiness is being separated unto God), personal and corporate prayer, attested by giving, soul-winning, and preparing for the second return of Jesus Christ. There are so many versions of the Bible, but all we have the do is go back to the original King James Version, read it and obey what God says; there are no seven principles for revival here. All that needs to be done in obedience to the Word of God, and we would experience what some of the Old Testament and New Testament saints experienced—the supernatural power of God.

Here are some Scriptures that can trigger a revival in an individual, people, church, or country,

> *Now Moses kept the flock of Jethro his father in law, the priest of Midian: and he led the flock to the backside of the desert, and came to the mountain of God, even to Horeb.*
>
> *And the angel of the LORD appeared unto him in a flame of fire out of the midst of a bush: and he looked, and, behold, the bush burned with fire, and the bush was not consumed.*
>
> *And Moses said, I will now turn aside, and see this great sight, why the bush is not burnt.*
>
> *And when the LORD saw that he turned aside to see, God called unto him out of the midst of the bush, and said, Moses, Moses. And he said, Here am I.*
>
> *And he said, Draw not nigh hither: put off thy shoes from off thy feet, for the place whereon thou standest is holy ground.*
>
> *Moreover he said, I am the God of thy father, the God of Abraham, the God of Isaac, and the God of Jacob. And Moses hid his face; for he was afraid to look upon God.*
>
> — Exodus 3:1–6

The key to the children's of Israel deliverance was keyed up in one man's spiritual curiosity. Moses was like any other man of our day; as a matter of fact, he had the responsibility of caring for sheep, and a strange and unusual phenomenon caught his eyes; strangely enough, the fire that was burning on the bush really caught his attention the bush was not burnt or consumed. Moses did not react like some people of our day, "I am losing my mind under this hot desert sun, or I imagine things, I am delirious, I think I am going to find a shade tree and go and lay down under it," Moses had a spiritual curiosity, here it is,

> *[…] I will now turn aside to see what this great sight, why the bush is not burnt.*
> *And when the LORD saw that he turned aside to see, God called him out of the midst of the bush, and said, Moses, Moses, And he said, Here am I.*
>
> — Exodus 3:3–4

There are four points I would like to emphasize here that caused Israel's deliverance, and these are: (1) He witnessed or saw something beyond the natural; in other words, he witnessed the supernatural. (2) His spiritual curiosity causes him to turn aside to see what this great sight is all about. (3) God called him out of the bush; in other words, he heard God speaking to him. (4) When God spoke, Moses said, "Here am I." His availability was God's opportunity to manifest who He is and manifest His supernatural power to the then known world, for that generation to teach their children's children and generations to come of the true and living God and for this generation worldwide to read about God and His power and to serve Him in spirit and in truth.

It is the author's intent that someone would have a sense of spiritual discernment and discern what God is wanting to do and do like Moses *"turn aside or turn around"* from a quagmire of worldliness, materialism, fleshiness, fame, name, fortune, and flowing with the crowd. Then and only then will we begin to experience a revival or move of God like never before. By Moses turning around, he heard from God Himself; and, brother or sister, do we need to hear from God at this time in a world of catastrophic situations and its dire and pandemic in every condition. It is the author's prayer that people turn around and seek or go after God, but this kind of thinking and writing or preaching might not set good, which might not be convenient to some ministers and Christians, but turning around and going after God and His purpose and would cause the supernatural power of God to move in the Church and bring an about a biblical revival.

The author cannot recall at the spur of the moment anyone preaching on this Scripture lately,

> *If my people, which are called by my name, shall humble themselves, and pray, and seek my face, and turn from their wicked ways; then will I hear from heaven, and will forgive their sin, and will heal their land.*
>
> — 2 Chronicles 7:14

After Solomon had finished the temple, God visited Solomon, and God, Himself, spoke the above words to Solomon. This particular scripture is always the key to revival; revival is God Himself intervening in the Church, to manifest Himself, His power and glory, to bring about a change for our betterment, and to bless us. Revival is God saying to an organized, sophisticated, traditional, systematic, programized church that my way is better than your way; it is for your benefit and beneficial to the church in every way.

It is for you to experience the fullness of God's power, to destroy the works of the flesh, pride, and the power of Satan, for the fruits of the spirit to be manifested, for the gifts of the spirit to be operating in the church. Revival is an opportunity for multitudes of souls to be saved and be swept into the kingdom of God. It is an opportunity for the love of God to be manifested among different races of people working in love and unity to have and experience what Jesus and the apostles had. Revival is also a God-given opportunity to change the political system, stop crimes, abortion, and perverted lifestyles, bring prosperity, bless the farmers that the crops or harvest be plentiful, animals to multiply for employment to skyrocket and the economy improves more than ever before and much more. By the way, when there is revival, the church and the country people live in prospers in every way.

"IF MY PEOPLE WHO ARE CALLED BY MY NAME,"

This is God talking to Christians as well as other people or mankind, His creation, shall humble themselves; we are living in a day and time where it seems that 89 percent of the church world is becoming hung up on positions, titles, degrees, archbishop, bishops, and doctors of divinity. Members pride themselves on belonging to a megaChurch, congregation, or building. If you are and there is a need for such, please be sure that you are saved, filled with the Holy Spirit, and doing something for Jesus. Be certain that you have a relationship with God and be ready for the second return of Jesus Christ. But what is God telling His creation or the Church; to experience revival, people must *humble themselves* before the Almighty God.

For the benefit of people who are spiritually hungry, literally, the word "*humble*" comes from the Hebrew word "*anav*," which means to be poor, not financially or materially poor but poor or broken in spirit. Jesus had the right idea about being humble; here are His words pertaining to humility,

> *And said, verily I say unto you, except ye be converted and become as little children, ye shall not enter the kingdom of heaven*
>
> *Whosoever therefore shall humble himself as this little child, the same is greatest in the kingdom of heaven.*
>
> *And whoso shall receive one such little child in my name receiveth me.*
>
> *But whoso shall offend one of these little ones which believe in me, it were better for him that a millstone were hanged about his neck, and that he were drowned in the depth of the sea.*
>
> — Matthew 18:3–6

If you did not get the revelation, what is Jesus saying if you will see the glory of God? Revival miracles, signs, wonders, supernatural happenings like in the Bible, you must humble yourself like a little child. What is it about a little child? They are *innocent*, one of the worst deterrents to revival in the church; we have too many smart alecks who act like they know it all. Most everyone wants their opinion to be heard without giving the other guy an opportunity. Writing these words certainly is without animosity, but there is a minister of God, TV ministries, and other people who are consistently conducting Christian programs. There are men and women of God in America and other parts of the world who know how to get a hold of God and pray until the heavens are open and miracles, signs, and wonders occur with revival and biblical results following; check the people; behind these results, they have an innocent spirit. Where are the days of innocence when people came to church with a humble spirit and a right attitude? Without being numbers conscious, without the megachurch spirit.

"AND PRAY AND SEEK MY FACE"

Prayer is the birthplace for revival; this word here is not just talking about and saying prayers, reciting prayers, or traditional prayers, but the type of praying that is vigilant, continuous, interceding, standing in the gap prayers, prayer that goes with a broken spirit and a contrite heart. Prayer that Christians pray until they get answers for what they are praying for; it also means praying until revival breaks out. Recently I ministered in a certain church or congregation, and I mentioned "pray and seek my face" (God's face); after this, a dedicated Christian man who has been a member of that church for over fifteen years came up to me and asked, "Evangelist Seebran, what does it mean to seek God's face?" He was honest, and I was surprised, but I sensed his hunger for God, so I explained to him what it means to pray and seek God's face. Seeking God's face means "to desire, hunger, thirst for God." This also means to be in prayer, to humble ourselves before Him, to be in God's presence, also to find out His will in our lives, to seek Him for a breakthrough spiritually, socially, financially, physically most of all for a New Testament revival like the ministry of Jesus and the apostles.

"AND TURN FROM THEIR WICKED WAYS, GOD'S PEOPLE!"

Turn from their wicked ways! This is the reaction some ministers are met with when this Scripture is preached about or ministered. Some people become quite adamant, as they would say, "How could God's people have wicked ways?" Anyone who has any spiritual inclination should realize when God spoke these words, He wanted to bless His people and send revival.

This Scripture was never meant to embarrass anyone. Turn from what! I am a Christian; I have not committed murder, sold or into drugs, harlotry, pimping pornography, gambling, robbing, stealing, wild parties, cursing, swearing, rape, pornography, child molestation, homosexuality, perversion, stealing, Satan worship, witchcraft, voodoo, and all such like related wicked ways.

Well, what are some of the wicked ways that God's people have to turn from? What about some preachers who are self egotistical and want everyone to support and help them and have no heart to help other ministers who want to do something for God? Some denominations do not confess to be saved and baptized with the Holy Spirit, who will gather on a given weekend and build a church building for that particular congregation that was in need of help. What about the sin of prayerlessness, sins of omission, commission (not praying, giving, or going to preach the Gospel), laziness, stinginess, worldliness, perversion, pornography, alcoholism, gossiping, destructive criticism, disobedience to God, disobedience, and lack of respect and honor to parents, prejudice this sin surely had hindered revival in past centuries.

> *[...] Adultery, fornication, uncleanliness, lasciviousness,*
> *Idolatry, witchcraft, hatred, variance, emulations, wrath, strife, seditions, heresies, Envying, murders, drunkenness, reveling, and such like: of the which I tell you before, as I have also told you in time past, that they which do such things shall not inherit the kingdom of God.*
> — Galatians 5:19b–21

It is not the intent of the author to give the idea that he is contrary, and the author does not want to convey the idea that all Christians are guilty of such sins or, as God calls it, wicked ways. But the above paragraph is to give an idea of some of the sins or wicked ways that are being practiced by some so-called Christians that obviously can and will hinder a revival. This is the reason why God spoke these words to Solomon. Suppose people will turn from all such wicked ways (more can be mentioned, but the above is to give you an idea of what the Holy Spirit is speaking to a nation and, of course, the Church. If sinners and Christians turned from these wicked ways, America and other countries of the world would experience real revival. National sin and the sins of Christians always paralyze a Nation and the Church. We have come to a point in America that real Christians can hardly differentiate the real from the false; to a point, so goes the world, so goes the church.

"THEN WILL I HEAR FROM HEAVEN AND HEAL THEIR LAND…"

If ever there was a time our land needed healing is now. The foundations of our faith in God in America are being attacked by Satan, demons, and men and women are given over to evil; the threat of a total economic downfall hangs over America after one of the best economic recoveries in about thirty years.

So call religious movements are slashing the heads of men, women, and children daily, and they are doing this in the name of their god, while the free governments of the world cannot seem to do anything about this, except for President Trump and very few leaders of other countries.

The American people are being bombarded with threats daily, while at the present time, hardly anyone seems to care what happens to us. Every facet of our society is being threatened by radical religious organizations from within and without. The prophecy of the prophets, Jesus, and the apostles about some people of the world and some Americans becoming sodomites are being flaunted and condoned as a free lifestyle. Suppose it feels God do it, with little regard for God and godly men and women, while unashamedly certain men, as they say behind the cloth from archbishops, bishops, priests, and some protestants are sanctioning this type of ungodly lifestyle. War has had its grip on so many countries of the world, all of this and more.

> *[But God says] if my people, which are called by my name, shall humble themselves, and pray, and seek my face, and turn from their wicked ways; then will I hear from heaven, […] and heal their land.*
>
> — 2 Chronicles 7:14

Some people want life but not the one who gives and is our life, the blessings but not the blesser, prosperity but not the one who prospers, guidance but not the one who guides and protects, rain for farming but not the one who sends the rain, money, and provision for daily needs but not the one who supplies our needs, peace, and prosperity but not the one who gives peace and prosperity, happiness in the marriage and home, but God is the one who can be the center of marriage and family life (by the way, the author and his wife celebrated fifty-six years of marriage on November 14th, 2021). Most people of America want God's blessing on this country but have eliminated the Bible, the Ten Commandments, and prayer from government offices, public places, and schools and now trying to remove "in God we trust from our money," while in universities students, and children are carrying guns, knives, and other deadly weapons. Most Americans have sown a wind and now reaping a whirlwind.

There are four of the worst sins that have caused nations within past centuries to self-destruct and vanish from the face of the earth. These are the same sins that are causing our nation, America, to self-destruct. What are these sins? First of all, compromising leaders of organized religion; some of them stand up behind their podiums or pulpits with Bibles in their hands and sanction same-sex marriage as some government representatives and lawmakers who attend these churches go against the same Bible they swore to tell the truth and do opposite to what the same Bible speaks against. Secondly, abortion or killing unborn babies is wrong and is condemned by God's Word, the Bible. Nations that committed these mass murders within past centuries, for instance, Egypt and Rome. This is one of the sins that brought their leaders and nation down. Thirdly, rejection and persecution of God's ministers who live godly lives and stand up for righteousness and truth, rejection of prayer, discarding and throwing out the Bible from public places and schools, and allowing heathens to come into our country with their heathen gods and practices and rejecting the true and living God through Jesus Christ. Fourthly, most nations of the world do not understand God in relation to the Nation of Israel, but God's relationship to Israel goes back to Abraham.

The sin of laziness (which can be termed wicked ways) has gripped most church members, people who used to party all day and night when they were in the world for material things, pleasure, the flesh, and the devil. They have suddenly become conscious of one hour for church on Sunday morning would not attend the sweet hour of prayer during the week, who do not want to be bothered about praying half a night like our early church fathers, grandparents, and parents used to do. This is the reason they had what the author would call "real revival." We have a majority of Christians who have developed a lackadaisical, passive, "don't care" attitude. If George Muller had this attitude, thousands of orphans would have died in England. If David Livingstone had this attitude, the Congo would have never had the Gospel of Jesus Christ. If Mother Theresa had this attitude, millions of children and adults would have died in India. If Rees Howell had this attitude, he would have never prayed for England to be saved from the Nazis, and England was spared from hundreds of thousands being massacred. If David Brainerd labored among the American Indians up North in the ice and snow at times, even though he developed TB, but thank God his labor was not in vain, multitudes of Indians were saved.

We have the power to change things; yes, certain educational programs and methods and outreaches are necessary, important, and needed. But please remember that God is saying to His people, all who name the name of Jesus, as a matter of fact, all people, who will put this word of God into action,

> *If my people, which are called by my name, shall humble themselves, and pray, and seek my face, and turn from their wicked ways; then will I hear from heaven, [...] and heal their land. [Our land, America, needs healing (not just physical healing), but healing in every facet of our society would be made well and be healed.]*

— 2 Chronicles 7:14

It is impossible to comment on all the Scriptures like the one above, and mind you, the subject of if the price is right did not slip away from the author, but 2 Chronicles 7:14 had to be commented on, especially for the people who are desirous for revival in America and the world in general. Here are some other Scriptures, if obeyed and put into practice by the church, will obviously cause revival.

> *Why sayest thou, O Jacob, and speakest, O Israel, My way is hid from the Lord, and my judgment is passed over from my God?*
>
> *Hast thou not known? hast thou not heard, that the everlasting God, the Lord, the Creator of the ends of the earth, fainteth not, neither is weary? there is no searching of his understanding.*
>
> *He giveth power to the faint; and to them that have no might he increaseth strength.*
>
> *Even the youths shall faint and be weary, and the young men shall utterly fall:*
>
> *But they that wait upon the Lord shall renew their strength, they shall mount up with wings as Eagles, they shall run and not be weary and they shall walk and not faint.*
>
> — Isaiah 40:27–31

This Scripture does not necessarily mean to sit down and do nothing; the Scripture before verse 31 reveals the power and greatness of God. With all of our knowledge, educational or spiritual, we cannot comprehend God, the pathetic condition of mankind's physical and spiritual being. But sitting down and doing nothing will never alleviate mankind's physical and spiritual adverse conditions and calamities, but the prophet Isaiah is opening our eyes to God's recommendation for change and revival, and that is by, "But they that wait upon the Lord shall renew their strength; they shall mount up with wings of eagles, they shall run and not be weary; and they shall walk, and not faint" Isaiah 40:31.

Unfortunately, the author cannot recall when last I heard a preacher behind the pulpit or TV, read a chapter from this book, preached a sermon, or mentioned the book of Joel. (This book is a direct word from God.) The book of Joel is clearly one of the greatest books in the Bible. This book will initiate, inspire, inflame, and it is the key to revival. Talking about if the price is right, this is it. It is not possible or convenient to print this entire book (no sarcasm meant here, I wonder if some of God's people are willing to read this book), but it is the author's request that this is done, especially those who hunger, thirst, and are desirous of revival God's way. Read this book over and over; herein lies the revelation for blessings, prosperity, and revival.

Just to convey the importance of revival, the author felt compelled to read the book of Joel again, even though I have read this book over and over. To read this book was an inspiration, and to print chapters two and three, which is of a surety to inspire and challenge anyone who is desirous of a spiritual awakening or a biblical revival. Here are two chapters of this God-inspired prophecy that concerns our day, which is termed "the last days."

> *Blow ye the trumpet in Zion, and sound an alarm in my holy mountain: let all the inhabitants of the land tremble: for the day of the* L<small>ORD</small> *cometh, for it is nigh at hand;*
>
> *A day of darkness and of gloominess, a day of clouds and of thick darkness, as the morning spread upon the mountains: a great people and a strong; there hath not been ever the like, neither shall be any more after it, even to the years of many generations.*
>
> *A fire devoureth before them; and behind them a flame burneth: the land is as the garden of Eden before them, and behind them a desolate wilderness; yea, and nothing shall escape them.*
>
> *The appearance of them is as the appearance of horses; and as horsemen, so shall they run.*

Like the noise of chariots on the tops of mountains shall they leap, like the noise of a flame of fire that devoureth the stubble, as a strong people set in battle array.

Before their face the people shall be much pained: all faces shall gather blackness.

They shall run like mighty men; they shall climb the wall like men of war; and they shall march every one on his ways, and they shall not break their ranks:

Neither shall one thrust another; they shall walk every one in his path: and when they fall upon the sword, they shall not be wounded.

They shall run to and fro in the city; they shall run upon the wall, they shall climb up upon the houses; they shall enter in at the windows like a thief.

The earth shall quake before them; the heavens shall tremble: the sun and the moon shall be dark, and the stars shall withdraw their shining:

And the Lord shall utter his voice before his army: for his camp is very great: for he is strong that executeth his word: for the day of the Lord is great and very terrible; and who can abide it?

Therefore also now, saith the Lord turn ye even to me with all your heart, and with fasting, and with weeping, and with mourning:

And rend your heart, and not your garments, and turn unto the Lord your God: for he is gracious and merciful, slow to anger, and of great kindness, and repenteth him of the evil.

Who knoweth if he will return and repent, and leave a blessing behind him; even a meat offering and a drink offering unto the Lord your God?

Blow the trumpet in Zion, sanctify a fast, call a solemn assembly:

Gather the people, sanctify the congregation, assemble the elders, gather the children, and those that suck the breasts: let the bridegroom go forth of his chamber, and the bride out of her closet.

Let the priests, the ministers of the Lord, weep between the porch and the altar, and let them say, Spare thy people, O Lord, and give not thine heritage to reproach, that the heathen should rule over them: wherefore should they say among the people, Where is their God?

Then will the Lord be jealous for his land, and pity his people.

Yea, the Lord will answer and say unto his people, Behold, I will send you corn, and wine, and oil, and ye shall be satisfied therewith: and I will no more make you a reproach among the heathen:

But I will remove far off from you the northern army, and will drive him into a land barren and desolate, with his face toward the east sea, and his hinder part toward the utmost sea, and his stink shall come up, and his ill savour shall come up, because he hath done great things.

Fear not, O land; be glad and rejoice: for the Lord will do great things.

Be not afraid, ye beasts of the field: for the pastures of the wilderness do spring, for the tree beareth her fruit, the fig tree and the vine do yield their strength.

Be glad then, ye children of Zion, and rejoice in the Lord your God: for he hath given you the former rain moderately, and he will cause to come down for you the rain, the former rain, and the latter rain in the first month.

And the floors shall be full of wheat, and the fats shall overflow with wine and oil.

And I will restore to you the years that the locust hath eaten, the cankerworm, and the caterpiller, and the palmerworm, my great army which I sent among you.

And ye shall eat in plenty, and be satisfied, and praise the name of the LORD your God, that hath dealt wondrously with you: and my people shall never be ashamed.

And ye shall know that I am in the midst of Israel, and that I am the LORD your God, and none else: and my people shall never be ashamed.

And it shall come to pass afterward, that I will pour out my spirit upon all flesh; and your sons and your daughters shall prophesy, your old men shall dream dreams, your young men shall see visions:

And also upon the servants and upon the handmaids in those days will I pour out my spirit.

And I will shew wonders in the heavens and in the earth, blood, and fire, and pillars of smoke.

The sun shall be turned into darkness, and the moon into blood, before the great and the terrible day of the LORD come.

And it shall come to pass, that whosoever shall call on the name of the LORD shall be delivered: for in mount Zion and in Jerusalem shall be deliverance, as the LORD hath said, and in the remnant whom the LORD shall call.

Joel 2:1–32

This prophet does not mince words; he speaks of God's judgments; he prophesies as he delivers a word directly on the importance of fasting and prayer and the blessings that follow. The promise of the Holy Spirit, we have been told again and again here in America that fasting is optional (true to some extent), but the responsibility of the priest and ministers was to call the people to fast and pray, which will avert and deter God's judgments. Disobedience would mean, as the prophet describes, destruction would surely come on the land slowly but surely, bit by bit. The term locust and caterpillar is used to describe that the enemy would come in swarms and cause total and complete destruction. Outward expressions of sorrow and shame, fasting, weeping, and mourning; tears for trouble must be turned into tears for the sin that caused it. But rending the garments would be vain, except their hearts were rent by abasement and self-abhorrence; by sorrow for their sins, and separation from them. There is no question but that if we truly repent of our sins, God will forgive them, but whether he will remove affliction is not promised, yet the probability of it should encourage us to repent.

His promises are real answers to the prayers of faith; with him saying and doing are not two things. Some understand these promises figuratively as pointing to gospel grace and as fulfilled in the abundant comforts treasured up for believers in the covenant of grace. The promise began to be fulfilled on the day of Pentecost when the Holy Spirit was poured out, and it was continued in the converting grace and miraculous gifts conferred on both Jews and Gentiles. The judgments of God upon a sinful world only go before the judgment of the world on the last day. Calling on God supposes knowledge of him, faith in him, desire toward him, dependence on him, and, as evidence of the sincerity of all this, conscientious obedience to him. Those only shall be delivered in the great day, which is now effectually called from sin to God, from self to Christ, from things below to things above.

The judgments of God in the last and closing days before Jesus returns, the blessings the church shall enjoy. The restoration of the Jews and the final victory of true religion over all opposition appear to be here foretold. The contempt and scorn with which the Jews have often been treated as a people, and the little value set upon them, are noticed. None ever hardened his heart against God or His church and prospered long. Here is a challenge to all the enemies of God's people.

There are no escaping God's judgments; hardened sinners, in that day of wrath, shall be cut off from all comfort and joy. Most of the prophets foretell the same final victory of the church of God over all that oppose it. To the wicked, it will be a terrible day, but to the righteous, it will be a joyful day. What cause has those who possess an interest in Christ to glory in their strength and their Redeemer! The acceptable year of the Lord, a day of such great favor to some, will be a day of remarkable vengeance to others: let every one that is out of Christ awake and flee from the wrath to come.

There shall be an abundant divine influence, and the gospel will spread speedily into the remotest corners of the earth. These events are predicted under significant emblems; there is a day coming when every thing amiss shall be amended. The fountain of this plenty is in the house of God, whence the streams take rise. Christ is this Fountain; his sufferings, merit, and grace cleanse, refresh, and make fruitful. Gospel grace, flowing from Christ, shall reach to the Gentile world, to the most remote regions, and make them abound in fruits of righteousness.

After Jesus rose from the grave, He told the apostles and all of His disciples to go to the Upper Room; here are His words from Luke, "And, behold, I send the promise of my Father upon you: but tarry ye in the city of Jerusalem, until ye be endued with power from on high" Luke 24:49. He spent forty days with the disciples, and the disciples thought that He was going to restore the Jewish kingdom, but here are the words of Jesus,

> *And being assembled together with them, He commanded them not to depart from Jerusalem, but the wait for the Promise of the Father [The Holy Spirit], "which," He said, "you have heard from Me; for John truly baptized with water, but you shall be baptized with the Holy Spirit not many days from now."*
>
> — Acts 1:4–5

Please give attention to Acts 1:6, "When they therefore were come together, they asked of him, saying, Lord, wilt thou at this time restore again the kingdom to Israel?"

The disciple's minds were set on the worldly kingdom. The disciples wanted Jesus to overthrow the Roman emperors, the Roman government, and its oppressive political system against the Jews. They wanted Jesus to be their political leader, implement man-made rule and system of government, a palace, and huge buildings, with the iconic idea that we, the Jews, with Jesus as our leader, built all of this. Do you see how history repeats itself? This is the same spirit that is prevalent in our day; billions upon billions of dollars were and are being spent on buildings, and some of the leaders and people who built them possibly enter them once a week, and if there is any other activity, it might be the bridge club and the bingo assembled to bridge and bingo, while the weekly prayer meetings become obsolete. But here comes a stern warning from Jesus, "[…] It is not for you to know the times and seasons, which the Father has put in His own authority" Acts 1:7, NKJV.

Before going any further, if any ministry in America or any other part of the world that is teaching, preaching, and practicing biblical living and has the results that the prophets, Jesus, the apostles, and the apostle Paul and has a need for a building to house thousands of people, this surely is commendable. But having a mega building for fame and namesake, with so many ministers trying to split hairs over certain eschatological doctrines, plus the constant, continuous squabbles of when the rapture is going to occur, the introduction of feast days, with other preachers giving the idea that you cannot pray to God without a prayer shoal (I say this with respect) going back to judicial traditions. Most of these things take away from the Sacrificial Lamb, Jesus Christ, and His atoning work on the cross to emphasize more is said and sang about the piece of wood than Jesus who died on the cross. It is true that the Gospel of Jesus Christ started with the Jews in the East, then the Gospel of Jesus Christ swept the West and is now heading back to the East and the Jews, but the apostle Paul warns us to "keep the faith that was once delivered to the saints."

Jesus continues His stern warning to the apostles and early disciples to go to Jerusalem, tarry in Jerusalem, and wait on the promise from the Father, which Jesus spoke about. Here is the key: if you wait, if you tarry, if you pray, if you cry out to God, if you lay in sackcloth and ashes (I hear a resounding sound, "We don't need this today," who says? If we wait and pray to God all day and night as we used to, if we humble ourselves. If you do all of these, read and listen to the words of Jesus (and this comes not by voting and choosing a leader for politics in the church), "But ye shall receive power, after that the Holy Ghost is come upon you: and ye shall be witnesses unto me both in Jerusalem, and in all Judaea, and in Samaria, and unto the uttermost part of the earth" Acts 1:8.

In other words, Jesus is telling us if we tarry, if we wait, if we pray, if we fast, etc., we will have the power of God to shake the world. And this is possible when the price is right; yes, God is a God of grace, and it is true by His grace we are saved, but God's grace does not commend laziness in the kingdom of God. Instructions were given by Jesus, and the disciples willingly obeyed. With high expectations, they found themselves in the Upper Room, not the supper-room. For ten days, they waited, which means they read the Word, they rehearsed Jesus' words over and over as they repented, confessed their faults to one another, prayed for one another, prayed, fasted, and of course, waited and waited.

Could you imagine if Jesus had told His disciples of this day, some of them would have carried in the upper room food, snacks, cold cuts, bread, Pepsi, Coke, and other beverages? Some might have even carried their TV sets to watch their favorite shows and the Super Bowl! But in the Upper Room, the book of Acts, disciples knew the secret of having God's power in their lives, so much so they remembered the words of Jesus that the Holy Spirit would comfort, guide, lead, speak, and reveal the secrets of God to them. They remembered what Jesus said about the Holy Spirit would infuse them with power over the devil, demons, sicknesses, diseases, and most of all, to be a powerful witness to preach the Gospel of Jesus Christ.

They waited and waited and waited while they prayed, prayed, and prayed. They never had the attitude and said God is a God of grace and did nothing. What happened in the Upper Room on the tenth day in the Upper Room is biblical history, and we do not need to go very far to find out; all we have to do is read the book of Acts, what happened after Pentecost, twelve men and the book of Acts disciples shook the then known world. Could you imagine if the Church had continued like the disciples in the book of Acts, what would have happened? The Holy Spirit was outpoured on the book of Acts disciples, all because the price was right.

And when the day of Pentecost was fully come, they were all with one accord in one place.

And suddenly there came a sound from heaven as of a rushing mighty wind, and it filled all the house where they were sitting.

And there appeared unto them cloven tongues like as of fire, and it sat upon each of them.

And they were all filled with the Holy Ghost, and began to speak with other tongues, as the Spirit gave them utterance.

Acts 2:1–4

What were the results of these above four verses? Read the Bible from the book of Acts, probably lying on the coffee table.

God is a God of grace, and God's love and grace sent Jesus to die for us on the cross; by grace, we are saved, and by the grace of God, we live our daily lives, but the grace of God is not an excuse for laziness in the church Jesus Christ was grace Himself. How could anyone read the Gospels and not realize that Jesus Christ is grace Himself? He did not capitulate with the idea that He is the Son of God, and He would sit back with an attitude and say the work He came to do was already done and did nothing of what He came to do. Jesus did not procrastinate, and neither was He lackadaisical about the work the Father sent Him to do. He willingly submitted to the plan of His Father and did what He came to do for us human beings.

Studying the life of Jesus is intrinsically amazing, as the question is poignantly asked if Jesus was the Son of God and He prayed day and night, how much more you and I as human beings need to pray! Are we greater than Jesus? Well, for the benefit of the reader, just in case you missed them, here are some scriptures from the Gospels where Jesus prayed.

"Very early in the morning, while it was still dark, Jesus got up, left the house and went to a solitary place where he prayed" Mark 1:35, NIV. "After he had dismissed them, he went up on a mountainside by himself to pray" Matthew 14:23a, NIV. "One of those days Jesus went to a mountainside to pray, and spent the night praying to God" Luke 6:12, NIV. "One day Jesus was praying in a certain place. When he finished, one of his disciples said to him, "Lord, teach us to pray" Luke 11:1a.

God is a God of grace, and it is by the grace of God that we are saved, healed, and delivered from sin, the devil, and hell. God's grace and mercy are the reason the rain falls on the just and the unjust, God's grace is the cause that you are alive and well; you have food to eat, clothes to wear, and some money to help take care of you and your family. Surely it is the grace of God He has held back His judgments and has not destroyed this present world with all of the wickedness, sin, and evil that is being committed against God every single day. Someone might ask, "Well, what about all of the sufferings on the earth today?" To answer this question, the author would exercise some caution, but the reason there is some much suffering in this world today and the reasons are all biblical: (1) People have turned away from the true and living God. (2) The rich are not helping the poor as they should. (3) Thank God for the faithful ministers and people of God, but generally speaking, the Church of Jesus Christ is not really fulfilling the Great Commission as it should.

The author does not want to convey the idea of a know-it-all, every minister is at liberty to express his opinion, especially the claims that some of them make in the name of the Lord, but some of the teachings that are being taught about grace today do not correlate with biblical and balanced theology. Grace is definitely God's unrelenting love towards us, human beings, and God showed *His love and grace* by sending Jesus Christ to die on the cross, but there is something that is called faith and believing (believing is putting your faith into action), and there is something called mankind's or human responsibility. Therefore God's mandate for mankind is to believe repent and turn to God with all their mind, spirit and soul. Mankind's responsibility is to study the word of God, pray, fast (often), attend church, give, win lost souls, and be ready for the second return of Jesus Christ. This is the reason God would send an outpouring of the Holy Spirit like in the ministry of Jesus and the apostles; this is real revival when the price is right.

CHAPTER 17
Strong or Agonizing Praying

Even though prayer was mentioned and written about in an earlier chapter of this book, including the previous chapter, the author felt compelled by the leading of the Holy Spirit to continue on the subject when the price is right and interject in this chapter a vital key that will definitely produce biblical revival. Yes! The Bible does mention strong or agonizing praying. Negativity has been avoided as much as possible in every chapter of this book, but sad to say there are some people who are negative, sometimes adamant when it comes to subjects like strong or agonizing praying. This is not necessary; some would comment! If all of this was necessary for Abraham, Jacob, Moses, Hannah, Esther, Elijah, Isaiah, Jeremiah, Jesus, the apostles, the book of Acts Church, and the apostle Paul. Centuries have gone by; men like Praying Hyde, Rees Howell, George Mueller, John Wesley, and Charles Finney, who prayed strong and agonizing prayers that stopped wars, changed the course of nature, opened prison doors, stopped wicked people, deliverance from oppression, and shook cities and nations, the same can happen today by strong agonizing praying.

Some prophecies have to be fulfilled, but a certain crisis that is hitting so many countries like persecutions of Christians, beheading of thousands of people, murders, a wave of ungodly lifestyles, divorces, same-sex marriage, disrespect for human lives, pornography, apostasy, and a host of other abominations. What makes us think that these situations cannot be stopped if we really pray? With strong agonizing praying, intercession, and crying out to God day and night, pray as we ought to, God can do anything or stop the evil that is happening now. Ninety-eight percent of Christians laze back on their sofas and just watch the news of people being beheaded and do not even offer up a prayer to God to stop the evil that is going on in this world. All of what is written in this book should be taken seriously and put into practice, but pay attention to this statement "true, there are certain prophecies that have to be fulfilled, but there are certain things going on in America and the entire world that are not considered a fulfillment of prophecy, but its the devil taking every opportunity to seduce kill and to take lost souls to hell with him. But most of God's people are too lazy to pray, the kind of praying to stop some of these ungodly things from happening.

This chapter is intended to give every Christian a God-given desire to pray, especially strong agonizing praying. It must be stated here that this book is not intended just for reading pleasure, but it is the author's intention that this book would be an incentive to the reader to develop a life of prayer, especially in the area of strong agonizing praying. For prayer to be effective, you must pray. Reading about prayer (thousands of book has been written about prayer), talking about prayer, preaching about prayer, teaching about prayer is good, and saying prayers can be traditional; all of this is of no avail if people do not start praying strong agonizing prayers.

Out of concern and despite all that was written about revival, there is a vital need in the Church today that produces revival. Please bear in mind the type of revival that the author is speaking about is a revival of supernatural miracles, signs, and wonders that occurred in the lives of some of the Old Testaments saints, judges, prophets, Jesus, the apostles in the book of Acts, the apostle Paul, and of course the revivals that followed great men and women of God in centuries gone by.

Someone might quip, well! We are having revival today; thank God for some miracles that are taking place today, but this author's biblical concept of revival is not a few miracles, but the type of revival that this author is speaking about far supersedes a few miracles. Again! The author would reiterate what is needed today is the type of revival of supernatural miracles, signs, and wonders that occurred in the lives of some of the Old Testaments saints, judges, prophets, Jesus, the apostles in the book of Acts, the apostle Paul and of course the revivals that followed great men and women of God in centuries gone by. And this type of revival can happen today if God can find men and women who have a desire to abort the socialistic type of Christianity with all of its entertainment and do some strong agonizing praying.

The vital keys for biblical revival are strong agonizing prayer or praying combined with repentance, dedication, purity, holiness, and unwavering faith. Is strong or agonizing prayer biblical? Yes, it is! Turn with me to your Bible to Hebrews. "Who in the days of his flesh, when he had offered up prayers and supplications with strong crying and tears unto him that was able to save him from death, and was heard in that he feared" Hebrews 5:7. Aramaic Bible in plain English, "While also he was clothed in the flesh, he offered prayers, supplications, strong shouting and tears to him who was able to give him life from death, and he was obeyed." Strong crying and tears Luke 23:46.

Evidently, denote the manner of the *"prayers and supplications,"* and the thrice-repeated prayer in the garden recorded by the evangelists may be well conceived to have been thus loudly uttered, so as to be heard by the three disciples, a stone's cast distant, before sleep overcame them.

From the above scriptures and commentary from Hebrews 5:7 and a commentary from Luke 23:46, we get the idea of Jesus praying with strong or loud praying, weeping, and in agony. Of course, this is the agony that Jesus felt before the crucifixion. During this time, Jesus prayed so earnestly in agonizing prayer that the Bible says as He prayed, sweat came out from His body as drops of blood. Well! What's the point, preacher? Jesus had the victory in Gethsemane before getting to Calvary.

The devil thought He had Jesus whopped on the cross, but Jesus already whopped the devil in Gethsemane. Agonizing prayer is where we fight our greatest battles, but this is where we can be victorious before the victory. Revival history shows again and again that if there are two key elements to obtaining true revival, they would have to be *repentance* and *strong agonizing prayer*.

Anyone who has studied past revivals will tell you that above all else, the key requirements are repentance and heart-rending spirit fired up, praying this obviously would lead to revival. The author does not usually use other writers' thoughts and commentary, but some of you reading this book would be surprised to know that one of the most popular commentators, Matthew Henry, spoke these words, "When God intends great mercy for His people, the first thing He does is set them a-praying." And Leonard Ravenhill wrote that "the man who can get believers to praying would, under God, usher in the greatest revival that the world has ever known." What an amazing statement. Yet, all revival history confirms the truth of it. Truly, if we could get God's people to *agonize in prayer* for revival, as did believers of ages past, then the glory of God would surely come down. But there are many organizers than "agonizes" today.

The author is not in the habit of infringing on copyrights principles or copyrights laws, but while writing this particular chapter, I felt the leading of the Holy Spirit to read some commentaries and other Christian writers' views on this particular subject of strong or agonizing prayer or praying. Surprisingly, there were not too many articles on this subject. Anyhow! I came across one article during my research, of which the author gave permission to copy, print, and distribute this particular article. This article states the names of some great men of God of centuries gone by and recent years. Their names will be mentioned in the few paragraphs following. Portions of this article will be paraphrased.

As A. T. Pierson wrote,

"From the day of Pentecost, there has been NOT ONE great spiritual awakening in any land which has not begun in a UNION OF PRAYER, though only among two or three; no such outward, upward movement has continued after such prayer meetings declined."

Charles Finney is often regarded as possibly the greatest Revival preacher in the history of the church—a mighty preacher of conviction and repentance. But Finney had some very interesting views (almost 'scientific' in a spiritual sense) on how and why Revival came. He was convinced, through many years of Revival ministry, that God intended the church to live continually in a Revival state—that this was the "normal" state of the church. And he was also convinced that if the church would just meet the basic conditions for Revival—deep repentance and heartfelt, 'agonizing' prayer for the outpouring of God's Spirit, then Revival would ALWAYS result. He likened it to a field of wheat. If a farmer tills the soil (deep heart-searching repentance) and provides the right seed and conditions, then a great crop will always result. This is normal and expected. Finney said: "Revival is no more a miracle than a crop of wheat. Revival comes from heaven when heroic souls enter the conflict determined to win or die—or if need be, to win and die! 'The kingdom of heaven suffers violence, and the VIOLENT take it by force.'" John Wesley was of a similar mind: "Have you any days of fasting and prayer? Storm the throne of grace and persevere therein, and mercy will come down." Interestingly, when Finney's Revival Lectures" were published and Finney's "methods" and teachings were put into practice, there were outbreaks of true Revival all over the world. Deep repentance and agonizing prayer—the simple keys to true Revival. Some years later, a missionary to China named Jonothan Goforth, desperate to see God move amongst the seemingly-hardened locals, discovered Finney's writings. Before long he was 'revived' himself, and went on to see mighty outbreaks of Revival wherever he preached in China. Jonothan Goforth became one of this century's great Revival preachers, all through following the simple "methods" of Finney in seeing the convicting power of God unleashed. When we speak about 'Revival' here, we are not speaking about some mere evangelistic crusade or passing excitement. We certainly are not speaking about the kinds of movements that are sweeping through the church today under the labels of 'revival' or 'blessing.' We are talking about mighty moves of God, where conviction of sin and deep repentance often spread out of the churches and into the communities round about, utterly transforming thousands for Christ. One writer described this latter stage of Revival as being "a community saturated with God."

Jonathan Edwards said of the 1735 New England Revival, "The town seemed to be full of the presence of God. It was never so full of love, or so full of joy; and yet, so full of distress as it was then." When Revival spreads out into the community in this way (as happened with the 1904 Welsh Revival, and many others), it is not uncommon for bars to be transformed into prayer meetings, for large numbers of notorious criminals to be converted, and for judges to even be left without cases to put to trial! Such is the impact of a mighty general outpouring of the Spirit of God. In the Welsh Revival of 1904 under Evan Roberts, the entire nation was literally transformed, with HUNDREDS OF THOUSANDS converted in a matter of a few months *in this tiny nation. And it was all through prayer and repentance. One eyewitness said of this famous Revival in Wales that it was not the eloquence of Evan Roberts that broke men down, but his tears. "He would break down, crying bitterly for God to bend them, in an agony of prayer, the tears coursing down his cheeks, with his whole frame writhing. Strong men would break down and cry like children... a sound of weeping and wailing would fill the air."*

The following is a typical excerpt from Evan Roberts' preaching: "First, is there any sin in your past with which you have not honestly dealt, not confessed to God? On your knees at once. Your past must be put away and cleansed. Second, is there anything in your life that is doubtful—anything you cannot decide whether it is good or evil? Away with it. There must not be a trace of a cloud between you and God. Have you forgiven everybody—EVERYBODY? If not, don't expect forgiveness for your sins..." This, then, is the kind of Revival that we are talking about. A mighty outpouring, a deluge of the Spirit of God—a 'Pentecost' of God's convicting glory, where His presence floods down amongst men once more. And such outpourings always start with God's people, before they spread out into the community at large. In fact, right at the beginning, Revivals almost always begin with a small 'prayer core'—the believers who are wrestling in prayer—begging God in an agony of Spirit-led travail, to outpour His Spirit upon them, upon their fellow believers and upon their city or nation. What exactly is 'AGONIZING' PRAYER? Well, it is not too easy to describe. But I know it when it happens. When I was 17 years old, and I was first filled with the Holy Spirit and spoke in tongues, I had access to many old Revival books which I devoured with a Spirit-driven hunger. It did not take long for me to not that the keys to these past Revivals seemed to be deep repentance and this kind of 'wrestling, agonizing' prayer for the outpouring of God's Spirit. I simply decided that I was going to 'agonize' in prayer for Revival! And I did. Every day would find me on my knees for a period of time, with liquid fire on my lips, begging God to fill me more and more with His Spirit, to glorify Himself in the earth and to bring mighty Revival to our nation. Before long I noticed that there was often an awesome sense of being in the very throne room of God when I was praying. I could really tell that my prayers were being heard and that they were making an impact. Glory to God! And they were making an impact on me as well. When I look back now, I can see that basically every break-through in God that I have experienced has been because of this early, ongoing 'agonizing' prayer. It's been so crucial. Of course I do not ALWAYS pray this way. I think praying quietly in tongues is very important and effective also (and you can pray in tongues driving your car or whatever—it is REALLY important). And simply worshipping God and enjoying His presence is also a vital part of communing with God. But I believe that in connection with REVIVAL, this kind of 'wrestling, agonizing' prayer is essential.

However, in order to pray this way, we must have the Holy Spirit empowering and leading our prayers. This is why Finney and others would talk about the 'spirit of prayer' coming upon them: "... unless I had the spirit of prayer I could do nothing. If I lost the spirit of grace and supplication even for a day or an hour I found myself unable to preach with power and efficiency, or to win souls by personal conversation."

I remember a very significant moment in the book 'Anointed for Burial,' which is Todd and DeAnn Burke's account of the mighty Revival in Cambodia in the 1970s. It occurred when God had already been moving powerfully for some time. Todd wrote: "I briefly shared with them some of the things God had been showing me through my Bible readings. Referring to Genesis 32, I told them how Jacob wrestled with the Lord until He blessed him. 'If we expect power and blessing from the Lord, we are going to have to be willing to wrestle with Him in prayer and fasting, in self-denial, in taking up our cross,' I said. 'Then I shared with them from a devotional book by Hudson Taylor, "An easy-going, non-self-denying life will never be one of power." With that, everyone began to wrestle in prayer, and before long, the blessing came.' Several powerful outpourings of the Holy Spirit were the result. What a difference such concerted, 'agonizing' prayer could make in every city and nation today. God has promised Revival, but I believe that He is waiting for a people who will take hold of His promise and begin to make a stand together in prayer for its fulfillment. Friends, could we agree together to lay hold of God in this way? Believe me, it could make all the difference in the world. The key with such prayer is to firstly see the desperate need for true Revival, both in the church and the world, and then to ask God to send His Spirit to help us pray. 'Agonizing' prayer pleads with God that He might glorify Himself and that His Spirit might be poured out. It is for HIS GLORY that we pray in this way. Another key is truly having "clean hands and a pure heart" before God. No secret sin. No unforgiveness. Only those with clean hands and a pure heart can ascend to the holy place of God in prayer. My great hope is that God would inspire as many as possible to join in prayer to see His mighty purpose fulfilled in the earth. The fact that GOD IS NOT GLORIFIED in our world is the tragedy of this late hour. Friends, it is high time for this to change. And be assured that we can truly make a difference. The time has surely come to join together in 'agonizing' prayer for a mighty deluge of His grace and mercy in our day. If everyone reading this would simply begin to pray in this way, what glorious outpourings could result!

— Copyright (c) Andrew Strom, 1998

This chapter would not be complete without mentioning some biblical examples of strong agonizing prayer and some divine principles and guidance of how to pray for biblical revival in our day and time. If there is ever a time that we need biblical revival and results is now. The reason for saying this, and this is a fact while this book was being written, the supreme court had just voted in favor of same-sex marriage, feeling very uncomfortable that particular morning when the results of the supreme court ruling on same-sex marriage and all that goes along with it. I was very, what I might say, troubled that previous night and early in the morning; it was kind of an eerie cloudy dark grey sky morning as I whispered to my wife, "God is grieved because immorality is at its peak." Legalizing same-sex marriage is the worst sin committed against God; I glimpsed at the ruling, then I literally became sick to my stomach and almost vomited.

All of this transpired under the administration before President Trump's presidency. After President Trump left office, we are back under a new president whose administration is embracing the same agenda?

I turned off the television and did not look at or hear the news for two days because I did not want my mind, my spirit, and my soul to be tainted with scenes of people who were in favor of this ruling. Yes! God loves the sinner, but He does not love the sin and the sinning. For those of you reading this book, yours truly is a soul winner, and I have been in some of the streets of America, winning and helping the worst of sinners; this means sinners of the worst who practices every sin against God. I have witnessed, spoken, won their souls to Jesus and prayed them through to God, saw them walk out changed men and women, and today they are serving God; the same is applied to my life and ministry in fifty-five countries of the world, where I have seen God changed the worst of sinners. If holy ministers and Christians (few to find these days) would get back to strong agonizing prayer in every church building, storefronts, backwoods, homes, every nook, and cranny, like they used to pray a strong agonizing prayer, no unbiblical, ungodly ruling would be able to stand against this type of praying. *O God, give us these kinds of prayer warriors.*

Here are some examples of this type of praying. This scripture was in relation to Abraham when his nephew Lot and his family left Abraham to live in Sodom and Gomorrah. Jesus and two angels visited Abraham and Sarah and told Abraham, who was one hundred years old, and Sarah was ninety years old, that they would be blessed with a child.

> *And the* L*ord* *said, Because the cry of Sodom and Gomorrah is great, and because their sin is very grievous;*
>
> *I will go down now, and see whether they have done altogether according to the cry of it, which is come unto me; and if not, I will know.*
>
> *And the men turned their faces from thence, and went toward Sodom: but Abraham stood yet before the Lord.*
>
> *And Abraham drew near, and said, Wilt thou also destroy the righteous with the wicked?*
>
> *Peradventure there be fifty righteous within the city: wilt thou also destroy and not spare the place for the fifty righteous that are therein?*
>
> *That be far from thee to do after this manner, to slay the righteous with the wicked: and that the righteous should be as the wicked, that be far from thee: Shall not the Judge of all the earth do right?*
>
> *And the* L*ord* *said, If I find in Sodom fifty righteous within the city, then I will spare all the place for their sakes.*
>
> *And Abraham answered and said, Behold now, I have taken upon me to speak unto the* L*ord**, which am but dust and ashes:*
>
> *Peradventure there shall lack five of the fifty righteous: wilt thou destroy all the city for lack of five? And he said, If I find there forty and five, I will not destroy it.*
>
> *And he spake unto him yet again, and said, Peradventure there shall be forty found there. And he said, I will not do it for forty's sake.*
>
> *And he said unto him, Oh let not the* L*ord* *be angry, and I will speak: Peradventure there shall thirty be found there. And he said, I will not do it, if I find thirty there.*
>
> *And he said, Behold now, I have taken upon me to speak unto the* L*ord**: Peradventure there shall be twenty found there. And he said, I will not destroy it for twenty's sake.*
>
> *And he said, Oh let not the* L*ord* *be angry, and I will speak yet but this once: Peradventure ten shall be found there. And he said, I will not destroy it for ten's sake.*

And the LORD went his way, as soon as he had left communing with Abraham: and Abraham returned unto his place.

— Genesis 18:20–33

The key to this chapter is verse 22, the angels went to judge Sodom and Gomorrah, but Abraham stayed with God. Reader, here is some godly instruction: before Jesus left Abraham, He told the two angels that were with Him the wickedness of Sodom and Gomorrah had come up before God and to visit and investigate the wickedness of those cities, then gave them the instruction to judge that city. Abraham heard this and became very troubled; the reason was his nephew Lot and Lot's wife and two daughters were in Sodom and Gomorrah. Abraham knew God was going to send fire and brimstone to destroy Sodom and Gomorrah; he was concerned about his nephew Lot and his family, and here is the key to this entire chapter expressed in verse 22, *"And the men [angels] turned their faces thence and went toward Sodom: but Abraham stood yet before the LORD"* Genesis 18:22. This means he stayed and prayed, interceded, and stood in the gap for his nephew and his family. Abraham could have taken the passive attitude and said to himself, "There is nothing I can do about stopping God's judgment; if my nephew had listened to me, he would have never been in that situation." He realized fire and brimstone were inevitable, but he interceded (do you realize that even though America is considered a Christian nation, some ministers and their congregation still do not realize what the word intercession means) intercession means serious praying like what Jesus did in the garden of Gethsemane, this is the kind of praying that would change you, your husband, wife, children, neighbors, community, city, state, nations and the world, believe me, this kind of praying would deliver people from Hell and get them to heaven, someone might say it does not take all of this, but it does not take the kind of entertainment, kind of only good life, the best life, the feel-good do it kind of Christianity, what has this produced? A kind of Christianity that knows where most of the church knows nothing about being visited by God, angels, fellowship with Jesus, and a relationship with God.

Here is the key for the survival of Christianity do not compromise regardless of whatever situation arises; always maintain your relationship with God, maintain your faith in God, and stand up for biblical and Christian principles always. Again, what is the key? Abraham stayed with Jesus and prayed for his nephew's escape from Sodom and Gomorrah. Abraham prayed strong prayers, interceded, and cried out to God. He started out by interceding and strong praying as he was specific, asking God if there were fifty righteous people in Sodom and Gomorrah. He continued praying before Jesus; from fifty, he went down to five; there were not even five righteous people in Sodom, Lot, Abraham's nephew, his wife, and two daughters. Abraham's prayer worked except for Lot's wife, who went against God's instructions to not look back. She turned into a pillar of salt. What is so scary about this is the fact that archeologists discovered a pillar of salt not too far on the hill from Sodom and Gomorrah.

MOSES

He was one of the greatest prophets in the Bible, but what is it that really made Moses great? Was it because of the miracles where he was used by God to perform? No, but what is it that really stood out about Moses? The answer is found in Exodus.

> *And Moses besought the Lord his God, and said, Lord, why doth thy wrath wax hot against thy people, which thou hast brought forth out of the land of Egypt with great power, and with a mighty hand?*
>
> *Wherefore should the Egyptians speak, and say, For mischief did he bring them out, to slay them in the mountains, and to consume them from the face of the earth? Turn from thy fierce wrath, and repent of this evil against thy people.*
>
> *Remember Abraham, Isaac, and Israel, thy servants, to whom thou swarest by thine own self, and saidst unto them, I will multiply your seed as the stars of heaven, and all this land that I have spoken of will I give unto your seed, and they shall inherit it for ever.*
>
> *And the Lord repented of the evil judgment] which he thought to do unto his people. [Because of Moses' strong and agonizing prayer, God spared the Israel from total destruction.]*
>
> — Exodus 32:11–14

What a man! What a leader! What a pastor! What an intercessor! Could you imagine this prophet told God to take his life if God did not change his mind from wiping out the children of Israel? But he stood in the gap for the children of Israel, and God spared them because one man prayed for them.

JOSHUA

Amazing is the word whenever an individual reads the account of when the Sun stood still for an entire day. Every believer reading this passage of Scripture cannot read the account of the Sun sun standing still without pausing for a while and wonder of about this supernatural phenomenon.

> *Then spake Joshua to the Lord in the day when the Lord delivered up the Amorites before the children of Israel, and he said in the sight of Israel, Sun, stand thou still upon Gibeon; and thou, Moon, in the valley of Ajalon.*
>
> *And the sun stood still, and the moon stayed, until the people had avenged themselves upon their enemies. Is not this written in the book of Jasher? So the sun stood still in the midst of heaven, and hasted not to go down about a whole day.*
>
> *And there was no day like that before it or after it, that the Lord hearkened unto the voice of a man: for the Lord fought for Israel.*
>
> Joshua 10:12–14

While reading this passage of Scripture, there is a possibility the reader might think that Joshua might have just lifted up his hands while fighting and commanded the Sun to stand still. Still, after much research, Joshua pulled aside and spoke to God; remember, five kings were coming against him and Israel in battle; they were winning. Still, if the Sun had gone down, the enemies would have had time to retreat and fortify themselves and come up against Joshua and the army of Israel.

After Joshua prayed, he had the power to command the Sun and the Moon to stand still so they could have some daylight to win the battle, and they did. The Sun and the Moon stood still, but here is what catches the attention of the author whenever I read this passage of Scripture: "And the Lord hearkened unto the voice of a man…" "And there was no day like that before it or after it, that the LORD hearkened unto the voice of a man: for the LORD fought for Israel" Joshua 10:14.

God has given us the power of prayer, not just to solve our problems and meet our needs (He is always willing to help us), but God wants us to exercise power of prayer to accomplish great feats for God's glory.

HANNAH

Anyone remembers this handmaiden of the Lord? I hardly hear preachers preach about this woman and church members hardly know from a biblical standpoint who this woman is. Recorded in the first chapter of 1 Samuel is the record of a woman by the name of Hannah.

In those days, not having children was a reproach followed by shame and embarrassment. By the way, in our day and time, some women would rather care for a poodle dog than take the time and care for a child. Hannah's shame and embarrassment among other women during those times; by the way, in our day, some women would care for a poodle dog or dogs than care for a child.

What did Hannah do to remedy her barren condition? She went straight to the house of God or the temple and stayed there for several days and prayed. This record in the Scriptures of pray or praying is so outstanding that the author felt the inspiration to mention the Scripture reference and stipulate point by point how she prayed for a child.

Here is the record from the Bible Hannah praying for a son,

> *So Hannah rose up after they had eaten in Shiloh, and after they had drunk. Now Eli the priest sat upon a seat by a post of the temple of the LORD.*
>
> *And she was in bitterness of soul, and prayed unto the LORD, and wept sore.*
>
> *And she vowed a vow, and said, O LORD of hosts, if thou wilt indeed look on the affliction of thine handmaid, and remember me, and not forget thine handmaid, but wilt give unto thine handmaid a man child, then I will give him unto the LORD all the days of his life, and there shall no rasor come upon his head.*
>
> *And it came to pass, as she continued praying before the LORD, that Eli marked her mouth.*
>
> *Now Hannah, she spake in her heart; only her lips moved, but her voice was not heard: therefore Eli thought she had been drunken.*
>
> *And Eli said unto her, How long wilt thou be drunken? put away thy wine from thee.*
>
> *And Hannah answered and said, No, my lord, I am a woman of a sorrowful spirit: I have drunk neither wine nor strong drink, but have poured out my soul before the LORD.*
>
> *Count not thine handmaid for a daughter of Belial: for out of the abundance of my complaint and grief have I spoken hitherto.*
>
> *Then Eli answered and said, Go in peace: and the God of Israel grant thee thy petition that thou hast asked of him.*
>
> *And she said, Let thine handmaid find grace in thy sight. So the woman went her way, and did eat, and her countenance was no more sad.*
>
> *And she said, Oh my lord, as thy soul liveth, my lord, I am the woman that stood by thee here, praying unto the LORD.*

Chapter 17: Strong or Agonizing Praying

For this child I prayed; and the LORD *hath given me my petition which I asked of him:*
Therefore also I have lent him to the LORD; *as long as he liveth he shall be lent to the* LORD.
And he worshipped the LORD *there.*

— 1 Samuel 1:9–18, 26–28

Eli, the priest (same with some preachers today), did not have the spiritual discernment and understanding that the anointing of the Holy Spirit was upon Hannah to pray. Pray and praying like Hannah in most gatherings and congregations today is like a foreign language.

Here is a synopsis of Hannah's prayer which resulted in one of the greatest prophets in Israel's history.

- She separated herself from everything else and went and stayed in the house of God or in the temple to pray.
- She was concerned about her barren situation and did not care about anyone who did not understand what she was doing, ^but she poured out her soul (prayed strong agonizing prayer) unto the Lord.
- She wept sore (do not let some of these faith preachers talk you of weeping before God, like making some statements "God does not honor your boohooing colloquial language for crying or weeping." This is the reason for the lack of revival today; crying, tears, and weeping is a sign of brokenness before God, and God honors brokenness.
- She vowed a vow and said, "God, looks upon my problem, and give me a man child, then I will dedicate him to you; give him back to you (God) all the days of his life."
- She continued praying; anyone with spiritual discernment, this means preachers and people alike, would start prayer meetings in their church buildings and be consistent (real praying) one night each week and start praying about the adverse situations in America and the world.

Don't tell me God will not answer prayer! Yes, He will. Yes! God will answer your prayers because He loves you, but most of the time, when there is no revival and prayer go unanswered, it's because thousands upon thousands of people make no commitment to God to work in His kingdom, to do something for God's glory and does nothing or gives nothing (thank God for those who does) or does nothing about winning lost souls. But when Hannah prayed and made a vow to God that she would give back her child to God, this prayer moved God to move for her by praying the way she did. She solved God's problem for the nation of Israel and solved her problem (Israel was in a backslidden state); her answer would be God's answer for the nation of Israel; her answer would be God's prophet who would bring Israel to God and obviously fulfill God's plan and purpose.

With the lack of spiritual discernment and the carnality in Eli, the priest, he could not discern Hannah was praying a deep agonizing prayer, her lips moved, but her voice was not heard (a sign of grief and broken-heartedness). Hannah was not drunk from drinking strong drinks like Eli and his sons, but she was under God's anointing to pray the way she did; it is very disheartening when preachers cannot discern the Spirit of

God moving in and through people. This is one of the greatest problems of our day, the lack of understanding of what is of God and what is not. Hannah was engrossed in what the author would term Holy Ghost praying; she did not care who was looking.

- She prayed from deep within her heart, her lips moved, but her voice was not heard. This was not saying prayers; this was not a grocery list of requests traditionally articulately rendered, but she was infused, immune lost in the spirit of prayer. The beautiful and amazing thing about Hannah's prayer touched God, and she got results. Hannah's prayer should be a model prayer for all TV evangelists, pastors, ministers, the fivefold ministry gifts, leaders, and church members today. Hannah's testimony was for this child, "I prayed to, and God has given me my petition." One of the most encouraging things of the Christian life is when we pray specific prayers, and God answers us.

ESTHER

A Jewish maiden became a Persian queen. She, as a Jew, risked her life for her people who were doomed for destruction? Here is the record of Esther's desperate determination to save her people from certain annihilation.

> *Then Esther sent this reply to Mordecai: "Go, gather together all the Jews who are in Susa, and fast for me. Do not eat or drink for three days, night or day. I and my attendants will fast as you do. When this is done, I will go to the king, even though it is against the law. And if I perish, I perish."*
>
> *[After Esther and her maids, Mordecai and the Jews fasted and prayed, God turned around the plan of the devil to destroy the Jews, and they were saved. Such is the power of strong and agonizing prayer.]*
>
> — Esther 4:15–16, NIV

ELIJAH

No one knew about this prophet until the sins of the people of Israel had reached the extent that God could not take it anymore and was ripe for God's judgment. Elijah was a real prophet (unlike some so-called prophets of today who crave the spotlight and cannot function unless they have the praises of men). Elijah lived in a cave for many years; he was taught by God to come out of seclusion and pace the streets of Jerusalem as he heralded these words, "Now Elijah the Tishbite, from Tishbe in Gilead, said to Ahab, 'As the Lord, the God of Israel, lives, whom I serve, there will be neither dew nor rain in the next few years except at my word'" 1 Kings 17:1, NIV.

This rugged prophet's words would have been met by the church world of today, as they would comment, who does this bald, bearded unrefined, unpolished, unecclesiastical, untrained man who knows no grammar and does carry a card with our denomination and certainly. He is not a member of the ministerial association; he cannot even deliver a proper, homiletically refined sermon; who does this crazy man think he is? Well! In simple everyday language, Elijah knew God, he had a personal relationship with God, and he certainly knew when to deliver a word from God most of all, he had the authority from God to stop the rain; he knew what it was to send up a prayer to God, and he surely knew how to pray for God to send the rain. Prophets like Elijah were not popular with kings, queens, and the administration of that day, but what amazes me about Elijah is that he had "thus saith the Lord," and certainly, Elijah's word was not the figment of man's imagination but the word he spoke was direct from God.

Have you ever thought that Elijah could have spoken the word and the rain would have come pouring down, just like he stopped the rain? But God had a reason for Elijah's choosing to go up to Mount Carmel and pray for rain. Here is the record from the Bible,

> *And Elijah said unto Ahab, Get thee up, eat and drink; for there is a sound of abundance of rain.*
>
> *So Ahab went up to eat and to drink. And Elijah went up to the top of Carmel; and he cast himself down upon the earth, and put his face between his knees, (and he prayed)*
>
> *And said to his servant, Go up now, look toward the sea. And he went up, and looked, and said, there is nothing. And he said, Go again seven times.*
>
> *And it came to pass at the seventh time, that he said, Behold, there ariseth a little cloud out of the sea, like a man's hand. And he said, Go up, say unto Ahab, Prepare thy chariot, and get thee down, that the rain stop thee not.*
>
> *And it came to pass in the mean while, that the heaven was black with clouds and wind, and there was a great rain. And Ahab rode, and went to Jezreel.*
>
> *And the hand of the LORD was on Elijah; and he girded up his loins, and ran before Ahab to the entrance of Jezreel.*
>
> — 1 Kings 18:41–46

Here is a revelation from verse 42, "So Ahab went up to eat and to drink. And Elijah went up to the top of Carmel; and he cast himself down upon the earth, and put his face between his knees [and he prayed]" 1 Kings 18:42.

Ahab is a type of or an example of the worldly church, always eating and drinking, concerts and partying spirit, but Elijah is a type and an example of the true church of Jesus Christ, who has a desire to pray. Two thousand years ago, the apostle James was so inspired and touched by the prophet's Elijah praying for rain that he had to mention this in the book he wrote,

> *Elias was a man subject to like passions as we are, and he prayed earnestly that it might not rain: and it rained not on the earth by the space of three years and six months.*
>
> *And he prayed again, and the heaven gave rain, and the earth brought forth her fruit.*
>
> — James 5:17–18

Someone might comment, "Well! Elijah was God's prophet." True! That's the reason when he prayed, the rains came.

The apostle James surely messed up the carnal thinking of some modern-day church folks today, "Elias was a man subject to like passions as we are, and he prayed earnestly that it might not rain: and it rained not on the earth by the space of three years and six months" James 5:17.

Far from the trend of thought today, "we are only human and are liable to make mistakes or its only prayer and a prayer meeting." I will not pray tonight or attend the cooperative prayer meeting at church; again, with the excuse of the century, I am only human, and it's only a prayer meeting.

But Elijah was a man (human); the difference is that he prayed earnestly (like he really wanted God to send the rain), and God did answer his prayer and sent the rain, look at the results in the lives of Elijah, Ahab, and Jezebel, Elijah was caught up in a chariot to be with God in heaven, and Ahab and Jezebel went to, you know where the hell! Not that the author delight in people going there, but there is a choice to make. The difference is a praying prophet and a backslidden prayerless Ahab, Jezebel, and people. What is it that is so desperately needed in the church of today, *praying people who know how to send up a prayer to god and get answers?*

It is impossible to mention all of the dedicated men and women of the Bible who prayed strong agonizing prayers and were rewarded with supernatural results. Most of the church world of today seemingly are solely sold out and interested in the prayer of Jabez. Jabez's prayer was a great and inspiring prayer, but Jabez's prayer was for Jabez himself, and nothing is wrong with Jabez or Jabez's prayer. But the kind of prayer that is being written about is the type of prayer that would change you, your family, your household, neighbors, community, city-state, and nation, also other countries and people. There are other men and women, even kings, who prayed strong agonizing prayers and were rewarded with supernatural results.

Some of these men and women were kings, such as King David; Solomon, he prayed, and God sent the glory cloud that the priest ministers, sacrifice attendants, musicians, and the officiating priest or preacher could not minister as thousands of people witnessed the power of God came down like a mist (glory cloud) when Solomon prayed. Solomon should have kept praying like this all his life; possibly, this type of praying would have kept him from all the heathen wives; he realized this and, of course, rededicated his life to God before he died.

HEZEKIAH

He was given a death sentence by God, Himself, gruesome as it may sound, yes! A death sentence by God, recorded in the Old Testament of the Bible, Hezekiah was given a death sentence by the prophet Isaiah. He knew when the prophet gave him a word from God that he was going to die, God meant he was going to die. But Hezekiah went to church, turned his face toward the wall, and laid on the altar as he wept, repented, and prayed; guess what! His praying changed God's mind about him dying; he prayed so hard he canceled his own death sentence. God sent the prophet and told him that he would not die. Not only would he not die, but God told the prophet to tell him that he would add to his life fifteen years. My! What an example of strong agonizing praying.

> *In those days was Hezekiah sick unto death. And Isaiah the prophet the son of Amoz came unto him, and said unto him, Thus saith the LORD, Set thine house in order: for thou shalt die, and not live.*

Then Hezekiah turned his face toward the wall, and prayed unto the LORD,

And said, Remember now, O LORD, I beseech thee, how I have walked before thee in truth and with a perfect heart, and have done that which is good in thy sight. And Hezekiah wept sore.

Then came the word of the LORD to Isaiah, saying,

Go, and say to Hezekiah, Thus saith the LORD, the God of David thy father, I have heard thy prayer, I have seen thy tears: behold, I will add unto thy days fifteen years.

— Isaiah 38:1–5

DANIEL

Daniel was a praying man. He prayed so much that praying kept him close to God; why do you think he was delivered from the lion's den? With his unrelenting faith in God and a life of prayer, God used him in revelations, dreams, and visions, which is beneficial for the church of today, but what is it that saved him from being devoured by the lions when he was thrown in the lion's den? It was faith in God and prayer that God saw him faithful and saved him. Strong agonizing prayer is God's way of using you in his kingdom and solving your problems, meeting your needs and healing your sicknesses and diseases, and sending revival. Shadrach, Meshach, and Abednego's refusal to bow down like everyone else before the image that Nebuchadnezzar built almost cost them their lives, their faith in God was immensely strong they had no fear for king Nebuchadnezzar and his iron fist administration. Their testimony was, "Even if God does not deliver us, we will not bow."

What is it that kept them from bowing to this monstrous image? When the king's decree was law and certain death if disobeyed, everyone must bow down to this image! Daniel, who was one of the king's personal attendants, knew of the decree of the king's command that no man must pray to another God or worship or bow down before the image; Shadrach, Meshach, and Abednego, including Daniel, prayed together' praying gave them the strength and power they needed. Praying was their source of strength that gave them the power to overcome, and this was the main reason when they were into the fiery furnace. Jesus was waiting in the fire and delivered them. Daniel's strength came from God because of his prayer life; when they threw him in the lion's den, God kept him from being eaten alive. All because they prayed and did not bow.

In part one of this chapter, mentions were made of Jesus praying in agonizing prayer in the Garden of Gethsemane, the apostles praying in the upper room until the Holy Ghost fell on them; this prayer meeting in the Upper Room where the apostles were gathered changed them, changed the atmosphere and Jerusalem, the religious order of that day thought the apostles and early church were lunatics, but the results of this prayer meeting and they being baptized with the Holy Spirit caused three thousand of men and women to be saved and be baptized with the Holy Ghost. Paul the apostle's life was changed because of the other apostles praying, he became the apostle to the Gentiles; read some of these words,

> *Now when Daniel knew that the writing was signed, he went into his house; and his windows being open in his chambers toward Jerusalem, he kneeled upon his knees three times a day, and prayed, and gave thanks before his God, as he did aforetime.*
>
> — Daniel 6:10

The greatest power allotted to every believer is the power of prayer, one of the greatest corporate prayer meetings recorded in the book of Acts.

> *It was about this time that King Herod arrested some who belonged to the church, intending to persecute them.*
>
> *He had James, the brother of John, put to death with the sword.*
>
> *When he saw that this met with approval among the Jews, he proceeded to seize Peter also. This happened during the Festival of Unleavened Bread.*
>
> *After arresting him, he put him in prison, handing him over to be guarded by four squads of four soldiers each. Herod intended to bring him out for public trial after the Passover.*
>
> *So Peter was kept in prison, but the church was earnestly praying to God for him.*
>
> *The night before Herod was to bring him to trial, Peter was sleeping between two soldiers, bound with two chains, and sentries stood guard at the entrance.*
>
> *Suddenly an angel of the Lord appeared and a light shone in the cell. He struck Peter on the side and woke him up. "Quick, get up!" he said, and the chains fell off Peter's wrists.*
>
> *Then the angel said to him, "Put on your clothes and sandals." And Peter did so. "Wrap your cloak around you and follow me," the angel told him.*
>
> *Peter followed him out of the prison, but he had no idea that what the angel was doing was really happening; he thought he was seeing a vision.*
>
> *They passed the first and second guards and came to the Iron Gate leading to the city. It opened for them by itself, and they went through it. When they had walked the length of one street, suddenly the angel left him*
>
> *Then Peter came to himself and said, "Now I know without a doubt that the Lord has sent his angel and rescued me from Herod's clutches and from everything the Jewish people were hoping would happen.*
>
> *When this had dawned on him, he went to the house of Mary the mother of John, also called Mark, where many people had gathered and were praying.*
>
> *Peter knocked at the outer entrance, and a servant named Rhoda came to answer the door.*
>
> *When she recognized Peter's voice, she was so overjoyed she ran back without opening it and exclaimed, "Peter is at the door!"*
>
> *"You're out of your mind," they told her. When she kept insisting that it was so, they said, "It must be his angel."*
>
> *But Peter kept on knocking, and when they opened the door and saw him, they were astonished.*

Peter motioned with his hand for them to be quiet and described how the Lord had brought him out of prison. "Tell James and the other brothers and sisters about this," he said, and then he left for another place.

— Acts 12:1–17, NIV

What an example in the power of prayer, not saying traditional ritualistic pharisaical trying to impress some great official kind of prayer, the prayer that was sent up for Peter. As a matter of fact, none of the other apostles were present in this prayer meeting recorded above, but it was some simple church folks or disciples when they heard Peter was in prison, did not have the attitude that it was the will of God Peter stay in prison overnight and next day, bless God! And they would kill him, but they got together and prayed a strong agonizing prayer, and God sent an angel and delivered Peter. This is the kind of praying we need today.

CHAPTER 18

Purity Is the Key to Revival

Jesus and the apostles taught holiness; as a matter of fact, they lived holy lives with the thought of holiness in mind; it is a fact that every genuine Christian has a desire and should have a desire to do something within the kingdom of God, most of all they want to be used of God. But the trend of thought these days in most Christian circles the more educated you are with a string of degrees attached to an individual name or the more popular, famous, this is the most sought after person for speaking engagements on Christian TV stations, seminars, conferences, churches, and other meetings (not that the author believes in accommodating a novice or some crank to fill these positions). But observation has prompted the author to inform the reading audience that any minister is teaching or preaching holiness, purity, and living it! You rarely see or hear them! Wisdom to the wise is sufficient! Why? It's all because they are different. But the crowd likes it when you are going in their direction; if not, they do not want to associate with that person.

It is requested the reader study the Gospels Matthew, Mark, Luke, and John; read the book of Acts and the Epistles or writings of the apostle Paul and compare it with today's Christianity. Any honest reader could recognize the difference. I could hear a resounding sound from some people, "Is this author trying or wanting to take us back to the way of life, lifestyle, dress code, conditions, culture of Jesus and the apostles?" The answer is no! Please understand what is being referred to about Jesus and the apostles, the power of God was manifested through the prophets, Jesus, and the apostles, and of course, our early church fathers; what was the reason they lived pure empty and holy lives. As a matter of fact, their lives were not put on or shared; there was no show or entertainment within or about them; let me put this in plain everyday language: *God worked through them.*

What was the reason? Not just holy life but pure is the answer: the word pure comes from the Hebrew word "*barar*," which means *to be clean inside and out*, but the author had to choose another word translated from the Hebrew word "*barar*," and that word is empty, empty of all man-made traditions, philosophy, thinking and plans, when it comes to God using someone this is a prerequisite requirement. An individual education, ability, and profession obviously can be an asset in God's service or being used by God; here is the revelation: God can only use someone who is filled with *Himself* and not *oneself*. "Blessed are the pure in heart: for they shall see God" Matthew 5:8.

Does this mean literally seeing God? This means every believer who lives a clean, pure, holy life would be a vessel or an instrument for God's power to flow through. The words "holiness," "purity," "sanctification," and "clean" are seldom heard from the pulpits today, God is a God of grace and mercy, but in some ministries, grace is being taught as a license to sin. We have a generation of Christians that has the attitude if it feels good—do it. When last did you hear the words "pure," "purity," or "holiness" mentioned from the pulpits? If you did, this is commendable. Even though purity and holiness are more lived than spoken, and when purity and holiness are spoken about, the person speaking or preaching about this should be living it.

We are living in a time when a majority of the church (notice, I did not say "the church") has adopted some philosophy and ways of the world. As the world goes, so goes a majority of the church. An entire chapter could be written right here about this! If Jesus and the apostles, including the apostle Paul, were alive in the flesh in our day and time and had entered some of these church buildings today.

I wonder what they would have done! Surely they would witness the worldliness, entertainment, concerts, parties, bingos, the bridge club, and TVs brought into the church buildings; some now have a large screen to show ball games and worldly movies with actors and actresses scantily dressed and impure words flying in the church building on a Sunday night. Most of them has replaced the old-time Sunday night evangelistic meeting, where lively singing about the blood of Jesus, stirring convicting salvation word or message used to be preached, then an altar call used to be given as people came running down to the altar to surrender their lives to Jesus and be saved (if you find an altar call in any church these days). Thank God, in most churches, an altar call is a thing of the past.

Loose living, beer, and other alcoholic drinking are now being condoned in some church buildings, as so many are channeling pornographic movies on their TV, computers in their homes, and phones. "Shocking" is the word as so many denominations, organizations, religions would openly support an administration that condones abortion, legalize certain harmful drugs, and, worst of all, at the present time, judges who passed a law of same-sex marriage that is now legal. Jesus and the apostles would have loved the souls of those who are willing to turn to God in righteousness, but of certain would have pronounced judgment on this so-called Christian nation.

Everything written in this book is of utmost importance, but then it must be realized that God wants to manifest Himself through us, not for the purpose of uttering wired sounds and looking for some new sensations, shakes, and shouting; yes! In revival, there might be some of these, but in revival, the fruits of the Spirit should be witnessed, the gifts of the Spirit should be in operation, souls should be saved, lives should be changed, people should be healed, miracles, signs, and wonders should will be evident, cities towns states and nations should be shaken, and the only way this can come about is by God's people living *pure lives*, this is one of the greatest requirement today in the Body of Christ, the Church.

While all of the foundational principles are of utmost importance, such as the born again experience, baptism with the Holy Spirit, Bible study, prayer, church attendance, tithing, winning lost souls, supporting missions, or reaching the people that have never heard of Jesus, feeding the hungry, clothing the naked, shelter for the homeless, strengthening the saints preparing for eternity or getting ready for the second return of Jesus. To a certain extent, all of this is of no use if there is no real praying and purity because praying and purity is a channel for God's power to be manifested through us. Biblical revival is imperative and desperately needed at this time. But praying and purity must precede a biblical revival, and if a biblical revival is to continue until it shakes the very foundation of sin and produces the same results as Jesus and the apostles, then purity is a must and is required by God.

The word "holy" is mentioned six hundred and eleven times; "sanctification"—seventy-three times, "pure"—one hundred times in the Bible. God, through the inspiration of the Holy Spirit, had a specific reason for these words being written in the Word of God, the Bible. Ministers and church folks preach the will of God; some ministers and church folks wrestle within their spirits as they say and pray, "God, what is Your perfect will for my life?" Some say, "I am searching for the will of God in my life!" Some would even travel hundreds of miles to get a word from a prophet to confirm the will of God in their lives. Nothing is wrong with all of this; I know there are people who are honest and want to do something for God or be in ministry, but really what is the perfect will of God?

Here is the perfect will of God for every believer in Christ Jesus,

> *I beseech you therefore, brethren, by the mercies of God, that ye present your bodies a living sacrifice, holy, acceptable unto God, which is your reasonable service.*

And be not conformed to this world: but be ye transformed by the renewing of your mind, that ye may prove what is that good, and acceptable, and perfect will of God.

— Romans 12:1–2

For this is the will of God, even your sanctification, that ye should abstain from fornication: [Christians must avoid the sins of the flesh and every other sin that corrupts their relationship with God.]

— 1 Thessalonians 4:3

Flee also youthful lusts: but follow righteousness, faith, charity, peace, with them that call on the Lord out of a pure heart.

— 2 Timothy 2:22

Dearly beloved, I beseech you as strangers and pilgrims, abstain from fleshly lusts, which war against the soul.

— 1 Peter 2:11

Now the end of the commandment is charity out of a pure heart, and of a good conscience, and of faith unfeigned.

— 1 Timothy 1:5

Being pure in heart involves having a singleness of heart toward God. A pure heart has no hypocrisy, no guile, and no hidden motives. The pure heart is marked by transparency and an uncompromising desire to please God in all things. It is more than an external puritan behavior; it is an internal purity of soul. "Blessed are the pure in heart" Matthew 5:8a.

The Greek word for "*heart*" is "*kardeeah*." This can be applied to the physical heart. But it also refers to the spiritual center of life. It is where thoughts, desires, a sense of purpose, will, understanding, and character reside. Being pure in heart involves having a singleness of heart toward God. A pure heart has no hypocrisy, no guile, and no hidden motives. The pure heart is marked by transparency and an uncompromising desire to please God in all things. It is more than an external purity of behavior; it is an internal purity of soul. The only way we can truly be pure in heart is to give our lives to Jesus and ask Him to do the cleansing work. Psalm 51:10 says, "Create in me a pure heart, O God; and renew a right spirit within me."

Is this possible in our day and time? Yes, it is! This can only be done through the finished work of Jesus Christ on Calvary's cross and His precious blood that was shed for us and to appropriate this in our lives daily.

Purity was required by God from the very beginning; when God created Adam and Eve, did you realize that God, Himself, used to come down in the Garden of Eden and kept company or fellowship with Adam and Eve! Think for a while! God, Himself, used to come down from heaven and walk and talk with Adam and Eve. But what is it that broke that relationship between Adam and Eve? It was deception and sin. Reading through the Bible from Genesis to Revelation, the one thing that God requires is holiness, cleanliness, sanctification, and purity in an individual, so He can speak to him and manifest his power and to work signs, wonders, and miracles to be a witness to an individual, people, or nation. Purity is of utmost importance if prayers are going to be answered, desires granted, and to be used by God.

Few books have been written on this subject of sanctification, purity, and holiness, more books have been written on other subjects, but it is of no use unless Christians realize how important being pure affects our lives in every way, and when there is "pureness," what our lives would mean? Answered prayers, the word of God, would flow in and out of our lives as the power of God would be manifested through us and cause results like Jesus and the apostles. Everyone loves reading the Psalms; reading the Psalms is so inspiring and comforting, but one of the psalms, in particular, has caught the author's attention, especially in relation to prosperity, God's blessings, answered prayers, God's power manifested through our lives, God coming down and manifesting His power and even showing up Himself which is real revival.

Reading and studying the Psalms is of immense spiritual experience from a godly biblical Christian point of view. The Psalms are also prayers offered up to God from King David and other leaders and singers during King's David reign, one of these Psalms that really caught my attention. Please be reminded that this Psalm was rendered by King David when the people had no temple to gather together to worship God; on the Sabbath day, the king, priest, and people gathered at the bottom of the hill inside and by the gate of Jerusalem. The priests led in worship as everyone was getting ready to march with songs, hymns, and praise to Jehovah God; as everyone was getting the moment of worship, no one was appointed to read the Torah, and this is the reason for this Psalm.

"The earth is the Lord's, and the fullness thereof; the world, and they that dwell therein. For he hath founded it upon the seas, and established it upon the floods" Psalm 24:1–2. King David begins this Psalm by recognizing God, who created everything, and reminds us that we, human beings, belong to God. He also reminds us that God caused the earth and everything to rise out of the vastness of the oceans. "Who shall ascend into the hill of the Lord? or who shall stand in his holy place?" Psalm 24:3

Three thousand years have passed by; there is no temple, but the worshippers of the true and living God gathers at the gate of the city of Jerusalem to begin a procession to the mount of worship, which is called the Hill or Mount Zion. King David is troubled because he needs a man of God, a priest, or a prophet, to represent them to God and perform all priestly duties. As he prays for a man to represent them before God, He asks a question, "Who shall ascend into the hill of the Lord? or who shall stand in his holy place" (the platform or place where the man of God stands to minister). Here comes an answer from God to David, "He that hath clean hands…" Psalm 24:4a

Three thousand years have passed by; there is no temple, but the worshippers of the true and living God gathers at the gate of the city of Jerusalem to begin a procession to the mount of worship, which is called the Hill or Mount Zion. King David is troubled because he needs a man of God, a priest, or a prophet, to represent them to God and perform all priestly duties. As he prays for a man to represent them before God, He asks a question, "Who shall ascend into the hill of the Lord? or who shall stand in his holy place" (the platform or place where the man of God stands to minister). Here comes an answer from God to David, "He that hath clean hands…" Psalm 24:4a

If we are going to experience a biblical revival, every preacher should take heed and give their undivided attention to these words—*"He that hath clean hands."* Thank God for the ministers of God who are living a pure, sanctified, and clean life; clean hands represent a sanctified and clean life before God, hands that are not practicing iniquity, voodoo, witchcraft, and masonry. Ministers should be honest in every way in their lives and ministry; they should be blameless and honest in their dealings about money and everything else. "[…] and a pure heart" Psalm 24:4b.

Everything else written in this book is pertaining to revival, but here is one of the most important keys to revival, a pure heart. Just as a physical and healthy heart is of utmost importance and beneficial to every human being to remain alive, it is the same principle that governs the spiritual heart. It is a fact that millions of human beings, especially in America, are dying of heart-related disease; the majority of the church is dying of spiritual heart disease. Within the heart of a human being is the region in which purity shows itself, in particular in Christians. Purity is in the heart, the seat of thought, desire motive, not an outward act, but it is what comes out of the heart of a person. Please note that Jesus emphasized the heart. The pure may be spotless or faultless in general; those whose very thoughts are clean; or the pure in motive, the single-minded, whatever is in your heart is what you are. Salvation occurs in the heart. Before anything else occurs, we must believe in our hearts. Notice in this very same statement that a pure heart and clean hands must be accompanied by separation from the lust for worldly things. Purity is a distinguishing virtue of Christianity.

The pure in heart can only be purified and be cleansed by the "blood of Jesus Christ" when an individual believes and accepts God's provision for his salvation. The blood of Jesus Christ refers to the entire sacrificial work of Jesus Christ on the cross. When an individual recognizes what Jesus Christ did for them on the cross and believes and accepts Jesus Christ into their hearts as Lord and Savior, these people are cleansed from vain thoughts, unprofitable reasoning, earthly and sensual desires, and corrupt passions. They are purified from pride, self will, discontent, impatience, anger, malice, envy, covetousness, and just worldly gains and ambitions. Their hearts are made pure this might not occur immediately in the lives of some, but purity, pureness, holiness, and sanctification is something that must be an individual effort to live pure by God's grace, strength, and help. "Pure" in the Old Testament comes from many Hebrew words; the Hebrew word "*tahor*" means to be clean, pure empty. In the New Testament, "pure" is translated *Katharos*, which means you will be blessed, be a vessel for God to work through, and your prayers answered; most of all, "purity" means a vessel for revival.

Three thousand years have passed by; there is no temple, but the worshippers of the true and living God gathers at the gate of the city of Jerusalem to begin a procession to the mount of worship, which is called the Hill or Mount Zion. King David is troubled because he needs a man of God, a priest, or a prophet, to represent them to God and perform all priestly duties. As he prays for a man to represent them before God, He asks a question, "Who shall ascend into the hill of the Lord? or who shall stand in his holy place" (the platform or place where the man of God stands to minister). Here comes an answer from God to David, "He that hath clean hands…" Psalm 24:4a

One of the greatest joys in the Christian life is to see and experience God working among His people. Does this mean we will see God literally? This unquestionably would be awesome! But seeing God means his saving grace in our lives, the baptism with the Holy Spirit, walking and having fellowship with God, praying and getting answers, ministering to people who need God, and seeing their lives changed by God's power. Praying for drug addicts and seeing them delivered, a cancer-stricken person healed, the lame walk, the blind see, the deaf hearing, and every other type of sicknesses and disease healed. Seeing God means the entire fivefold ministry functioning in the church, the nine gifts of the Holy Spirit operating, and the fruits of the Spirit manifesting in people's lives. Seeing God is having a right relationship with God and experiencing the supernatural like in the book of Exodus, Elijah, Elisha's ministry, more so the ministry of Jesus as recorded in Matthew, Mark, Luke, and John, the book of Acts, and of course the ministry of the apostle Paul.

Foremost seeing God is a personal relationship with God, spending time in His presence daily. Yes, God wants to solve our problems and meet our needs, but seeing God is to be an envelope in His presence, not just coming to Him to solve our problems and meet our needs. His presence is of utmost importance, and Jesus made all of this possible when He died on the cross. "[…] who hath not lifted up his soul unto vanity" Psalm 24:4b.

Continuing on the spiritual and natural abilities of a minister, a minister should not be proud, even in social status, should not be proud of his appearance, achievements, abilities, accomplishments; most of all, he should not have his proprieties set on material things. The Hebrew word for vanity is "*shav*," which means emptiness. Ministers must be aware even though we need certain material things in this life, they must not ascertain that extravagance is God's blessing. Materialism and only materialism is "*hebel*"—Hebrew for vapor, things that do not last. Ministers that have their eyes solely on material things are deluded, empty, futile, idolatrous, useless, vain, vanity or vanities, worthless. "[…] nor sworn deceitfully" Psalm 24:4c.

The meaning of the word "deceit" is trying to make someone believe something that is not true, the act of deceiving someone. A statement intended to make people believe something that is not true, deception, fraud, double-dealing, and trickery, meaning the acts or practices of one who deliberately deceives. Double-dealing suggests treachery or at least action contrary to a professed attitude. The Hebrew word for deceit is "*Mirmah*"—deceit, from the original "*Ramah*," meaning deception, dishonest. Generally speaking, deceit is double tongue saying certain things with the intention of swaying individuals to a wrong way of thinking and doing.

The scripture above emphasizes that the man who speaks for God must turn the searchlight within his own soul before he can represent God to the people. They should be above reproach, blameless, trustworthy, obviously up-front, honest, and not deceitful. He shows it inwardly and whatever is inside of him comes outwardly. Outwardly they work for righteousness, and inwardly there is a free and a clear conviction with a clear conscience; there is no hypocrisy. If there is deceit within the man of God, somewhere, somehow, deceit would reveal itself in the things he says and does because the fruits of deceit will reveal themselves when the power of God is present.

Preachers and people that are free from deceit are described as gracious in their deportment (how they conduct themselves); and speech (you can tell when a person is a deceiver; at times, they a slick and smooth, but when refused, they become very adamant)—they are honest, loving, forgiving, discerning, wise, respectful, trustworthy, generous, and just. These characteristics certainly describe a man who can enter into God's presence and then represent God to His people. God has a set standard for a man who represents Him to His people. King David realizes all of this; this is the reason he cried out, "Who shall stand on his holy hill." The idea of fame, fortune, personality, charisma, popularity, riches, prosperity for prosperity's sake, and giftedness is driving a nation, ministries, and people within the church further away from God; you're not accepted if you are not an entertainer with professionalism. If the Church of Jesus Christ is to experience a real Jesus and apostolic revival, most ministers, ministries, and members of the

Body of Christ must be open-hearted, approachable, and hospitable, combined with up-front honesty and transparency. "He shall receive the blessing from the Lord, and righteousness from the God of his salvation" Psalm 24:5.

All of the above quality and qualifications brings us to this verse; he shall receive the blessing from the Lord. Fifty-six years of ministry, this author has heard every type of sermon on the subject of blessing and prosperity, and please be reminded that these particular scriptures are referring to God's people and the priestly office. These scriptures are not referring to a worldly or Babylonian system of making money and securing material things, even though a certain sector of the Church could learn about investing and generating monetary gains. Please note, he shall receive the blessing of the Lord. God or the Lord's blessing is to know that you are saved and assurance of eternity, peace, joy, contentment, real happiness, favor, material and financial blessing, a daily relationship with God. Most of all, what you are doing and accomplishing in this life is not of your own, but by God's help and strength giving you the ability to do right, you will be blessed and prosperous. "This is the generation of them that seek him that seek thy face, O Jacob. Selah" Psalm 24:6.

King David is referring to the people of his generation who had a desire for God and wanted to see the power and glory of God. Seeking the "*seeking the face of God*," so many people ask the question, what does it mean to *seek God's face*? Seeking God's face is an old colloquial statement throughout the Old Testament that expresses a desire within an individual or people who has a desire to know God in a more intimate way; that person or people are not satisfied with solely blessings or material things. This is certainly commendable of King's David generation; they have a yearning and desire for God.

What a vast difference with the generation of today! Prosperity seems to be the popular trend with ministers and church folks of today, it is God's will for His people to prosper, but prosperity without God and purpose is no prosperity. "*Seeking God's Face*" means having a desire to know God and having a daily relationship with God. Too often, our generation goes to meetings, church, look at TV ministries with the idea in mind for material things, blessing, help, protection, healing, deliverance, financial blessings, etc. (nothing wrong with either of these), but please be reminded let us seek the "blesser" and not only the blessings. The pivotal point here, which God lovingly regards, is to seek to know His mind, His will, and to seek Him and to please and know Him.

> *Lift up your heads, O ye gates; and be ye lift up, ye everlasting doors; and the King of glory shall come in.*
>
> *Who is this King of glory? The* Lord *strong and mighty, the* Lord *mighty in battle.*
>
> *Lift up your heads, O ye gates; even lift them up, ye everlasting doors; and the King of glory shall come in.*
>
> *Who is this King of glory? The* Lord *of hosts, he is the King of glory. Selah.*
>
> — Psalm 24:7–10

The gates into the city of Jerusalem were originally installed in the form of pullies, which had to be lifted up by weights and pullies, obviously which had to be drawn up by a few men or an ox if too heavy.

When this Psalm was written, these gates could have been strenuously lifted up, then suddenly dropped down in the event of enemies attacking Jerusalem. The ornamental top of the gate was referred to as the head; this would be the same setting into the place of worship or the house of God. Please recall this Psalm begins with a processional to worship either to a tent or a house chosen for the place of worship; this procession started just outside the gate, the congregation was anxious to go to the place of worship, the gates into the city when worship was about to begin were traditionally closed, here comes the cry of worship, "Lift up your heads O ye gates," which means pull up the gates "and be lifted up ye everlasting doors" making reference to open the doors of the place of worship, where the ark of the covenant was resting.

This Scripture also means that the place of worship should always be open, and because of His people worship, praise, honor, and give glory to God, the King of Glory shall come in. This should be the desire of every minister and Christians for the King of Glory, who is Jesus, to come into our lives and the place of worship. Purity brings people into a place for God to manifest Himself among His people. Ritual, formality, and tradition have their place, but it does not produce life. But when God's people are holy, clean, and living pure lives, then Jesus Christ Himself will come into our lives and in the places of worship. This is what revival is all about—Jesus, Himself, manifesting Himself in power and glory. *Who is the King of Glory?* Jesus Christ, Himself; He is the King of Glory. Purity is the key to revival, and revival is all about Jesus and not about exalting men or women, but then revival begins into the heart of humble men and women.

Can the church experience Christianity beyond the norm or status quo of today? Purity or clean living is the answer. Or, most of all, God is looking for a pure people to manifest Himself through and to a deceptive and ungodly generation of people. Purity certainly is not a conflagration of set down rules and regulations but can be attained by a total dedication of individual life to God. It's this simple when Jesus comes into an individual life, the Holy Spirit indwells that person, and the world, flesh, and the devil go out.

The moment a person comes to Jesus Christ and is born again, they are cleansed by the precious blood of Jesus Christ and are sanctified (made clean); from then on, sanctification is progressive in that individual's life, but here is the key it is the person's or individual responsibility to choose and stay away from a life of the sins of the flesh, the vices of the worldly things, and the devil. It is an individual responsibility to remain pure by refusing iniquity; this means everything that would take away from a godly life that God intends for you to live. "He that worketh deceit shall not dwell within my house: he that telleth lies shall not tarry in my sight" Psalm 101:7.

CHAPTER 19

Manifestation of God's Power

Being used of God is one of the greatest honors because the man or woman whom God chooses God honors them as they honor God. He has a plan and purpose for their lives, but the age-old question is, He cannot use or manifest His plan and purpose without dedicated people. God has to have a man or a woman because God has committed the preaching of the Gospel of Jesus Christ to those who will answer His call and obey Him.

In the Garden of Eden, after our first parents plunged the entire human race into sin, this affected mankind's relationship and communion with God; from that time to the present, God has and is always on the lookout for a man, a man He can trust with His power to bring mankind back to God, obviously, the man or woman He chooses must be willing to be a channel for His power in miracles, signs, and wonders, power to vindicate the word He gives them to validate that God is with them.

We have a generation of ministers and Christians who are as prone to excuses, explanations, and excesses of arguments as they are spending millions of dollars in conferences talking about what is not needed than what is necessary. The apostles' prayer contradicted the excuses, explanation, and excesses arguments when they prayed, as recorded in the book of Acts. "Saying, What shall we do to these men? for that indeed a notable miracle hath been done by them is manifest to all them that dwell in Jerusalem; and we cannot deny it" Acts 4:16.

> *For to do whatsoever thy hand and thy counsel determined before to be done.*
>
> *And now, Lord, behold their threatenings: and grant unto thy servants, that with all boldness they may speak thy word,*
>
> *By stretching forth thine hand to heal; and that signs and wonders may be done by the name of thy holy child Jesus.*
>
> *And when they had prayed, the place was shaken where they were assembled together; and they were all filled with the Holy Ghost, and they spake the word of God with boldness.*
>
> *And the multitude of them that believed were of one heart and of one soul: neither said any of them that ought of the things which he possessed was his own; but they had all things common.*
>
> — Acts 4:28–32

This prayer they prayed was not in a one-week conference costing thousands upon thousands of dollars in some fancy conference center but in a humble home of one of the believers. Please note that the place was shaken; this meant the apostles also shook, but the emphasis here was not the apostles shaking; this seems to be the trend of our day by some, shaking and sensations. But what is needed is God's power manifested through the gifts of the Holy Spirit, in particular miracles of healing and meeting the needs of people.

Some ministers seemingly cannot function without titles and positions. Worst of all, talk, motivational speeches, lectures, teaching, Hebrew and Greek translations combined with English interpretation flow from the mouths of ministers, teachers, and evangelists like never before. Mind you, nothing is wrong with this: talk, talk, talk morning, noon, and night. We wake up in the morning and go through the day, then go to sleep at night pestered with talk. Mind you, the author understands that these stations and media have to keep some kind of talk going to keep their network going.

Chapter 19: Manifestation of God's Power

There is talk on television, radio, the workplace, universities, and schools; people gather to talk in conferences, seminars, and rallies. Before all ball games, there is talk in the gym or workout places and the workplace. Wives talk to husbands, mutter, and grunt, and it's a miracle when a wife can get her husband to talk. But some talk, children listen to their parents' talk or lecture day and night.

While this book is being written, politicians are running and ripping throughout the US, talking, making speeches to get their policies across to crowds, town hall meetings, and obviously on television, radio, and all other media to be elected president. Every Sunday and during the week, preachers are talking, preaching, or teaching. The purpose of all the talk obviously is to motivate the hearers into action and accomplishments. But do you realize with all the talk that only 11 percent of all who speak and listen produce any results?

With respect to whom respect is due, we have some of the finest preachers and speakers in America, but motivational speeches, talk, lectures, and preaching are of no effect until the hearers listen, believe, and spring into action and produce results that will convince their listeners into commitment followed by the action of results. Personally speaking, yours truly, the author of this book, has become weary of just talk.

Of all the apostles that followed Jesus, besides the one that betrayed Jesus, the eleven apostles talked their way into electing an apostle named Matthias, whom we never read about. Just a name that fizzled out into oblivion which was the result of just prayerlessness, talk, and lack of leadership through the Holy Spirit.

Paul, the apostle, was God's chosen to replace Judas; after his supernatural conversion, no one wanted to have anything to do with him; the eleven apostles stayed away from him because of his tainted reputation of killing Christians. There was a chosen vessel of God named Ananias, who was not an apostle but heard God's voice to go to a street called straight and lay hands on Saul; all of this occurred after his supernatural experience and conversion to Christianity.

God restored the sight of Saul, who later became Paul, the apostle; all of this is recorded in the Bible, the book of Acts, chapters 8 and 9. Well, the apostle Paul was used of God in miracles, signs, and wonders among the Jews, but his ministry was ordained of God, and he was mightily used of God to reach the Gentiles.

Here are the words of the apostle Paul,

> *And I, brethren, when I came to you, came not with excellency of speech or of wisdom, declaring unto you the testimony of God.*
>
> *For I determined not to know any thing among you, save Jesus Christ, and him crucified.*
>
> *And I was with you in weakness, and in fear, and in much trembling.*
>
> *And my speech and my preaching was not with enticing words of man's wisdom, but in demonstration of the Spirit and of power:*
>
> *That your faith should not stand in the wisdom of men, but in the power of God.*
>
> — 1 Corinthians 2:1–5

The Greek word for demonstration is "*apodeiksis,*" which means *proof, results,* and *manifestation.* The Hebrew word for demonstration is "*hadh-gah-mah,*" which means *you talk about it*; now show me a sample or let me see some proof. The Bible was translated from the original Hebrew and Greek; amazing is the word how the original words translated from the original Hebrew and Greek can magnify and enhance the original translation.

The apostle Paul did not mince words when he wrote these words; as he wrote in the book,

And I, brethren, when I came to you, came not with excellency of speech or of wisdom, declaring unto you the testimony of God.

For I determined not to know any thing among you, save Jesus Christ, and him crucified.

And I was with you in weakness, and in fear, and in much trembling.

And my speech and my preaching was not with enticing words of man's wisdom, but in demonstration of the Spirit and of power:

That your faith should not stand in the wisdom of men, but in the power of God.

— 1 Corinthians 2:1–5

Before preceding, the author does want the reader to get the idea that the author is illiterate when it comes to ministry or church administration, etc. All the ministry gifts, for instance, the fivefold ministry gifts, are important and are ordained by God for the edification and growth of the church, the Body of Christ. Church administration from Sunday school, youth meeting, Bible study, Sunday and weekly services, and outreaches are of most importance to the ministry and Church. But something is lacking when sick people are not being healed, the gifts of the Spirit are not in operation, and most of all, souls are not being saved. The reason for this is that people are content with traditional Christianity, or rightfully so, just being religious. It has been discovered that in this kind of Christianity, most of them are lukewarm (more of this in the following chapter) and do not know whether they are going to heaven or not.

The ministry of Jesus, especially in the area of the supernatural, must always be emphasized; someone might say, "Well! He was Jesus or God in the flesh, and nothing but the supernatural was expected of Him." But read, study the words of Jesus, "Ye have not chosen me, but I have chosen you, and ordained you, that ye should go and bring forth fruit, and that your fruit should remain: that whatsoever ye shall ask of the Father in my name, he may give it you" John 15:16.

These words were instructions of Jesus to the apostles, but they were for all believers throughout all generations, even to us in this present day. But the apostles in the book of Acts, especially after the outpouring of the Holy Spirit on them in the Upper Room, their lives were transformed, and anyone reading the book of Acts should come to the conclusion that they picked up exactly where Jesus left off to confirm this here is a scripture from the book of Mark, "And they went forth, and preached the word every where, and the Lord [Jesus] went with them every where, *confirming the word with signs [miracles, signs, wonders, supernatural] following.* Amen" Mark 16:20.

There are myriads of books written in the past and present about revivals that occurred within the past centuries, it is not the intent of the author to write about these revivals, but reading and studying about these revivals or move of the Holy Spirit is inspiring and gives an incentive within the spirit of all Christians to hunger and desire to experience the same for today.

Just to briefly mention, in the year 1725, under the leadership of Ludwig Von Zinzendorf, a German who conducted a prayer meeting that lasted for one hundred years that produced missionaries who went around the world preaching the uncompromising Gospel of Jesus Christ; 1784, a revival that lasted thirty years after John Erskine published Jonathan Edwards' request for earnest daily prayer; this move of God affected Britain and the United States. In the year 1830, Charles G. Finney, who lived in the presence of God, prayed, prayed, and prayed, where ever he went. People were so convicted that they just fell down on their knees and cried out to God most of the time without an altar call.

September 1857, Jerry Lanphier, a convert of Charles Finney, this revival started in Canada of which this businessman started a prayer meeting on a Wednesday night that went on for many years as revival fire caused ten thousand businessmen to be saved and stirred as revival fires burned that caused thousands to turn to God. What about the name D. L. Moody; I guess some modern-day Christians heard about this revivalist and real soul-winner who shook cities in the year 1857, which drew hundreds of thousands of rich, poor, and middle class to turn to God. Early in the nineteenth century, 1905 revival broke out in Wales, the United Kingdom. This revival ignited and affected Europe; according to revival history, God only knows of the hundreds of thousands that were saved, healed, and delivered. At the same time as the Wales revival men such as Smith Wigglesworth, who ministered to King George, Queen Elizabeth's father, it is told of Smith Wigglesworth that he was called the apostle of faith. Some of the greatest miracles occurred under his ministry: hundreds of thousands of souls turned to God. It is said of this man of God that his ministry was like the book of Acts.

While the revival was going on in Wales, the United Kingdom, here, at home, in the United States, some Christian ministers were longing for revival; God began to raise up simple men like Charles Parham, a Bible teacher, who inspired and taught J. Seymour, a black man. On April 8th, 1906, he led a prayer meeting on 312 Azusa Street in downtown Los Angeles, which broke out into a move of God's Spirit. According to the records of this revival, which is hardly mentioned in our day, almost everything that happened in the book of Acts happened in this revival.

After this revival, God raised up a man by the name of William Branham, whose name so many are afraid to mention because of doctrinal differences. Some of the people following his ministry kept their eyes on him more than Jesus, but he truly has always had an open heart in studying the life and ministry of men that were supernaturally used by God. William Branham (his life and ministry) was a real prophet, a seer; the gifts of the Holy Spirit were manifested through his life. Besides everything else about his ministry, God used him in the word of knowledge and discernment like never witnessed before; there was no guessing, unlike today where some ministers would say in a crowd of thousands or in a TV audience there is somebody out there with a stomach problem or some kind of sickness. "You are being healed" not so with this man of God; he told people exactly what their problems were. At times, he would speak by the gift of the word of knowledge and call out people's names, sicknesses, and addresses, not knowing them; he would read people like a book, and the beautiful thing about God's gift in him—cancers and other diseases would die or be healed immediately. A real prophet heard directly from God; this was the case of this prophet of God.

His ministry ushered in the healing ministry in the '30s, '40s, '50s, and '60s; during this time, God raised up men like Oral Roberts and women like Kathryn Colman, who were used of God here in the US, while T. L. Osborn is one of the greatest soul-winners of our times. In over two hundred or more countries, this man of God reached millions for Jesus. I remember in one of his meetings in Cuba on a Ball Field, with five hundred thousand people or more in attendance, Jesus was seen walking over the people; the greatest miracles happened in these meetings. Other ministers from the voice of healing were mightily used of God in healings, miracles, and in particular, reaching millions of souls around the world to Jesus Christ.

During this era, A. A. Allen would walk into the invalid tent and see people who looked like skin and bones on their last breath, but there was no fear, doubt, unbelief, excuse, or hesitancy in this man of God. He would lay hands on them as the power of God would hit these people. These sick and dying people stood up, jumped up and down, and ran as they were healed by the power of God. A few organizations, denominations, and independents of that day ridiculed this man of God, as they gossiped and criticized and blamed him for being a drunk of alcoholic drinks, but whatever he was drinking, yours truly would like to have some of it, because whatever he was drinking produced some of the greatest miracles.

Some readers might question, "Well! Why did the author leave out the ministers, pastors, evangelists, and great men of God that are being used of God now, here, in America, and other countries?" Reinhard Bonnke, who recently passed, was a man of God. God used him in a supernatural way when he led millions of souls to Jesus in Africa and other parts of the world with every type of miracle and healing following the Word of God that he preached. How could anyone forget the awesome sight of the films that he showed on TV, looking at these films with a sea of people as the African people echoed a wave of roaring praises unto God?

There are ministers here in the US and other countries that are reaching millions of souls to Jesus Christ (not talking about TV; this is expected), pastors of megachurches who are doing a great work for God which is commendable; God bless them, but I did not obtain permission to mention their names; some I have not met, some of them I would like to meet, some of them I dare not meet because their bodyguards would not allow me (no animosity here). Some of them do not want you to meet them because their attitude tells you, "Don't ask me to come into a minister" or "Don't ask me for anything." Another reason is, I am often in other countries winning souls. Then there are some of them that the only gift that operates in their lives is the gift of suspicion. Praise God for them anyhow, but generally speaking, we do need a revival like in past centuries and years went by.

In sync with the previous page about past revival and the great men and women of God, whom God used in bringing about revival in the past centuries, the early 1900s, there are men and women of God, pastors, and other ministries; there are no reasons why they should not be inspired to have this type of revival? Before continuing, the author is doing everything to avoid negativity, but if I may let me run a negative wire here to follow with the positive, there are reasons why modern-day Christians and ministers are not desirous of this type of revival. The number reason is some of them do not want to pay the price for this type of revival; the second reason is most of this generation of Christians are too intellectually inclined to condone this type of revival but thank God if they humble themselves like these people, God would send this type of revival. The third reason is some of them do not want to let go of worldliness, materialism, the flesh, and the devil.

There should be a hunger and thirst for God and to see the miracle-working power of God that shook the world in the '40s, '50s, '60s, until the late '70s (most of all, a hunger and thirst for the ministry of Jesus as recorded in the Gospels and the book of Acts). There was such a desire and yearning for God and His power; this move of God produced some of the mightiest men and women of God who were used of God in the miraculous. The tailwind of this move of God inspired some younger ministers of that time who are now being used of God in the miraculous, but they are so few.

We read of God's creative power and the moving of the Holy Spirit in the book of Genesis. The book of Exodus never ceases to inspire, excite, and leaves yours truly in a state of wonder of the miracles and power of God. Moses, of course, was used of God in manifesting and demonstrating God's power in Egypt and to the Israelites. His consecration, prayer life, meekness, and willingness to assume and willingly carry out the tedious responsibility of leading the Hebrew people to the Promised Land was not an easy task, but what is it that made the difference in the lives of the Hebrew people, it was the miracles, signs, and wonders which God worked through Moses and there are times God, Himself, showed up.

The Ten Commandments and all of the inspiring words and wisdom that Moses received were passed down to the Israelites to adhere to and live by, but what is it that stood out in the minds of the children? It was the miracles, these signs, wonders, miracles, and supernatural manifestations of God's working power that stayed with them. The Egyptians had a particular god for each and everything; Jehovah God had to prove to the Egyptians that their gods were false or just idols. God's intention was to prove to the Egyptians that He was real and His power was real. Most of all, He wanted Israel to witness His power so that they would believe in Him. God's overall purpose was not just a show, but that He was greater than the gods of the Egyptians; He counteracted every god that they believed in. His overall purpose is that He is *Elohim* (*El above all*), and He alone is Jehovah God; He alone has power, and He is God above all.

These few paragraphs obviously are to enlighten the reader. The first plague was turning the Nile River water into blood; this was God's judgment against the false god *Apis*, who was the god of the Nile River, Isis, the goddess of the Nile, and *Khnum*, guardian of the Nile. The Nile was also believed to be the bloodstream of the goddess of *Osiris*, whom the Egyptians believed was reborn each year when the river flooded. The Nile River was the basis of the Egyptians' national and overall economy; they were deeply devastated as millions of fish died when the river turned into blood.

The Egyptians were suddenly helpless as their source of food was gone, and the water was unusable. Pharaoh was told, "Thus saith the LORD, In this thou shalt know that I am the LORD: behold, I will smite with the rod that is in mine hand upon the waters which are in the river, and they shall be turned to blood" Exodus 7:17.

The second plague, bringing frogs from the Nile, was a judgment against *Heqet*, the frog-headed goddess of birth. Frogs were thought to be sacred and not to be killed. God had the frogs invade every part of the homes of the Egyptians, and when the frogs died, their stinking bodies were unbearable, which caused a small percentage of the Egyptians to doubt the god of the frogs.

> *And the LORD did according to the word of Moses; and the frogs died out of the houses, out of the villages, and out of the fields.*
> *And they gathered them together upon heaps: and the land stank.*
> — Exodus 8:13–14

The third plague, gnats, was a judgment on *Seb*, the god of the desert. Unlike the previous plagues, the magicians were unable to duplicate this one and declared to Pharaoh, "Then the magicians said unto

Pharaoh, This is the finger of God: and Pharaoh's heart was hardened, and he hearkened not unto them; as the LORD had said" Exodus 8:19.

The fourth plague, flies, was a judgment on *Uatchit*, the fly god. In this plague, God clearly distinguished between the Israelites and the Egyptians, as no swarms of flies bothered the areas where the Israelites lived.

> *Else, if thou wilt not let my people go, behold, I will send swarms of flies upon thee, and upon thy servants, and upon thy people, and into thy houses: and the houses of the Egyptians shall be full of swarms of flies, and also the ground whereon they are.*
>
> — Exodus 8:21

The fifth plague, the death of livestock, was a judgment on the goddess *Hathor* and the god *Apis*, who were both depicted as cattle gods. As with the previous plague, God protected His people from the plague while the cattle of the Egyptians died. God was steadily destroying the economy of Egypt, and Pharaoh sent spies to find out if the Israelites were suffering along with the Egyptians, but he was disappointed to find out that the Israelites were protected by God Himself,

> *Behold, the hand of the Lord is upon thy cattle which is in the field, upon the horses, upon the asses, upon the camels, upon the oxen, and upon the sheep: there shall be very grievous murrain.*
>
> — Exodus 9:3

The sixth plague, boils, was a judgment against several gods over health and disease, *Ptah* and *Hathor*. This time, the Bible says that the magicians "could not stand before Moses because of the boils." Clearly, these religious leaders were powerless against the God of Israel. Before God sent the last three plagues, Pharaoh was given a special message from God. These plagues would be more severe than the others, and they were designed to convince Pharaoh and all the people; Pharaoh was even told that he was placed in his position by God so that God could show His power and declare His name through all the earth, "And Pharaoh sent, and, behold, there was not one of the cattle of the Israelites dead. And the heart of Pharaoh was hardened, and he did not let the people go" Exodus 9:7.

As an example of His grace, God warned Pharaoh to gather whatever cattle and crops remained from the previous plagues and shelter them from the coming storm. Some of Pharaoh's servants heeded the warning.

> *For now I will stretch out my hand, that I may smite thee and thy people with pestilence; and thou shalt be cut off from the earth.*
>
> *And in very deed for this cause have I raised thee up, for to shew in thee my power; and that my name may be declared throughout all the earth.*
>
> — Exodus 9:15–16

> *He that feared the word of the Lord among the servants of Pharaoh made his servants and his cattle flee into the houses.*
>
> — Exodus 9:20

The seventh plague, hail, attacked *Nut*, the sky goddess; *Isis*, the crop fertility god; and *Seti*, the storm god. This hail was unlike any that had been seen before. It was accompanied by a fire that ran along the ground, and everything left out in the open was devastated by the hail and fire. Again, the children of Israel were miraculously protected, and no hail damaged anything in their lands. Before God brought the next plague, He told Moses that the Israelites would be able to tell their children of the things they had seen God do in Egypt and how it showed them God's power. "Behold, to morrow about this time I will cause it to rain a very grievous hail, such as hath not been in Egypt since the foundation thereof even until now" Exodus 9:18.

The eighth plague, locusts, again focused on *Serapia*, which is the goddess of protection. The later crops, wheat, and rye, which had survived the hail, were now devoured by the swarms of locusts. There would be no harvest in Egypt that year.

The ninth plague, darkness, was aimed at the sun god, *Re*, who was symbolized by Pharaoh himself. For three days, the land of Egypt was smothered with unearthly darkness, but the homes of the Israelites had light.

> *And the LORD said unto Moses, Stretch out thine hand over the land of Egypt for the locusts, that they may come up upon the land of Egypt, and eat every herb of the land, even all that the hail hath left.*
>
> *And Moses stretched forth his rod over the land of Egypt, and the LORD brought an east wind upon the land all that day, and all that night; and when it was morning, the east wind brought the locusts.*
>
> *And the locust went up over all the land of Egypt, and rested in all the coasts of Egypt: very grievous were they; before them there were no such locusts as they, neither after them shall be such.*
>
> — Exodus 10:12–14

The ninth plague was the plague of darkness which was against the god of *Amon-Re* and *Aton/Aten* or really the moon god; this god was supposed to give them light in every way, whom they worshiped every night in particular when the moon was full.

> *And the LORD said unto Moses, Stretch out thine hand toward heaven, that there may be darkness over the land of Egypt, even darkness which may be felt.*
>
> *And Moses stretched forth his hand toward heaven; and there was a thick darkness in all the land of Egypt three days:*
>
> *They saw not one another, neither rose any from his place for three days: but all the children of Israel had light in their dwellings.*
>
> — Exodus 10:21–23

The tenth and last plague, the death of the firstborn males, was a judgment on *Isis*, the protector of children. In this plague, God was teaching the Israelites a deep spiritual lesson that pointed to Christ. Unlike the other plagues, which the Israelites survived by virtue of their identity as God's people, this plague required an act of faith by them. God commanded each family to take an unblemished male lamb and kill it. The blood of the lamb was to be smeared on the top and sides of their doorways, and the lamb was to be roasted and eaten that night. Any family that did not follow God's instructions would suffer in the last plague. God described how He would send the death angel through the land of Egypt, with orders to slay the firstborn male in every household, whether human or animal. The only protection was the blood of the lamb on the door. When the angel saw the blood, he would pass over that house and leave it untouched. This is where the term Passover comes from. Passover is a memorial of that night in ancient Egypt when God delivered His people from bondage.

> *And it came to pass, that at midnight the LORD smote all the firstborn in the land of Egypt, from the firstborn of Pharaoh that sat on his throne unto the firstborn of the captive that was in the dungeon; and all the firstborn of cattle.*
> — Exodus 12:29

"Purge out therefore the old leaven, that ye may be a new lump, as ye are unleavened. For even Christ our passover is sacrificed for us" 1 Corinthians 5:7. Jesus became our Passover when He died to deliver us from the bondage of sin. While the Israelites found God's protection in their homes, every other home in the land of Egypt experienced God's wrath as their loved ones died. This grievous event caused Pharaoh to finally realize that the God in Israel was real and released the Israelites.

By the time the Israelites left Egypt, they had a clear picture of God's power, God's protection, and God's plan for them. For those who were willing to believe, they had convincing evidence that they served the true and living God. Sadly, many still failed to believe, which led to other trials from God. The result for the Egyptians and the other ancient people of the region was a dread of the God of Israel. Even after the tenth plague, Pharaoh once again hardened his heart and sent his chariots after the Israelites. When God opened a way through the Red Sea for the Israelites, then drowned all of Pharaoh's armies there, the power of Egypt was crushed, and the fear of God spread through the surrounding nations

> *And she said unto the men, I know that the Lord hath given you the land, and that your terror is fallen upon us, and that all the inhabitants of the land faint because of you.*
>
> *For we have heard how the Lord dried up the water of the Red sea for you, when ye came out of Egypt; and what ye did unto the two kings of the Amorites, that were on the other side Jordan, Sihon and Og, whom ye utterly destroyed.*
> — Joshua 2:9–10

> *And as soon as we had heard these things, our hearts did melt, neither did there remain any more courage in any man, because of you: for the LORD your God, he is God in heaven above, and in earth beneath.*
> — Joshua 2:11

This was the very purpose that God had declared at the beginning. We can still look back on these events today to confirm our faith in and our fear of this true and living God, the Judge of all the earth. The judgments of God upon the Egyptians; for instance, the Egyptians had a god for everything.

The day and time came for the Hebrews to leave Egypt; obviously, they were already packed and prepared, excitement and expectancy permeated the atmosphere, with everything that they earned plus the gold, silver, and money that God caused the Egyptians to place in their hands before leaving, were tacked away, and they held whatever they can in their hands ready to march to their freedom. Three million Hebrews formed a band as they scuttle together out of Egypt towards the Promised Land. With thankful hearts and praises to God, they started their tedious journey towards the wilderness; marching towards the wilderness, expectancy turned into a nightmare of bewilderment as they stood before the Red Sea. The Red Sea in front of them, mountains on each side, and now Pharaoh's army behind them; alas, what now!

Some members of the congregation began murmuring and complaining, "You, Moses, brought us into the wilderness to kill us!" The Red Sea in front of them with its boisterous gloomy deathly waters hitting against the rocks and waves rolling onto the shore, but with a word from God to take them to the Promised Land and a command from God to Moses to stretch the rod in his hands towards the Red Sea and speak to it to open up. Moses did, and the Red Sea opened up as God froze the waters on both sides, paved a path on the marshy seafloor, and hardened it for the Hebrews to walk on; this act of God was a supernatural miracle from a supernatural God, a miracle of miracles with a series of supernatural miracles that would accompany Israel to the Promised Land.

The four hundred years between the Old and the New Testament were not silent years as some people seem to think; at the closing of the book of Malachi in the Old Testament, the nation of Israel was back in the Land of Palestine after being held captive in Babylon. During the four hundred years between the Testaments, the political situation was war and a transition of power from one world power to another.

- *The Persian period*—536 to 333 BC
- *The Greek period*—333 to 323 BC
- *The Egyptian period*—323 to 204 BC
- *The Syrian period*—204 to 165 BC
- *The Maccabean period*—165 to 63 BC
- *The Roman period*—63 BC

Knowledge of the period between the Old and New Testaments is important and necessary if we are going to understand Jesus' life, teaching, and ministry in the four Gospels.

Religiously speaking, in Jerusalem, the temple had been restored, although it was a much smaller building than the one that Solomon had built and decorated in such marvelous glory. Within the temple, the line of Aaronic priests was still worshiping and carrying on the sacred rites as they had been ordered to do by the Law of Moses. Religiously speaking, the spiritual condition of the Jews began to dwindle as the excitement of returning to Palestine and the erection of the second temple eroded into a conflagration of tradition, rituals, formality, and animal sacrifices culminating in millions of Jews being empty and unsatisfied.

This emptiness among the Jews drove thousands of them into fractions of religious zealots like the Pharisees, Sadducees, Scribes, Hellenistic, Judaism, and more of these religious sects. The Greeks, with their knowledge, and the Romans' ingenuity for building roads, waterways, and dams, prepared the way for the unusual to happen. Spiritual darkness loomed over most of the Jewish people who lived under the tyranny of the Roman government; their only hope was the *Messiah*.

The Roman Empire conquered all of the then known world political power at the closing of the four hundred years, who now ruled over the Jews suppressed by Roman rule as they continued in their animals' sacrifices while observing the law of Moses. All of the splinter groups like the Scribes and Pharisees implemented strict religious laws on the populace, while there were multitudes of Jews who studied, heard, and knew that a Messiah would come and deliver them. Their hopes were high as they waited for the promised One.

Shepherds, who were the lowliest of all tradesmen of that day, sometimes these shepherds for several days and nights, would leave the city and graze their sheep on the hills and small mountain tops of Jerusalem. They were tired and being gathered in one area with their sheep talking and sharing shepherds' stories and eating their food that they had prepared to last about a week or more while their sheep grazed the hills of Jerusalem. Suddenly on the hillside or sloops of the mountainside, the stars were shining and glistening, and the Moon and all of the other planets were circling around the Earth. In the hush of the winds and the stillness of the night, the shepherds heard the most beautiful singing of an angelic choir as angels were singing, the angel Gabriel announced,

> *And there were in the same country shepherds abiding in the field, keeping watch over their flock by night.*
>
> *And, lo, the angel of the Lord came upon them, and the glory of the Lord shone round about them: and they were sore afraid.*
>
> *And the angel said unto them, Fear not: for, behold, I bring you good tidings of great joy, which shall be to all people.*
>
> *For unto you is born this day in the city of David a Saviour, which is Christ the Lord.*
>
> *And this shall be a sign unto you; Ye shall find the babe wrapped in swaddling clothes, lying in a manger.*
>
> *And suddenly there was with the angel a multitude of the heavenly host praising God, and saying, Glory to God in the highest, and on earth peace, good will toward men.*
>
> *And it came to pass, as the angels were gone away from them into heaven, the shepherds said one to another, Let us now go even unto Bethlehem, and see this thing which is come to pass, which the Lord hath made known unto us.*
>
> — Luke 2:8–15

After centuries of tradition, ritual, formality, religious ceremonies, sacrifices, and man-made rules and regulations and hope for some Jews, the birth of Jesus significantly altered history and ushered in the supernatural. His birth was a miracle and, of course, supernatural. Jesus' birth, growth, teachings, actions, words, and of course, the miracles were now imminent as Jerusalem witnessed the supernatural power of God like never before. What is it that irritated the ecclesiastical order of the day? First, it was Jesus' claim that He was the Son of God. Secondly, it was the healings and miracles out of love and compassion to help and deliver hurting humanity. The supernatural miracles that Jesus performed were undeniable attestations that He was the Son of God, "But if I do, though ye believe not me, believe the works: that ye may know, and believe, that the Father is in me, and I in him" John 10:38.

Could you imagine a Bible without miracles! What about the ministry of Jesus and the apostles! Imagine reading the New Testament without the miracles! One of the most outstanding miracles of Jesus, which is considered to be supernaturally recorded in the Gospel of John, is pertaining to the "raising of Lazarus from the dead." Lazarus, of course, was a rich man, a friend of Jesus; he became sick and died, after which they laid him in a tomb. He was dead for three days, but Jesus stood up in front of the tomb where Lazarus laid; here is the account from the Word of God, the Bible,

Now a man named Lazarus was sick. He was from Bethany, the village of Mary and her sister Martha. (This Mary, whose brother Lazarus now lay sick, was the same one who poured perfume on the Lord and wiped his feet with her hair.)

So the sisters sent word to Jesus, "Lord, the one you love is sick."

When he heard this, Jesus said, "This sickness will not end in death. No, it is for God's glory so that God's Son may be glorified through it."

After he had said this, he went on to tell them, "Our friend Lazarus has fallen asleep; but I am going there to wake him up."

On his arrival, Jesus found that Lazarus had already been in the tomb for four days

and many Jews had come to Martha and Mary to comfort them in the loss of their brother.

When Martha heard that Jesus was coming, she went out to meet him, but Mary stayed at home.

"Lord," Martha said to Jesus, "if you had been here, my brother would not have died. But I know that even now God will give you whatever you ask."

Jesus said to her, "Your brother will rise again."

Martha answered, "I know he will rise again in the resurrection at the last day."

Jesus said to her, "I am the resurrection and the life. The one who believes in me will live, even though they die;

and whoever lives by believing in me will never die. Do you believe this?"

"Yes, Lord," she replied, "I believe that you are the Messiah, the Son of God, who is to come into the world."

"Where have you laid him?" he asked. "Come and see, Lord," they replied.

Jesus, once more deeply moved, came to the tomb. It was a cave with a stone laid across the entrance.

"Take away the stone," he said. "But, Lord," said Martha, the sister of the dead man, "by this time there is a bad odor, for he has been there four days."

Then Jesus said, "Did I not tell you that if you believe, you will see the glory of God?"

So they took away the stone. Then Jesus looked up and said, "Father, I thank you that you have heard me.

I knew that you always hear me, but I said this for the benefit of the people standing here, that they may believe that you sent me."

When he had said this, Jesus called in a loud voice, "Lazarus, come forth!"

The dead man came out, his hands and feet wrapped with strips of linen, and a cloth around his face. Jesus said to them,

"Take off the grave clothes and let him go."

— John 11:1–4, 11, 17, 19–27, 34, 38–44 NIV

There is one verse that the author would like to interject from this entire chapter that is of utmost importance, "Then Jesus said, 'Did I not tell you that if you believe, you will see the glory of God?'" John 11:40, NIV.

Some of the people that were gathered around when Lazarus walked out of the tomb saw him walk out of the tomb and still did not believe. Unbelief is one of the worst hindrances to the power of God. Unbelief is a devil thing that has blinded most of the church world from witnessing the Power of God. Believing is one of the greatest assets in any Christian life; the above verse attested to this when God placed Adam and Eve in the Garden of Eden. He placed everything in that Garden for them to enjoy, but one instruction He gave them was—"But of the fruit of the tree which is in the midst of the garden, God hath said, Ye shall not eat of it neither shall ye touch it, *lest ye die*" Genesis 3:3.

What happened to Adam and Eve in the Garden of Eden? They died spiritually; in other words, their unbelief. Plunge the entire world into sin; what is it that is crippling the hands of most of the church today, and what is it that is hindering the people of the world today? It is unbelief. Jesus said, "If you believe, you will see the glory of God" John 11:40b, NIV.

When Jesus performed the miracle of raising Lazarus, just think about this for a moment, Lazarus was dead for four days; his body was already in the process of decaying; who would have thought Jesus would and could have done this. But read the words of Jesus; this is what He said, "I knew that you always hear me, but I said this for the benefit of the people standing here, that they may believe that you sent me" John 11:42, NIV.

This miracle happened because Jesus wanted the people to believe in Him, and when you believe in Him, miracles happen. Believe in Him first, not believe in the miracle; the miracle has to have a source and a cause to happen, Jesus is the source and the cause for the miracle to happen, and it all happens by believing and believing in Jesus. If you don't believe in Jesus, there will be no miracle; this is the main reason why the world is going to pieces; they do not believe in Jesus.

Believing is faith walking and talking; faith believes, which means action acting on what the word of God tells you to do; there is nothing like believing and unbelieving or doubt at the same time. To proceed further, you will never see God in His fullness or His power by accepting part of His word and leaving out part of the word. Believe all of it, and you will see the glory of God.

> *And on the morrow, when they were come from Bethany, he was hungry:*
>
> *And seeing a fig tree afar off having leaves, he came, if haply he might find any thing thereon: and when he came to it, he found nothing but leaves; for the time of figs was not yet.*
>
> *And Jesus answered and said unto it, No man eat fruit of thee hereafter for ever. And his disciples heard*
>
> *And when even was come, he went out of the city.*
>
> *And in the morning, as they passed by, they saw the fig tree dried up from the roots.*
>
> *And Peter calling to remembrance saith unto him, Master, behold, the fig tree which thou cursedst is withered away.*
>
> *And Jesus answering saith unto them, Have faith in God.*

Chapter 19: Manifestation of God's Power

For verily I say unto you, That whosoever shall say unto this mountain, Be thou removed, and be thou cast into the sea; and shall not doubt in his heart, but shall believe that those things which he saith shall come to pass; he shall have whatsoever he saith.

Therefore I say unto you, What things soever ye desire, when ye pray, believe that ye receive them, and ye shall have them.

— Mark 11:12–14, 19–24

These words above are some of the most powerful words ever recorded that Jesus spoke in the Bible, particularly verses 23 to 24.

For verily I say unto you, That whosoever shall say unto this mountain, Be thou removed, and be thou cast into the sea; and shall not doubt in his heart, but shall believe that those things which he saith shall come to pass; he shall have whatsoever he saith.

Therefore I say unto you, What things soever ye desire, when ye pray, believe that ye receive them, and ye shall have them.

— Mark 11:23–24

There is something in particular about verses 23 and 24; the author's statement is not that he intends to be negative (but, as mentioned in an earlier chapter, there are times you must apply the negative to interject the positive). Listening to ministers in general and Christians everywhere, TV preachers, these two verses are the most popular verses. You hear them morning, noon, and night on TV, radio, the internet, podcasts, Zoom, etc., but are we really seeing results in what we are speaking, saying, praying to come to pass? One of the greatest joys of the Christian life *is answered prayer in any form.*

Speaking it and getting it, blabbing it and grabbing it, saying it and claiming it are superfluous statements that certain sector of the church has come up with. It is spoken loosely, but what you are speaking, blabbing, and grabbing, is it coming to pass? Or in other words, *are we seeing results?* If we are not seeing and having results, then something is wrong, then what is wrong!

Did you notice in the very same chapter 11, verses 13 and 14, that Jesus curses the fig tree? The word curse does not mean profanity but comes from the Hebrew word "*arar,*" which means *nothing is going to happen for you; you will not get through,* and *what you are going after will not come to pass*; here is the reason,

And they come to Jerusalem: and Jesus went into the temple, and began to cast out them that sold and bought in the temple, and overthrew the tables of the moneychangers, and the seats of them that sold doves;

And would not suffer that any man should carry any vessel through the temple.

And he taught, saying unto them, Is it not written, My house shall be called of all nations the house of prayer? But ye have made it a den of thieves.

— Mark 11:15–17

From the verses above, you will get the idea why the power of God was *not* being manifested; it was a forgone fact the priests and other religious leaders were just as guilty of the people that were buying, selling, trading; money lenders, money changers, and lenders we doing brisk business.

Where? In the temple of Jehovah God. Worst of all, prayer, which is the key to the working of God's power, was a no-no in the house of God. Jesus will not allow anyone to carry any kind of boxes or containers for business in the house of God. How could God manifest Himself in the house of God when it seems like everything in the church is so high and excessively commercialized. So much could be written about this, but this is not the purpose of the chapter. The key to the manifestation of God's power, faith, and miracles is the source of all of God's blessings. Jesus said it right here,

> *And he taught, saying unto them, Is it not written, My house shall be called of all nations the house of prayer? But ye have made it a den of thieves.*
>
> *Therefore I say unto you, What things soever ye desire, when ye pray, believe that ye receive them, and ye shall have them.*
>
> *And when ye stand praying, forgive, if ye have ought against any: that your Father also which is in heaven may forgive you your trespasses.*
>
> *But if ye do not forgive, neither will your Father which is in heaven forgive your trespasses.*
>
> — Mark 11:17, 24–26

There is something in particular that all Bible-believing Christians should understand, which correlates with the Scriptures above, especially verse 23, in order for God to answer prayer, miracles to happen, healings to occur, for your desire to come to pass, degree a thing and it comes to pass revival to come about, to heal the sick, to cast out devils, to experience God's blessings in every way and other godly and supernatural occurrences to come about. Please let it sink down in your spirit what Jesus is saying; if it's going to happen, you have to desire it, pray it, speak it, or say it, then it will come to pass; nothing will happen to keep your mouth shut.

Here is another key for all of the above to happen—it is forgiveness; there are two avenues of forgiveness, and they are (one) if you have honestly repented of your sins and accepted Jesus Christ as your Lord and Savior and living the Christian life, even made mistakes, and you have repented, the blood of Jesus Christ cleanses you from all sins. Do not go around being condemned; accept God's forgiveness; (secondly) forgive those that have done you wrong. Do not go around thinking that God would answer your prayers, send revival or bless you in every way if there is unforgiveness in your heart. The words of Jesus above, verses 25 and 26, are relevant and so explicit in relation to God's blessing and revival within the Church.

There is a place and a position in God that every ministry and all professing Christians should and could aspire in their walk with God, and that is getting to the point that your spirit should become mellow that it is impossible to harbor unforgiveness or become bitter because unforgiveness leads to bitterness. Yours truly, the author, has told the audiences or congregation that I minister to that I have come to a pace in God that it's impossible for me to become bitter, and believe me, it was not easy getting to this position. Read my next book following this one as to how I got to this point.

CHAPTER 20

You're Assurance for Heaven

Going to heaven is not as easy as it's written about, preached by some, spoken, or mentioned! Being baptized in water, a handshake from the preacher, becoming a member of a church or congregation, and doing good works or charitable deeds is commendable, but this does not guarantee an individual or people getting to heaven. Getting to heaven is certainly serious business. The fact is, almost every person that you speak to about heaven wants to go to heaven, but getting to heaven means an individual or people must make a commitment of their lives to God which begins at repentance, which means to be exceedingly sorry for their sins and a total turn around from a life of sin, worldliness, the sins of the flesh and the devil. Salvation means genuine repentance according to the Gospel of John, chapter 3; this is about the conversation that Nicodemus had with Jesus and Jesus' answer about being "born again," this was dealt with in an earlier chapter, page 118.

When a person is born again or saved, this means they have repented for their sins and the results of a sinful nature. Justification, regeneration, transformation, and sanctification (which is progressive as a person grows spiritually) are evident in the new life of a person now saved. What really happens when a person repents, becomes saved, or is born again? The blood of Jesus Christ cleanses that person from their sin, guilt, and condemnation of their past sins, then the Holy Spirit impregnates and transforms the human spirit. Then the Holy Spirit unites with the human spirit, and the seed life image of Jesus Christ is birthed into a person, and they are born again or saved.

But the completion of a person's salvation of being saved or born again does not stop at repentance and accepting Jesus Christ as Lord and Savior. As an individual continues to live a Christian life, their life would be a life of inner peace, contentment, true happiness, love, joy, growing in faith, a relationship with God, and an assurance of eternity, but it is the responsibility of the individual Christian by God's help to maintain and live a Christ-like life. Thank God for the Christians that have the fortitude, guts, gumption, stamina, and strength with a commitment to God to live a holy and clean life after they are saved and want to make it to heaven.

There are people that are born again, saved, and profess Christianity, who consistently indulge in the sins of the flesh, worldly and ungodly lifestyle, and encourage or practice voodoo, witchcraft, etc. and expect to make it to heaven. We are living in a day when a percentage of the church world is more materialistic conscious than God-conscious. Thousands and thousands of people are indulging and taking drugs to sustain their busy lifestyle; divorces are the highest in church circles; pornography has become a lucid problem to thousands; social drinking of hard liquor by some is now a pastime with the excuse a little will not hurt; fornication and adultery are smeared upon with the excuse we are human. Some are channeling unclean movies and pornography in their homes, with killing and murder scenes, combined with consistent swearing and cursing; they are going to the movies and enjoying the same with no conviction; it's wrong! What about the abortion issue, which is literal murder, homosexuality, and lesbianism? Same-sex marriage is now supported by law and sanctioned by some denominations, organizations, independents, some clergy, so-called pastors, priests, and heads of organizations, some of them think they are going to heaven, and some of them say they are going to heaven, most of them want to go to heaven. Yours truly's desire is that they go to heaven, and God's plan of redemption opened the way for them to go to heaven. By the way, like everything else, people's choice depends on where they go, heaven or hell.

Chapter 20: You're Assurance for Heaven

This is not a book of don'ts or a form of legalistic point of view for those of you who do not understand legalism. It means to be like the religion of the Pharisees, keep the law of Moses; you will not make it in the kingdom of God or some other religion that emphasizes dress codes, mythology, besides conviction; common sense would tell you those who practice such, according to the Bible, will not make it to heaven unless they are genuinely saved or born again. Every reader should meditate upon these words penned by the apostle John two thousand years ago, "Whosoever is born of God doth not commit sin; for his seed [if he or she is saved or knows God] remaineth in him: and he cannot sin, because he is born of God" 1 John 3:9.

The above scripture penned by inspiration of the Holy Spirit is a different type of language that you hear from modern-day preachers and Christians, for instance, "we are humans, we will make mistakes, we are flesh." But look carefully at the above word, "Whosoever is born of God [born again] doth not commit sin" 1 John 3:9.

For his seed remain in him, whenever a person is born again, the Holy Spirit implants or sows God's spirit within the human spirit, that they cannot sin (remain in sin), but it is the individual responsibility to walk with God so that seed of the life of Jesus Christ that was sown within that person would remain in that person that they will not consistently commit and live in sin because they were born again by God's spirit.

All of the books that were written and being written, the surmountable booklets, instructions, and convert classes that are being conducted in different congregations, stadiums, and ball fields are filled with thousands of people when an altar call is given. Thanks be to God for the people who respond by the thousands to give their lives to Jesus Christ, which is followed by instructions on how to live for God. All of this is certainly commendable and glorifying to God. But if a person or people who are born again and saved and the Holy Spirit sows the seed of eternal life within their heart, believe me, as long as that individual intends to walk and live for God, God will keep them. Forget about once saved, always saved, live as you like, do as you like, and you will make it to heaven.

Really speaking, people that are truly born again or saved will not deliberately want to sin or commit sin; yes, they will be tempted because temptation is not a sin, but wanting or desirous of committing the sin or sinning is wrong, but if an individual or people realize they have sinned against God they can repent and come back to God,

> *My little children, these things write I unto you, that ye sin not.*
> *And if any man sin, we have an advocate with the Father, Jesus Christ the righteous:*
> *And he is the propitiation for our sins: and not for ours only, but also for the sins of the whole world.*
> *And hereby we do know that we know him, if we keep his commandments.*
> — 1 John 2:1–3

Paul, the apostle, had to warn us in this day that the sins of the flesh, the spirit of the world (ungodly people), and the devil, please be reminded, he wrote this to the church,

Now the works of the flesh are manifest, which are these; Adultery, fornication, uncleanness, lasciviousness,

Idolatry, witchcraft, hatred, variance, emulations, wrath, strife, seditions, heresies,

Envyings, murders, drunkenness, revellings, and such like: of the which I tell you before, as I have also told you in time past, that they which do such things shall not inherit the kingdom of God.

But the fruit of the Spirit is love, joy, peace, longsuffering, gentleness, goodness, faith,

Meekness, temperance: against such there is no law.

And they that are Christ's have crucified the flesh with the affections and lusts.

If we live in the Spirit, let us also walk in the Spirit.

— Galatians 5:19–25

Paul the apostle, of all the other apostles, was last but not least on his way to Damascus to persecute the Christians (Acts, chapter 8), had a life-changing experience when he encountered Jesus Christ; he was immediately changed by God's power. After he was baptized and received the Holy Spirit, he was introduced to the other apostles. He started to preach the Gospel of Jesus Christ, but God had a greater plan for his life; God led him to the desert and mountains of Arabia, and God, Himself, taught Paul. He gave him revelations, dreams, and visions where he said he saw things which he could not speak or write about; these are the inspired words of the apostle written to the Church.

But I certify you, brethren, that the gospel which was preached of me is not after man.

For I neither received it of man, neither was I taught it, but by the revelation of Jesus Christ.

For ye have heard of my conversation in time past in the Jews' religion, how that beyond measure I persecuted the church of God, and wasted it:

And profited in the Jews' religion above many my equals in mine own nation, being more exceedingly zealous of the traditions of my fathers.

— Galatians 1:11–14

But when it pleased God, who separated me from my mother's womb, and called me by his grace,

To reveal his Son in me, that I might preach him among the heathen; immediately I conferred not with flesh and blood:

— Galatians 1:15–16

It is not expedient for me doubtless to glory. I will come to visions and revelations of the Lord.

I knew a man in Christ above fourteen years ago, (whether in the body, I cannot tell; or whether out of the body, I cannot tell: God knoweth;) such an one caught up to the third heaven.

And I knew such a man, (whether in the body, or out of the body, I cannot tell: God knoweth;)

— 2 Corinthians 12:1–3

How that he was caught up into paradise, and heard unspeakable words, which it is not lawful for a man to utter.

— 2 Corinthians 12:4

What is the message, word, or revelation that the Church of Jesus Christ desperately needs that would guarantee the believer in Jesus Christ and give a confidence of assurance of going to heaven? Here is the revelation that God gave Apostle Paul for the Church. A revelation is when God chooses to pull back the curtain, to reveal the truth, to show a mystery and secrets and make them known. Any time that unknown spiritual reality becomes known, the initiative is with God. This revelatory word is our assurance to make it to heaven, it has been in the Bible all the time, but hardly anyone takes the time to read, meditate, and preach this word, which will give people the hope of going to heaven; here it is, "To whom God would make known what is the riches of the glory of this mystery among the Gentiles; which is Christ in you, the hope of glory" Colossians 1:27.

The above Scripture is a revelation to us; the apostle Paul is saying to us what was hid is now made known, which God is now revealing to us, what is the riches of the glory of this mystery, which God has made known to us. Christ in you—the hope of glory.

Again what is the message, word, or revelation that the Church of Jesus Christ desperately needs that would guarantee the believer in Jesus Christ and give a confidence of assurance of going to heaven; Christ in you—the hope of glory. The mystery is, God and God's secrets were hidden but now are made known unto us. Even though we were strangers and foreigners, heathens, to be exact, because of Jesus Christ coming to earth, God condescended in His Son, Jesus Christ, and sent Jesus Christ on earth in the flesh to reveal what and whom God is like. The three and a half years Jesus was on earth, He revealed God to us and whom God is like and what He wants to do for us; that is, He wanted us to understand that God loves and cares for us, He wants to give us peace, real joy, and true happiness, also solve our problems, meet our every need, heal our sicknesses and diseases. Most of all, live a God life here, on earth, and hope for the future, which is eternal life.

The mystery is that when Jesus Christ died on the cross, His death on the cross was the ultimate price the Son of God had to pay for the sinful nature that humankind inherited from the beginning. The resurrection of Jesus Christ and now Jesus is sitting at the right hand of the Father to represent us before God as our High Priest and to make intercession for us. After a person is saved and baptized with the Holy Spirit, it is their responsibility by the help of the Holy Spirit to keep his or her relationship with God. Once saved, always saved, but it is an individual responsibility again, with the help of the Holy Spirit, to stay saved, and individual should not expect to go to heaven after they are saved and then go back into a life of sin and remain in sin and be consumed with the idea of going to heaven! You begin your Christian life with Christ; continue the Christian life with Christ; Christ has to be in you all the time; this is Christ in you, the hope of glory, your hope of going to heaven.

Christ is your means that the individual Christian and the Church would have revival all the time; most of the church world must wake up and realize we do not always have to have a mysterious prophet, TV preacher, evangelist, pastor, teacher, apostle some with blessed oil, water blessed clothe or handkerchief or a singing gospel artist or choir to pump (not against any of these) them up and bring their crowds into a hype. This God-given revelation means you get saved, you will be saved, and stay saved, and the church can always be in a state of revival and be ready for the second return of Jesus Christ and make it to heaven.

Paul, the apostle, mentions this as a mystery; what is this mystery "God dwelling in human vessels," "We have this treasure in earthen vessels [us human beings]" 2 Corinthians 4:7.

What is a mystery or something mysterious? Something not recognized or known, keeping things secret, especially in a way that makes other people curious or desirous of wanting to discover what is hidden or what you have, something hid but now revealed or made known.

The Holy Spirit inspired the apostle John and gave the greatest revelation and awe-inspiring Word recorded in 1 John 3:1–3 pertaining to and relevant to the church preparing for the second return of Jesus Christ. The Church of Jesus Christ should observe and give heed to these Scriptures, which relate to the Church's readiness in relation to preparation and being ready for the second return of Jesus Christ.

> *Behold, what manner of love the Father hath bestowed upon us, that we should be called the sons of God: therefore the world knoweth us not, because it knew him not.*
>
> *Beloved, now are we the sons of God, and it doth not yet appear what we shall be: but we know that, when he shall appear, we shall be like him; for we shall see him as he is.*
>
> *And every man that hath this hope in him purifieth himself, even as he is pure.*
>
> — 1 John 3:1–3

BRIEF COMMENTARY ON 1 JOHN 3:1

The apostle John expresses God's love for the world, in particular, the human race; if anyone knew about God's love, it was the apostle John because he was the closest of the apostles to Jesus. He witnessed Jesus dying on the cross firsthand; he realized that this was God's love to the extreme. Jesus Christ had to pay the ultimate price for the sins of the human race; this was God of showing His love to us, the reason why John quoted the words above. Please remember these scriptures are written to the Church of Jesus Christ, especially for those who are interested in going to heaven. "Beloved, now are we the sons of God, and it doth not yet appear what we shall be: but we know that, when he shall appear, we shall be like him; for we shall see him as he is" 1 John 3:2.

There is a revelation here; the word revelation comes from the Hebrew word "*apokalupsi,*" which means *a disclosure of truth* or *God's secrets revealed* to us by the Holy Spirit to give us clarity or understanding of His Word to live and walk in truth so we can make it to heaven. If you are going to be used of God and manifest God's power here on earth and be caught up to meet Jesus Christ in the air, according to 1 Thessalonians 4:13–17.

> *But I would not have you to be ignorant, brethren, concerning them which are asleep, that ye sorrow not, even as others which have no hope.*
>
> *For if we believe that Jesus died and rose again, even so them also which sleep in Jesus will God bring with him.*
>
> *For this we say unto you by the word of the Lord, that we which are alive and remain unto the coming of the Lord shall not prevent them which are asleep.*
>
> *For the Lord himself shall descend from heaven with a shout, with the voice of the archangel, and with the trump of God: and the dead in Christ shall rise first:*
>
> *Then we which are alive and remain shall be caught up together with them in the clouds, to meet the Lord in the air: and so shall we ever be with the Lord.*
>
> — 1 Thessalonians 4:13–17

We must realize that after accepting Jesus Christ as Lord and Savior, we become sons of God (this means men and women). The apostle John is emphasizing that in order to be caught up with Christ when He returns, we have to possess the image and nature of Jesus Christ to be caught up to meet Him in the air when He returns.

This statement is biblical and a far different view from the modern-day modernistic church that thinks they will do as they like, live as they like, say what they like; if it feels good, do it and then expect to go to heaven. This must be emphasized again and again if an individual or the church, in general, is going to be caught up (some say ruptured). According to the word of God, we must have nature of Christ to see and go to be with Jesus when He returns the second time.

"And every man that hath this hope in him purifieth himself, even as he is pure" 1 John 3:3. Every person who calls themselves a Christian that has a hope and assurance of going to be with Jesus must do everything possible to live a clean, sanctified, pure, holy, and Christ-like life if they are going to make it to heaven. A Holy Spirit-filled life is a prerequisite requirement of the assurance of eternity. The apostle Paul prayed like a woman who was experiencing birth pains (most of the modern-day church really does not know what the meaning of this is) for the church of Galatia until the nature of Christ was formed in them. This means that if they were going to heaven, they must have the nature of Christ. If members of the Body of Christ will make it to heaven, obviously, we must have the nature of Christ.

Here are the words of the prayer of the apostle Paul for the Church of Galatia and for all the Churches, "My little children, of whom I travail in birth again until Christ be formed in you" Galatians 4:19.

Here are the words of Jesus' requirement of going to heaven,

> *Then the kingdom of heaven shall be likened to ten virgins who took their lamps and went out to meet the bridegroom.*
> *Now five of them were wise, and five were foolish.*
> *Those who were foolish took their lamps and took no oil with them,*
> *but the wise took oil in their vessels with their lamps.*
> *But while the bridegroom was delayed, they all slumbered and slept*
> *And at midnight a cry was heard: 'Behold, the bridegroom is coming; go out to meet him!'*
> *Then all those virgins arose and trimmed their lamps.*
> *And the foolish said to the wise, Give us some of your oil, for our lamps are going out.*
> *But the wise answered, saying, No, lest there should not be enough for us and you; but go rather to those who sell, and buy for yourselves.*
> *And while they went to buy, the bridegroom came, and those who were ready went in with him to the wedding; and the door was shut.*
> *Afterward came also the other virgins, saying, Lord, Lord, open to us.*
> *But he answered and said, Verily I say unto you, I know you not.*
> *Watch therefore, for ye know neither the day nor the hour wherein the Son of man cometh.*
> — Matthew 25:1–13

Who spoke these words? Obviously, Jesus Christ addressed these words to people of the entire church world and likened the entire church to "Ten Virgins." Virgins, of course, represent those who name the name of Jesus Christ and call themselves Christians, practice good works, feed the hungry, etc. Most of all, with their testimony of what they were doing, they confess that they are ready to meet Jesus at His second return and go to be with Him in heaven when He returns the second time. Half the Church or five virgins whom Jesus called foolishly took their lamps (which represent themselves, their testimony, and works), but they had no oil in their lamps. But the wise virgins took oil in their lamps; oil represents the Holy Spirit which is the seal of God. Oil represents readiness, preparation, and completion. All ten virgins said they were ready for the second return of Jesus Christ, but while Jesus tarried or did not return as of yet, most of the church world slumbered and slept, but when Jesus was about to return, all the virgins said they were ready to meet the Lord in the air, but only five of the virgins went to be with Jesus; why? They had oil in their lamps; in other words, they were baptized and filled with the Holy Spirit.

Is all of the above biblical or scriptural? Obviously so! God used the apostle Paul as He inspired him to pen these words that only the spiritually wise can comprehend, recorded in the book of Ephesians. "In whom ye also trusted, after that ye heard the word of truth, the gospel of your salvation: in whom also after that ye believed, ye were sealed with that Holy Spirit of promise" Ephesians 1:13.

Everyone who claims they are a Christian, please remember being a Christian is not a profession, confession, religion, tradition, or someone who belongs to a denomination, organization, or some far east religion with all of its formality. Being a Christian is to be born again, according to Jesus' words in John, chapter 3, as was emphasized in chapter 3 of this book. It means to be transformed by the power of God, someone who is living a clean, holy life, separated from the world, the flesh, and the devil; someone who most of all has a daily relationship with God and is filled with the Holy Spirit ready and looking for the return of Jesus; they are the one that is going to be with Jesus.

CHAPTER 21, PART 1

Stranger in His Own House

You recall from chapter 10, "Prophecy: Where We At!", mention was made of the seven church ages; the history and backdrop of the seven church ages begin with the apostle John who was banished on the Isle of Patmos. During this time or while in banishment on the Isle of Patmos, God visited John and gave him a revelation of Jesus Christ, supernatural visitations which comprised of visions, revelations, and prophecies pertinent to that time, our day, the future, and the end of the world.

At the same time, Jesus gave John a word or message to deliver to the seven local congregations—"Seven Local Congregations" scattered throughout Asia Minor. The apostle John had to deliver a word or message from Jesus Christ to each of these churches or, better stated local congregation; every one of these local congregations had a particular message or word from Jesus Christ that was applicable to their natural most of all their spiritual conditions. The word or message that was to be delivered to them came in the form of encouragement, exhortation, rebuke, listening, repenting, and a stern warning to get back to God and their original faith in Jesus Christ and the apostles.

Author's note: It must be understood that each of these church ages and its message from our Lord Jesus Christ was prophetic, and its message was applicable to the church of that day and through the centuries gone by to the present time. Someone might ask, "Well, how do we know that these church ages refer to and are applicable to different periods of time to the present? Did the Church exist from the time of the apostles in the book of Acts to the present time? The answer is yes! Anyone studying church history can read the messages from Jesus Christ to the different churches and can understand and discern that each message or word from Jesus corresponds, correlates, and fits that particular age. It is very interesting to see and read what God had to say about our present church age; to respond to its message will bring about constant revival. As a matter of fact, according to Jesus and the apostles, revival is a constant and ongoing occurrence within the Church; here is a shocking statement Jesus and the apostles never had to have a revival; they were always revived.

> *The Revelation of Jesus Christ, which God gave unto him, to shew unto his servants things which must shortly come to pass; and he sent and signified it by his angel unto his servant John:*
>
> *Who bare record of the word of God, and of the testimony of Jesus Christ, and of all things that he saw.*
>
> *Blessed is he that readeth, and they that hear the words of this prophecy, and keep those things which are written therein: for the time is at hand.*
>
> *John to the seven churches which are in Asia: Grace be unto you, and peace, from him which is, and which was, and which is to come; and from the seven Spirits which are before his throne;*
>
> *And from Jesus Christ, who is the faithful witness, and the first begotten of the dead, and the prince of the kings of the earth. Unto him that loved us, and washed us from our sins in his own blood,*
>
> *And hath made us kings and priests unto God and his Father; to him be glory and dominion for ever and ever. Amen.*
>
> *Behold, he cometh with clouds; and every eye shall see him, and they also which pierced him: and all kindreds of the earth shall wail because of him. Even so, Amen.*
>
> *I am Alpha and Omega, the beginning and the ending, saith the Lord, which is, and which was, and which is to come, the Almighty.*

> *I John, who also am your brother, and companion in tribulation, and in the kingdom and patience of Jesus Christ, was in the isle that is called Patmos, for the word of God, and for the testimony of Jesus Christ.*
>
> *I was in the Spirit on the Lord's day, and heard behind me a great voice, as of a trumpet,*
>
> *Saying, I am Alpha and Omega, the first and the last: and, What thou seest, write in a book, and send it unto the seven churches which are in Asia; unto Ephesus, and unto Smyrna, and unto Pergamos, and unto Thyatira, and unto Sardis, and unto Philadelphia, and unto Laodicea.*
>
> *And I turned to see the voice that spake with me. And being turned, I saw seven golden candlesticks;*
>
> *And in the midst of the seven candlesticks one like unto the Son of man, clothed with a garment down to the foot, and girt about the paps [breast] with a golden girdle.*
>
> *And his feet like unto fine brass, as if they burned in a furnace; and his voice as the sound of many waters.*
>
> *And he had in his right hand seven stars: and out of his mouth went a sharp two edged sword: and his countenance was as the sun shineth in his strength.*
>
> *And when I saw him, I fell at his feet as dead. And he laid his right hand upon me, saying unto me, Fear not; I am the first and the last:*
>
> *I am he that liveth, and was dead; and, behold, I am alive for evermore, Amen; and have the keys of hell and of death.*
>
> *Write the things which thou hast seen, and the things which are, and the things which shall be hereafter;*
>
> *The mystery of the seven stars which thou sawest in my right hand, and the seven golden candlesticks. The seven stars are the angels of the seven churches: and the seven candlesticks which thou sawest are the seven churches.*
>
> — Revelation 1:1–20

"His head and his hairs were white like wool, as white as snow; and his eyes were as a flame of fire" Revelation 1:14. The author will attempt a brief study of each church age, starting from the first church age to the last, which is the seventh church, Laodicea. This last Church Age is of utmost importance due to the fact it's the pivotal point of this book, and the word of message from Jesus Christ is the focal point for our church age, which is the church of Laodicea.

If you would recall, in chapter 10, "Prophecy: Where We At!", there was a chart showing the church ages. And as the author explained later on in this book, the "Church Ages" would be dealt with from a brief point of view with emphasis as to point out our last hope for a restoration of the church in its fullness.

The Church May Ice in the Summer

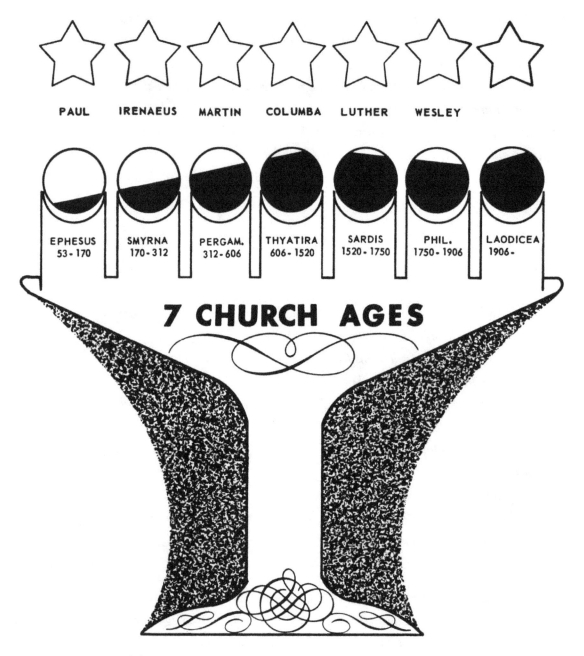

THE SEVEN CHURCH AGES

The chart above give you an idea of the seven church ages, beginning with the first church age, Ephesus, and ending with the church age Laodicea (which is our church age). Each of these church ages covers a period of time with a word or message from Jesus Christ and its relevance to God's people in the form of exhortation, correction, rebuke, encouragement, and strengthening of faith in God (notice what the author is saying faith in God) rewards of serving Jesus Christ, holding on to end and believe it or not judgment; why judgment?

Because in our day, it seems like the fear of God is gone from people, and they have forgotten that; yes! God is a God of love, but He is also a God of judgment.

Chapter 21, Part 1: Stranger in His Own House

Ephesus, AD 53 to 170

Ephesus, which comes from the Greek word *"rfasas,"* Ἔφεσος, Ephesos, Turkish—Efes, derived from the Hittite word *"Apasa,"* was an ancient Greek city of the coast of Ionia Southwest of the present-day Selcuk in Izmir Province of modern-day Turkey. One of the greatest of the Ionian cities, it became the leading seaport of the region. The founder of the city was a prince of Athens named Androklos. According to Greek mythology, the ancient city of Ephesus was established by Greeks in the eleventh century bc by Androklos, the son of the legendary king of Athens. Ephesus was host, according to Greek mythology, to the temple of Artemis, which housed the goddess Diana, the fertility god whom the Ephesians worshipped.

This temple was known as one of the Seven Wonders of the World. Ephesus was a Roman colony and the capital of the Roman province of Ephesus was a Roman colony and the capital of the Roman province of Asia. Its ruins can still be seen if you go to modern Turkey today. Ephesus was one of the religious centers of the Roman Empire at the time and accommodated a population of 300.000 people or more.

AD 52, the apostle Paul on second missionary journey together with Aquila and Priscilla, who were deported from Rome, sailed to Ephesus; they stopped at Ephesus, where he met with some other believers, stayed for several months, ministered in the Jewish synagogue, during this period of time he taught and established a church teaching them of Jesus Christ, His life, teachings, death and resurrection, and His intercessory work in heaven.

The believers in Ephesus…their hunger for God was expressed in eagerness, enthusiasm, and expressive zeal in their love for God and one another as the Ephesians Church grew at a rapid rate. The apostle Paul's stay was for a short period as he left for Jerusalem and then returned to Ephesus, continuing to lead this church in one of the greatest moves of God. He stayed in Ephesus for several years as revival continued, and the love of God flowed to saints and sinners. He also ordained pastors and leaders, taught them about Jesus and the apostle's doctrine after three years, then he left for Rome, his final journey. Many years later, the apostle John delivered the message from Jesus Christ to the Ephesians Church. Please read Acts, chapters 18 to 20.

> *Unto the angel of the church of Ephesus write; These things saith he that holdeth the seven stars in his right hand, who walketh in the midst of the seven golden candlesticks;*
>
> *I know thy works, and thy labour, and thy patience, and how thou canst not bear them which are evil: and thou hast tried them which say they are apostles, and are not, and hast found them liars:*
>
> *And hast borne, and hast patience, and for my name's sake hast laboured, and hast not fainted.*
>
> *Nevertheless I have somewhat against thee, because thou hast left thy first love.*
>
> *Remember therefore from whence thou art fallen, and repent, and do the first works; or else I will come unto thee quickly, and will remove thy candlestick out of his place, except thou repent.*
>
> *But this thou hast, that thou hatest the deeds of the Nicolaitans, which I also hate.*
>
> — Revelation 2:1–6

The Ephesians Church, which is the book of Acts Church, the book of Acts should really be called the Acts of the Holy Spirit through the apostles. Notice how Jesus commended the Church of Ephesus,

> *I know thy works, and thy labour, and thy patience, and how thou canst not bear them which are evil: and thou hast tried them which say they are apostles, and are not, and hast found them liars: And hast borne, and hast patience, and for my name's sake hast laboured, and hast not fainted.*
>
> — Revelation 2:2–3

Someone reading this book would think there was no fault in this church, but with all the commendation from Jesus Christ, the stern warning also came to the word or message "you have left your first love." Here comes a fact that should be a deep realization for the Church of today, revival is the cry of every preacher today but has it ever dawned on you that the apostles and those that closely walk with Jesus never needed revival because they were not caught up with the mechanics, tradition, ritual, formality, tradition, entertainment, programs, hypes; they kept their first love which is revival.

Smyrna, AD *170 to 312*

The city of Smyrna, today Izmir in Turkey, was located forty-nine miles north of Ephesus. It was one of the chief cities of Roman-dominated Asia and competed with places such as Pergamos and Ephesus for the title "First City of Asia." Although the city was settled in the eleventh century BC, it did not begin to reach its height of importance until after Alexander the Great, who laid the foundation for a new city. The actual enlargement and fortification of the city were carried out under Antigonus from 316 to 301 BC and Lysimachus from 301 to 281 BC. The city of Smyrna was also a seat of the worship of the pagan idols Cybele called "the Mother of the gods" and of Dionysus of Bacchus. It was also a seat of the worship of the city of Rome, with a temple built to worship the goddess Roma in 195 BC. Emperor worship was practiced with a temple built to honor the Roman Emperor Tiberius in AD 28.

The name Smyrna means "myrrh," which is a resin obtained from the Commiphora myrrha tree. Myrrh, which means bitter, is often remembered as one of the three gifts the wise men gave to Jesus after he was born. Smyrna was known for its schools of science and medicine. It boasted of, on the slope of Mount Pagus, a theater that could seat up to twenty thousand spectators. The city also celebrated Olympian Games, which were very popular with the local populace. The church in Smyrna, called the "suffering church," was established by the apostle Paul (Acts, chapter 19).

This church was being severely persecuted at the time this letter was written, Smyrna had a large Jewish population, and many of the Jews were hostile toward the church. Most of the book of Acts, Christians died because of persecution; some died a natural death and went on to be with Jesus, the world became spiritually darker, and the new Christians who believed in Jesus and the apostles' ministry were severely persecuted and suffered under the brutal Roman Empire; here is the message to the church of Smyrna:

> *And unto the angel of the church in Smyrna write; These things saith the first and the last, which was dead, and is alive;*

> *I know thy works, and tribulation, and poverty, (but thou art rich) and I know the blasphemy of them which say they are Jews, and are not, but are the synagogue of Satan.*
>
> *Fear none of those things which thou shalt suffer: behold, the devil shall cast some of you into prison, that ye may be tried; and ye shall have tribulation ten days: be thou faithful unto death, and I will give thee a crown of life.*
>
> *He that hath an ear, let him hear what the Spirit saith unto the churches; He that overcometh shall not be hurt of the second death.*
>
> — Revelation 2:8–11

The word or message from God to the Church of Smyrna,

> *I know thy works, and tribulation, and poverty, (but thou art rich) and I know the blasphemy of them which say they are Jews, and are not, but are the synagogue of Satan. Fear none of those things which thou shalt suffer: behold, the devil shall cast some of you into prison, that ye may be tried; and ye shall have tribulation ten days: be thou faithful unto death, and I will give thee a crown of life.*
>
> — Revelation 2:9–10

As was mentioned, this church was being severely persecuted when the apostle John delivered this word or message from Jesus. Certain Jews in this church were strict adherents or followers of Moses and believed in the Law (this means ceremonial, civil, and sacrificial); these Jews were persecuting the true believers in Jesus Christ. Jesus called them the synagogue of Satan. Through John, Jesus' message to this church was that they would be cast into prison for the name of Jesus, be severely tried, and be imprisoned for 10 days; however, they were encouragemed to be faithful unto death, and God would give them a crown of life.

Pergamos, AD 312 to 606

The Church of Pergamos was situated in the city of Mysia, a city in Asia Minor, a district watered by three rivers, a perfect city for every type of idolatry, commerce, trade, and licentiousness. This city had a library that was second to none; people came from everywhere to read and study in Pergamos. Given over to every type of sin, this city had one of the most illustrious temples and practiced the sin of Aesculapius. "What is this?" some of you might ask. Inside this temple was a huge snake that roamed around freely whom the citizens of that city fed daily as they gathered to worship it; in this ungodly and heathenistic atmosphere, there was a group of believers who were not fooled by the grandeur, beauty, and veneer of this satanic worship, which filled this temple.

Here is the message that the church of Pergamos,

> *And to the angel of the church in Pergamos write; These things saith he which hath the sharp sword with two edges;*
>
> *I know thy works, and where thou dwellest, even where Satan's seat is: and thou holdest fast my name, and hast not denied my faith, even in those days wherein Antipas was my faithful martyr, who was slain among you, where Satan dwelleth.*

> *But I have a few things against thee, because thou hast there them that hold the doctrine of Balaam, who taught Balac to cast a stumbling block before the children of Israel, to eat things sacrificed unto idols, and to commit fornication.*
>
> *So hast thou also them that hold the doctrine of the Nicolaitans, which thing I hate.*
>
> *Repent; or else I will come unto thee quickly, and will fight against them with the sword of my mouth.*
>
> *He that hath an ear, let him hear what the Spirit saith unto the churches; To him that overcometh will I give to eat of the hidden manna, and will give him a white stone, and in the stone a new name written, which no man knoweth saving he that receiveth it.*
>
> — Revelation 2:12–17

Here again, Jesus commends the Pergamos Church for their insistent works ministering to the needs of the people; their works were not the works of the religious Jews to earn salvation like the church of Galatia, but they were really meeting the needs of the people and doing something for God in the midst of a people that were totally given over to sin. So wicked were the people of Pergamos that Jesus called the city a synagogue of Satan or where Satan worship was held.

There were people within the congregation that were harboring the worshipers of Balaam or Balac (Numbers 31:16). Seduced into sexual immorality and food sacrificed to idols, and some were involved in the deeds of the Nicolaitans; these were not supposed as some suggest an apostate follower of Jesus Christ, but the Nicolaitans were the not followers of any man but from a Greek word "Nicolah," which means "let us eat," as they were always in the habit of wanting to worship with true believers desiring and wanting to eat lavish meals offered to idols. So wicked was this city and some compromising believers that Antipas, a faithful believer in Jesus Christ, was martyred.

This is the first church that Jesus told them to listen to, there are times people are listening, but they are listening naturally but not spiritually. When listening to God and His word, strange as it may sound, we have to listen with our hearts, which are the center or core of our life. "He that hath an ear let him hear what the Spirit saith unto the churches"; listening to what the spiritual ear is of utmost importance because this is where God speaks to every one of us; listening through the physical ear is like listening through one ear, and it is going through the other ear, but those who really listen, listens to what God is saying or listening to the what the Holy Spirit is saying. Jesus did not leave the faithful Christians of Pergamos without some encouragement, yes! They were being persecuted, but He promised to bless and reward them, "To him that overcometh will I give to eat of the hidden manna, and will give him a white stone, and in the stone a new name written, which no man knoweth saving he that receiveth it" Revelation 2:17b.

Christians…being persecuted…Jesus made it clear in the Gospels that Christians will be persecuted, but when persecuted, the desire to quit is obvious; Jesus is telling this church to not give up, do any quit but to be faithful to Him to end, then He promises the overcomers will be given the hidden manna.

When Moses led the children of Israel from being in bondage in Egypt when they came out of Egypt and desired the food of the Egyptians, some of the food was garlic and onions, but God had something better for them; this food was called manna that God, Himself, made and rained it down among their camps. He knew the manna He rained on them was much better for them than the food they were eating in Egypt. It was much better for their physical well-being. When they ate the manna, they did not get sick; they were stronger and healthier.

God has something that is better for you, and that is the hidden manna; ask me what the hidden manna is. I do not know, God alone knows, but all you have to do is whatever persecution you are going through, please do not give up your faith in Jesus Christ; just be an overcomer, and you will find out what the hidden manna is.

The author has visited monuments, graves, stones, and memorial plaques and has seen the inscription or epitaphs of soldiers, VIPs, and presidents' names inscribed on some of the most beautiful granite, beautiful stones, or marble. I have ever seen, well! Your names will be written on the most beautiful white stone with your name on it; the most beautiful thing about this is you will have a new name; I guess you are curious, what is your new name!

Thyatira, AD 606 to 1520

Surrounded by many rivers, Thyatira was the least of the cities in Asia Minor; it was noted for its financial stability and cooperation, guilds of potters, tanners, weavers, dyers, and robe makers. In the book of Acts, chapter nine, there is a true story of a woman named Lydia who had died, and Peter the apostle raised her up from being dead; she was a seller of purple (clothing for royalty); this dedicated woman supported the apostle Paul's ministry, of course, she was converted to Jesus Christ through the ministry of the apostle Paul.

The people of this city worshipped the sun god; this they did to please the emperors of that time. Worst of all, this entire city and its people worshipped one woman after another who sat on a tripod chair uttering messages while entranced by the devil, demons, and evil spirits; thank God for dedicated women of God. God's purpose and plan include women, but the word that came to this church warned against the spirit of Jezebel (women wanting to rule over the men), which is so prevalent in our day and time. Here is the word that came to this church for Jesus.

> *And unto the angel of the church in Thyatira write; These things saith the Son of God, who hath his eyes like unto a flame of fire, and his feet are like fine brass;*
>
> *I know thy works, and charity, and service, and faith, and thy patience, and thy works; and the last to be more than the first.*
>
> *Notwithstanding I have a few things against thee, because thou sufferest that woman Jezebel, which calleth herself a prophetess, to teach and to seduce my servants to commit fornication, and to eat things sacrificed unto idols.*
>
> *And I gave her space to repent of her fornication; and she repented not.*
>
> *Behold, I will cast her into a bed, and them that commit adultery with her into great tribulation, except they repent of their deeds.*
>
> *And I will kill her children with death; and all the churches shall know that I am he which searcheth the reins and hearts: and I will give unto every one of you according to your works.*
>
> *But unto you I say, and unto the rest in Thyatira, as many as have not this doctrine, and which have not known the depths of Satan, as they speak; I will put upon you none other burden.*

> *But that which ye have already hold fast till I come. And he that overcometh, and keepeth my works unto the end, to him will I give power over the nations:*
>
> *And he shall rule them with a rod of iron; as the vessels of a potter shall they be broken to shivers: even as I received of my Father.*
>
> *And I will give him the morning star.*
>
> *He that hath an ear, let him hear what the Spirit saith unto the churches.*
>
> — Revelation 2:18–29

The church of Thyatira, of all the churches, received one of the strangest and diabolical words from God, "Jesus looked at them with eyes like a flame of fire, and His feet were like fine brass." This means judgment; he also commended them for their works, charity, service, and faith. This Church, in the eyes of man, was no one considered them to be nothing, but in the eyes of God, they were first in His sight because of a few faithful saints. Here comes a warning from Jesus to this church of Thyatira. As you must have noticed from the chart, the spiritual darkness was at its worse (just for the benefit of those of you who did not notice the chart, the lighter part in the circle represents spiritual light or revival, and the darker part of the circle represents spiritual darkness).

As was explained earlier, women are in God's plan and purpose; women were used of God as recorded in many books of the Bible, but please note here that in this particular church age, God rebuked this church for allowing the spirit of Jezebel, please note the spirit of Jezebel, the question is, what is the spirit of Jezebel? The spirit of Jezebel is usurping authority over the man.

> *Notwithstanding I have a few things against thee, because thou sufferest that woman Jezebel, which calleth herself a prophetess, to teach and to seduce my servants to commit fornication, and to eat things sacrificed unto idols.*
>
> — Revelation 2:20

There are so many false teaching that is so prevalent in church circles promulgated by men, for instance, Christlam, which is a mixture of Christianity and Islam, merging together, of course, this is a seducing spirit from the pit of hell, not that the author does not love the people or better yet the souls of the people belonging to either of this newfound religion, but what is it that goes with this newfound religion, certain men given over to seducing spirits.

Recorded in the Bible are women whose life exemplified a life of godliness, wisdom, and what they did is an example for women of today. Women throughout the centuries gone by, even to the present time, have been some of the best contributors within the kingdom of God who should be preached and spoken about. But recently, we have witnessed a different kind of spirit manifesting in women that is rather alarming. Much can be written about this, but in keeping with a biblical trend of thought in this particular church age, we have seen the spirit of Jezebel manifesting itself in the political, economic, and, sad to say, the church. Specifics will be left out for certain reasons.

This particular church age of Thyatira speaks in particular of the spirit of Jezebel; the author has a sense of humor and does like a sense of humor in his writings. Have you ever heard any parents naming their daughter Jezebel? No, not really, but I know of a certain couple that named their daughter Jezebel; guess what? Their daughter's name perpetuated her to be that of Jezebel in many so many ways, came out to be in life exactly like and more as the name suggested, all you have to read—the book of 1 Kings in the Bible from chapter 15 (some people don't know), and you would realize who Jezebel was.

What is the meaning of the name Jezebel? Coming from ancient Hebrew, the name *Jezebel* come from the name *level*, meaning *where the prince is referring to Baal, the false god*. This name also means *not exalted* or *not being in a position where one could be seen and heard*. An individual who goes around bullying, forcing, cunning, even as sex objects and sex to manipulate and reach the position of a certain goal just to be seen and heard. It also means to take a position of power of importance by cunning deceit.

The Jezebel spirit's ultimate goal is always to take control and be motivated by its own agenda, which is relentlessly pursuing attacks, dominating and manipulating, especially if it's male authority. Like Jezebel in the Bible, Jezebel usurped political authority in the kingdom; this spirit is to conquer and neutralize its enemy, whether in the political, business, or church, as it causes a leader within the same to flee from it, appointed place with character assassination in mind. The Jezebel spirit attempts to seek out people of influence to win their ears, gain credibility, and win endorsement for their toxic cause. People under Jezebel's influence are often insecure and wounded, with pronounced egocentric needs.

They are often trying to fill a love deficit, always have deep, unhealed wounds from sources such as rejection, resistance, fear, insecurity, self-preservation, and bitterness, which, in turn, spreads its defilement to many. The Jezebel spirit functions subtlety; this spirit is master of manipulation by guilt and undermining or discrediting another's influences. The spirit of Jezebel uses flirtation and is extremely jealous of anyone perceived to be a threat. Obviously, they are proud, independent, and rebellious.

Rebellion is the sin of witchcraft (1 Samuel 15:23) and will attempt to control others through any means other than the Holy Spirit. Jezebel's spirit is always in alignment with a religious spirit. Both Jezebel in the Old Testament and Revelation in the New Testament operated under cover of religion. Its religious deeds are done for all to see. True and pure spiritual gifts attract people to Jesus, not to the people who exercise the gifts. The families of people under Jezebel's influence are often out of order. Those under Jezebel's influence control their partners, and because their children take sides, they grow up insecure, disrespect their fathers, feel manipulated, and become distrustful toward true authority.

From a personal point of view, the author will withhold names or specific situations, time or places, and even illustrations where this spirit of Jezebel exists and is being manifested. More divorces are occurring right at this moment because some women have forfeited a godly and biblical example of being a model wife, mother, even as a dedicated woman to God within the home; believe me, this Jezebel spirit is prevalent in the political, entertainment industry, news media, and so much so the church. The spirit of Jezebel obviously is infesting some men who do not know how to take her rightful place in the home, political world, workplace, and even the church.

The spirit of Jezebel is like a malignant tumor; when it's there, it produces a hard stone-like spirit, as the apostle Paul said in one of the epistles having a seared conscience, as God gave them space, time, and grace to repent, but most of them did not because they did not repent. He would allow them to go into a mixture of religion and false doctrine, and because of this, they will go into great tribulation. God told this church He would kill their children with death (this can mean spiritual and natural death). They were reminded that God searches the reins and the heart (where they were going and what they were doing), and He will reward them according to their works; their works here mean they were doing their own works and not the work of God.

The spirit of Jezebel is like a malignant tumor; when it's there, it produces a hard stone-like spirit, as the apostle Paul said in one of the epistles having a seared conscience, as God gave them space, time, and grace to repent, but most of them did not because they did not repent. He would allow them to go into a mixture of religion and false doctrine, and because of this, they will go into great tribulation. God told this church He would kill their children with death (this can mean spiritual and natural death). They were reminded that God searches the reins and the heart (where they were going and what they were doing), and He will reward them according to their works; their works here mean they were doing their own works and not the work of God.

God chooses to encourage the faithful Christians of Thyatira because of their uncompromising stand for the truth, their stance against the doctrine of Jezebel, and they did not go into the depth of Satan's work. He will not judge them, but He encourages them to hold fast or stand up for Jesus or hold on to their faith in God and do what they suppose to do for Him. He will allow them to rule over nations (meaning in the new world); those who overcome will reign on earth with Jesus during the millennium.

> *Blessed and holy is he that hath part in the first resurrection: on such the second death hath no power, but they shall be priests of God and of Christ, and shall reign with him a thousand years.*
> — Revelation 20:6

That will be something truly special. Jesus will be sitting in Jerusalem, and He'll have His bridal flock spread out over the earth, healing and restoring, and you can be alone in putting all of this in order. He will rule them with a broken disciplinary life, and He will give them the morning star. There are so many Christians in this day and time who does not know what the morning star is. First of all, the "morning star" is that bright planet Venus, which at some seasons of the year appears so beautifully in the east, leading on the morning as the harbinger of the day. It is one of the most beautiful objects in nature and is susceptible to a great variety of uses for illustration. It appears as the darkness passes away; it is an indication that the morning comes; it is intermingled with the first rays of the light of the sun; it seems to be a herald to announce the coming of that glorious luminary; it is a pledge of the faithfulness of God.

In which of these senses, if any, it is referred to here, is not stated; nor is it said what is implied by its being given to him that overcomes. It would seem to be used here to denote a bright and brilliant ornament, something with which he who "overcame" would be adorned, resembling the bright star of the morning. It is observable that it is not said that he would make him like the morning star, as in Daniel 12:3, "And they that be wise shall shine as the brightness of the firmament; and they that turn many to righteousness as the stars for ever and ever."

Sardis, AD 1520 to 1750

Sardis was the capital of ancient Lydia, it passed from kings and monarchs to the Persians, then to Alexander the Great, and then the Romans took over this city and ruled until the Romans' downfall. The people of Sardis were gifted in the art of coloring or wood dyeing; they invented carpets, and of course, the art of dyeing carpets originated here. Most of all, the city of Sardis was exceptionally noted for minted gold and silver. The gold coin and silver coins were first minted here. The religion of this city was a mixture of all religions; in particular, their main religion was the religion of Cybele, which is the origination of the "mother and son" worship, which attributed to the Sun god, the moon goddess, lord of heaven, the queen of heaven. These were the same gods that Rome adopted and are passed on to some major religions of today. Here is the message to this church given to John by Jesus Christ Himself.

> *And unto the angel of the church in Sardis write; These things saith he that hath the seven Spirits of God, and the seven stars; I know thy works, that thou hast a name that thou livest, and art dead.*
>
> *Be watchful, and strengthen the things which remain, that are ready to die: for I have not found thy works perfect before God.*
>
> *Remember therefore how thou hast received and heard, and hold fast, and repent. If therefore thou shalt not watch, I will come on thee as a thief, and thou shalt not know what hour I will come upon thee.*
>
> *Thou hast a few names even in Sardis which have not defiled their garments; and they shall walk with me in white: for they are worthy.*
>
> *He that overcometh, the same shall be clothed in white raiment; and I will not blot out his name out of the book of life, but I will confess his name before my Father, and before his angels.*
>
> *He that hath an ear, let him hear what the Spirit saith unto the churches.*
>
> — Revelation 3:1–6

Of all the churches throughout this period of time, Sardis received a word from Jesus Christ that was concise, brief, and to the point; the geographical setting of Sardis and its cosmopolitan background where this church existed was the perfect setting for a brief message from Jesus this was not the angel Christ. Remember, the angel that this word of the message was addressed to is not the same angel of the Lord that led the children of Israel to the Promised Land. The angel here is the pastor, bishop, and overseer of churches.

What was the word from God to this Church of Sardis? "He that hath the seven spirits of God, and the seven stars…" Over fifty-six years of ministry, there are so many commentaries pertaining to this subject that I have read; thank God for them, but none of them correlated with the spirit of God within the author's spirit. Then what are the seven spirits of God? It is the Spirit of God or the Holy Spirit working in seven different directions. Seven is God's complete number.

Throughout the seven churches or congregations, One Holy Spirit, who is God, is working in completion to bring about His purpose and glory throughout the seven churches. In God's eyes, seven is completion, and please bear in mind where are, or the author is doing a brief study here on seven churches. Do you think that there were only seven churches or congregations throughout Asia Minor? During this time, there were more; how many? No one really knows. So Jesus singled out seven churches or congregations at this time whose spiritual conditions (remember, the book of Revelation is a book of prophecy, which is the future of the ongoing book of Acts Church), the message or word from Jesus to the churches in this era, the same conditions that existed and the word or message from Jesus was for the churches as time progresses, even to our day and time. Who holds the seven churches in His hands? God. What are the churches supposed to be doing? Shining, shining as stars that Jesus has in His hands.

Jesus tells this church to be watchful and strengthen the things that remain; this church, in particular, was being persecuted by false religions, zealous Jews of the law, the Roman government had unleashed persecution against the book of Acts church, who had to flee to other neighboring countries and cities. God's people were being killed, but the word came from Jesus to the Christians that were strong to strengthen or encourage those that were weak to be strong in their faith in Jesus Christ because they were getting discouraged and were about to give up. Study Christianity in the year 1520–1750; it does correspond with this church.

The admonition came from Jesus to them to be watchful and repent and do what they were supposed to do and that is do everything possible to help those that were being persecuted. Twice they were told to be watchful and to listen to what God was saying to them; else, He would visit them in judgment. There were people in Sardis who were living pure and holy; if I may use the word so beautiful to hear Jesus tell the few saints that were holy and pure that He would walk with them when the people of some churches or congregations today hear about purity and holiness. It's like a language that they cannot understand, but purity and being holy is an opening to hear from God and Him walking with and having fellowship with Jesus. Is this not the pivotal transcending purpose of an individual or people who are saved and washed in the precious blood of Jesus? And this is to "walk and have fellowship with God."

Philadelphia, AD 1750 to 1906

Philadelphia was approximately eighty miles from Lydia, the second-largest city in all of Asia Minor, built upon several hills and boasted of being the wine capital of the world. The population consisted of Jews and Christians of Jewish origin. This city exists today and is under the Turkish name *Alasehir*, which means the city of God. This church age was considered to have the opportunity and privilege as never before for the penetration of the Gospel of Jesus Christ. As a matter of fact, God raised up the Wesley's. There were circuit riders who carried and preached the Gospel of Jesus Christ on horseback to multitudes of people, not particularly the church buildings but in parks, roadways, cemeteries, and some large buildings.

John Wesley, who was used of God, traveled four thousand five hundred miles on horseback within a year; he was used of God in an exceeding mighty way. Wesley did not care too much about denominational barriers and did not care that his name be linked with the Wesley Organization; as far as prosperity and money, his motto was "get all you can, save all you can, and give all you can for the Gospel of Jesus Christ's sake." Revivals broke out everywhere he ministered in the pattern of the book of Acts and the apostles' ministry, of which this denomination does not mention in this day. The Philadelphians church had one of the greatest opportunities, "*an open door.*" Open door for what? This church age witnessed one of the greatest revivals and open door for the preaching of the Gospel, as some of the greatest men and women were raised up by God, who was used of God in local churches throughout Asia, Europe, Africa, and America. What was the word that came from Jesus to this church?

Chapter 21, Part 1: Stranger in His Own House

And to the angel of the church in Philadelphia write; These things saith he that is holy, he that is true, he that hath the key of David, he that openeth, and no man shutteth; and shutteth, and no man openeth;

I know thy works: behold, I have set before thee an open door, and no man can shut it: for thou hast a little strength, and hast kept my word, and hast not denied my name.

Behold, I will make them of the synagogue of Satan, which say they are Jews, and are not, but do lie; behold, I will make them to come and worship before thy feet, and to know that I have loved thee.

Because thou hast kept the word of my patience, I also will keep thee from the hour of temptation, which shall come upon all the world, to try them that dwell upon the earth.

Behold, I come quickly: hold that fast which thou hast, that no man take thy crown.

Him that overcometh will I make a pillar in the temple of my God, and he shall go no more out: and I will write upon him the name of my God, and the name of the city of my God, which is new Jerusalem, which cometh down out of heaven from my God: and I will write upon him my new name.

He that hath an ear, let him hear what the Spirit saith unto the churches.

— Revelation 3:7–13

Commenting on this church age from 1750 to 1906, this was a church and people obviously who had one of the greatest opportunities or an open door for the preaching of the Gospel of Jesus Christ. It must be noted here that Jesus was addressed as He that is Holy. This reminds us that the Church of Jesus Christ should be holy. He that has the key of David, Jesus, first of all, was born out of a covenant promise and the lineage of David and the authority and kingship of which Jesus will be greater.

He will open a door, and no man could shut it and shut it where no man could open; this also indicated the open door for the preaching of the Gospel of Jesus Christ like never before in all of the ages past, which is mentioned in the second verse "*I have set before thee an open door.*" Without a doubt, the Philadelphian church age had superseded every other church age as pertaining to the preaching of the Gospel of Jesus Christ. Jesus encouraged this church, even though they had little strength; they kept His word and did not deny Him.

Jesus called the unbelieving Jews who really, even up to this time (some of them), could not accept the fact of Him dying on the cross as a common criminal. He called them a synagogue of Satan because of their religiosity and so zealous about the law of Moses. He tells them in due time, because of a revival and their desire to come back to Jerusalem, they will be saved by an act of God. The fact is some of them kept his word; He will protect them from the great tribulation. Jesus exhorts them that He is coming back quickly and do not give up or else they will lose their reward.

Here comes an encouraging word for the faithful Christians that overcome all trials, testing, and persecutions; He will make them a pillar in the temple of God, in building temples in ancient time there for six or seven pillars, which was the main support of the building or temple that held up the building, Jesus told the faithful saints that if they overcome, they will be the main support and example of encouragement to the church and the name of God, and New Jerusalem would be seen upon them; also they would have a new name. Since these church ages represent an era or a given period of time or dispensation, the ministers and the people of God who gave themselves for the preaching of the Gospel and were faithful to God will also have the honor of having the same.

The brief study about the six church ages was no intention of taking away the seriousness of the Word or messages from our Lord Jesus Christ to the apostle John. These six churches or congregations (some of them) listened because they heeded the warning from Jesus Christ and were blessed and used of God in a tremendous and supernatural way. Most of all, they were effective in the propagation of the Gospel of Jesus Christ, in particular in the church of Philadelphia. "He that hath an ear, let him hear what the Spirit saith unto the churches" Revelation 3:22.

Was the warning for most of these churches, the messages or words from John to convey to angel pastor, leader, or bishop were not allowed or written through the inspiration of the Holy Spirit for dispute, to argue, debate, and to hold conferences or great seminars but to give heed, listen, and put into action (the author do not like the word "practice") the word that was given to each of these churches, then we will experience biblical results.

This book was not written to prove who is right or wrong. As was written earlier, world situations, the crumbling of America, the eradication of truth, the dishonesty of some leaders in government, the greed for power by any means to rule, the deception that has permeated the masses of people to come out in the open and march and the apoplectic attitude to destroy what is good and right, some women who are not subjected to their husbands as the spirit of Jezebel is being manifested by some women in the churches and government, homosexuality, same-sex marriages, abortion is at the top of the agenda.

To add insult to injury of all people, some Americans, high tech companies, and elected officials (some of them) came to America as nothing. America took care of them, helped them support them financially, and now they are enemies of our godly constitution and principles as they are endeavoring to introduce a government of socialism; this is but an inkling of occurrences in this hour.

With all of this written and obviously more could be written, we need revival; not just saying the word "revival" and not doing anything about it is not liable. Biblical revival at this present time is absolutely necessary. Is there any hope for the church in this hour where every prophecy is being fulfilled? Signs of the antichrist government are popping up everywhere. The second return of Jesus Christ is at the door; is there any hope for a biblical revival? Yes, there is hope. Some say no! But let's find out what the Bible says now that we are in the final chapters of the end of the world as we go on to part 2 of "Stranger in His Own House," which obviously is our church age, the church of Laodicea.

CHAPTER 21, PART 2
Stranger in His Own House

Laodicea, AD 1906 to the Present Time

First-century Laodicea sat astride two major trade routes. The first road ran from Rome eastward into Asia Minor, then beyond to Cilicia, where Paul was born. At Derbe, it split: One leg went to the south through Damascus and on into Egypt; the other leg struck across the east to Mesopotamia, the ancient home of Babylon. Connecting the city to southern Europe through Byzantium, the second route entered Laodicea from the north and continued to the Mediterranean.

The founders built the city in the Lycus Valley, where these routes crossed. This provided Laodicea with unlimited opportunities for trade but caused other significant problems. Ideally, prosperous cities are built close to abundant natural resources, especially water. Great cities are usually founded on deep natural harbors or on the banks of navigable rivers where water is abundant. Unfortunately, Laodicea was not established near an adequate water supply. More driven by trade, its builders located it where the roads crossed. However, the city had much in its favor, and of special note were its three main industries. The Laodiceans produced glossy black wool that was prized by the wealthy all over the world.

No one knows whether its rich color came from a particular strain of sheep that they bred in the area or whether they dyed it, but the quality of the wool is indisputable. In fact, they cornered the market in this commodity, producing tremendous wealth. Their second business was medicine. Laodicea boasted of one of the most renowned medical schools in the world, and with it came all of its associated industries like pharmaceuticals. They produced a world-famous eye salve, reputed to cure certain kinds of eye diseases. Another salve supposedly healed ear problems. People came from all over the Roman world in search of remedies for their ailments.

These two industries produced a third that multiplied their already vast wealth in banking. Laodicea became a center of currency exchange and money lending. Cicero, it is said, cashed huge bank drafts there. So huge were its assets that, when it was demolished by a first-century earthquake, the city refused Rome's offer of help, rebuilding with its own funds. Laodicea had a monopoly in textiles, a world-renowned medical industry, and a prosperous financial center. Writers of the ancient world spoke openly of their envy of Laodicean wealth. Record after record attests to their status.

Their one weakness was the IR water supply. Water had to be piped into Laodicea, which was cold water that came from an abundant supply from Colossae. By the time this water ran from ten or so miles from the cold springs from Colossae, it was lukewarm. About six miles away in Hierapolis were hot springs, but that water, too, was lukewarm when it reached Laodicea. Whether they piped in the cold or the hot water, it arrived at Laodicea lukewarm. Reading the above facts about Laodicea is certainly amazing, and someone might be tempted to think that God does not know our natural circumstances, yes! He does; please note how Jesus zeroed in and used the city of Laodicea's acute water crisis or problem to convey the word or message to the Church of Laodicea, again, which is symbolic of our church age.

Here is the message or word to Laodicea,

> *And unto the angel of the church of the Laodiceans write; These things saith the Amen, the faithful and true witness, the beginning of the creation of God;*
>
> *I know thy works, that thou art neither cold nor hot: I would thou wert cold or hot.*

> *So then because thou art lukewarm, and neither cold nor hot, I will spue thee out of my mouth.*
>
> *Because thou sayest, I am rich, and increased with goods, and have need of nothing; and knowest not that thou art wretched, and miserable, and poor, and blind, and naked:*
>
> *I counsel thee to buy of me gold tried in the fire, that thou mayest be rich; and white raiment, that thou mayest be clothed, and that the shame of thy nakedness do not appear; and anoint thine eyes with eyesalve, that thou mayest see.*
>
> *As many as I love, I rebuke and chasten: be zealous therefore, and repent.*
>
> *Behold, I stand at the door, and knock: if any man hear my voice, and open the door, I will come in to him, and will sup with him, and he with me.*
>
> *To him that overcometh will I grant to sit with me in my throne, even as I also overcame, and am set down with my Father in his throne.*
>
> — Revelation 3:14–21

The angel of the Church is always referred to as the prophet or overseer of a particular age; the amen, the faithful and true witness, the beginning of the creation of God, is Jesus Christ. Jesus is speaking as He says, "I know thy works." The Hebrew word for works here is "*abad,*" which means to willingly serve, minister, praise, and worship God with all of your body, soul, mind, or spirit. Their lack of zeal, enthusiasm, yearning, lack of desire for God, and routine traditional ritualistic Christianity produced neither cold nor hot spiritual conditions within their spirit. In other words, they were "lukewarm." What does Christ mean by this metaphor? Coldwater stimulates and invigorates. Nothing refreshes more than drinking a glass of cold water on a hot day. And hot water? It is useful for health; yes, to a certain extent. Not only do we mix it with teas, herbs, broths, and the like, but it also works as a solvent, good for cleaning just about anything.

What does lukewarm water do? Christ's complaint against the Laodiceans is revealed here: It is good for nothing! The Laodicean is useless to Him. Lukewarm water is an emetic: it makes one vomit. In terms of God's work, a lukewarm Christian is useless. The other traits of Laodiceanism spring from this characteristic of uselessness. As Head of the church, Christ cannot use them in the spiritual condition in which He found them. We should think of this in terms of biblical symbolism: Water represents God's Holy Spirit. Neither cold nor hot means stagnation; nothing living can live or survive in stagnant water. Please be reminded that this condition exists in our church age.

The stern warning comes from Jesus Christ Himself; "I will spue thee out of my mouth" was passed on to the apostle John, which he was to deliver to the Laodicean Church. This word from Jesus was a warning if they did not repent. Warning messages, a word from God, some godly visions, supernatural visitations, and dreams are not to be taken for granted; it is God's ways of showing His mercy and love to us humans and the church that He is giving us a chance to get our act together and straighten up. Negative! are the comments of hundreds of thousands of so-called preachers and Christians. "*I will spue thee out of my mouth*"—this is Jesus speaking. It indicates a future warning to straighten up a present deathly spiritual condition and, if obeyed, would result in revival and God's blessings upon the church.

There are certain denominations, organizations, and some full gospel Christians (who are not really full gospel; do not believe the book of Revelation). Visions, dreams, revelations, the fruits of the spirit, the gifts of the spirit, miracles, healing, signs, and wonders of the Holy Spirit and the manifestations of God's power are something of the past, they say, and since the apostles died.

There are ministers standing on their church platform, behind the pulpit who are denying the existence of God (they should not be there because if you do not preach about God or Jesus Christ, who will you preach about?); some of them openly support a homosexual lifestyle, transgender sexes, no fear for God and authority, who has become reprobates according to Bible (Romans, chapter 1). God has already spued some of them out of His mouth because they are sickening in God's stomach. But there are people who are in a lukewarm condition within the church; please heed this warning and turn to God with all your heart, spirit, and body.

The above word or message from Jesus to John, to the Laodicean Church, our church age in this present day and time adequately fits the church of today. Before going any further, it must be understood that the author of this book believes in God's promises to bless and prosper His people in every way; this means spiritually, materially, socially, physically, mentally, and financially. Acts of God, the supernatural, are God's ways of manifesting His love and power is to believe in God.

Deuteronomy 28:1–13 explicitly explains and reverberates that in choosing God and His word, how we would have His covering, protection, blessings, and how to break the spirit of poverty and all curses from our lives. Third John 1:2 teaches us that it is always God's will to bless and prosper His people.

At the beginning of this chapter, since this particular scripture was addressed to the church of Laodicea, our church age, our Lord and Savior, Jesus Christ, rebuked us not for the blessings of God upon our lives but for being content in their constant persuasive consciousness of riches, and being rich they constantly boasted that their riches and with this kind of attitude they shut God out and His power from being manifested in the church. Tradition, ritual, and formality are the norm when Christians are lukewarm.

How fitting is this word from Jesus Christ to this our church age, this self-condemning message that was reiterated to the Laodicean Church, "Because thou sayest, I am rich, and increased with goods, and have need of nothing" Revelation 3:17a?

This is what prosperity does to some Christians who do not know God and His power. There are denominations, organizations, independents, and ministries; some of them boast of having the elite and richest of people who are worth millions upon millions who are just the opposite of Peter and John in the book of Acts, chapter 3; silver and gold we have, but we do have the power to heal and dying and sick world.

With the millions upon millions of dollars, some of these organizations boast, but the lack of power is imminent among them each week as they gather in their millions stain glass church buildings (no envy here), even though there is a percentage of the American Church doing everything for missions evangelism to carry the Gospel to the unreached. Why are 49 percent of the people world are yet unreached and unevangelized? With the kind of money that some organizations, denominations, independents, and ministries boast and bring in, could you imagine, for example, a country like Haiti, just two hours or less from Miami, this country would have already been evangelized. Sometimes the author is liable or tempted to think because there are no TV cameras and a Hollywood type showmanship charismatic style type kind of preaching, some ministers and ministries do not want to go there and do what really needs to be done. Worst of all, there is no money to get there. It might be true that these people might have the beggar

Chapter 21, Part 2: Stranger in His Own House

mentally, but what will you do if you have nothing? Also, someone needs to teach these same people to give and watch how God would bless them.

The author just wanted to pour out his soul right here, thank God for the faithful who has compassion for lost souls and are doing something to win lost souls, but generally speaking, there is a percentage of so-called Christians who are so conscious of mega edifices and church buildings, and mega crowds (nothing wrong if a minister and ministry has a need to seat thousands) but have forgotten the sole purpose of why Jesus died on the cross; *lost souls.*

What this generation of churchgoers needs—is to read the words of our Lord and Savior Jesus Christ repeatedly, in the Gospel of Matthew 16:26a, "For what is a man profited, if he shall gain the whole world, and lose his own soul?"

Which is translated as *one soul* is worth more than all the world's church buildings, monies, gold, silver, gemstones, oil, and material things. Please keep in mind the Laodicean Church describes in Revelation 3:17.

This message adequately fits and accurately describes the spiritual condition of the church today. Most of this modern-day church is content with their traditional ritualistic Christianity and, in particular, absorbs with riches, but here comes the charge from Jesus Christ Himself,

> *Because thou sayest, I am rich, and increased with goods [material things and money] and have need of nothing; and knowest not that thou art wretched, and miserable, and poor, and blind, and naked.*
>
> — Revelation 3:17

If I, the author, should have the privilege of ministering in one of these modern-day churches today, which would be a miracle and stand behind the pulpit to minister and preach these words, "Because thou sayest, I am rich, and increased with goods, and have need of nothing; and knowest not that thou art wretched, and miserable, and poor, and blind, and naked" Revelation 3:17, there is a possibility that I will be stopped by the pastor or deacon board and be ushered out the door. One of the worst things that can happen to a person is when they are sick and don't realize they are sick, and worst of all, some of these denominations, organizations, religions, and independents are sick, spiritually wretched, miserable, poor, blind, and naked. Nakedness in public is an embarrassment.

The church that thinks and acts like riches and material things are more important than desiring, hungering, thirsting, seeking, and wanting more of God is wretched, miserable, poor, blind, and naked and is an embarrassment to God.

The word counsel is spoken directly to the Laodicean Church from Jesus Christ. Like some churches today, they get counsel from the politician, governor, mayor, and businessmen (thank God for prominent dedicated saved men of God within the church), but most of the time, there is a tendency to push ungodly prominent men into the business of church because of the fact to impress the populace of a city, but they don't know a thing about God and spiritual things. But Jesus is telling this church to come to Him for counsel and advice, one of the ways this can be implemented is by allowing Holy Spirit to lead, and this does not mean to accommodate spookiness and weirdoes. There are times within the church people whom we consider spooky and weirdoes have the answer for God's blessings and revival in the Church.

The word "counsel" means to take counsel together and give advice. There is only one market from which you can buy the goods Jesus offers, from "Him." The Hebrew word for buy is "*Qanah*," which means to acquire what the other has; it means to give something to get something. Surrender yourself, and the material things that you possess to gain eternal life are worth more than all the material things of this world. The Laodiceans do not have to run to the malls of wealth in Laodicea to obtain satisfaction. Jesus wants to do business with the Laodiceans. First, He counsels them "to buy" a certain kind of "gold," a "refined" gold of character that comes from the fires of testing. This is not a monetary transaction but a spiritual transaction, a spiritual transaction in exchange for a quality of life.

One of the most misunderstood and least addressed subjects in the church today is trials, testing, persecution, and tribulation. The Hebrew word for trial is "*maccha*," which literally means to turn away from your faith in God for trivial things such as the flesh (fornication), etc. The meaning of the word test or testing comes from the Hebrew word "*nasah*," which means to prove the reality of your faith in God; for example, God tested Abraham's faith in God when He asked him to sacrifice Isaac on Mount Moriah. Persecution means to be subjugated and hated for your faith in God through Jesus Christ. Tribulation means when there exists harsh persecution, like arrest, jail sentences, and killing of Christians in certain nations or countries. And white garments that you may be clothed, that the shame of your nakedness may not be revealed, and white garments that you may be clothed, that the shame of your nakedness may not be revealed.

The Laodicean Church knew nothing of trials, testing, persecution, or tribulation. If all of these were happening during the time of the existence of the Laodicean Church, most of them would have backslidden and denied Jesus. Trials, testing, persecution, and tribulation, were not in their thoughts and vocabulary; most of all, they lived such a luxurious life while all of the other churches around them were going through the worst of trials, testing, persecution, and periods of tribulation. This church could not understand, figure out, or comprehend what was going on. They thought that the other churches were not serving God, hence the reason for their suffering. No Christian should deliberately go around initiating and looking for persecution, but a real Christian faith would be tried in some way, which brings out the real Christ in you.

Second, Jesus wanted the church of Laodicea to trade or surrender their prideful lifestyle of boasting and wearing their famous glossy black goat's wool. No other part of Asia had the ability to make possessed and wears this kind of clothing. Spiritually speaking, Jesus was talking to this church to trade their rich, wooly, shiny, glossy clothing, which indicated unclean hearts, and trade it for His white garments, which are purity, righteousness, holiness, and clean hearts. By doing this, they will cover their spiritual nakedness and be righteous to stand before God. Could you imagine that this church was naked and did not realize they were naked until the word from Jesus Christ came to them? They realized they were naked and were shameful before God. Jesus exhorted this church to "anoint your eyes with eye salve, that you may see" Revelation 3:18, NKJV.

The third thing about the church of Laodicea required was eyes to see; they were spiritually naked and did not realize they were naked. Naked people parading the streets are considered not being in their right mind; one of the worse things about nakedness is when a person is naked and does not realize they are naked. This is a generation of Christians of which some of them are naked and do not realize they are naked.

There was a Phrygian powder used by eye specialists, eye doctors, and oculists that was made in Laodicea that was unlike any of that day. Kings, princes, emperors, and Roman soldiers used to come to Laodicea to buy this powder or eye salve to cure their eyes because it was the best to cure eye diseases.

Again, spiritually speaking, they needed to come to Jesus and anoint their eyes with His eye slave. What Jesus is saying is that you are spiritually naked and blind, but you need my eye salve would help open your eyes. To make this easier for the reader to understand, when an individual wakes up in the morning, you would sit up at your bedside, you open your eyes, you can hardly see or focus; what do you do? You rob your eyes gently, and the eye salve circulates around your eyes, then you can see clearly or focus. Jesus is saying to the Laodicean church, which is our church age, "Don't depend on the eye salve that you made but anoint your eyes with the salve that I give you, who is the Holy Spirit, then you can see clearly."

Jesus, through John, is exhorting Laodicean Church again, which is our church age, that He loves them, and because of His love, He rebukes them (stern warning with intent to correct). The Hebrew word for "chasten" is "*yasar*," which means discipline with the intent of becoming the individual that God wants you to be. Rebuke and chastening can cause a person to be driven away from God if misunderstood; God was trying to bring this church or us closer to Him, hence the reason for His harsh discipline. Rebuke and chasten is God's way of saying, "I desire you to draw you into a relationship with God, do not settle for and idolize material things." Jesus' discipline emanates from love to us. He loves us unconditionally. There are no strings attached to His love. Jesus says, "When I rebuke your tepid hearts, I do it for your good. If I left you on your course of destruction, I would be like the mother who keeps her child from harm."

People are zealous about everything, their routine at home, their housework, and daily chores, work, business, vacation, family reunion, pleasure trips, exited in pursuant of ball games and parties, but here Jesus tells the church the same zeal you muster up for these natural and material things, "Hurry up and be zealous and repent to gain spiritual or godly things."

Jesus challenges the Laodicean church to be "zealous." This word means to be eager, earnest. Jesus wants them to be deeply committed to His values with the accompanying desire to do it. He wants them to set their hearts on His plan for them. The word "repent" is literally to perceive afterwards. This implies changes after previously thinking about something. This is the basis of moral and spiritual choice of values. Repentance is a complete change of view and way of life as a result of looking at what Jesus values.

The English convey the idea of sorrow or contrition, but the Greek does not necessarily portray this idea. The Greek idea is more on the total change in thought and behavior based on a fundamental change in terminal values, the values of God; the church is asking the world to repent, but the church must first repent. The Greek indicates that we are to make a decision decisively. Do not delay. Come to grips with this immediately. To repent is not to vow that we will never do it again. Neither is it a promise to do better next time. Of all the six local churches, the church of Laodicea was given the sternest of the word, message, or warning by the apostle John from Jesus Christ.

Wrapped up in their own works, neither cold nor hot, which is a stagnant condition within the church, lukewarm, Jesus was about to spue (vomit, gurgitate); please note Jesus was about to vomit them out of His mouth because they boasted of their materialism and riches. Worst of all, they adamantly insisted they had need of nothing. One of the worst things that can occur in a person's life is the fact that they are sick and do not realize that they are sick; naturally and spiritually speaking, this spirit can be detrimental. Please remember that we are dealing with *our church age*. There are people in our church age that are doing their best to please God, but generally speaking, a lukewarm condition is the worst stage, spiritually speaking.

Negativism has been sincerely avoided throughout this book, but at this juncture, it is imperative to mention the condition of the church in this day and age to bring the members of the Body of Christ to the point of being ready to receive with open hearts "what the author would term our last call for a revival that would prepare the church for the second return of Jesus Christ." The author is well aware that we are living in a day and time when knowledge has increased, modern-day technology is at the point of lighting speed that we have to adapt to the thinking of a modern day generation of people if we are going to reach them with the Gospel of Jesus Christ. But this does not mean we should compromise the basic standards of our faith in Jesus Christ and let down our biblical principles, in particular, "Holiness" (a word hardly mentioned from the pulpits today, this does not just mean hair and dress codes). But simply remembering the exhortation and warning from the apostle Paul, "Follow peace with all men, and holiness without which no man shall see the Lord" Hebrews 12:14. "Jesus Christ the same yesterday, and to day, and forever" Hebrews 13:8.

Something is wrong when certain artist and entertainment is the key attraction for the attendees to fill up the church building. In most churches, the Sunday Night evangelistic meeting where there was lively singing and testimonies combined with a good salvation word or message is hardly anymore. Thank God for the minister who does, but you could hardly find a prayer line where the preacher laid hands on those that are sick, to deliver them from drugs and other problems. The mid-week Bible study and prayer meeting are considered old-fashioned, a thing of the past, and least attended. The Friday night, all night or half-night of prayer and intercession have been substituted for ball games, the bridge club, and other entertainment, plus going to the movies or cinemas to digest all of the foul languages and smutty scenes; some would rather stay at home and look at these things because it's being channeled into their homes.

Some Christians would rather wait for the popular TV ministries to come to town, to go to church (not that anything is wrong about this), to hear sermons on prosperity, the good life, the great life, and the best life. Hardly anyone wants to hear a good word, message, or sermon on missions, evangelism, frontline evangelism, or soul-winning and living a dedicated life to win lost souls. Ask the majority of church members and professing Christians if they are ready for the second return of Jesus Christ. The answer from a majority of them is, "I am not sure." A lukewarm, neither cold nor hot need of nothing worldly modernistic church generates uncertainty about being saved and unreadiness for the second return of Jesus Christ.

Get the picture: imagine a church building with five hundred people, all of them already seated with the program or brochure in their hands, then the worship leaders appear on the platform and start singing (while everyone is still seated to be entertained); then someone possibly prays for the meeting, then there are the announcements, then comes the time for the tithes and offerings while the choir or someone sings a special, or the choir sings another song and the pastor or guest speaker walks up to the pulpit and announces his text and topic which is already programmed into the computer gleaming from the projector unto the screen. The pastor or preacher delivers his sermon for twenty minutes or half an hour (in some churches, the pastor is not allowed to preach longer while someone on the board watches the clock); after the preaching, the doxology is pronounced, and everyone heads for the door to spend more time in the restaurant or to attend their favorite ball game or visit with friends. Talking to a pastor in Miami about the Sunday Night meeting, his excuse was after the Sunday Morning meeting, "I do not have a Sunday evening meeting." "Why?" I quipped. His answer was, "I like to get in my boat and go fishing on Sunday evening!" This might not be a trend in all gatherings, but a typical example in most pastors, churches, or congregations.

Being born again or salvation, baptism with and in the Holy Spirit, living a life of faith, keeping a relationship with the Almighty God, fulfilling our calling within the Body of Christ, and preparing for eternity is the responsibility of the member of the Body of Christ and the responsibility that upon the ministries and members of the Body of Christ. To make a point before going on, ask most or a certain member of any gathering or, as modern-day Christians call it, a church to pray for you. The blunt and short-cut answer is "it is done." In other words, they are telling you, "I am too lazy to pray for you, or I am not going to pray." Grace, faith, and love do not mean ministers and Christians have to sit around and do nothing. Here is the truth; it is true that when Jesus died on the cross, He said, "It is finished," but that does not mean we do not have to do anything to obtain all of the above in this paragraph; we definitely have to reach out to God in faith in God and believe. Faith and believing is an act, and so is prayer, some fasting, and doing something within the kingdom of God.

The Church, in general, cannot continue and remain in its stagnant lukewarm condition. The most wonderful thing about God is that He goes to extreme limits to show His grace, mercy, and love to the Church; because of His love, the Church is without excuse and is given every opportunity to get to the place it ought to be and to implement or fulfill and complete God's plan for the Church before the second return of Jesus Christ. By the Church fulfilling and completing its God opportunity means that the members of the Body of Christ, which is the Church, have the opportunity to redeem their souls from destruction and be ready for death and the second return of Jesus. Within the pages of the Bible, from Genesis to Revelation, as recorded, God always extends His mercy towards men and women or mankind within every dispensation the opportunity to redeem themselves from impending judgment. The same within our church age, the Laodicean Church.

What is the hope for the church to redeem itself? It's right there, in the book of revelation, after God's stern rebuke to our church, the Laodicean Church. "Behold, I stand at the door, and knock: if any man hear my voice, and open the door…" Revelation 3:20a.

Eighteen words from Jesus Himself hold the key to one of the greatest moves of God or a revival like in the ministry of Jesus recorded in the Gospels and the Apostles and in the book of Acts. But this revival is conditional. "[…] if any man hear my voice, and open the door, I will come in to him, and will sup with him, and he with me" Revelation 3:20b.

I have heard of pastors, evangelists, missionaries, preachers, personal workers, and councilors use this scripture above to make an altar call for people to open up their hearts to accept Jesus Christ as their Lord and Savior to be saved (nothing is wrong with this), but this said scripture is not directed to sinners. Again, please recall we are dealing with Seventh Church Age, which is the final church age. This scripture is directed to the church of today, the Laodicean Church Age, which is us.

It must be noted that the above Scripture was not addressed to non-Christians, but to the Church or those who profess to be Christianity. Fifty-six years of ministry, the author has seen pictures over and over again of Jesus standing outside the door of a church building, knocking, wanting to get into the church building. Even though this might be true to a certain extent, please understand that the building is not the church, even though the building might be worth millions.

The heartbreaking fact about this Scripture is that Jesus is standing outside the door of the Church building doing everything possible to get in and, of course, knocking to get into the heart of individual Christian or into the hearts of a body of people who comprise the Church. This is not fiction but facts, sound, godly biblical facts. Jesus should not be standing outside knocking, trying to get into the building, or most of all, people's hearts. He should already be in the building, and most assuredly, He should already significantly be living in people's hearts, and when He is in people's hearts, He will be in the church building. How could Jesus be in the Church building when He is not in people's hearts who are the Church?

We have a generation of so-called Christians who have become so obsessed with the names of certain popular ministers and buildings with multiplied of thousands of members. But is God with them and in them? There were twelve apostles after Jesus went back to heaven (only twelve) that shook the then known world. Here we are in a day and time we hear of congregations comprising of thousands but cannot shake the block around them. What was the secret of the book of Acts or early Church, "Jesus living in them and with them"? Herein lays the key to one of the greatest revivals, which will revolutionize the church, and we can experience an unprecedented move of the Holy Spirit that will prepare us for the second return of Jesus Christ. If we can open up and let Him in, instead of Him outside the door knocking, again, He should not be outside knocking; He should be inside. Jesus knocking and individuals or the church opening up and letting Him in is the last and only hope for revival in the Church.

There are so many voices today within the Church; so many really do not know where to turn to because there is an aura of confusion as to who is wrong or right. Never before in the history of the Church have there been so many denominations, organizations, independents, and religions with their respective leaders claiming they are right.

There are so many Christian TV stations combined with thousands of Christian radio stations and tens of thousands of Christian ministers filling the airways with preaching, teaching, and lectures about God, Jesus Christ, the Holy Spirit, end-time events, and more. There are church buildings of every size and structure in almost every street, with people filling them every Sunday morning. There are more translations of the Bible than at any time in history. Praise God; we are a nation that is so privileged, but with all of these blessings, where are the supernatural visitations, miracles, signs, and wonders of the Old and New Testaments, most of all experiencing the results of Jesus ministry in the four Gospels, plus the results like unto the apostles' ministry in the book of Acts. What is the problem? Is anyone listening?

Before going any further, let us take into consideration ungodly unbiblical conditions that are going on in America and the world today. While this book is being written, I thank God for America and Americans. Americans profess that this is a Christian nation, but never before have we witnessed so many so-called Christian leaders and churches turning to false doctrines which do not correlate with the Bible, the word of God. The latest is Chrislam (Christianity and Islam merging), witches, warlocks, witchcraft, and now Halloween (even some Christians are involved in this demonic celebration). Some wars and such like upheavals are being waged in most of the countries of the world; hurricanes Irma, Maria, and Hosea caused severe devastations in the United States and some Islands in the Caribbean; a 7.1 earthquake struck

Mexico City, where hundreds have died. Go to Matthew, chapter 24; religions of the East are being magnified and accepted by a sector of our society.

When President Donald Trump won the election, he was fairly elected, but some people's candidates were not elected. Most of the news media was voicing their poison and venom daily of their dissatisfaction that the election was not legitimate. Unrest, destruction, murders, shootings, and killings seem to be a daily trend in our cities and streets; there is no regard for law-abiding citizens and human lives, while abortion means nothing to some popular movie stars and TV personalities; while Hollywood, most of the time, magnifies loose living such as homosexuality, same-sex marriage, adultery, and loathes anyone who propagates and wants to live a clean life.

Some of them have even openly called for the assassination of our leader with no conscience, while some are calling for impeachment even before the new president took office. Protest, demonstrations, marches with the help of certain movie stars openly threatening to blow up the white house and assassinate the president, lawsuits are being filed by the hundreds of opposing parties while investigations are being conducted almost daily. This investigation means nothing and is a waste of taxpayers' money. Some were professing elected officials who were elected in other areas of government; some of them profess Christianity and even go to church; they have forgotten the words of the apostle Paul pray for those in authority.

The last administration was met with such apoplectic opposition as left-wing radicals were calling for his resignation and impeachment without due cause, upheavals in every city seem to be the order of the day, while wars are being waged in so many countries, hurricanes, earthquakes, etc. is a complete fulfillment of Matthew 24, Luke 21, as the words of Jesus take us closer to the second return of Jesus Christ.

Going back to our study in revelation the Seven Church Ages, the word hear means to listen; the word "to hear" or "listen" comes from the Hebrew word "*Shema*," which means *to hear or listen*, encompasses a whole spectrum of ideas, which means to perceive, taking heed, responding and obeying what you have listened and is listening to. God wants the Church of Jesus Christ to experience a revival like unto the ministry of Jesus and the apostles, but sad to say, the Church or Body of Jesus Christ is looking for this kind of revival to start within their denomination, organization, and their leaders from head office but they want it their way. But unless they do as the word says, revival will never happen.

When there is a move of God, and the Holy Spirit is working in the lives of people, we must be led by the Holy Spirit. This does not mean that people should be out of control and going into all kinds of spasms, spookiness, and isms; leaders in revival must lead people into Christ-like and biblical manifestations of the Holy Spirit, which will glorify and win people to Jesus Christ. Then we must be reminded that you cannot organize God; this is what happened in past revivals. They tried to put a label on God's revival or moving of the Holy Spirit and formed denominations, organizations, and religions, and their revival died.

When God made mankind, He made them with a body, spirit, and soul. The body is that part of you that is external but temporal; the word body comes from the Hebrew word "*Soma*," which is interpreted as *a temporary thing*. The Spirit of man was placed there by God to retain God's spirit; when a person repents for their sin and accepts Jesus Christ as Lord and Savior of their life, God's Spirit enters that individual, and they are "*born again*" (John, chapter 3). The Hebrew word for Spirit is "*Puema*," "*God breathes into*." This act of God makes that man, woman, young man or woman, a child (boy or girl at the age of accountably) a son or daughter of God.

Now we come to the soul of mankind. The soul and the spirit of mankind are so closely related, but yet there is a distinction. This brings us to the Hebrew word "*Nephesh,*" which means the *soul*; this is the real you, your will, your emotion, your heart. Notice what was mentioned as your heart—is the center of you, the real person; the heart is where you make choices for what's right or wrong; worst of all, a closed heart is one of the worst things that any human can have; an open heart, especially towards God and His plan and purpose, is priceless.

This is the key message of this book; right here is Jesus standing outside the church door knocking at your hearts' door; the focal point here is with emphasis, "He is outside knocking when in truth and in fact He should already be on the inside your heart, and when He is inside your heart, automatically would be in the building."

He is knocking to get into His own Church or people's heart and lives. Just think for a moment: Jesus knocking to get into His own church or people's lives when He should already be in our hearts and lives; this is the reason why so many moves of God and revivals have died in the past. Why? God is not in our hearts and lives.

What is the word or message to the Laodicean Church, the Seventh or our Church age? Remember, the author mentions there will be no more church age, then what is the message to us, "Behold, I stand at the door, and knock: if any man hear my voice, and open the door" Revelation 3:20a.

Jesus is standing at the door knocking, not a physical church door; yes, He is outside the physical church door knocking, and as a cover of this book is suggesting, this means He is at our hearts' door knocking, trying to get in. The author wants you to get it, folks; if He is in your hearts, He would be in the building. Have you ever wondered why people would come down by the altar after a pastor, evangelist, or missionary makes an altar call, then people confess they are saved (I am no judge), then you have to follow them up, convert classes for a year, then baptize them in water, then organize special classes to teach them the seven or ten principles of a successful Christian life, be baptized with the Holy Ghost. After so many years, so many are wrestling with the fact of whether to speak in tongues or not when it's recorded in the Bible. Then beg them to pray, be in church, read their Bibles, do something for God, win souls, and, if possible, be ready for the second return of Jesus Christ.

The God fact is, look at Christianity or, to be exact, notice most denominations, organizations, independents, full gospels, and others; after two thousand years of Jesus' death on the cross and resurrection, they still do not know what to believe, and I am talking about some so-called Christians. All of these religious organizations have special guests, evangelists, some TV preachers coming to town, Christian artists, comedians, dinners, moppet shows, bridge clubs, TV in their church buildings, ball games, Christian artists and singing groups, etc. to pull people in their church buildings but if Jesus was really living in peoples' hearts, the houses of God should be filled regardless.

The COVID-19 virus is one of Satan's greatest ploys, and a socialist devil inspired aspiration to hinder the church, and some pastors and preachers fell for it if they really had the fullness of the Holy Ghost; no virus is more powerful than the anointing and the power of the Holy Spirit to allow these devil's inspired government officials to deliberately hinder the church. All it took was Jesus in you and some old fashion prayer meeting day and night to stop what a certain country and its leaders unleashed on the world, killing millions. Forty years ago, yours truly decided to move out from the city. We are now living in a small town in Georgia where we have a gathering, and not one day since the pandemic did we close down our building, and everyone was there praising God, and we continue our regular meetings, not one member was sick with the COVID-19 virus. Because we did not believe in a heartless power hungry foreign government which does not have a heart for their own people, who knows nothing about the worth of a soul, and now a Marxist influenced US government administration whose lust for power and greed has stolen an election to be in power to control US citizens in every way they can. Don't you think we need a move of God and revival in America and the world?

It must be reiterated He should not be outside knocking. He should have already been inside of the heart of God's people. But even though He is outside of the church door knocking, but His mercy, grace, and love for the Church whom He died and purchased by shedding His own blood, He is giving us the Laodicean Church, one more mercy call, as He is saying, "Behold I stand at the door and knock, if any man open." This statement from Jesus Himself is not condemnation but an invitation for the last hope to experience revival and a move of God like unto the ministry of Jesus in the Gospels and the apostles in the book of Acts.

There is no condemnation in this statement but an extended love, mercy, and grace to a modern-day church so organized that they have shut God out. Now the invitation is given to let Him in, into your hearts. Open minds open hearts, especially towards God, is a door swung wide open for a modern-day revival. Revival can only begin with open hearts. This is what our Lord and Savior is speaking to the Church of today. Closed hearts destroy and kill, but open hearts are the floodgates that open up the heavens from the throne of God that can fill the church with rivers of living water that will bring the church back to the restoration of God's love and power that would sweep the church of Jesus Christ in a biblical scriptural revival that would prepare the church for the second return of Jesus in resurrection power. Note what was said! Prepare the Church for His resurrection power; Jesus is not coming back for a backslidden church; He is coming back for a church that is like Him in nature, His image, and His likeness.

This invitation to open hearts to receive Jesus in His fullness is open to all; this means all denominations, organizations, and independent Christian people. The word here for the church is to put aside your man-made doctrines, dogmas, rituals, and traditions and open your heart's door to what God wants, forget about your man-made systems and the dictates from head office or head hierarchy, and open your hearts to what Jesus Christ is saying. One of the worst hindrances to revival is the fact that so many are man conscious than God-conscious. If any man opens up his heart, it is the word for revival. All God is looking for is one man, one woman that will open up their hearts; this does not mean just one in the singular but different ones everywhere with open hearts. Yes, at the same God can use one man and one woman with open hearts. God is looking for a man or woman to channel His power, respect to whom respect is due, but it is due time to forget what anyone says and open up your heart to what God is saying to usher in a last-day revival.

Jesus on the inside means He is working on the outside. "[…] I will come in to him, and will sup with him, and he with me" Revelation 3:20b. From the fall of mankind to the present moment, God's desire (believe it or not) is to commune with mankind when mankind (note what is being written) wants to and chooses to commune and spend time with Him. From the first Church Age, which was Ephesus, the key message to this Church was to "return to your first love." Believe it or not, returning to your first loves is always revival, and now to our last Church Age. God's key message is, "If any man hear my voice, and open the door, I will come in to him, and will sup with him, and he with me" Revelation 3:20b.

It is my prayer that you see or discern and see the similarity of these messages the first Church to the present God has been trying to get mankind back to Himself and the Church of Jesus Christ back into fellowship with Him. The simple fact is from the very beginning, mankind, generally speaking (besides a few who desires God), has the audacity to think he or she can function without God, this for some who are professing Christianity. This has been and is the problem with this modern-day Church. Jesus gave this word or message to John to deliver to the Church of Laodicea. "I will come in to him, and will sup with him, and he with me" is to get the church in fellowship with Him. Why did God create Adam and Eve? For fellowship with Him, why did Jesus die on the cross, reconcile mankind back to God, and to have fellowship with God? "I will come in to him, and will sup with him, and he with me"—these words were addressed to the last day church, not sinners, but to the eleventh hour last day church in its lukewarm condition.

God through Jesus Christ is extending His love, mercy, and grace as Jesus takes the initiative and says to the Laodicea Church in its backslidden condition, "If any man hears my voice, and opens the door, I will come in to him, and will sup with him, and he with me."

True sheep would recognize their shepherd's voice, and the church of Jesus Christ would recognize Jesus' voice. Remember, He is still knocking; spiritually speaking, knocking should be interpreted as the Holy Spirit drawing, wooing, speaking, pulling, tugging at your heart's door that He, Jesus, wants to come into our hearts or the hearts of God's people, the Church. "I will come into him," notice what the Word says, "[…] come into him […]." "[…] and will sup with him, and he with me."

Any born-again believer who is saved, baptized in water by immersion, and baptized with the Holy Spirit, should have a desire for and to have a constant intimate relationship with God. When a person becomes saved, God's spirit hooks up with that person's spirit as they begin to develop a relationship with God; this means they can talk to God, walk with God, fellowship and love God as God loves and has fellowship with him. The word "*sup*" comes from the Hebrew word "*Meggamah*," which means *you are welcome, sit down, have something to eat*, and *have fellowship and to talk or communicate with me as I talk or communicate with you*. This also means to talk with me because I want to talk with you. This statement would surprise a lot of people; whether you have a desire for God or not, any Christian should want to be with God. This chapter is not about ministers, ministries, and staff members, members of the Body of Christ, who are so involved and absorbed in the activities of ministry, programs, and church work that they do not have time to be with God. But this is the cold fact that is hindering and killing revival; they are working in the name of Christ but lacking to spend time with Him; this is spiritual death.

Being with the Master, Jesus Christ, masters everything else; someone might ask, "In what way He can come in and sup with me and I with Him?" It begins with a simple word, "prayer." We have a generation of Christians who are versed in every aspect of activities within the church, from who is the best preacher, the best choir, the best Christian artist, the best entertainer, the best Christian comedian, and more, but when it comes to prayer, hardly anyone knows what it is. We also have a generation of Christians which has lost this aspect of the Christian life and is searching for something from ministry to ministry (not that anything is wrong with some ministries) to obtain satisfaction. They should be praying and having fellowship with God for themselves, so they can be of greater service in the kingdom of God, be happy and satisfied. Excuse the blunt way of stating this, but Jesus was blunt and straightforward when He took a rod and whopped the money changers and tax collectors in the outer court of the house of God when He said, "My house shall be called the house of prayer; but ye have made it a den of thieves" Matthew 21:13. The house of God should be a place of worship, fellowship, communion, or you talking to God and God talking to you.

Getting back to Jesus coming in to "*sup*" with Him, He with you begins with a simple fact called "prayer." This is an act from us, Christians, who are really saved; forget about the 90 percent of the grace message that is being preached today. Prayer is an act and action that a Christian should do in order for Jesus to come in *sup* with you and you with Him; this also means you can have fellowship with Him anytime or anyplace, but reference is being made a here of a particular place and time where you can meet with God and He with you.

This is not talking about when you first get saved but to *sup* with Jesus, and He with you is for Christians who are already followers of Jesus Christ. The question was asked before, and it is being asked again; how can anyone call themselves a Christian and has no desire to spend time with God? The answer is prayer and fellowship with God; yes, the author and God realize there are activities within and without the confinements of the walls of the Church building are of utmost importance, but the activities that are considered important can only be successful when being with Jesus and Jesus being with and in you comes first.

The Old and New Testaments are filled with references to where Old and New Testaments' saints were, where the Spirit of God was in and with them, and they impacted Israel and the nations around them. Anyone reading must realize that the Bible is a book of miracles, supernatural miracles; that is because there were men and women who desired and wanted God in and with them, who believed and accepted and invited God in their lives, which, in turn, caused supernatural miracles—beginning with Abraham, who saw two angels and Jesus in the middle walking on Abraham's land coming towards his tent. What did Abraham do? Ran them off because his gift of suspicion told him they were coming to kill him? No, he had enough discernment to realize that Jesus and two angels were coming to him; Abraham received and accepted them, and God had dinner with Abraham and Sarah; what was the result? Jesus made them young again so Abraham could father a child, and Sarah could birth a child so that God's promise to Abraham should be fulfilled that he would be the father of Israel and many nations (Genesis, chapter 30).

Even though the apostles spent three and half years with Jesus, after Jesus' death, resurrection, and ascension, they did not go around with an attitude and boasted of the years they spent with Him on earth. They humbled themselves and opened up their hearts like everyone else that was with them in the upper room and let Jesus in. This is by and through the baptism of the Holy Spirit. From the upper room, they impacted the entire then-known world around them. This is the key into the supernatural and a last-day revival within the Church, a revival that would usher in the miraculous like certain men and women of the Old Testament saints, prophets, Jesus, and apostles. All the historic supernatural revivals that occurred within past centuries and as close to forties through sixties, they knew what it was to pray and spend time with God. He was saying to function effectively in the ministry, "You have and must spend time with Me—Jesus." "I will come in and sup with you" can also mean God wants to have fellowship with you, with me! Yes, just like at the beginning when God made Adam and Eve, God used to come down in the cool of the day and spend time with Adam and Eve; that was the reason He made them. What makes you think that God does not want to do the same with you and obviously the Church of Jesus Christ? With thousands of Church activities, plus conferences, seminars, retreats, young people activities, concerts, banquets, suppers, bridge club's gatherings, games, women's program, men's gatherings, ball games, and now large plasma TV screens in the church building, including children activities and program in the Church. He does not have room to get in. A story is told about a certain famous preacher who won thousands of souls outside the church building; in the city where he lived, there was the largest church building with hundreds of members; this particular preacher's daily prayer was, "God, open the door for me to get in this church to preach and minister to these people." God spoke back to him and said, "Son, I can't even get in." A word to the wise is sufficient.

The word fellowship comes from the Greek/Hebrew word "*koinonia,*" which means *joint conversation, fellowship, to share one another feelings, to know each other secrets, to confide in each other.* This is what Jesus is indicating to the Laodicean Church of today; I want to fellowship with you, even the church. An individual can pray and have fellowship with Jesus at the same time. In fifty-five years of ministry, I could never figure out why a great percentage of church folks want to pray when some crisis, trouble, or problems arise. This applies to some people that do not care about God and His work; it would be commendable if God's people, in general, have a desire to pray and obviously want to live and do something for God when they are well, healthy, strong or even in the youth of their lives. It must be understood that pray and fellowship with God are of utmost importance God because this prepares you for eternity either by death or the second return of Jesus Christ.

CHAPTER 22

Peter's Shadow: An Embarrassment or a Challenge

By now, you should realize that the author's intention, goal, and objective is to challenge the church of Jesus Christ to return to the basics and foundational principles of Christianity, which could and should lead to having the power of God and the supernatural. Just in case you missed what is meant by the basics and foundational principles of Christianity, as was emphasized in an earlier chapter, please be reminded that the basics and foundational principles of Christianity are being born again, baptism with the Holy Spirit, studying the word of God, prayer, fasting (once in a while), church attendance, holiness, doing something within the local church, preparing for the second return of Jesus Christ and most of all, winning lost souls in the local community and, in particular, those that have never heard the Gospel of Jesus Christ, this means here and overseas.

Also, the author's intention, goal, and objective are to challenge the church of Jesus to pray and believe God to restore all of the gifts of the Spirit, the fruits of the Spirit, and the power of miracles, signs, and wonders that the prophets, Jesus, the apostles, the apostle Paul had, as recorded in the Bible. Also, to believe God to restore what the church of Jesus Christ experienced during the forties through the sixties.

Believe me, with the billions of books on the subject of prayer, revival, having a successful church and ministry, prosperity, marriage, the good life, the wonderful life, prophecy and end-time events, the Rapture and the second return of Jesus Christ and more. Except for a sprinkle of revival here and there and a few men and women of God who are experiencing a biblical revival in America and certain countries, certain men and women of God have ministered to crowds of one or two million people in a single meeting, but generally speaking, what needs to be done is that every member of the Body of Christ should read the Gospels, the book of Acts, the writings of the apostle Paul, believe it, act upon it, and we will experience the same results the people had, as recorded in the Bible; this is real revival.

Could you imagine the millions of dollars spent and is being spent in travel and time-consuming hours of paying for expensive five-star or fewer hotels, motels, aristocratic resorts for a week or more of seminars, conferences, retreats, tours, cruisers to lecture, preach, teach, talk, and chatter might serve its purpose. Some organizations, denominations, and independents do the same just for the fact of lecturing, preaching, and teaching to disprove the fact that the days of the ministry gifts, the gifts of the Holy Spirit, have passed, that we do not need miracles, healings signs and wonders; it's all in the past and worst of all, some of them teach that since Jesus and the apostles died, we do not need all of this anymore.

No wonder God had to raise up the poorest of the poor, one of the greatest men of God and a simple farm young man and his wife, a man of God they called a drunk and an insignificant woman in the forties, fifties, and sixties sent them throughout America and the world with the power of God and biblical results, and they shook the world as millions of souls came to know Jesus Christ as Lord and Savior. After this, America went into a spiritual slump, but thank God at the present time, there are few men and women whose names I did not get the permission to mention in this book, but they have read and are reading the Bible, believing the Bible and experiencing biblical results.

Jesus Christ is coming back for a church that is without spot or wrinkle. One of the books that the apostle Paul wrote was the book of Ephesians; in chapter five of the same book, Paul allegorizes how Jesus loves the Church in general as a husband loves his wife, and even though He loves the Church (in general), He is coming back for glorious church. In other words, He is coming back for a church that was like in its original state, which is the book of Acts Church. Please understand the author is not suggesting walking hundreds of miles like Jesus and the apostles and doing without the necessary conveniences, dressing as they did, doing without the printed word, going about deliberately looking for persecution, or getting involved in extensive political activities. Just continue in God's service, continuing with the basics of the Christian faith, but don't just settle for the norm or status quo but be like the early church that lived holy lives, had constant angelic and supernatural visitations, witnessed and manifested the power of God in signs, wonders, and miracles.

The original Church, first of all, was baptized in and with the fire and power of the Holy Spirit with all of the ministry gifts, gifts of the Holy Spirit, fruits of the Holy Spirit, and certainly with miracles, wonders, and signs following. But please keep in mind the Holy Spirit fell, or the Church was baptized with Holy Ghost. Forget about all of the philosophy, physiology, and fancy phraseology that is stigma-ed as a church today, but the huge question is, is it the same identical church from the day of Pentecost today? Because the Bible says that God hath set some in the Church, does the church exist today? Yes, but let us keep in mind the words of the apostle Paul in one of his epistles, "That he might present it to himself a glorious church, not having spot, or wrinkle, or any such thing; but that it should be holy and without blemish" Ephesians 5:27.

Jesus is coming back for a glorious church; the word glorious comes from the Hebrew word "*hadar*," which means splendor, glory, majesty, honor, beauty, and excellence. These words sum up the book Acts church or the church in its original state. The Church of today should do everything possible to recapture what the apostles and early Church had. All that has to be done is to read the book of Acts, the power that was manifested attested to the fact that people were sick with every type of sicknesses and disease. Angelic visitation and supernatural or divine interventions, most of all the greatest of all miracles, thousands upon thousands of souls were saved. Someone might ask what the secret of the book of Acts Church is. Holy and righteous living! God works through dedicated, holy, and righteous people.

The Scripture chosen correlates with this chapter; it is what caught the author's attention, and this Scripture is taken from the book of Acts, where the apostle Peter was preaching the Gospel; here is the account from the book of Acts.

> *Insomuch that they brought forth the sick into the streets, and laid them on beds and couches, that at the least the shadow of Peter passing by might overshadow some of them.*
> *There came also a multitude out of the cities round about unto Jerusalem, bringing sick folks, and them which were vexed with unclean spirits: and they were healed every one.*
> — Acts 5:15–16

The author will forgo all of the disputes, arguments, some controversy pertaining to this particular Scripture and ask a question, why would the people bring the sick and place them in the streets when Peter was passing by so that the sick would be healed? They recognized or saw the power of God in Peter; the record of this supernatural phenomenon of Peter's shadow is recorded in the scripture above and cannot be denied.

This is the problem with some ministers and people within the church today is unbelief! It is easier to believe and have the same results than to debate and argue and have nothing or no results. The question is not Peter's shadow but the results of people being healed. Any right-thinking preacher and people should rather see people healed than suffering. God heals people, not the devil. Arguments, disputes, and being indifferent about this Scripture are absurd; people were not healed by the shadow of Peter; this is not what Dr. Luke intended to say when he wrote the book of Acts; all he was trying to project was the results, people were healed when Peter passed by, and his shadow overshadowed the sick people, and they were healed. His shadow was a point of contact for the power of God to heal the people that were sick, just like the woman who touched the hem of Jesus' garment and was healed.

As was mentioned earlier, the power of God with the anointing of the Holy Spirit was vindicating that God was with Peter and that even his shadow was a point of contact for the healing of the sick people. Any Bible-believing minister or believer in Jesus Christ should rejoice in the fact that God is so caring that He is willing to use one of His dedicated apostles shadows so people can be healed and set free from the bondage of sin and sicknesses. Embarrassment here is a godly shame and so much more a challenge that God wants me to fulfill Christ in bringing healing to suffering people for whom He died on the cross. If God could use a piece of weed for normalizing water for the children of Israel to drink while on their way to the Promised Land, a donkey to hear his voice, or Jesus spitting spit and making mud (some modern-day pastor or people would have said Jesus was nasty) for the healing of a blind man's eyes, He could sure use the shadow of Peter to heal thousand of people of their sickness.

Amazing how some commentators, ministers, pastors, and members of the Body of Christ would overlook the results of souls being saved, lives being changed, miracles, signs, and wonders taking place and argue and debate over a shadow; the reason is that they are too embarrassed and ashamed to admit that the shadow of an apostle has more power than they do.

As a matter of fact, all kinds of excuses are being uttered in some so-called Christian circles that the book of Acts is not for today and the reason this is being said is that their denomination or organization has no power to do the miracles that Jesus said we could and should do.

HOW DO WE EXPLAIN THIS SCRIPTURE?

"Verily, verily, I say unto you, He that believeth on me, the works that I do shall he do also; and greater works than these shall he do; because I go unto my Father" John 14:12. The words of Jesus from the above Scripture express the fact that the works that Jesus did, the apostles and the present-day believers should do, it must be reiterated believers would do even greater works, and this does not mean immaculate concrete structures with stained glass windows, expensive chandeliers padded pews, air condition, piped organs, huge choir, ministers with titles and degrees before and after their names; all Jesus was talking about we will have the power of God to heal hurting people.

Peter and Peter's shadow should be a reminder, a wake-up call, and so much more a challenge to the reader that we need the power of God. Peter's shadow is also a reminder to the church, especially to the full Gospel or, as some would say, the Pentecostal or Charismatic believers, and the invitation and door are open to all denominations, organizations, and independents that when the apostles and other believers waited in the Upper Room and on the tenth day were baptized with the Holy Spirit, they knew that God came into the Upper Room in a mighty rushing wind, cloven tongues as of a fire sat upon each of their heads, and they were baptized with the Holy Ghost or Spirit as they spoke in other tongues. But when they left the upper room, they did not emphasize the cloven tongues as of a fire on their heads, the sensations that they experienced or speaking in tongues, but Peter's shadow should be a reminder that they had received the fire and power to see the results like seven thousand people were immediately saved and all kinds of healing and miracles followed them as they preached the word.

Most of the Church of today are so engrossed with revelation, being deep, visions, dreams, breaking codes, splitting hairs over prophecy what or who is right or wrong, yes! Be watchful of false teachings and doctrines and do not be caught up in the entertainment syndrome that is sweeping most of the church of today and a word of caution and encouragement to the ministers and ministers who are not what you might term the spotlight and are not being heard or seen on television and other media, but align yourself with God's plan and get in position and atmosphere where you can receive the power of God and manifest the power of God and bring healing and deliverance to mankind in body, spirit, and soul.

I remember as a little boy, I had fun and was sometimes puzzled by my shadow. We lived in an area when the Sun rose from its rising to its setting; it shone directly on the cascading hills and valleys onto our yard and house. There were hardly any houses in between from our house, stores, businesses, and of course, the school building, which was a seven-minute walk as I walked to school. Walking to school, I recall I did some tricks with my shadow. When the sun was about quarter way risen, the sun shone on me walking east, so it cast about fifteen feet or more back of me; midday or walking home for lunch and going back to school, my shadow was very short and stayed with me from school to home mid-evening the Sun would shine on me walking in a westerly direction the Sun shone directly on me which cast my shadow back of me again it looked about fifteen to twenty feet tall which gave me an egotistical psychological feeling about myself that I was tall and important.

Dr. Luke, who is the author of the book of Acts, like every Bible scholar, realizes certainly noticed Peter's shadow followed Peter as even his shadow overshadowing the people who were sick with all kinds of sicknesses and diseases being healed. Shadows go either way and have their origination when an individual is directly in the open with the sun shining over them. Their shadow protrudes behind, in front, or on either side, or on whosoever is around them.

It would be interesting to study the diametric of Peter's shadow, which means the length and breadth of which way he passed by, but realistically speaking, a shadow vanishes, so what's the point, preacher? You can debate, argue, or waste time and money having a conference over whether Peter's shadow healed the people or not, but surely there were people being healed as Peter passed by, but what is the most important thing about Peter's shadow, it is the results, which was the healing, miracles, and the people that were being helped. Biblical revival is something so needed in our day, but is it Peter's shadow the center of attention here? No! But the power of God and the people that were being saved, healed, and delivered. Results are what we are looking for, results and revival.

I am certain that the apostle Luke before he wrote the book of Acts, spoke or mentioned to the other apostles about what he saw or witnessed about Peter passing through the crowd of sick and suffering people, but he must have said to them, "Guys, something peculiar happened today!" As we were ministering to the sick, the power of God was so strong or imminent; I saw with my own eyes as Peter was passing by through a crowd of people; they were being healed, and all types of miracles happened as Peter passed by.

Is it the miracles that caught my attention? No! This is what caught my attention, as Peter was passing by, he did not lay hands on anyone, he did not touch anyone, no one had to confess their sins to him, but just his shadow touched the people, and the lame got up and walk, blind eyes were open, limbs straightened out, deaf ears were unstopped, cancers and growth melted, all kinds of miracles, signs, and wonders happened. Here is the response by the other apostles, Luke, "I think you are losing it; in other words, we think you are going out of your mind, or I think you are in another world." Yes, Dr. Luke was in another world; he was in Jesus' world, which will bring the Church to what God wants for the Church of today.

None of the other apostles or disciples said this to him, "Luke, I think the hot sun had your kind of delirious! I think you were losing your mind!" Or, "As we say in this day and time, you are losing it! We think you need to get back to the altar and pray that God would help your mind; child, please, you know exaggeration would get you nowhere, brother, please! I think that the education and qualification you graduated with and now being a doctor is beginning to mesmerize or rattle your brains." None of the apostles or disciples criticized or castigated him; all they did was believe what Luke was telling them. This is the reason he went ahead and recorded Peter's shadow passing over the people, and they were healed. All Luke is saying to us is that the power of God was so strong that even Peter passing by and his shadow passing over the people without touching the sick people, they were healed. Even after he wrote the book of Acts, not even the apostle Paul's disciples disputed what he mentioned about Peter's shadow.

Why is it in this age, day, and time? Certain people are so adamant about disputing what's recorded in the word of God they spend more time doubting than believing and accepting. Is it because we cannot measure up or come up to par with biblical standards? Throughout this book, surely the emphasis was on the basics or foundational principles of Christianity, of which the author does not mind reintegrating. Here is a brief reminder; to enter the kingdom of God or heaven, an individual has to be born again, being baptized in water by immersion, baptism with the Holy Spirit with the evidence of speaking in other tongues, honor their pastor or leader, assemble together or attend the house of God, read their Bible, pray; personal devotion is of utmost importance, do something in the local assembly, pay your tithes, love and help one another, be a witness or share your faith in Jesus Christ, get involved in missions or be a missionary, especially to those that have not heard the Gospel of Jesus Christ, this can be done by praying, giving and going; most of all, always be ready for the second return of Jesus Christ. But when it comes to the supernatural (from a godly and biblical point of view), we hesitate.

I have preached over and over in revivals in America and other countries, "If you don't care for your own soul, you will not care for the souls of others, and if you don't care for your own body and let it be ridden with sickness and diseases, you will not care for those that are sick and suffering."

One of the things that I have noticed in so many ministries and churches is the lack of altar calls in most churches for the salvation of the souls of men; even worse, there is no prayer line to minister to the sick and suffering. But if these same ministers and pastors would begin to pray and seek God for His power, make altar calls for the salvation of the souls of men and women, young people and children, and minister to the sick and suffering, this would obviously change your ministry for the greater and experience revival.

Peter's shadow is a reminder and a challenge to get back to the ministry of Jesus and the apostles,

Chapter 22: Peter's Shadow: An Embarrassment or a Challenge

The Spirit of the Lord is upon me, because he hath anointed me to preach the gospel to the poor; he hath sent me to heal the brokenhearted, to preach deliverance to the captives, and recovering of sight to the blind, to set at liberty them that are bruised.

— Luke 4:18

Now when the sun was setting, all they that had any sick with diver's diseases brought them unto him; and he laid his hands on every one of them, and healed them.

And devils also came out of many, crying out, and saying, Thou art Christ the Son of God. And he rebuking them suffered them not to speak: for they knew that he was Christ.

— Luke 4:40–41

And when the day of Pentecost was fully come, they were all with one accord in one place.

And suddenly there came a sound from heaven as of a rushing mighty wind, and it filled all the house where they were sitting.

And there appeared unto them cloven tongues like as of fire, and it sat upon each of them.

And they were all filled with the Holy Ghost, and began to speak with other tongues, as the Spirit gave them utterance.

And there were dwelling at Jerusalem Jews, devout men, out of every nation under heaven.

But this is that which was spoken by the prophet Joel;

And it shall come to pass in the last days, saith God, I will pour out of my Spirit upon all flesh: and your sons and your daughters shall prophesy, and your young men shall see visions, and your old men shall dream dreams:

And on my servants and on my handmaidens I will pour out in those days of my Spirit; and they shall prophesy:

And I will shew wonders in heaven above, and signs in the earth beneath; blood, and fire, and vapour of smoke:

The sun shall be turned into darkness, and the moon into blood, before that great and notable day of the Lord come:

And it shall come to pass, that whosoever shall call on the name of the Lord shall be saved yourselves from this untoward generation.

Then they that gladly received his word were baptized: and the same day there were added unto them about three thousand souls.

— Acts 2:1–5, 16–21, 41

Howbeit many of them which heard the word believed; and the number of the men was about five thousand.

— Acts 4:4

And God wrought special miracles by the hands of Paul

So that from his body was brought unto the sick handkerchiefs and aprons, and the diseases departed from them and the evil spirits went out of them.

— Acts 19:11–12

> *[...] Eye hath not seen, nor ear heard, neither have entered into the heart of man, the things which God hath prepared for them that love him.*
>
> — 1 Corinthians 2:9

One of the greatest needs in the church of Jesus Christ in this day and time is the need for results, answers, and a manifestation of God's power; something is radically wrong with the believer in Jesus Christ who professes Christianity and lives a Christian life and does not want answers, results, and longs to witness a manifestation of God's power; they are missing out what God has for them and are dying a slow spiritual death. Anyone reading some of the prophets, Matthew, Mark, Luke, or John, the book of Acts, the epistles, and the writings of the other apostles should have a yearning, deep desire hunger for what they read about, but the majority of the church folks are looking for programs, tradition, ritual, formality, and entertainment. It's like the apostle Paul said,

> *But she that liveth in pleasure is dead while she liveth.*
>
> — 1 Timothy 5:6

The above Scripture might apply to the people of the world, but please be reminded the apostles were writing this to the Church. The Scriptures in the previous pages, plus three hundred or more promises with records of the manifestations of the power of God, are of utmost importance and dire need within the Church of Jesus Christ. There are more educated people in the world than ever before, medical science and medical breakthroughs have astounded the modern world, and there are more educated pastors with degrees gracing their names but the people of the world and in the worst shape than they have ever been. More sicknesses, diseases, and now a pandemic in COVID-19 virus are killing millions. No one has the audacity, especially certain ministers within the church, to say we don't need what Jesus and the apostles had, and that is the power of God manifested not just talk but the power of God.

To make a point, the author recalls: when my children, all three of them, were going to school, we lived in Jacksonville, Florida, and my wife, Sherry, had to come off the road and stay with them at home while I was on the road traveling and doing evangelistic meetings in different cities, even going overseas doing evangelistic meetings in different countries. I recall ever so often I would call my wife and tell her I would be home on certain weekends, sometimes Mondays and Tuesdays.

I would tell my wife to request the school principal and teachers of their respected class to give them a leave of absence from school for a day or two, this they graciously granted because they knew I was a minister traveling a lot, and I wanted to spend time with them. I remember when I was home with them, we would all pack up and go to the main street to a fish market and buy some shrimp for bait, then proceed to the Jacksonville Pier and fish; all of us would bait our hooks and start fishing.

There are times I remember we catch fish like crazy; you might chuckle and say, "Here comes another fish story about the big one that got away!" Not really, but I recall there were times we would pull up one fish, two or three of them on the same tackle with four hooks. No exaggeration here, one of my boys pulled up four fish on the same line because it had four tackle and hook; why did he pull up four fish at the same time, or did we catch fish one after another? Because the fish were hungry!

Then there were times we did the very same thing go to the same Pier, bait the hook, and go fishing at the same place and fish all day and catch nothing; we would pack and go home going into the house my wife, Sherry, would immediately clean, season, and cook the bait which was the shrimp we carried for bait, and everyone one of us ate them for dinner. What was the reason we caught no fish? The fish was not hungry.

King David and Jesus used two life-sustaining desires or instincts of mankind to express their quest or desire for God; either of these holds the key to the supernatural, revival, and a move of God's spirit and power. What are these? Is it hunger and thirst? Here is how King David and Jesus expressed this, "My soul thirtieth for God, for the living God: when shall I come and appear before God?" Psalm 42:2 "Blessed are they that hunger and thirst after righteous for they shall be filled" Matthew 5:6.

Thirst is a sensation of dryness in the stomach and throat associated with a craving for water and other liquids. The Hebrew word for thirst is *"tasama"* or *"dipsao,"* which means a desperate desire for water or liquids to quench the thirst within your being. The Hebrew word for hunger is *"raabh,"* which means an uneasy craving within your stomach for want of food. The above Scriptures adequately express a longing, yearning, craving for God and His power for greater than the status-quo, a hunger, and thirst for God also to experience miracles, signs, and wonders for the benefit of revival and winning souls to Jesus.

Something is not quite normal when some Christians are not spiritually thirsty and hungry for God. The foundational principles of Christianity should be s stepping stone into the supernatural, like unto the ministry of Jesus and the apostles. How many revivals has the author conducted? And during preaching or teaching, I would ask the congregation, "How many of you are thirsty or hungry," and I was aghast to get a negative look with some of them answering, "We don't understand what are you talking about!" Then I would endeavor to explain what the biblical term for thirst and hunger means.

The author does everything possible to avoid talking about himself, but at this point, it is necessary to mention in fifty-six years of ministry, God's love, mercy, and grace kept me, and I can convey my personal experience. I got saved and baptized with the Holy Spirit at the age of sixteen; at the age of twenty-one, I graduated from Bible college. Then at the age of twenty-three, I was pasturing my own church with a wife and three children with about three hundred people who later grew immensely. Upon leaving or resigning our first church with the concern for lost souls, we entered the missionary evangelist field; we pioneered and established many churches while pastoring a few of them; during this time, I studied and earned a master's degree and a doctorate at this present time we are involved in missionary evangelistic work presently working in Brazil and other countries of the world, so far by God's help and blessing we have preached and ministered the Gospel of Jesus Christ in fifty-five countries and have ministered to hundreds of thousands of people in a single meeting.

God be glorified for all that was accomplished, but in fifty-six years of ministry during this time, no one or anyone had to ask, beg, plead, preach, talk, counsel me to attend church, read my Bible, pray, witness, win souls, give or pay my tithes, do something within the local congregation then work with my pastor in every way. What was the reason, especially when it comes to praying? What was the reason? Hunger and thirst for God. This hunger and thirst drove me to do these things. Now that I am older, the hunger and thirst which is a yearning, longing in my soul to see and experience the power of God manifested, even though I have seen many supernatural things in my life and meetings, I am hungry and thirsty, have a yearning and longing for God and to experience more and more of God's power.

Thirst and hunger are natural instincts in every human being; from the moment a baby is born, the pangs of hunger and thirst are evident with crying. Spiritually speaking, if there are hunger and thirst for God in us, God's people, the cries of prayer would be evident in us until revival breaks out. If you are truly born again and baptized with the Holy Spirit, obviously, there would be a hunger and a thirst for God. Getting down to the nitty-gritty, as we say in Georgia, and for those of you living in other States and foreign countries who do not understand the word nitty-gritty, this actually means getting serious or down to business with the Almighty God.

Again if you do not know what this means, let this preacher explain. Your spirit or soul feels like a wilderness, desert, dry and empty; suddenly, deep down within your being, your spirit, or soul, there is a longing, yearning, wanting, reaching out for God and His power, even to witness signs, wonders, miracles, according to biblical standards like in the ministry of the Prophets, Jesus, and the Apostles. This is called hunger and thirst, which is the key to revival and experiencing the power of God.

HOW ABOUT NOW

"[…] faith is the substance of things hope for, the evidence of things not seen" Hebrews 11:1. Reading this book is absolutely commendable, but so many preachers preach, teach, explore, and explain hundreds of thousands of Christians read and quote it; some cannot understand and are quite puzzled about it. Yes, this Scripture is expressing what faith is; faith is something that you have; it is the evidence (faith) of things that you are expecting or believing God for, but expecting and believing God for something or having results is not in the future, but in the now, it is true that we have experienced great moves of God in the past, but the past is in the past, the future is in the future, but you cannot dwell or be melancholy about the past or look to the future and forget about the now. What you have read in this book, thank God, but the author's wish and desire, even praying for that we will experience what the Prophets, Jesus, and the Apostles and some revivals of the past would happen now.

It must be reiterated at the closing of this book that Jesus standing outside knocking is not a condemnation, but God's mercy is beckoning that we open the door and let Him in. Not tomorrow, end of the week, next week, next month, or next year but now.

CPSIA information can be obtained
at www.ICGtesting.com
Printed in the USA
BVHW021528100223
658272BV00017B/1344